Cambridge Series on Judgment and Decision Making

Conflict and Tradeoffs in Decision Making

What makes some decisions easy and others difficult? Current research in judgment and decision making indicates that conflict plays a crucial role in decision-making processes. The chapters in this book address questions about the causes of conflict and its effects on decision making and emotions, particularly (but not only) the emotion of regret. Several chapters address the role of attribute tradeoffs, such as that between money and risk, in the measurement of values for policy purposes. The chapters provide overviews of several current research programs and present new data. Methods involve answers to hypothetical scenarios, other questionnaires, interviews, and observations of behavior outside of the laboratory. Although most contributions are informed by psychology, some also take an economic or sociological approach.

Elke U. Weber is Professor of Management and Psychology at Columbia University. She is Associate Editor of *Organizational Behavior and Human Decision Processes* and coeditor of *Risk, Decision, and Policy*.

Jonathan Baron is a Professor of Psychology at the University of Pennsylvania. He is author of *Thinking and Deciding* and *Judgment Misguided* and coeditor of *Psychological Perspectives on Justice* (with Barbara Mellers).

Graham Loomes is a Professor of Economics at the University of Newcastle upon Tyne.

Cambridge Series on Judgment and Decision Making

Publications Board
Jonathan Baron, Chair
University of Pennsylvania

Michael Birnbaum
California State University

William M. Goldstein
University of Chicago

Past Members
Hal R. Arkes, Chair
Ohio State University

John S. Carroll
Massachusetts Institute of Technology

Kenneth R. Hammond
University of Colorado, Boulder

Don N. Kleinmuntz, Chair
University of Illinois at Urbana-Champaign

Lola Lopes
University of Iowa

James Shanteau
Kansas State University

The purpose of the series is to convey the general principles of and findings about judgment and decision making to the many academic and professional fields to which these apply. The contributions are written by authorities in the field and supervised by highly qualified editors and the Publications Board. The series will attract readers from many different disciplines, largely among academics, advanced undergraduates, graduate students, and practicing professionals.

Jane Beattie, 1960–1997.

Conflict and Tradeoffs in Decision Making

Edited by

Elke U. Weber
Columbia University

Jonathan Baron
University of Pennsylvania

Graham Loomes
University of Newcastle upon Tyne

PUBLISHED BY THE PRESS SYNDICATE OF THE UNIVERSITY OF CAMBRIDGE
The Pitt Building, Trumpington Street, Cambridge, United Kingdom

CAMBRIDGE UNIVERSITY PRESS
The Edinburgh Building, Cambridge CB2 2RU, UK
40 West 20th Street, New York, NY 10011-4211, USA
10 Stamford Road, Oakleigh, VIC 3166, Australia
Ruiz de Alarcón 13, 28014 Madrid, Spain
Dock House, The Waterfront, Cape Town 8001, South Africa

http://www.cambridge.org

First published 2001

Printed in the United States of America

Typeface Palatino 10/13 pt.   *System* LATEX 2_ε [TB]

A catalog record for this book is available from the British Library.

Library of Congress Cataloging in Publication Data
Conflict and tradeoffs in decision making / edited by Elke U. Weber, Jonathan Baron,
Graham Loomes.
    p.   cm. – (Cambridge series on judgment and decision making)
Includes bibliographical references and indexes.
ISBN 0-521-77238-9 (hb)
1. Decision making. 2. Conflict (Psychology)   I. Weber, Elke U.   II. Baron, Jonathan,
1944–   III. Loomes, Graham.   IV. Series.
BF448.C655   2000
153.8′3 – dc21   99-087061

ISBN 0 521 77238 9 hardback

Contents

Contributors

Sema Barlas   *1153 Oak Ridge Dr., Streamwood, IL 60107*

Jonathan Baron   *Department of Psychology, University of Pennsylvania, Philadelphia, PA 19104*

James R. Bettman   *Fuqua School of Business, Duke University, Durham, NC 27708*

Helga Dittmar   *Social Psychology, University of Sussex, Falmer, Brighton BN1 9SN, UK*

Deborah Frisch   *Department of Psychology, University of Oregon, Eugene, OR 97403-1227*

William M. Goldstein   *Department of Psychology, University of Chicago, Chicago, IL 61820*

David A. Houston   *Department of Psychology, University of Memphis, Memphis, TN 38152*

J. Jeffrey Inman   *Department of Marketing, University of Wisconsin–Madison, Madison, WI 53706*

Michael Jones-Lee   *Centre for the Analysis of Safety Policy and Attitudes to Risk (CASPAR), Department of Economics, University of Newcastle upon Tyne, Newcastle upon Tyne NE1 7RU, UK*

Graham Loomes   *Department of Economics, University of Newcastle upon Tyne, Claremont Tower, Newcastle upon Tyne NE1 7RU, UK*

Mary Frances Luce   *Marketing Department, Wharton School, Philadelphia, PA 19104*

Rosemary Murray   *75 Havelock Rd., Brighton BN1 6GL, UK*

John W. Payne   *Fuqua School of Business, Duke University, Durham, NC 27708*

Rik G. M. Pieters   *Department of Marketing, Tilburg University, 5000-LE Tilburg, The Netherlands*

Deborah Sherrill-Mittleman   *Department of Psychology, University of Memphis, Memphis, TN 38152*

Mark D. Spranca   *Rand Corporation, Santa Monica, CA 90407*

Detlof von Winterfeldt   *Decision Insights, Inc., Irvine, CA 92612*

Elke U. Weber   *Department of Psychology and Graduate School of Business, Columbia University, New York, NY 10027*

Matthew Weeks   *Department of Psychology, University of Memphis, Memphis, TN 38152*

Marcel Zeelenberg   *Department of Business Administration, Tilburg University, 5000-LE Tilburg, The Netherlands*

Preface and Dedication

On March 25, 1997, Jane Beattie died of cancer after a year-long illness. She is survived by her husband and three children. Her students and colleagues will also miss her deeply. She was a wonderful person; her positive attitude and her intellectual contributions inspired us all.

When she died, her former colleagues resolved to do something in her memory. After much discussion by electronic mail, we settled on a book and a memorial fund. The fund, which supports foreign scholars' travel to the United States, is now administered by Joshua Klayman of the University of Chicago for the Society for Judgment and Decision Making. (Contributions are welcome.)

The book evolved in the course of discussions with the Society and with Cambridge University Press. We decided to focus on the major theme of Jane's work (putting aside her interest in hypothesis testing), conflict and tradeoffs, and to attempt to represent the work of the major scholars in this field, some of whom never had the chance to collaborate with Jane, so that the book would also serve as a coherent presentation of the state of the field. The book also includes chapters in which Jane herself played a major role, sometimes as an author and sometimes as an author of collaborative work that is reviewed. We hope that this book will serve as a fitting memorial.

What follows are (slightly edited) memories of Jane, written soon after her death, for the newsletter of the European Association for Decision Making. The first was written by Jon Baron, with help from Elke Weber and Graham Loomes, and is intended as an overview. Two other recollections follow.

Overview

Jane was my advisee in graduate school and my closest collaborator from the time she received her Ph.D. until her illness. Before I met her, she was an undergraduate at Sussex University and had worked for 2 years. She came to the psychology department at the University of Pennsylvania in 1983 at the recommendation of Dan Osherson: He recommended us to her and her to us, we all listened, and we were all grateful. Jane had another reason. Her boyfriend, David Weir, was also considering the University of Pennsylvania for graduate work in computer science. When she and David decided to marry, her spirits soared and her productivity increased.

Early in her graduate career she was interested in hypothesis testing, and she retained this as a secondary interest. Her first-year research project was a variation of the four-card problem, and the results were published in the *Quarterly Journal of Experimental Psychology*. She also worked with me and Jack Hershey on my own main interest at the time, biases in seeking information. Her office mate was Deb Frisch, with whom she formed a lasting friendship.

Jane soon got interested in what was to be the main theme of her work from that time on: tradeoffs in decision making. She wanted to know why some tradeoffs were difficult and why people did not like to make them. She hoped to find measures that would be sensitive to the difficulty, and she and I were still working on follow-ups when she became ill.

After she taught at Swarthmore for a year while David was finishing his Ph.D., they both got jobs in Chicago. David was in the computer science department at Northwestern University. Jane joined one of the best groups in her field, the Center for Decision Research, within the Graduate School of Business at the University of Chicago. There she worked with Bill Goldstein and Sema Barlas, following up her thesis on tradeoff difficulty. She also began a project with Mark Spranca, Jack Hershey, and me on what we called *decision aversion*, the desire to avoid making certain kinds of decisions. We collaborated entirely by e-mail. This was a new idea, and we all got somewhat carried away. We generated several megabytes of correspondence. Jane was always among the most computer literate people I knew, and I picked up many habits from her, such as that of using LATEX (a computer program for formatting text).

During their years at Chicago, Jane and David's first son, Sam, was born, and David developed lung cancer, of which he has now been free for a decade.

Several factors led them to move back to England, including a desire to be near their parents and the greater availability and higher quality of child care. This decision involved tradeoffs, though, mainly in the form of a large salary cut for Jane. Jane was a (nonprobationary) lecturer in psychology and then in experimental psychology (1991) at the University of Sussex. Their second son, Gavin, was born, and Jane pursued several interrelated lines of research. With Helga Dittmar, she studied impulse buying in women and men. With me, she worked on in-kind versus out-of-kind compensation. With Rosemary Murray, she worked on decisions concerning fetal testing, yet another example of decision difficulty. With Marcel Zeelenberg, she worked on the psychology of regret.

In 1994 she also began a project with a group of economists – Graham Loomes, Robert Sugden, Chris Starmer, and Robin Cubitt – studying the consistency or inconsistency of preferences under risk and over time. While this work was in progress, she and Loomes joined with Michael Jones-Lee and Nick Pidgeon to investigate the value(s) people place on health and safety benefits in a variety of contexts. Amid all this activity, David and Jane's third child – a daughter, Hayley – was born.

In the spring of 1996, the team working on the health and safety project came to Pittsburgh to meet with several Americans consulting on this project, including me. Jane was to come too, and then Jane and I were going to spend some time working on range effects. I hadn't seen her for years, although we had been corresponding by e-mail almost daily. She had to cancel the trip at the advice of her doctor. At first, everyone thought it was Hodgkin's disease, and we hoped that she would recover soon. It turned out to be much worse: cancer with an unknown primary tumor. Jane and her doctors did everything possible – and there were some optimistic periods – but to no avail.

As is clear from this history, Jane was a wonderful collaborator. It is very encouraging that she has been recognized for her accomplishments, which were essentially all collaborative. She was good at everything and could fill in wherever her collaborators were weak, whether it was writing, statistics, or creative ideas. She was responsible and directed, yet warm and understanding. I also think she had extrasensory perception. For one of our papers, the reviewers asked us to check the interrater reliability of some coding that we had done on subjects' justifications. So I selected 20 cases at random, coded them, and sent them to her by e-mail. I was hoping for 70% agreement, as I felt that I had very little confidence in my own coding. A day later, her codes came back, and agreement was 100%.

Her death, just before her 37th birthday, brought great sadness to everybody who had the pleasure to know her. It has left a big gap in our lives. Things like this aren't supposed to happen, but they do. We were looking forward to many years of collaboration and friendship, but that is not to be. Her family, of course, feels the greatest loss.

Other Tributes from the Newsletter of the European Association for Decision Making

Jane Beattie became a member of the Executive Board of the European Association for Decision Making (EADM) at the Subjective Probability, Utility, and Decision Meeting (SPUDM) conference in Jerusalem in 1995. Her first task as a member of the executive board was to serve on the editorial committee of the selected proceedings, which were published in *Acta Psychologica*. Because of her illness, this was unfortunately the only time EADM was able to profit from her expertise and critical mind. I first met her in 1993 at the SPUDM conference in Aix-en-Provence, where she impressed us all with her presentation about decision aversion in relation to prenatal testing. A year later, she visited the Netherlands and also gave a talk at our Medical Decision Making Unit in Leiden. With the multidisciplinary audience that attended her talk, she had a lively discussion about the relevance of decision aversion and anticipated regret for medical treatment decisions now that patient involvement is becoming increasingly important. We on the board were very much looking forward to working with her. She had a clear mind, but above all she was a very pleasant person. Although we knew she was very ill, her death came as a shock. In her EADM has lost a valuable member, and we will miss her. We wish her family the strength to carry this loss.

Danielle Timmermans
Secretary/Treasurer EADM

Jane Beattie participated in a European network on decision making, and I was one of the lucky Ph.D. candidates who made several visits to Sussex to discuss research with her. Working with Jane was a superb experience. I first met her when she came to the University of Amsterdam to give a colloquium about her work on decisions about prenatal testing. At that time, Jane and I talked for half an hour about our common research interests. Around Christmas 1994 I visited Jane in Sussex for the first time when she was awaiting the birth of her youngest child, Hayley. Despite her busy professional and personal life, Jane found time (or better, made time) to discuss our ideas in detail. I recall our meetings as hard work and great fun. Hard work because Jane was a good sparring partner, asking the right questions at the right time (and providing the right answers as well). Great fun because Jane was generally optimistic, good-humored, and very supportive. We had written a research proposal that would enable me to move to Sussex and work more closely with her after I had finished my Ph.D. Tragically, this never happened. We did get the proposal funded, but Jane was already ill and had to stop working. We kept in touch during her illness by phone and e-mail. On these occasions, Jane was always cheerful and interested in other people. It was difficult to perceive her as an extremely ill person. I realized how serious her illness was after I visited her in early February 1997, a few weeks before she died. It still was a big shock when I learned about her death on 25 March. Jane was a truly good person. Losing her, both as a friend and as a colleague, is hard. I will miss her deeply.

Marcel Zeelenberg

1 Introduction

Jonathan Baron and Elke U. Weber

Experienced conflict and difficulty characterize some decisions, but not all of them. Which decisions can be characterized in this way? What makes some tradeoffs appear hard, whereas others are made easily? How does conflict affect the experience of decision making and the way in which decisions are made? What is the relation between decision conflict and emotions, such as regret, and between decision conflict and moral conflict? Do people try to avoid making certain decisions because of the conflict? Does experienced conflict interfere with consistent judgment of tradeoffs of the sort required for public policy? What can be done to help people avoid the negative effects of conflict? What can be done to make difficult tradeoffs more consistent? And finally, at the other end of the spectrum, what can be done to get people to acknowledge and deal with difficult tradeoffs and associated conflict instead of avoiding them by making impulsive decisions?

These were some of the questions that occupied Jane Beattie and her collaborators before her untimely death in 1997. Her former collaborators and colleagues felt that an edited book on this important subject would provide a useful contribution to the literature as well as a fitting memorial to Jane.

The book includes chapters by Jane's former collaborators as well as other colleagues working on the topic of conflict and tradeoffs in decision making. The chapters attempt to review relevant literature as well as to report new findings, so that the book may serve as an introduction to the topic for students as well as experienced researchers. The chapters review existing relevant research and also include new results. They range from providing answers to important theoretical questions to providing demonstrations of practical importance of these issues in private and public decision-making applications.

In this chapter, we introduce the major themes of the book and provide some background.

In a sense, most of our behavior does not involve decision making. We do things without thinking. We do not consider options or evaluate consequences. At times, though, we catch ourselves in a moment of confusion. We don't know what to do or what to advise others to do. Some of these moments are characterized by a feeling that some fact is missing. If we had it, we would know what to do. At other times, we feel a sense of conflict. Different reasons pull or push in different directions. Such conflict is the topic of this book.

Psychology has been concerned with such conflict for a long time. It was part of the psychology of learning. Early cognitive theories of learning were satirized as having the rat "lost in thought at the choice point" (Atkinson, 1964, p. 149). Kurt Lewin (1951) classified conflicts in terms of approach and avoidance. *Approach* meant that some outcome was better than the status quo, and *avoidance* meant that it was worse. Approach-approach conflicts were between two better outcomes; approach-avoidance conflicts involved whether to change the status quo when the only alternative was better in some ways and worse in others.

Another line of work grew out of studies of stress in World War II by Irving Janis and others, culminating in the *conflict-theory model of decision making* (Janis & Mann, 1977). According to this view, decisions are easy, involving little stress, when doing nothing (not changing from the status quo or default) involves little risk or when there are serious risks of *not* changing but no risk of changing. These patterns are called *unconflicted adherence* and *unconflicted change*, respectively. When either option (change or no change) has risks and when the decision maker hopes to find a better solution and sufficient time to do so, he or she will engage in *vigilant* decision making, that is, will seek information and weigh the options. Vigilant decision making occurs in situations of moderate stress. If it is not realistic to hope to find a better solution because all options are expected to be worse than the status quo (although one might still be better than others), the most common decision-making style is *defensive avoidance*, that is, not thinking about the decision at all. Finally, if there is time pressure, a condition of frantic and disorganized search called *hypervigilance* may result, in which the decision maker considers one option after another, with little search for evidence. When the decision maker does seek evidence, the search is unsystematic and the most useful evidence is often overlooked. Defensive avoidance and hypervigilance are examples of high-stress decision making. A unique feature

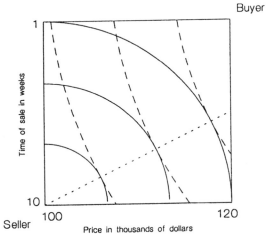

Figure 1.1. Representation of buyer and seller indifference curves for price and selling date of a house sale. The dotted line represents the Pareto frontier.

of the conflict-theory model, for which much support exists, is the claim that decision making is highly influenced by situational factors. The same person may make rational, methodical decisions in one situation and very poor decisions in others. The theory also claims that the quality of decision making affects the outcome (Herek, Janis, & Huth, 1987).

Meanwhile, also since about 1950, part of psychology – what we shall call the *judgment and decision-making (JDM) approach* – came under the influence of economics (see Edwards & Tversky, 1967). Since the late 19th century, economists had been thinking of choice among bundles of goods as based on quantitative tradeoffs. Edgeworth (1881) showed how choices involving two goods could be represented in terms of in-difference curves, as shown in Figure 1.1, which represents house sales that differ in price and selling date. Each curve represents options that were equally preferred. Of two points on the same curve, the one in the lower right would be better in terms of money but worse in terms of time of sale. A point above the curve would be preferred to any point on the curve.

The ideal consumer is characterized as choosing the combination of amounts of the two goods that will maximize the total utility. This involves equating the marginal utilities of the goods consumed. For ex-ample, a classic tradeoff is between leisure time and money. (Money, of course, is really a proxy for other goods to be consumed later.) If you have 20 hours of leisure per week and you are offered a chance to work

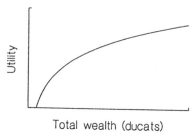

Figure 1.2. Utility of a person's total wealth, according to Bernoulli.

5 additional hours for $250, you have to figure out if that is worthwhile. The more of your time you sell in this way, the more valuable the remaining time becomes. As a result, you require a higher payment to give it up. You reach an optimal amount of leisure when the additional $50 is worth less to you than the utility of an additional free hour.

We often think of these curves as resulting from two utility functions, one for money and one for time. The term *utility* was originally coined by Jeremy Bentham (1789), who argued that actions should maximize utility. "By utility is meant that property in any object, whereby it tends to produce benefit, advantage, pleasure, good, or happiness, (all this in the present case comes to the same thing) or (what comes against to the same thing) to prevent the happening of mischief, pain, evil, or unhappiness. . . ." (p. 2). Evidently, Bentham had a broader concept in mind than simply pleasure and pain, but he did not dwell on its breadth.

A similar concept was developed much earlier by Bernoulli (1738) in order to explain (in essence) why people were not willing to pay $500 for a 50% chance to win $1,000. Bernoulli proposed that the utility of $1,000 was less than twice that of $500, so the expected utility of the bet – 50% of the utility of $1,000 – was less than the utility of $500. Bernoulli's idea of utility was quantitative. He thought of it as something that could be measured on a numerical scale. Figure 1.2 shows Bernoulli's idea of the utility of money.

This idea, in combination with Bentham's idea of maximizing utility as the proper basis for action, led to the kind of theory that Edgeworth developed. Edgeworth's indifference curves could be explained in terms of these utility curves for the two goods in question. Free time, like money, would also have a utility function. The indifference curves in Figure 1.1 can be derived from the utility functions. Each indifference curve connects points with the same total utility. The total utility is the sum of utility on the time function and the money function.

The money-versus-leisure decision is a classic tradeoff. Money and leisure are both good things, but the world is constructed so that more of one means less of the other. It is this sort of perversity that puts us in situations of conflict and requires us to make hard decisions. This much was known by early psychologists, but the new idea is that these things can be thought of quantitatively, in terms of the utility of different goods or the utility of different attributes of options. The field of judgment and decision making, as we know it today, grew out of this infusion of economic thinking into psychology. In this way, it is different from the work of the learning theorists and of Lewin.

Major credit for making psychologists aware of economic theory must go to Ward Edwards (1954). Edward and his students (and a few others) began a program of research into the psychology of judgment and decision making. The idea was, and is, to compare judgments and decisions to economic models that specify the optimal responses. Models of optimal responses are now called *normative*.

The chapters in this book are mostly about tradeoffs that can be analyzed quantitatively in this way. They are in the JDM tradition begun by Edwards rather than in the earlier psychological tradition exemplified by Lewin. Nor are they in the economic tradition. Economists tend to assume that individual decisions are rational and then go on to work out the implications of this assumption for aggregate behavior. The JDM tradition represented in this book, on the other hand, takes a more data-driven approach; that is, it attempts to explain and predict decision-making behavior, whether such behavior appears to be rational or irrational. Two classes of questions are addressed. The first category contains questions about the role of tradeoffs and conflict in choice behavior. What makes tradeoffs difficult? How do people resolve conflicts when they make everyday decisions? The other category contains questions about the measurement of tradeoffs, that is, the measurement of the relative utilities of two goods, such as time and money or money and risk. Such measurement is undertaken for the evaluation of public programs, such as those directed at risk reduction.

Jane Beattie was interested in both of these problems. In graduate school, her interest in tradeoffs was triggered in part by research of her advisor, Jon Baron, who had just written a paper on "Tradeoffs Among Reasons for Action" (1986) and in part by Barry Schwartz's book *The Battle for Human Nature* (1986), which argued against the moral appropriateness of making tradeoffs in some situations (and hence against the economic way of thinking). In Jane's thesis, she saw the two problems as related. She thought that the measurement of tradeoffs would be more difficult, and hence less internally consistent, when the tradeoff itself was difficult.

Role of Tradeoffs in Choice Behavior

One of the psychological questions addressed in the literature and in Jane's thesis concerns difficulty. Some tradeoffs are made so easily that the decision maker does not even notice making them; others seem extraordinarily difficult. Perhaps the first psychologist to address this issue quantitatively was Roger Shepard (1964). Shepard had been studying perceptual judgments, including judgments of the similarity of visual forms that varied in two dimensions, such as the size of a circle and the angle of a radius drawn inside the circle. Shepard found that for this pair of dimensions (but not for all pairs of dimensions), subjects did not give consistent weights to the two dimensions. They attended to one dimension or the other but rarely to both. Shepard suggested that people might have a similar problem making decisions that involved conflict between two attributes. He thought of the problem as a general one. As people thought about a tradeoff, they would first think about one attribute, then the other. The weights of the two attributes would depend on the decision maker's "frame of mind," which would fluctuate without a stable middle point.

In her thesis, Jane Beattie (1988) suggested that Shepard's problem might apply to some pairs of attributes more than others. The difficulty of making a tradeoff might be especially great when this kind of fluctuation occurred. Beattie tested various hypotheses about the determinants of tradeoff difficulty and its effects. In particular, she presented students with scenarios like the following: "You have a term paper due tomorrow and cannot get an extension. You have an eye infection and have been told not to do any reading or writing, but if you leave the paper your grade will suffer." The subject then considered two options: "You are put in pain but your grade does not suffer" versus "You are not put in pain, but you get a worse grade." Scenarios involved tradeoffs between commodities (apartments, computers, etc.), noncommodities (health, pain, grades, etc.), and currencies (time and money). Subjects rated each scenario on "decision difficulty" (the dependent variable) and on the following scales:

Q1 Is it ever wrong to trade off these two alternatives?
Q2 How sure are you that you would make the right decision?
Q3 How important is the first alternative to you?

Q4 How important is the second alternative to you?

Q5 How easy is it to imagine a decision involving these two alternatives in which you didn't care which alternative happened?

Q6 How easy is it to imagine a decision involving these two alternatives in which you found it very difficult to choose which alternative you wanted to happen?

Q7 How long do you think you would have to spend thinking about a decision with these two alternatives?

Q8 How experienced are you at making decisions involving these two alternatives?

Q9 To what extent do you think this is a moral decision?

Q10 How vaguely described is this decision?

Q11 How similar are these two alternatives?

Q12 Do you have rules for making decisions of this kind?

Subjects differed in which of these measures accounted for their decision difficulty judgments. In general, though, the most important predictors were certainty (Q2), ease of imagining that one did not care (Q5), ease of imagining that one could not choose (Q6), morality (Q9), similarity (Q11), and the product of Q3 and Q4, which was high when both alternatives were important. When the alternatives were more similar, the tradeoff was easier. People have difficulty trading off attributes that seem quite different and hence hard to compare. Moral decisions were more difficult for some people but easier for others; Beattie suggested that the latter applied rules. Although these results were preliminary, they inspired further research by Beattie and others.

An extension of Beattie's work with Sema Barlas is included here as chapter 2. Beattie and Barlas proposed a set of psychological categories to account for differences in decision difficulty (commodities, noncommodities, and currencies). They found that these categories, along with other features of the decision (e.g., similarity and importance of alternatives), can be used to predict the difficulty of the decision. They also found sex differences in category structure, with women requiring a two-dimensional solution (importance of alternative and degree of personalness) and men a one-dimensional solution (importance). Decisions between categories were easier than those within categories, and decisions involving noncommodities were more difficult than those involving other items. Category information also predicted choice behavior in a "choices between equally preferred alternatives" paradigm (noncommodities were chosen most often) and reaction time needed to choose (decisions involving noncommodities took longest).

Beattie, Baron, Hershey, and Spranca (1994) developed a new concept of decision difficulty, which they called *decision attitude*. Your attitude toward a decision is whether you want to make that decision or avoid it. Notice that avoiding a decision is not the same as doing nothing. (Otherwise, decision attitude would be the same as attitude toward the default option.) Decision attitude was measured in two ways. First, subjects were asked to rate how much they would like to be in each of three situations: getting A without choosing it, getting B without choosing it, or choosing between A and B. Second, subjects were asked whether they wanted to choose A or B or whether they wanted some random device to make the decision. The second question is actually a choice of a more complex kind, but subjects tended to see it as a way of not deciding because its results matched those of the first method. In most cases, subjects wanted to make the decision themselves, that is, they were *decision seeking* in the sense of rating making the decision as better than getting either of the two options. Some decisions, though, created real *decision aversion*, for example, deciding which of your children would get a medical treatment when only one could get it, or even deciding which of someone else's children should inherit an antique piano. Even making a risky decision for another person, like deciding which of two medical treatments to give, induced some aversion. Generally, decision aversion was most apparent when the decision required violating the rule of equal treatment and when it could cause a bad outcome for someone else. These properties seem to be moral ones, based on principles of equity and self-determination (autonomy). Beattie et al. (1994) looked at the influence of other factors, such as anticipated regret for decisions affecting the self, and losses versus gains, but failed to find any effects.

In 1996, however, Jane supervised an undergraduate project (Shepard, 1996), which yielded more promising results concerning gains and losses and which should be replicated. The study used a version of the Asian Disease Problem (Tversky & Kahneman, 1981):

> Imagine that the United States is preparing for the outbreak of an unusual Asian disease that is expected to kill 600 people. Two alternative vaccines to combat the disease exist. Assume that the exact scientific estimates of the consequences of the vaccines are as follows:
>
> Vaccine A: 200 saved
> Vaccine B: 600 saved (33% chance)
>   No one saved (67% chance)

Imagine three possibilities. In each case, you are a citizen of the United States and must be vaccinated against the disease.

Situation 1: Only vaccine A is available.
Situation 2: Only vaccine B is available.
Situation 3: Both vaccines A and B are available, and you must choose which one you want.

In half of the conditions, "600 − x saved" was replaced with "x die," ostensibly the same event. In half of the conditions, the subject took the perspective of a "medical officer responsible for administering the vaccine program." The number of subjects showing decision seeking or aversion (as defined by Beattie et al., 1994) was:

Condition	Seeking	Neutral	Aversion
Officer/saved	6	7	12
Officer/die	3	2	20
Citizen/saved	10	9	6
Citizen/die	19	5	1

Most subjects were decision seeking when making decisions for themselves and decision averse when making decisions for others. Both of these effects were (almost significantly) greater in the loss frame than in the gain frame (despite the apparent error).

The hypothesis that tradeoffs are more difficult when dimensions are dissimilar was tested further in the work of Beattie and Baron (1995), which concerned the judgment of appropriate penalties for causing harm. Subjects preferred penalties that were more similar to the harms. For example, if a logging company negligently cut down 100 square miles of protected forest (because the company did not check to make sure it could legally cut the timber in question), subjects preferred a penalty in which the company returned about the same amount of forest of the same type to the government to a penalty in which the company returned even a larger amount of a different kind of forest (or money). When setting the optimal penalty of each kind, subjects asked for a greater area of different-type forest than of same-type forest. They also indicated that they found the judgments of different-type forest penalties to be more difficult.

As Zeelenberg, Inman, and Pieters point out in chapter 6, psychologists have known about the role of regret in decision making for some time. Regret research in the JDM tradition is more recent. Bell (1982) and

Loomes and Sugden (1982) simultaneously proposed that many of the deviations of observed choices from expected-utility theory could be explained in terms of anticipated regret. These deviations had also been explained by features of prospect theory (Kahneman & Tversky, 1979), so for these cases *regret theory* became an alternative to prospect theory.

The idea (based on Savage, 1954) is that we experience outcomes of choices by comparing them to outcomes that would have occurred if we had chosen differently. If we buy shares of a stock and its price goes down, we regret the purchase because we compare the outcome to what would have happened if we had done nothing. If we consider buying shares, do not buy them, and the price goes up, we regret our omission. (Kahneman and Tversky, 1982, found that people expect to feel stronger regret as the result of action than as the result of an omission.)

Notice that this kind of comparison is one of two kinds that we could make. We could also compare outcomes to what would have happened if the situation had turned out differently. Thus, we could compare the price of the stock to what it would have been if interest rates had not gone up, and so on. This kind of comparison leads to disappointment as distinct from regret. In chapter 6, Zeelenberg, Inman, and Pieters review evidence that people distinguish regret and disappointment.

Regret, not disappointment, is the more important issue in decision conflict. Decisions are often difficult because we fear that we will regret whatever choice we make. A similar fear of disappointment surely exists and makes people averse to taking risks, but disappointment alone cannot lead to self-blame. It is the possibility that another choice option may lead to a better outcome that causes true conflict.

The domain of Bell and Loomes and Sugden's theory of regret were choices between gambles. The idea is that when people think about gambles, they think of the decision in terms of options, probabilistic states of the world, and outcomes. For example, the states of the world might be the different numbers that might come up in a lottery. The options are which numbers you bet on. The outcomes are the amounts you would win. The outcome depends on your bet and on the state of the world. Regret theory proposes that people choose the option that minimizes the regret that they anticipate experiencing after the selected lottery is played. They do so by comparing the outcome of each choice in each state of the world to the outcome of the other choice in the same state.

The theory turned out to be less useful than was originally thought as an account of choices among gambles (Starmer & Sugden, 1993), but the basic idea was borne out by a great deal of subsequent research. We can study the role of anticipated regret by looking at the effects of *resolution* of the uncertainty, that is, whether or not the decision maker finds out what would have happened if another option had been chosen. The original theory assumes that, ex ante, the decision maker always imagines the consequences of all options and compares them to each other in every possible state of the world. This could be true, but it turns out not to be true. It matters whether people think they will know about outcomes ex post (Boles & Messick, 1995; Josephs, Larrick, Steele, & Nisbett, 1992; Ritov & Baron, 1995; Zeelenberg, Beattie, van der Pligt, & de Vries, 1996). For example, Zeelenberg and his colleagues (1996) gave subjects a choice between a "risky" gamble and a "safe" gamble. The gambles were chosen to be equally attractive (as determined in a matching task). An example of a risky gamble is a 35% chance to win 130 Dutch guilders (vs. nothing), and a safe gamble is a 65% chance to win 85 guilders. When subjects expected to learn the outcome of the risky gamble even if they chose the safe one, 61% of them chose the risky gamble. When they expected to learn the outcome of the safe gamble even if they chose the risky one, only 23% chose the risky gamble. What subjects tended to avoid was losing the gamble they chose and learning that they would have won if they had chosen the other gamble. This result indicates not only that people pay attention to resolution but also that regret has a larger effect than rejoicing. Attention to rejoicing would lead to the opposite result: Subjects would think that they might win the gamble they had chosen and lose the other gamble.

In chapter 6, Zeelenberg et al. discuss yet another property of regret: its influence on subsequent behavior. Present evidence indicated that regret can mediate the effect of learning from experience. Thus, when we make choice A, learn that choice B would have been better, and experience regret, we are more likely to change to B at the next opportunity than if we do not experience regret. This result fits nicely with the findings of Markman, Gavaski, Sherman, and McMullen (1993), who found that knowing that there will be another opportunity to make the same decision makes people attend more to how they might have done better, thus increasing their susceptibility to regret itself. Zeelenberg et al. point out that the effect of regret on subsequent behavior is specific to regret, as distinct from disappointment. They also show that actions lead to greater regret than inactions (at least in the short term) and to greater effort to undo the effects of the bad decision, for example, to make amends to those who were hurt.

Murray's chapter (chapter 7, based on work originally supervised by Beattie) examines the role of anticipated regret and other factors on the aversiveness of making decisions about prenatal testing. Screening tests, carried out on samples of maternal blood at 16 weeks' gestation, can provide estimates of the risk of giving birth to a child with Down syndrome and spina bifida. Pregnant women and their partners can then use these risk estimates to help them decide whether to have further tests such as amniocentesis in order to obtain a definite diagnosis. Murray reports findings from an interview study of 40 pregnant women that examined how they decided whether to accept or decline one such test, the Triple Test. Psychological factors such as decision aversion, regret, and omission/commission bias, which have been shown to be important in laboratory studies of decision making, were found to be influential in this real-life decision. Only some of the women who took part in the study welcomed the opportunity to make a choice about testing. Others found it difficult and unpleasant to anticipate what they might do if they got a positive test result, and they felt they had to think about such possible later choices in order to decide whether or not to have the Triple Test. Predicting their future preferences was extremely difficult for some women, and the data from follow-up interviews showed that such preferences often changed over time. Although the Triple Test decision was presented to them as a choice they could make, many women felt that they would be going against the "norm" to decline the test; this led to a greater sense of responsibility and anticipation of self-blame in some of those who refused it. Those who could vividly imagine future situations in which they might regret their choices reported finding the Triple Test decision particularly difficult.

The Markman et al. (1993) study just described is one of many that illustrate how people reframe decisions to focus more on one feature of the outcome of one option at the expense of other features. Such reframing is affected by various properties of the decision itself. The features can be positive or negative, by comparison to some natural reference point, and the reference point itself may be labile. Houston, Sherill-Mittleman, and Weeks, in chapter 3, discuss the various factors that make people attend to positive and negative features and how such attention mediates the effect of these factors on decision making.

Houston et al. discuss several factors that can affect the resolution of choice dilemmas by systematically enhancing the salience of the good features of a pair of alternatives at the expense of the bad features, or vice versa. Such differences in feature salience can, in turn, affect which features contribute disproportionately to a judgment. In a way, Houston et al. resurrect Lewin's idea of different types of decision conflict (approach-approach, approach-avoidance, etc.) and turn it into an empirical theory rather than just a framework for description.

In particular, Houston et al. report evidence that people tend to ignore common features of choice alternatives. If the common features are bad, then people view the decision as a choice between sets of good features, and vice versa. Moreover, when people are asked to compare one option to another, the unique features of the subject get more attention. This effect, combined with the first, yields a rich set of predictions. Attention to positive versus negative features also depends on whether subjects are told to choose one option or reject one option. This effect further enriches the predictions of the theory. The theory makes predictions not only for choice but also for regret. Regret is greater when the choice is based on the less bad of two sets of unique bad features. This is because the bad features of the chosen option cannot be forgotten. Houston et al. discuss research on the practical implications of this approach for consumer behavior and for political choice. For example, the theory explains why negative political advertising reduces the tendency to vote.

Luce, Payne, and Bettman, in chapter 4, summarize another research program concerned with tradeoff difficulty. Like Zeelenberg et al., they examine both the determinants and the effects of emotional responses to decisions and their outcomes. They are concerned with emotions in general, not just regret. Their view of conflict is in the tradition of the conflict-theory model of Janis and Mann (1977), but they are more explicit in defining the nature of threat-producing outcomes and effects, and they also draw on more recent work on the psychology of emotion.

Two effects are of interest. One is that emotional conflict leads to simplified decision strategies, in which (for example) the decision is based on the single most important attribute rather than on a consideration of the tradeoffs among all relevant attributes. The other is that emotional conflict leads people to favor the status quo or default option (just as negative political advertising may lead people not to vote). Both of these can be seen as clearer statements of what *defensive avoidance* means.

Luce and her colleagues define tradeoff difficulty as the degree to which making an explicit tradeoff between two attributes (i.e., calculating an explicit exchange rate) generates threat or negative emotion. *Threat,* in this case, refers to a loss on some dimension relative to some natural reference point, such as a loss of safety. Luce et al. find that measures of attribute-level loss aversion seem to predict tradeoff difficulty more precisely than do measures of attribute-level importance. *Loss aversion* refers to the extra weight given to losses as opposed to equivalent gains (Kahneman & Tversky, 1979). Luce and her colleagues measured loss aversion in several ways, all based on comparison of explicit tradeoffs involving losses to tradeoffs based on nominally equivalent gains (e.g., a 20% decrease in salary vs. a 20% increase).

Another type of conflict is that between impulses and deeper values. Buying on impulse is an example. Impulse buying has been of theoretical and practical significance to economics, consumer behavior, and psychology. Economic and marketing approaches have traditionally assumed a rational decision maker. Impulse buying presents a challenge to this assumption, as such purchases are often ones that consumers wish – on reflection – not to have made. The clinical psychological literature has been concerned with examining the excessive impulse-buying behavior of "compulsive" or "addicted" consumers.

Dittmar's chapter (chapter 5, based partly on work done collaboratively with Jane Beattie) develops a social psychological model, which proposes that people buy on impulse in order to acquire material symbols of personal and social self-identity. This model explains, among other things, why certain types of goods (e.g., clothes) are bought impulsively more than others (e.g., basic kitchen equipment). Results of several studies, using a variety of methods, support the model's prediction that the motivation to bolster self-image is a significant – if not the only – factor in impulse buying.

Typical of such conflicts is that the deeper values, those that the consumer would endorse after reflection, are affected more in the long term. This leads to two predictions, both of which are supported by the results. One is that impulse buyers will often experience regret after their purchasing. Indeed, the judgment that the decision was wrong, on reflection, is almost the essence of the phenomenon, and the step from this realization to the emotion of regret is a short one. The other is that impulse purchases will be characterized by high discount rates. That is, the buyer will behave as though the value of the good declines quickly over time. The results show that high discount rates characterize both the kinds of goods that are typically bought on impulse and, in general across a variety of goods, the people who buy them.

Measurement of Tradeoffs and Its Applications

Shepard (1964) was pessimistic about the possibility of measuring tradeoffs. Despite his pessimism, psychologists developed several methods for measuring the kinds of tradeoffs that economic theory required. Of interest to the theory is the extent to which a change in one dimension can be compensated for by a change in another dimension.

That defines the relative weight of the two dimensions. To return to our earlier example, the two dimensions could be money and leisure time. The question would be, how much salary would you give up in order to increase your leisure time by 5 hours per week? At your current level of income and leisure time, if you would give up $25,000 per year, then the tradeoff between time and money for you is about $100 per hour ($25,000 / [50 weeks × 5 hours per week]). Note that the tradeoff measure requires two units, one for each dimension.

One technique for assigning relative weights is to ask respondents simply to evaluate multidimensional stimuli holistically with ratings or rankings. For example, each respondent rates many antipollution policies that differ in yearly deaths prevented and in yearly cost per driver for inspections. Utilities on each dimension and relative weights of dimensions are inferred from these responses. A large variety of methods use this approach. The two most common ones are *functional measurement* (e.g., Anderson & Zalinski, 1988) and *conjoint analysis* (Green & Srinivasan, 1990; Green & Wind, 1973; Louviere, 1988). Conjoint analysis is based on the theory of conjoint measurement, in which utility functions for each of the dimensions can be inferred from the indifference curves (Krantz, Luce, Suppes, & Tversky, 1971), although, in practice, the full process of inference is often approximated with a regression model.

In these methods, the tradeoff between a given change on one dimension and a given change on the other should be unaffected by the range of either dimension used within the experimental session. If a change from 50 to 100 lives is worth a change from $20 to $40, then this should be true regardless of whether the dollar range is from $20 to $40 or from $2 to $400. The *marginal rate of substitution* between lives and money is $20 ($40 − $20) for 50 lives (100 − 50), or $0.40 per life. We shall call this the tradeoff between money and lives. (Of course, the tradeoff may depend on where in the range it is measured, but it should not depend on the range itself.)

Beattie originally thought that tradeoff difficulty would increase the susceptibility of these multiattribute rating tasks to extraneous influences, such as the effect of the stimulus range. The idea was that, for some decisions, people would have definite ideas about just how willing they were to give up one thing for something else. In other decisions, however, people might be uncertain about their preferences for dimensions and thus about their willingness to trade off. In these cases, people would be easily influenced by extraneous factors. Thus, when tradeoffs are difficult, people might give less weight to each unit of an attribute (e.g., $1 for money) when the range of the attribute is larger. The extraneous influence here is that subjects think in terms of the proportion of a range rather than the unit itself.

Beattie and Baron (1991), using a functional measurement task, found no effects of relative ranges on rates of substitution, using several pairs of dimensions, so long as (arguably) the dimensions were understandably related to fundamental values, that is, to values that really mattered (e.g., effect on winning vs. injury rate of basketball players, risk of endometrial cancer vs. risk of osteoporosis in women considering estrogen replacement therapy). They found range effects only when the dimensions were presented as arbitrary numbers (e.g., a score on a test), so that the range itself provided information about their relation to the values of fundamental interest (e.g., ability). Mellers and Cooke (1994) found range effects even under conditions like those in which Beattie and Baron (1991) found none. Baron, in chapter 10 in this volume, also finds range effects, using familiar tradeoffs such as those between time and money.

Measurement of tradeoffs has been important for a number of practical problems, and several methodological approaches to these problems have developed. In the field of marketing, research has been concerned with the tradeoff of attributes of consumer goods, such as price and quality, and the various dimensions of quality. Conjoint analysis has been widely used for these purposes.

A second method is *multiattribute decision analysis* (Keeney & Raiffa, 1993). In this method, respondents make explicit and implicit tradeoffs between dimensions. A researcher typically elicits these tradeoffs in an extended interview with each respondent, using a variety of methods. One method might require the respondent to make two ranges equally important by manipulating one end of one of them. For example, "How many square miles of forest saved is equivalent to spending $1 million of the government's budget?" The two ends of the forest range are the current amount of forest land and the current amount minus the amount to be given. The two ends of the money range are the current government budget and the current budget plus $1 million. The differences are assumed to have equal utility.

Another method is to ask for a probability: "What probability of losing 1,000 square miles of forest is equivalent to the government spending an additional $1 million?" If the answer is 20%, then it is assumed that the utility of losing $1 million is 20% of the utility of losing 1,000 square miles. A third method is to ask for a direct judgment: "What is the ratio of an an extra $1 million to losing 1,000 square miles of forest?" When different methods are used, the resulting answers can be checked against each other.

A variant of the first method is to use money as one dimension, in the form of a payment by the respondent. The researcher asks, "How much are you willing to pay to save 1,000 square miles of forest?" Economists have called this method *contingent valuation* because it is like asking someone about his or her willingness to pay in a contingent, or hypothetical, market (Mitchell & Carson, 1989). (Another form of the method uses willingness to accept instead of willingness to pay.) It has been applied extensively to measure the value of goods for which real markets do not exist, such as natural resources (wilderness areas, etc.) and human life and limb. In the latter application, people are asked how much they would pay to reduce their risk of death or injury by some (small) amount. If you are willing to pay $10 to reduce your risk by .00001, then your life is worth approximately $10/.00001 to you, or $1 million. We cannot ask you directly how much you would pay for your life, or even to avoid a large risk of death, because the value of money to you is presumably lower if you die, so this value depends on the probability of death.

The contingent valuation method suffers from a major problem, observed by Kahneman and Knetsch (1992) in the context of natural resources and by Jones-Lee, Loomes, and Phillips (1995) in the context of life and injury. The problem is that it is insensitive to quantity. People are willing to pay about the same amount for a risk reduction of 4 in 100,000 for road injuries as they would pay for a reduction of 12 in 100,000. Likewise, they are willing to pay about the same amount to clean up the pollution in one lake as to clean up the pollution in many lakes. This phenomenon does not seem to be artifactual (Baron, 1997; Beattie et al., 1998).

Multiattribute decision analysis suffers from similar problems, although practitioners are more aware of them. In particular, it is difficult to get subjects to pay attention to quantities when they compare dimensions. For example, when subjects are asked, "Which is more important, money or risk?" they often answer the question without thinking about the quantities. Questionnaire designers ask such questions routinely, and respondents answer them without realizing that the questions are almost meaningless. They should respond, "How much money for how much risk?" Even when subjects are told about the ranges – for example, the difference between a risk of 4 in 100,000 and 8 in 100,000 and a difference in taxes between $10,000 and $10,200 – they tend to be undersensitive to variations in the range. Doubling the range of money, for example, should approximately double its judged relative importance, but this rarely happens. Keeney (1992, p. 147) calls underattention to range "the most common critical mistake."

Underattention to range can be reduced. Fischer (1995) found complete undersensitivity to range when subjects were asked simply to assign weights to ranges (e.g., to the difference between a starting salary of $25,000 and $35,000 and between 5 and 25 vacation days – or between 10 and 20 vacation days – for a job). When the range of vacation days doubled, the judged importance of the full range of days (10 vs. 20) relative to the range of salaries ($10,000) did not increase. Thus, subjects showed inconsistent rates of substitution, depending on the range considered. Subjects were more sensitive to the range, with their weights coming closer to the required doubling with a doubling of the range, when they used either matching or direct judgments of intervals. In matching, the subject changed one value of the more important dimension so that the two dimensions were equal in importance, for example, by lowering the top salary of the salary dimension. In direct judgment, subjects judged the ratio between the less important and more important ranges, for example, "the difference between 5 and 25 vacation days is one-fifth of the difference between $25,000 and $35,000." (This is also called the method of *swing weights*.)

This kind of result leads one to wonder what people mean when they say that risk is twice as important as money. As Goldstein, Barlas, and Beattie point out in chapter 8, people make statements about relative importance in negotiations (formal or informal) and in other situations in which they communicate their desires to each other, as well as in tasks designed to measure utility. Even when subjects are asked explicitly to compare a range on one dimension with a range on another, they seem to be influenced by some concept of importance that is insensitive to the ranges. What could people mean when they say that one dimension is more important than another?

One approach to this question, used by Goldstein and his colleagues, is to ask whether person B can reconstruct person A's importance judgments after being told person A's rank ordering of options. That is, importance judgments may have a communicative function even if they do not reflect explicit tradeoffs. The first experiment reported in the chapter manipulated the duration of a vacation prize and the amount of extra cash available for expenses. In different sets of vacations, the prizes had a different constant amount added, so that their range was either from $600 to $900 or from $1,100 to $1,400. Subjects had to guess the importance judgments of other (hypothetical) subjects concerning the two dimensions from knowing how the other subjects ranked or priced the vacations.

Studies of preference reversals suggest that objective attribute importance depends on the response mode by which people express their preferences. Goldstein et al. investigated whether subjective judgments of relative importance also depend on the preference-response mode. They found changes in subjective importance that did not parallel the changes in objective importance (effect on choices). They also found evidence that people's interpretations of subjective importance depended on the preference-response mode. People did not (consistently) interpret importance to mean marginal rate of substitution. The problem of what people mean by importance is left unresolved by their results, but their method is a novel and useful approach that should be used in further studies.

One kind of tradeoff judgment has considerable importance for public policy, namely, that between monetary expenditures and risk to life and limb. The general result is that such tradeoffs raise a host of fundamental problems. Here, people's uncertainty/imprecision about their preferences, and the difficulties they have in conceptualizing very small changes in already small probabilities of unfamiliar and disquieting health outcomes, make their judgments vulnerable to many sources of bias and distortion – giving undue weight to factors that should not matter while neglecting or underweighting other factors that should.

In 1995, a multidisciplinary team embarked on a large and ambitious project commissioned by a consortium of U.K. government departments and agencies, coordinated by the Health and Safety Executive. Their objectives were (1) to reexamine (and perhaps reestimate) the money value used by the Department of Transport to represent the benefit of reducing the risks of premature death and injury in road traffic accidents and (2) to explore whether the same value should be used in other hazard contexts, such as public transport, domestic fires, radiation, and occupational health. Chapter 9 by Jones-Lee and Loomes describes the current state of this project, of which Jane Beattie was an active member. Drawing on team members' previous experience of the difficulties associated with (1), most of the research during the first 18 months demonstrated the robustness of numerous "unwelcome" influences. More recent work has explored other approaches that appear (at this early stage) to hold more promise – although many difficulties remain, and fundamental issues about how far "true" preferences exist and how far stated preferences are constructed in response to the particular questions being asked (and what implications this may have for the way policymakers use such data) are still far from resolved. Such issues are likely to stimulate an extensive and controversial program of research for many years to come.

In chapter 10, Baron further explores the measurement of tradeoffs between values, such as that between money and risk or between health quality and length of life. One way to measure such tradeoffs is to ask respondents for attractiveness ratings of stimuli consisting of pairs of attributes, such as a reduction of 1/100,000 in the annual risk of death for $100. Holistic ratings of this sort are useful if the tradeoffs are independent of irrelevant factors such as the range of values on each attribute within the session or the magnitude of the highest value. Range is the difference between the highest and lowest items on a dimension; magnitude is the difference between the highest item and zero. In this sense, Goldstein, Barlas, and Beattie (chapter 8) manipulated magnitude and held range constant in their first study. Unfortunately, such independence is not always found.

Another approach to eliciting consistent tradeoffs is to ask respondents to resolve the inconsistencies inferred from their responses to tasks that require comparisons of intervals on each dimension. This approach seems more promising. Two experiments illustrate each approach.

An important application of value measurement is multiattribute decision analysis. In the last few years, decision analysis has been used extensively as an aid to negotiation among interested parties (stakeholders) in complex decisions such as those involving conflicts between commerce and the environment. Chapter 11 by von Winterfeldt, a major proponent of this application, describes a systematic process for framing and analyzing decisions involving multiple stakeholders with conflicting objectives. The process, called *stakeholder decision analysis*, has evolved through many applications of decision analysis to highly controversial decisions. It consists of several steps, including framing the decision problem, eliciting values and objectives from stakeholders, developing measures for objectives, estimating and evaluating consequences, decision making, and implementation. While based on decision analysis, the steps in this process are largely qualitative and are equally useful for other formal analyses like dominance analysis, cost-effectiveness analysis, and cost-benefit analysis. Chapter 11 illustrates the stakeholder decision analysis process with a detailed example of a major infrastructure improvement decision concerning the reduction of electromagnetic fields from electric power lines.

Another applied problem involving tradeoffs is in the development of decision aids. In chapter 12, Spranca presents some work on the development of a computer decision aid for helping recipients of Medicaid (a U.S. health program for the poor) choose their health-care providers. The tradeoffs at issue involve dimensions such as the cost of extra payments, the convenience of the services, and the possibility of staying with one's current doctor. The chapter presents some key design features and the history of a computerized decision support tool that was developed by the RAND Corporation and the American Institutes for Research and Digital Evolution to help Medicaid recipients in Florida choose a health plan. The tool creates a personal summary table. The inputs for this table come from users' personal judgments of how well plans performed on major attributes, one attribute at a time. The tool stops short of using the computer to integrate information for users. This idea met with resistance from insurers, which feared it might work against them, and from others who felt it would be paternalistic. Another possible objection could be that many people just do not think that decisions should be made by weighing attributes and making tradeoffs (Kahn & Baron, 1996).

Spranca also discusses two other applications of decision aids, one dealing with testing for breast cancer genes and the other dealing with treatment of depression. The genetic testing problem raises issues of anticipated regret, very similar to those raised in chapter 7 on fetal testing.

Chapter 13 by Frisch concerns another kind of conflict, that between people's intuitive decisions and normative models, most notably expected utility theory. People's intuitions have been shown to violate description invariance (framing effects), procedure invariance (preference reversals), transitivity, and the independence axiom of expected utility theory. People's intuitive probability judgments sometimes violate the laws of Bayesian probability theory. Researchers disagree about how to interpret the conflict between intuitions and mathematical models. In particular, they disagree about whether the mismatch is due to a flaw in the models or a flaw in the people.

Chapter 13 argues that mathematical normative models can be viewed as tools for clarifying one's intuitions. Formal models do not eliminate the need for intuition. Arguably, the decision about whether to accept *axioms* is based on their intuitive compellingness, and the decision about whether two outcomes are the same or different also must be based on intuition (e.g., whether "receive $500" is the same as "receive $1,000 and then lose $500").

Frisch argues that this emphasis on intuition as essential can be viewed as a female perspective. In the field of judgment and decision making, there is much controversy about *intuition* versus *normative models*. Analogously, perhaps, in the field of moral development, there is a contrast between Kohlberg's *rights and justice* approach and Gilligan's *responsibility and caring* approach. However, in both domains, Frisch says, the disagreement is exaggerated. The question of how to develop a model of decision making that acknowledges the validity of both perspectives (the importance of logical consistency as well as intuition and emotion) is addressed through the idea of using intuitions and formal models as means of mutual clarification.

References

Anderson, N. H., & Zalinski, J. (1988). Functional measurement approach to self-estimation in multiattribute evaluation. *Journal of Behavioral Decision Making, 1,* 191–221.

Atkinson, J. W. (1964). *An introduction to motivation.* Princeton, NJ: Van Nostrand.

Baron, J. (1986). Tradeoffs among reasons for action. *Journal for the Theory of Social Behavior, 16,* 173–195.

Baron, J. (1997). Biases in the quantitative measurement of values for public decisions. *Psychological Bulletin, 122,* 72–88.

Beattie, J. (1988). *Perceived differences in tradeoff difficulty.* Unpublished Ph.D. dissertation, Department of Psychology, University of Pennsylvania.

Beattie, J., & Baron, J. (1991). Investigating the effect of stimulus range on attribute weight. *Journal of Experimental Psychology: Human Perception and Performance, 17,* 571–585.

Beattie, J., & Baron, J. (1995). In-kind vs. out-of-kind penalties: Preference and valuation. *Journal of Experimental Psychology: Applied, 1,* 136–151.

Beattie, J., Baron, J., Hershey, J. C., & Spranca, M. (1994). Determinants of decision seeking and decision aversion. *Journal of Behavioral Decision Making, 7,* 129–144.

Beattie, J., Covey, J., Dolan, P., Hopkins, L., Jones-Lee, M., Loomes, G., Pidgeon, N., Robinson, A., & Spencer, A. (1998). On the contingent valuation of safety and the safety of contingent valuation: Part 1 – Caveat investigator. *Journal of Risk and Uncertainty, 17,* 5–25.

Bell, D. E. (1982). Regret in decision making under uncertainty. *Operations Research, 30,* 961–981.

Bentham, J. (1948). *An introduction to the principles of morals and legislation.* Oxford: Blackwell. (Original work published 1843)

Bernoulli, D. (1954). Exposition of a new theory of the measurement of risk (L. Sommer, Trans.). *Econometrica, 22,* 23–26. (Original work published 1738)

Boles, T. L., & Messick, D. M. (1995). A reverse outcome bias: The influence of multiple reference points on the evaluation of outcomes and decisions. *Organizational Behavior and Human Decision Processes, 61,* 262–275.

Edgeworth, F. Y. (1881). *Mathematical psychics.* London: Kegan Paul.

Edwards, W. (1954). The theory of decision making. *Psychological Bulletin, 51,* 380–417.

Edwards, W., & Tversky, A. (Eds.). (1967). *Decision making.* Harmondsworth, U.K.: Penguin.

Fischer, G. W. (1995). Range sensitivity of attribute weights in multiattribute value models. *Organizational Behavior and Human Decision Processes, 62,* 252–266.

Green, P. E., & Srinivasan, V. (1990). Conjoint analysis in marketing: New developments with implications for research and practice. *Journal of Marketing, 45,* 33–41.

Green, P. E., & Wind, Y. (1973). *Multiattribute decisions in marketing: A measurement approach.* Hinsdale, IL: Dryden Press.

Herek, G. M., Janis, I. L., & Huth, P. (1987). Decision making during international crises. Is quality of process related to outcome? *Journal of Conflict Resolution, 31,* 203–226.

Janis, I. L., & Mann, L. (1977). *Decision making: A psychological analysis of conflict, choice, and commitment.* New York: Free Press.

Jones-Lee, M. W., Loomes, G., & Phillips, P. R. (1995). Valuing the prevention of non-fatal road injuries: Contingent valuation vs. standard gambles. *Oxford Economic Papers, 47,* 676–690.

Josephs, R. A., Larrick, R. P., Steele, C. M., & Nisbett, R. E. (1992). Protecting the self from the negative consequences of risky decisions. *Journal of Personality & Social Psychology, 62,* 26–37.

Kahn, B. E., & Baron, J. (1996). An exploratory study of choice rules favored for high-stakes decisions. *Journal of Consumer Psychology, 4,* 305–328.

Kahneman, D., & Knetsch, J. L. (1992). Valuing public goods: The purchase of moral satisfaction. *Journal of Environmental Economics and Management, 22,* 57–70.

Kahneman, D., & Tversky, A. (1979). Prospect theory: An analysis of decisions under risk. *Econometrica, 47,* 263–291.

Kahneman, D., & Tversky, A. (1982). The simulation heuristic. In D. Kahneman, P. Slovic, & A. Tversky (Eds.), *Judgment under uncertainty: Heurstics and biases* (pp. 201–208). New York: Cambridge University Press.

Keeney, R. L. (1992). *Value-focused thinking: A path to creative decisionmaking.* Cambridge, MA: Harvard University Press.

Keeney, R. L., & Raiffa, H. (1993). *Decisions with multiple objectives: Preference and value tradeoffs.* New York: Cambridge University Press. (Original work published 1976)

Krantz, D. H., Luce, R. D., Suppes, P., & Tversky, A. (1971). *Foundations of measurement* (Vol. 1). New York: Academic Press.

Lewin, K. (1951). *Field theory in social science.* New York: Harper.

Loomes, G., & Sugden, R. (1982). Regret theory: An alternative theory of rational choice under uncertainty. *Economic Journal, 92,* 805–824.

Louviere, J. J. (1988). *Analyzing individual decision making: Metric conjoint analysis.* Newbury Park, CA: Sage.

Markman, K. D., Gavaski, I., Sherman, S. J., & McMullen, M. N. (1993). The mental simulation of better and worse possible worlds. *Journal of Experimental Social Psychology, 29,* 87–109.

Mellers, B. A., & Cooke, A. D. J. (1994). Tradeoffs depend on attribute range. *Journal of Experimental Psychology: Human Perception and Performance, 20,* 1055–1067.

Mitchell, R. C., & Carson, R. T. (1989). *Using surveys to value public goods: The contingent valuation method*. Washington, DC: Resources for the Future.

Ritov, I., & Baron, J. (1995). Outcome knowledge, regret, and omission bias. *Organizational Behavior and Human Decision Processes, 64*, 119–127.

Savage, L. J. (1954). *The foundations of statistics*. New York: Wiley.

Schwartz, B. (1986). *The battle for human nature: Science, morality, and modern life*. New York: Norton.

Shepard, A. (1996). *The effects and interaction of 'framing' and decision attitude on choice*. Final Year Project, Department of Experimental Psychology, University of Sussex, Brighton, UK.

Shepard, R. N. (1964). On subjectively optimum selection among multi-attribute alternatives. In M. W. Shelley & G. L. Bryan (Eds.), *Human judgments and optimality* (pp. 257–281). New York: Wiley.

Starmer, C., & Sugden, R. (1993). Testing for juxtaposition and event-splitting effects. *Journal of Risk and Uncertainty, 6*, 235–254.

Tversky, A., & Kahneman, D. (1981). The framing of decisions and the psychology of choice. *Science, 211*, 453–458.

Zeelenberg, M., Beattie, J., van der Pligt, J., & de Vries, N. K. (1996). Consequences of regret aversion: Effects of expected feedback on risky decision making. *Organizational Behavior and Human Decision Processes, 65*, 148–158.

2 Predicting Perceived Differences in Tradeoff Difficulty

Jane Beattie and Sema Barlas

It is a truism that some decisions are more difficult than others. Yet classical models of decision making have little say to about when and why decisions seem easy or difficult. The most pervasive model of riskless decision making is multiattribute utility theory (MAUT) (Keeney and Raiffa, 1976). This model posits that choices (e.g., apartments) can be decomposed into values on relevant attributes (e.g., rent, distance from work). The values on all the different attributes are converted to a common psychological scale of utility. The utility values are then weighed by an attribute weight representing the importance of the attribute to the individual decision maker. Finally, these products are summed together to yield the overall utility of each object. The outcome (apartment) with the highest utility should be preferred or chosen. More precisely, for the choice set of objects $O = \{o_1, \ldots, o_k\}$, there is a set of attributes $A = \{a_1, \ldots, a_n\}$. u_{ij} is the utility of attribute a_j of object o_i. w_j is the weight of attribute a_j. The overall utility of object o_1 is

$$U_i = \sum_{j=1}^{n} w_j u_{ij} \tag{1}$$

The theory, as stated here, says nothing about why some decisions should be more difficult than others, although it would be easy to extend

Preliminary findings from Experiments 1 and 2 were presented by Beattie and Barlas (October 1990; August 1991). We thank Jon Baron, Colin Camerer, Helga Dittmar, Greg Fischer, Bill Goldstein, Jack Hershey, Robin Hogarth, George Loewenstein, Jay Russo, and John Sabini for helpful comments and discussions. Emily Reber, Maureen Markwith, and Laura Schlachtmeyer prepared the stories and collected the data. This research was supported in part by National Science Foundation Grant SES89-22156 to W. M. Goldstein and J. Beattie. Beattie gratefully acknowledges support from the University of Chicago Graduate School of Business faculty research fund.

it to do so in the following way. Decisions may be difficult when the choices have equal or almost equal utilities (i.e., the U_i values are approximately equal). This certainly seems to be true of some difficult decisions, as illustrated by the following example. Imagine being asked to choose between the following pairs of apartments characterized by monthly rent and distance from work in minutes of walking time.

Choice 1	Rent	Distance
Apt. 1	$2,000	10 min
Apt. 2	$400	11 min

Choice 2	Rent	Distance
Apt. 3	$410	10 min
Apt. 4	$400	11 min

All other things equal, the choice between 1 and 2 would be easy for most people (apartment 2 is better). The difference between apartments 3 and 4 is much smaller, however, and choosing is much more difficult. In this case, the difficulty stems from a lack of discriminability based on the similar utilities. In such cases, however, a paradox seems to arise. We have proposed that decisions are difficult when the choices are equally valuable, yet those should also be exactly the cases in which it matters little (in utility terms) which outcome one obtains. Hence close decisions should be easy. If two outcomes really are matched in utility, then it matters not at all how one decides: Any decision rule will be as good as any other, so agonizing is pointless. We may as well flip a coin.

While "closeness in utility" may explain why some decisions are difficult, it cannot capture all of our intuitions about when decisions are difficult. This point is well illustrated by the following example from Tversky (1972), based on an example of L. J. Savage. Imagine that you are finding it difficult to choose between a trip to Paris (P) and a trip to Rome (R). Thus we assume that you are indifferent between Paris and Rome:

$$P \approx R \tag{2}$$

Now you are offered a new alternative of "Paris + $1" ($P'$), which would obviously be preferred to the old Paris trip (being of unambiguously higher utility). Thus:

$$P' \succ P \tag{3}$$

By substitution, MAUT now predicts that you would easily choose the "Paris + \$1" package over the trip to Rome. It should be true that

$$P' \succ R \tag{4}$$

Yet this prediction may be wrong: The addition of the dollar may not make the choice between Paris and Rome noticeably easier. We may be left with the actual preference of

$$P' \approx R \tag{5}$$

which results in a violation of transitivity of preferences. It appears, then, that not all choices are substitutable for each other despite being of apparently equal utility.

We will argue that substitutability and comparability are two sides of the same coin and that both relate to decision difficulty. Items that are difficult to compare (P and R) may be those that are difficult to decide between, whereas those that are easy to compare (P and P') are easy to decide between. The reason P cannot be substituted for across the two different equations to yield a preference for P' over R is that P' and R are also not comparable. As Tversky (1972, p. 289) argued from this example, "[c]hoice probabilities ... reflect not only the utilities of the alternatives in question, *but also the difficulty of comparing them*" (our emphasis).

In this chapter we examine the question of why some decisions are perceived as more difficult than others, with particular attention to the issue of the comparability and substitutability of the alternatives. We argue that the standard decision theory notion of *closeness to the indifference point* cannot account for all differences in decision difficulty, and we develop an alternative theory of when decisions will be difficult. We concentrate on the perception that some pairs of attributes are more difficult to trade off than others. For example, imagine being asked to fill in the missing value in the following two decisions such that you are indifferent between the choices in each pair. Item 1 refers to two different apartments described on the attributes of monthly rent and distance from work. Item 2 concerns two options for highway programs and requires a comparison of the attributes of expenditure and lives saved.

Item 1	Rent ($)	Time (min)
A	330	10
B	400	?

Item 2	Expenditure ($)	Lives saved
C	5 million	7
D	4 million	?

The attributes in item 1 may seem easier to compare than those in item 2. This indicates that there may be differences in the difficulty of trading off the two different attribute pairs. Note that the members of each pair are set, by definition, to have equal utility ($U_A = U_B$ and $U_C = U_D$). Thus the difference in tradeoff difficulty can have nothing to do with deciding between objects that are differentially close in utility (as predicted by the MAUT account). In order to account for the differences in difficulty in making tradeoffs between these two items, we need a theory of how attributes are represented and compared with one another. In this chapter we categorize attributes or objects into three classes (commodities, noncommodities, and currencies) in order to predict when tradeoffs will be difficult.

Categorization of Objects

Investigators working in several different theoretical traditions have proposed different taxonomies or categories of objects (although not generally for the purpose of investigating decision difficulty). We now review these literatures briefly and use them as a point of departure for our own categorization and our investigation of its relation to decision difficulty.

From a philosophical point of view, Schwartz (1986) distinguished between commodities (which can rightly be exchanged in the market) and noncommodities. Commodities have several defining features (pp. 303–304): Producers and consumers are generally different people and are typically strangers; commodities are owned, are transferable, and are produced and exchanged for profit. Common examples are cars and electronic items. Noncommodities, on the other hand, either cannot be traded or transferred (e.g., I cannot give you my pain) or will lose some of their desirable properties if traded for profit (friendship cannot be bought and sold; and if I sell my grandmother's necklace, I cannot also transfer to you the sentimental value that I feel for it). In a similar spirit, Walzer (1983) distinguished between different *spheres of justice*. He argued that money and commodities can rightly be traded for one another but that other goods (noncommodities) become corrupted when traded in the marketplace: for example, political power, divine grace, and love.

In their development psychological theory, Foa and Foa (1974) proposed six classes of goods (love, status, information, money, goods, and services) arranged in a circle in a two-dimensional space of particularism and concreteness. *Particularism* refers to the degree to which the identity of the person involved in the exchange matters. This is similar to Schwartz's notion of consumers and producers being separate. Unlike Schwartz and Walzer, however, Foa and Foa distinguished between money and other goods. Turner, Foa, and Foa (1971) validated the category structure proposed by showing that items from closer categories are perceived as more similar than those from distance categories and are more likely to be offered as appropriate substitutes for the object.

From a social psychological viewpoint, Dittmar (1989) classified subjects' lists of favorite possessions into four categories: material processions (e.g., camera, clothes), pets, relationships (e.g., friend, lover), and nonmaterial possessions (e.g., health, memories). She found substantial gender differences in subjects' choices, with women listing more objects of sentimental value and men choosing more items relating to leisure and finances. In listing the reasons for their choices, men concentrated on practical usage. Women, however, also saw possessions as important symbols of interpersonal relationships. A similar method was used by Prentice (1987), who classified 70 favorite objects into a space defined by four dimensions: symbolic versus instrumental, recreational versus practical, cultured versus everyday, and prestigious versus common. She did not, however, analyze for gender differences in object selection or reasons for choice. The large number of dimensions required may reflect the pooling of qualitatively different data from male and female subjects.

In the decision-making literature, Frisch, Jones, and O'Brien (1992) conducted a retrospective study of real-life difficult decisions. They classified these decisions into two main categories: professional focus and personal focus. These categories were related to the mode of resolution of the decision. Frisch et al. (1992) also found that the category of the decision and postdecisional satisfaction interacted with the gender of the subject. Men were more likely to be highly satisfied with professional decisions than with personal or relational decisions, whereas for women there was no relationship between satisfaction and decision category.

Finally, researchers in consumer behavior have also been concerned with product classification, particularly with respect to a buyer's ability to make decisions between comparable and noncomparable alternatives. (Degree of comparability is defined in terms of the number of features shared by two products; thus VCRs and CD players are more comparable than VCRs and washing machines.) Johnson (1984, 1986) found that the difficulty of the choice between items increased as their comparability decreased. Bettman and Sujan (1987) found that novices were susceptible to priming effects for noncomparable alternatives, whereas experts were not. This line of research related the difficulty of the decision directly to the type of alternative used. Note, however, that all of Johnson's and Bettman and Sujan's choice items were consumer goods. Hence they would all be placed in the same category by the researchers whose work was described earlier.

Although the studies just cited derive from several different theoretical traditions, a number of common themes emerge in their classifications of goods. The following factors may be important: status or prestige (Foa and Foa, 1974; Walzer, 1983); usefulness (Dittmar, 1989; Prentice, 1987); relational/symbolic; particularism (Foa and Foa, 1974; Schwartz, 1986); recreation/action/leisure (Dittmar, 1989; Prentice, 1987). From Dittmar (1989) and Frisch et al. (1992), it appears that there may be differences in the ways in which men and women conceptualize objects related to the factors listed previously. Other than Frisch et al. (1992), however, none of these researchers have related their categories of objects to the difficulty of making a decision. Frisch et al.'s (1992) classification refers to categories of decision problems rather than of objects.

In the following experiments, we propose a categorization of objects to predict which decisions will be difficult. Our categorization draws heavily on the literature reviewed earlier and classifies objects as follows:

Commodities	Objects that are appropriately bought and sold in markets (e.g., cameras, CDs)
Currencies	Objects that act as stand-ins for commodities (e.g., money, coupons)
Noncommodities	Objects that either cannot be transferred (e.g., pain) or that lose some of their value by being traded in markets (e.g., friendship)

In the first two experiments, we ask subjects to make judgments of difficulty in deciding between objects drawn from different categories. We also ask them to rate other features of the decisions, such as attribute similarity and subjective importance, in order to discover whether these features can be used to describe the hypothesized categories. The third experiment investigates the characteristic features of the proposed categories more directly in the absence of judgments of decision difficulty. Before describing the experimental work, we briefly discuss why decision difficulty may have been neglected in previous research and why we believe it is important.

Why Study Decision Difficulty?

Experiential aspects of decision making such as the difficulty of the tradeoff have received relatively little research attention in the decision-making literature. Perhaps one reason is that it has been assumed that these factors are unimportant behaviorally. There is, however, some evidence that experiential factors may influence diverse aspects of the decision process. For example, stress can influence decision strategy and judgments (Mano, 1992). For example, positive and negative affect can influence probability judgments (Johnson and Tversky, 1983) and risk attitude (Isen and Geva, 1987)

We believe that differences in decision difficulty may also have important behavioral effects. First, people may avoid decisions that are difficult, leading them not to maximize their utility. Beattie, Baron, Hershey, and Spranca (1993) and Frisch et al. (1992) have shown that people prefer to avoid decisions between outcomes they find painful to compare. Schweitzer and Scalzi (1981) showed that treatment during the last year of life of patients with acute leukemia generally cost over $30,000 but apparently had little beneficial effect. Their interpretation was that health care policymakers have avoided considering alternative (less costly) therapies because this would involve a tradeoff between human suffering and financial resources. Yet in a resource-limited world such tradeoffs must be made, either implicitly or explicitly.

Second, the presence of decision difficulty may signal that subjects are making unreliable decisions. Butler and Loomes (1988) asked subjects to give certainty equivalents for simple gambles. They found differences in task difficulty, depending on the stimuli presented and a lack of precision in the values subjects reported. Many studies have shown nonnormative lability in attribute weights (e.g., Ebbesen and Konecni, 1980; Fischhoff, Slovic, and Lichtenstein, 1980; Shepard, 1964). If subjects are sensitive to this unreliability, they may find the decision difficult and may also be reluctant to decide. (However, Beattie and Baron, 1991, asked subjects to trade off a variety of attributes and found nonnormative lability in attribute weights even when subjects found the judgments difficult.)

Finally, some decisions may be difficult because people are unable to trade off the attributes. If this is so, conventional multiattribute decision aids are inappropriate for eliciting subjects' values. To make a trade-off requires some common scale or basis for comparison to be found (e.g., conversion of physical values to utility values). It is possible that some pairs of stimuli cannot be reduced to such a common scale. For example, certain psychophysical stimuli might seem hard to compare (e.g., can one match the brightness of a light to the level of a musical pitch?). However, we know of no psychophysical evidence suggesting that any dimensions actually are incomparable. In fact, the work of Stevens and his colleagues suggests the reverse (see Stevens, 1975, ch. 4, for a review of experiments on cross-modal matching). Stevens studied cross-modal matching in various sense modalities (e.g., loudness and shock) and found impressive consistency in subjects' judgments (even though subjects perceived the task to be difficult). Teghtsoonian (1971) even suggested that there may be a common psychological scale onto which many sensory magnitudes can be mapped. Thus there is no evidence that there are truly incomparable dimensions. In formulating the subjective expected utility model, Savage (1954) explicitly addressed the question of whether some dimensions might be incommensurable, but he decided that this "would prove a blind alley losing much in power and advancing little, if at all, in realism" (p. 21). However, there is little research to allow investigators to decide whether his claim is true, and it is still possible that decision difficulty may signal an inability to make tradeoffs. The studies presented in this chapter attempt to discover some of the causes of decision difficulty and its effects on behavior, including examining whether certain attributes may be incommensurable (e.g., those from different categories).

Experiment 1

We begin with the hypothesis that decision difficulty may be related to the types of objects involved in the tradeoff. The literature reviewed earlier suggests three major categories of objects: commodities (or market-tradables), currencies (social stand-ins for commodities), and noncommodities (market-inalienables). These categories were used in a pilot experiment by Beattie (1988, Experiment 7). She asked subjects to rate the difficulty of a decision between pairs of alternatives drawn from commodities (e.g., camera), noncommodities (e.g., health), and currencies (e.g., money). Subjects were also asked to list rules (if they had them) that they would use to decide between the alternatives. Decision difficulty was related to the category of the object and to the importance of the alternatives, their similarity, and the morality of the decision. In all cases where rules were given, noncommodities were chosen over commodities, and in all but one case, noncommodities were chosen over currencies (e.g., "...I found that trading objects of sentimental value remains painful, where money from savings is not often regretted – can be replaced").

These results suggest that noncommodities are treated differently than commodities and currencies. For example, subjects seem more likely to use lexicographic rules when deciding between these categories. However, this study involved only 10 subjects, and no formal statistical analysis of the category structure of the alternatives could be performed because not all pairs of alternatives were represented in the stimuli. In the present studies, we asked a smaller number of questions of a much larger number of subjects, permitting a more comprehensive analysis.

Experiment 1 tested the following hypotheses:

> *Hypothesis 1:* The objects presented will form psychologically distinct clusters or categories. Noncommodities will differ from commodities and currencies. The latter two may or may not differ from each other.
>
> *Hypothesis 2:* Decision difficulty will be related to the category to which the attributes belong. Decisions between commodities and currencies will be easier than those between noncommodities. Decisions involving currencies may be easier than those involving commodities.

We also investigated how the role of the decision maker affects the perception of decision difficulty. We manipulated whether the subject was the affected party or was making the decision on behalf of a close friend. We hypothesized that decision role could influence decision difficulty in a variety of ways. First, subjects might find decisions for a friend easier because they were not the affected party and thus would not have to cope with the consequences of the decision. Alternatively, they might find such decisions more difficult because they might not have adequate knowledge of the friend's preferences. We also thought that subjects might show a more pronounced interaction of decision difficulty with the categories from which the objects were chosen when they decided for a friend. This could be because, in making a decision for another person, one must often justify the choice overtly, promoting the use of lexicographic decision rules (which are easy to explain). These decision rules might be based on an ordering of the categories from which the items were chosen.

> *Hypothesis 3:*   The role of the recipient of the good (self vs. friend)
> may affect decision difficulty, as just described.

A list of items was constructed, and each item was classified a priori as a currency, commodity, or noncommodity. Commodities and noncommodities were classified using Schwartz's definitions (see earlier). Commodities were apartment quality, computer, clothes, camera, and vacation; noncommodities were health, pain, objects of sentimental value, midterm grades, and promotion. Currencies were time and money; both are used in sentencing criminals and thus are apparently viewed as substitutable for all other goods.

Pairs of alternatives were drawn from this list, and each pair was embedded in a short story describing a tradeoff between the two items. This gave the subject some context in which to imagine the decision. The level of each attribute was left deliberately vague to avoid differences between items in closeness to subjects' indifference points. (Subjects were asked to imagine a range of different values for each alternative to help them judge the difficulty of making the tradeoff described.) Subjects were then asked to rate the difficulty of the decision. They also evaluated the decision on a list of other features that were designed to help diagnose the differences between the categories (e.g., similarity of the alternatives, importance of the alternatives).

Method

Subjects. Subjects were 64 students at the University of Chicago (27 men and 37 women). All were solicited by advertisements on the campus and were paid a total of $20 each. Subjects were randomly assigned to one of four groups corresponding to different decision roles (16 subjects per group).

Stimuli. The stimuli were constructed from a list of 12 alternatives belonging to three categories (first used by Beattie, 1988). Pairs of alternatives were selected to yield tradeoffs that were expressed as short stories. Each possible pair was represented to yield 66 (12 choose two) stimuli. The stories were written by three psychology research assistants who were naive to the experimental hypotheses. In all cases, the level of the good (e.g., amount of money) that could be obtained was left unspecified.

Four parallel groups of stories were devised, differing only in the person who benefited from the choice made (either oneself or a close friend).

Group 1 involved decisions only for oneself (SS), Group 2 involved decisions made totally on behalf of the friend (FF), Group 3 rated tradeoffs in which "self" received the first alternative and "friend" received the second alternative (SF), and vice versa for Group 4 (FS). Due to the large number of stimuli involved, a within-subject design was obviously not feasible. However, we wished to encourage subjects across groups to anchor their use of the scales similarly. To this end, we included nine filler items from other groups' stimuli (three from each remaining group) so that all subjects rated some tradeoffs of each group type. Most of the fillers were located early in the trial sequence to maximize their effect. Data from the fillers were discarded.

Here is an example story from the SS condition.

> *Alternative 1*:   You are put in pain.
> *Alternative 2*:   You get a worse grade.
>
> You have a term paper due tomorrow. You have an eye infection and have been told not to do any reading or writing, but if you leave the paper your grade will suffer.

Procedure. Because of the large number of responses collected, the experiment was divided into three sessions of approximately 40 minutes each, scheduled with a gap of at least 2 hours between sessions. All subjects completed all sessions. Stimuli and instructions were presented by a computer, which also collected all responses. A Ross ordering (Ross, 1934) was constructed for the stimuli to minimize possible order and position effects. The computer randomly determined the starting point in the order for each subject.

> *Session 1:* Subjects were asked to read each story and rate its difficulty on a continuous scale running from −20 (extremely easy) to 0 (neutral) to +20 (extremely difficult).
>
> *Sessions 2 and 3:* Subjects reread each story and rated it on the following feature scales (each running from −20 to +20 and anchored with verbal labels specific to the scale).

1. How sure are you that you would make the right decision?
2. How important is the first alternative to you?
3. How important is the second alternative to you?
4. How easy is it to imagine that you didn't care which alternative you received?
5. How easy is it to imagine that you couldn't choose which alternative you wanted?

6. To what extent is this a moral decision?
7. How similar are the alternatives?

Session 2 presented the first 33 stories. Session 3 presented the remaining stories. (The difficulty ratings were separated from the feature scale ratings to avoid contaminating the subjects with our own hypotheses concerning why some decisions should be difficult.)

Instructions. The instructions gave subjects a brief introduction to the idea of making tradeoffs and informed them that we were interested in which kinds of things were difficult to trade off *in principle* (rather than because of the specific attribute levels). No examples of difficult-to-trade attributes were given to avoid suggesting our hypotheses to the subjects. Subjects were asked to imagine various values (high or low on each attribute) to help gauge the difficulty of the decision. In Groups 2–4, subjects were told that the "friend" mentioned was a very close friend whom they had known for a long time. They were also told not to introduce any extraneous facts into the story. Although the instructions may seem conceptually complex, debriefing interviews indicated that subjects understood the issues involved and were happy to answer the questions.

Results

Effects of Decision Role. The effects of decision role (friend, self) were not significant, so we collapsed across this variable for subsequent analysis.

For all the analyses that follow, the responses have been standardized within subject for each scale to reduce variability due to differences among subjects in scale usage after the filler items were discarded.

Psychological Validity of Categories. Multidimensional scaling (MDS) (Shepard, Romney, and Nerlove, 1972) and clustering analysis (complete linkage method; Anderberg, 1973) were used to assess the category structure of the alternatives. The standardized similarity judgments were pooled for all subjects, and the result was a two-dimensional solution (stress $= 0.116$) with two categories at the first level cut (see Figure 2.1a).

Although there is no statistical test for this, it appears that there was a reasonably good fit between the hypothesized categories and the psychological representation derived from the MDS and clustering analyses. The left-side category was composed primarily of the noncommodities, and the right-side category contained all of the commodities. The only confusion between these two categories was the "objects of sentimental value" (osv). Interestingly, these are the only noncommodities that are tangible, and they were located with the other tangibles (commodities), indicating that concreteness may in part underlie the difference between the two categories (as suggested by Foa and Foa, 1974). The most problematic category was clearly the currencies. Although "time" and "money" were located very close to each other in the similarity space, they were assigned to different categories. However, this may have been due to the small number of currencies used. This issue is taken up in Experiment 2.

In interpreting the two dimensions of the MDS, we hypothesized that dimension 1 was "importance." Objects rated high on the importance feature scale received low scores on dimension 1 and vice versa. Regressing subjects' importance ratings onto the scores on dimension 1 explained 87.4% of the variance in the importance ratings ($p < .0001$), and the correlation between the scores on dimension 1 and the importance ratings of the items was 0.92. The relationship between rated importance, category membership, and dimension 1 is shown in Figure 2.2. The interpretation of dimension 2 seemed problematic to us. To aid its interpretation, we analyzed the similarity data separately for men and women.

Gender Differences in Category Structure and Decision Difficulty. Several investigators have examined the effect of gender on attitudes toward material and nonmaterial goods (e.g., Csikszentmihalyi and Rochberg-Halton, 1981; Dittmar, 1989, 1992). Their findings suggested the possibility that women and men might differ in the bases for their similarity judgments and hence in the structure of their underlying categories. Thus we performed the MDS and clustering analyses separately for men and women (see Figures 2.1b and 2.1c). For both genders this yielded a two-cluster solution, but the constituents of the categories were different. Women separated all the noncommodities from the currencies and commodities, whereas men placed the objects of sentimental value with the commodities/currency grouping (money was also grouped with the remaining noncommodities). The other striking difference was that the solution for women was two-dimensional, whereas men required only one dimension. The stress for the two-dimensional solution for women was .147 (compared to .221 for the one-dimensional solution).

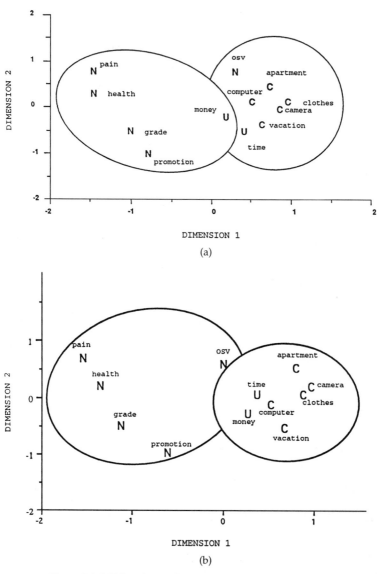

Figure 2.1. MDS analyses of judgments of similarity between pairs of attributes in Experiment 1 for (a) pooled data, (b) women, and (c) men (opposite). (Note: Men required only a one-dimensional solution, but the two-dimensional plot is shown to facilitate comparisons with the pooled and women's data.)

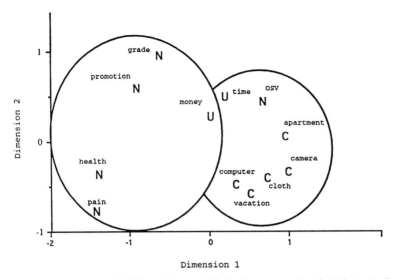

Figure 2.1c. MDS analysis of similarity between pairs of attributes in Experiment 1 for men.

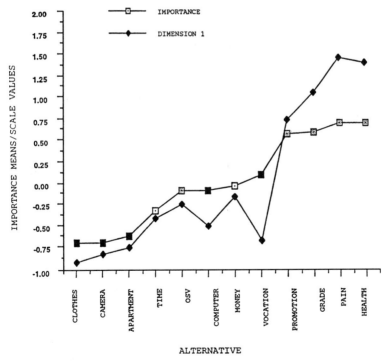

Figure 2.2. Relation between rated importance, category membership, and dimension 1 of MDS in Experiment 1.

The stress for the one-dimensional solution for men was .196. The r^2 when regressing rated importance on dimension 1 was .924 ($p < .0001$) for women (two-dimensional model) and .835 ($p < .003$) for men. It also appears that men and women find similar items important, as the correlation between men's and women's ratings of importance was .977 ($p < .0001$).

For women the second dimension appears to be a continuum from positional, high-status goods (e.g., promotion, grade, money) to personal or relational items (e.g., pain, objects of sentimental value). The difference in dimensionality between men and women presumably accounts for the difficulty in interpreting dimension 2 for the pooled data set. In fact, if a second dimension is forced into the model for the men's data, this dimension is uncorrelated with the second dimension for women ($r = .387$, $p > .22$). The second dimension for men appears to be uninterpretable and does not lead to a large stress reduction. It would be desirable to be able to test whether there are gender differences in the mean degree of decision difficulty experienced by men and women across all items. However, it is highly unlikely that we would be able to detect such an effect because subjects generally tend to spread their ratings over the entire available scale (Parducci, 1965), making such a between-subject comparison meaningless. Thus, even if experienced difficulty was actually much greater for one gender than the other, this would be unlikely to show up in the ratings. Indeed, our analyses found strikingly similar overall ratings of difficulty by men and women ($F(1,56) = 0.0$, $p < .96$, MSE $= 187.38$).

Predicting Tradeoff Difficulty from Categories. The MDS and clustering analyses suggest that the hypothesized categories have psychological validity. We now examine whether they can be useful in predicting decision difficulty. Table 2.1 shows the mean difficulty of the decision for each type of tradeoff (commodity–commodity, commodity–currency, etc.).

There were significant overall differences between the mean difficulty score dependent on the type of tradeoff (one-way, repeated measures ANOVA, $F(5,315) = 7.68$, $p < .0001$, MSE $= .24$). A set of transformations was performed to test some of the hypothesized differences in tradeoff difficulty. The first transformed variable contrasted the tradeoff difficulties within a category from those between categories. Tradeoffs within a category were found to be significantly more difficult ($F(1,63) = 21.61$, $p < .0001$, MSE $= 1.16$). The remaining three

Table 2.1. *Mean Rated Difficulty of Items from Different Category Combinations in Experiment 1*

	Commodity	Noncommodity	Currency	Mean
Commodity	0.011	−0.142	0.067	−0.062
Noncommodity		0.254	−0.006	−0.024
Currency			0.307	0.044

Note: Higher ratings indicate more difficult tradeoffs.

transformations concerned pairwise comparisons of the marginal difficulty of each category. The ordering of difficulty was as follows: currencies were most difficult, followed by noncommodities and then by commodities. Currency tradeoffs were significantly more difficult than commodity tradeoffs ($F(1,63) = 10.77$, $p < .002$, MSE $= .28$). The difference between currencies and noncommodities approached significance ($F(1,63) = 3.9$, $.05 < p < .06$, MSE $= .28$), as did the difference between commodities and noncommodities ($F(1,63) = 2.66$, $.10$, $p < .11$, MSE $= .17$). This ordering was, of course, quite different from that predicted earlier, when we hypothesized that the noncommodities would be involved in the most difficult decisions. This issue was examined further in Experiment 2.

Gender did not interact with the difficulty of making a decision between categories versus within a category or with the type of decision.

Predicting Decision Difficulty from the Feature Scales. Next, we turn to the relationship of decision difficulty to the feature scales. The "importance" feature was found to be highly correlated with dimension 1 of the MDS analysis. We now examine its contribution to decision difficulty in more detail. Our intuition was that the following relationships would hold. First, decisions involving important alternatives would be difficult. Second, decisions involving *similarity* of important alternatives would be difficult. (If only one alternative is important, then presumably the choice is easy. If neither alternative is important, then one may not care very much which alternative one gets.) Tetlock (1986) suggested that decisions in which *both* alternatives are very important to the subject

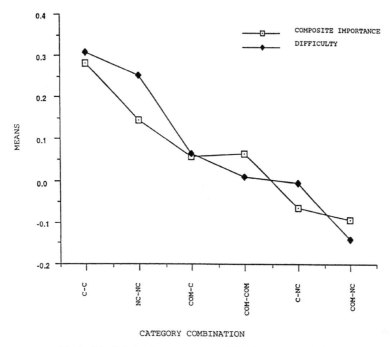

Figure 2.3. Relation between mean difficulty rating and the composite importance measure for each category combination in Experiment 1.

produce the greatest integrative complexity in solving social and political problems. Integrative complexity measures the sophistication of problem solving and is presumably related to the difficulty of reaching a decision.

To operationalize these hypotheses, we devised a measure of composite importance, CI, as follows:

$$CI = \frac{I_1 + I_2}{\sqrt{|I_1 - I_2| + .05}} \qquad (6)$$

Where I_i is the importance of attribute i. (The .05 value was added as a fudge factor to prevent division by zero, and the square root was used to normalize the distribution.) Note that the value of CI grows as (1) the joint importance of the alternatives grows (numerator) and (2) as the similarity of the importance grows (denominator). Figure 2.3 shows the relation of mean difficulty rating to the composite importance measures for each category combination. As can be seen, the difficulty of the tradeoff is strongly related to the composite importance of the attributes. A model that predicts tradeoff difficulty using the composite importance variable yielded a significant positive coefficient for the linear component, whereas the quadratic component had a significant negative weight ($p < .0001$ and $p < .0005$, respectively). The composite importance variables explained 54% of the variance in decision difficulty.

The composite importance measure was analyzed in conjunction with the other feature scales, and their relationship to the difficulty ratings was established as follows. The high correlations (multicollinearity) among feature scales made it difficult to interpret the effect of each feature on the difficulty of decision individually in a multiple regression analysis. To solve this problem, we used a stepwise regression analysis to determine the most useful set of features. The stepwise regression analysis suggested that the feature scales "How sure of making the right decision," "How moral a decision," "Composite importance," and "How difficult to choose" (in quadratic form) were most strongly related to tradeoff difficulty. The more unsure the subject was, the less moral the decision was, the more subjects cared which alternative they received, and the more important the decision was, the more difficulty subjects experienced.

In addition to the stepwise regression analysis, we performed a principal components analysis to examine whether there was any meaningful structure in the correlations between the feature scales. This analysis yielded two components with the following weights for each feature (after varimax rotation) (see Table 2.2). The first and second components

Table 2.2. *Loadings on Components Following Principal Components Analysis and Varimax Rotation in Experiment 1*

Feature	Component 1	Component 2
"How sure?"	−0.880	−0.287
"Didn't care"	0.140	0.929
"Couldn't choose"	0.890	0.010
"How moral?"	−0.003	−0.950
"How similar?"	0.552	0.724
Composite importance	0.869	0.166

explained 27% and 24% of the variance of the correlations between feature scales, respectively. The difficulty scores were regressed on the two components, which jointly explained 70% of the variance in the difficulty measure. Both components were significant ($p < .004$). Thus, we can reliably predict the difficulty of a decision from self-related features of the tradeoff.

The first component seems to represent the distinction between more and less important decisions. The negative loading of the "how sure" feature on this component implies that subjects were more sure of their important decisions but less sure of their unimportant decisions. This might be because they felt that they could use a lexicographic decision rule to aid their choice or because they felt that they would devote greater thought to the decision. The low positive loadings of the "similarity" and "did not care" feature scales support this interpretation. The second component appears to distinguish between moral decisions and decisions that are not associated with moral values. It appears that moral decisions involve very dissimilar alternatives (perhaps those from different categories). Subjects strongly cared which alternative they received, and moral decisions were associated with some uncertainty (negative loading of "how sure").

The relation between the features "didn't care" and "couldn't choose" is noteworthy. "Couldn't choose" loads strongly on the first component (important decisions) but weakly on the second component (unimportant decisions). The reverse is true for "didn't care," suggesting that our questions captured the distinction between indifference and difficulty. Certainly there are many decisions we might feel indifferent (and care little) about, such as which brand of toothpaste to buy. However, there are also many decisions that we find difficult but that we are certainly not indifferent about. For example, imagine being asked whether you prefer your older or younger child to die. The decision would be agonizingly difficult, but the psychological state attached to the decision is not indifference. Such a decision would surely receive the highest possible rating on "couldn't choose." We propose that indecision occurs (1) when any choice leads to an unacceptable outcome (as in choosing which child should die) or (2) when one is sure that one has a preference but finds the alternatives hard to compare (as in deciding between Paris and Rome). This distinction is similar to one made by Shafer (1986). He argued that one may be undecided for a wide variety of reasons (e.g., one has not yet considered the alternatives as part of the choice set or one does not wish to make a decision yet).

Experiment 2

Experiment 2 had two main purposes. First we wished to demonstrate that the perceived difference in decision difficulty has an impact on actual decisions, as Experiment 1 had asked subjects only to rate the difficulty of making the decision. Experiment 2 examined the relationship of decision difficulty to two measures: (1) the *choices* that subjects actually make and (2) the *time* required to decide.

Second, we wished to examine the role of currencies more thoroughly. Currencies were not assigned a separate category by the MDS analysis, perhaps because we tested only two members ("time" and "money"). In Experiment 2 we broadened the category and examined four members. In Experiment 1 we obtained the unpredicted finding that currencies were the most difficult category to trade off. After interviewing our subjects informally, we hypothesized that the difficulty involving these items lay in the fact that the level of the attribute was unspecified, rather than in the difficulty of trading off currencies per se. Subjects apparently felt that they could have made the decision easily if they had known how much money was involved, but found it difficult if they were imaging any amount from \$1 to \$1 billion. As an intuitive example, imagine being asked to decide whether you would prefer pounds sterling or dollars. Stated this way, the decision is difficult (almost nonsensical) because one does not know how many (i.e., what level) of each currency is involved. However, once the amounts and the exchange rate are known, the decision becomes almost trivially easy. Thus the difficulty seems to lie in the vagueness of the stimuli rather than in the difficulty of making the tradeoff per se. Currencies may be more susceptible to this problem than the other items, as the range of imaginable possibilities seems large.

To circumvent this problem in Experiment 2, we used the method of choices between equally valued alternatives devised by Slovic (1975). In series of experiments, Slovic asked his subjects to match the utility level of one alternative with the utility level of another alternative. He then asked subjects to choose between them. In terms of a utility framework, there is clearly no difference between the choices; hence one should have no reason to prefer one to the other. If one must decide, all decision rules (e.g., coin flip, random) should lead to equal satisfaction (decision costs aside). Yet Slovic found that subjects systematically chose the alternative with the highest value on what he hypothesized to be the most important attribute. Similar results were found by Tversky, Sattath, and Slovic (1988). Recall that "importance" played a key role in the categorization of alternatives and in the difficulty of making tradeoffs in Experiment 1. Based on Slovic's results, we might expect that subjects' choices will be determined by the category membership (and importance) of the alternatives involved.

Experiment 2 tested the following hypotheses:

> *Hypothesis 4:* Decisions involving noncommodities rather than currencies will now be the most difficult (following the utility-matching procedure).
>
> *Hypothesis 5:* Choice time will increase with the difficulty of the decision.
>
> *Hypothesis 6:* Subjects will tend to choose noncommodities over commodities and currencies (due to the greater importance of noncommodities).

Method

The method was similar to that of Experiment 1, with the following changes. Two new currencies were added to the list ("mall coupons" and "grocery coupons"). To avoid an excessively long experiment, an item was removed from each of the other categories (health from the noncommodities and camera from the commodities). This left the list length at 12 items, with 4 in each category. The number of feature scales was also reduced, based on those that had seemed particularly useful in Experiment 1. Subjects were asked only to rate the difficulty of the tradeoff and the importance and similarity of the attributes. The results of the role manipulation in Experiment 1 were confusing, in part because of differences found between tradeoffs for Friend-Self and Self-Friend (which should be logically similar). To strengthen the manipulation, we eliminated these conditions and ran only two groups: Self-Self and Friend-Friend. Forty-four subjects were run (19 men and 25 women). All of them completed the experiment and were paid $7. The experiment was run in a single session lasting approximately 50 minutes.

The instructions asked subjects to consider each story and imagine levels on each alternative such that they were indifferent between the two alternatives. Each time a story was presented, they were asked the following questions:

1. Which alternative do you choose? Remember that you are exactly indifferent between alternatives 1 and 2.
2. How difficult was it to make a decision involving a choice between these alternatives?
3. How important is the first/second alternative to you?

The time between the onset of the presentation of the story and the subject's choice was recorded.

Results

Effect of Decision Role. As before, no significant main effect of role on decision difficulty was found ($F(1, 40) = 2.71$, $p > .10$, MSE $= .04$). The results for choice reaction time showed a complex interaction with role, gender, and decision type ($F(1, 200) = 2.78$, $p < .01$). Follow-up analyses did not aid our interpretation of this interaction. Thus, the more straightforward role manipulation in this experiment did not produce meaningful differences in decision difficulty between subjects in different roles. Thus, as in Experiment 1, all ratings were standardized within subjects for the remaining analyses, and the data were pooled.

Category Representations. MDS and cluster analyses of the similarity judgments were performed for the pooled data and for men and women separately (see Figure 2.4). As in Experiment 1, the pooled data yielded a two-dimensional solution (stress $= .129$), this time with three clusters at the first level. The two left-side clusters contain the noncommodities, and the remaining items are placed together in a single category. Analyzing the data by gender led to a two-dimensional solution for women (stress $= .212$), whereas men required only one dimension to explain their ratings (stress $= .247$). For women, all the noncommodities were separated from the remaining items. As in Experiment 1, men apparently treat objects of sentimental value as similar to commodities rather than noncommodities. For men, women, and the pooled data, currencies and commodities were not well separated, leading to the conclusion that they are not psychologically distinct categories.

Dimension 1 again appears to be the importance of the attribute for men, women, and the pooled data. Regressing the mean importance ratings on dimension 1 explains 86% of the variance for the pooled data ($p < .0001$). Dimension 1 for men and women is highly correlated

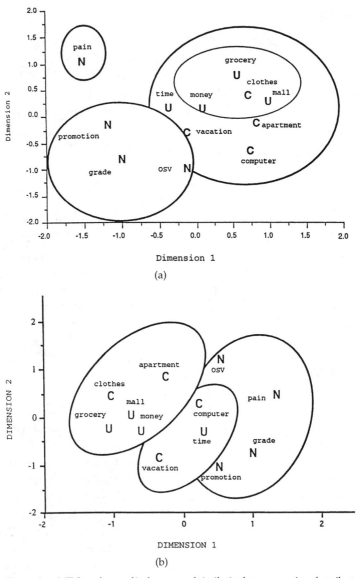

Figure 2.4. MDS analyses of judgments of similarity between pairs of attributes in Experiment 2 for (a) pooled data, (b) women, and (c) men (opposite). (Note: Men required only a one-dimensional solution, but the two-dimensional plot is shown to facilitate comparisons with the pooled and women's data.)

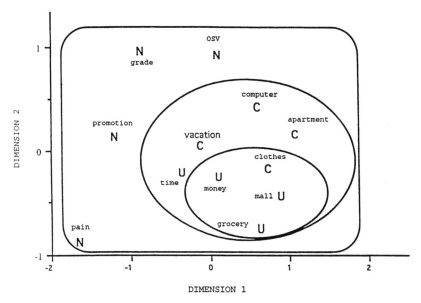

Figure 2.4c. MDS analysis of similarity between pairs of attributes in Experiment 2 for men.

($r = .80$, $p < .002$), indicating that it is measuring a similar construct for the two groups. The correlation of dimension 1 with importance was .874 for men ($p < .0002$) and .745 for women ($p < .006$). As before, the second dimension for the pooled data is uninterpretable due to the gender differences found, whereas dimension 2 for women again seems to be a continuum from positional (e.g., promotion) to relational (e.g., objects of sentimental value) goods.

Predicting Tradeoff Difficulty from Categories. The mean difficulty ratings for each category and each category combination are shown in Table 2.3. There is a significant overall effect of category type on decision difficulty (mixed, three-way ANOVA, $F(5,2400) = 7.09$, $p < .0001$, $MSE = .13$). Follow-up tests revealed, as before, that tradeoffs within a category were more difficult than those between categories ($F(1,40) = 7.00$, $p < .01$, $MSE = 1.05$). The marginal comparisons showed that decisions involving noncommodities were significantly more difficult than those involving currencies ($F(1,40) = 5.12$, $p < .03$, $MSE = .65$) and were marginally more difficult than those with commodities ($F(1,40) = 3.79$, $p < .06$, $MSE = .65$). The difference between currencies and commodities did not approach significance ($F(1,40) = 0.06$, $p < .80$, $MSE = .48$). Note

Table 2.3. *Mean Rated Difficulty of Trading Off Items from Different Category Combinations in Experiment 2*

	Commodity	Noncommodity	Currency	Mean
Commodity	−0.033	−0.030	0.020	−0.014
Noncommodity		0.313	−0.101	−0.061
Currency			0.015	−0.022

Note: Higher ratings indicate more difficult tradeoffs.

that these results support our hypothesis concerning the difficulty ordering of the categories. In this experiment the noncommodities were involved in the most difficult tradeoffs, whereas the currencies were the easiest, in contrast to Experiment 1. This suggests that the utility-matching manipulation was successful in removing the artifact of differences in vagueness of the stimuli between categories present in Experiment 1.

Effect of Category on Behavior. We hypothesized that difficult decisions would require longer reaction times. Hence we would expect that tradeoffs within a category would take longer and that those involving noncommodities would take particularly long. We examined this supposition using the choice reaction times for each category and category combination, having partialed out the effects of story length (see Table 2.4). The values shown are the residuals in milliseconds (hence the appearance of negative values).

Table 2.4. *Mean Residual Reaction Times Required to Choose, in Milliseconds (After Partialing Out Story Length), by Category Combination in Experiment 2*

	Commodity	Noncommodity	Currency	Mean
Commodity	291.25	−1393.22	781.06	−106.97
Noncommodity		1233.59	−337.49	−165.71
Currency			1007.58	483.72

There was a significant main effect of decision type on reaction times (three-way, mixed ANOVA, $F(5,200) = 2.69$, $p < .04$, $MSE = 1.75 \times 10^7$), as shown in Table 2.4, but no significant interaction of reaction time with gender. As predicted, decisions within a category took significantly longer than those between categories ($F(1,40) = 4.69$, $p < .04$, $MSE = 1.28 \times 10^8$). The marginal comparisons revealed that commodity decisions were significantly faster than currency decisions ($F(1,40) = 4.13$, $p < .03$, $MSE = 3.69 \times 10^7$). The choice reaction times for currencies were marginally longer than those for noncommodities ($F(1,40) = 2.58$, $p > .10$, $MSE = 4.46 \times 10^7$). The difference in reaction times between commodities and noncommodities was not significant ($F(1,40) = .04$, $p > .80$, $MSE = 6.22 \times 10^7$). The pattern of choice reaction time length for each category combination is very similar to that of rated decision difficulty for each combination (shown in Table 2.3). This suggests, broadly speaking, that the more difficult decisions tend to be those on which subjects spend most time.

Examining the noncommodities row is particularly revealing. Decisions involving two noncommodities were particularly difficult (mean rating = .313) and took a very long time (mean residual reaction time = 1233.59 ms). However, decisions involving noncommodities traded with other items (currencies or commodities) were the easiest of all. This suggests that in the latter cases, subjects may use the lexicographic choice rule of always choosing the noncommodity over the other alternative. Such a rule would be quick and easy to follow (Tversky, 1972). These data suggest that there are no hard-to-trade attributes per se, only difficult combinations of attributes (as determined by the categories into which they fall).

We now turn to the question of which items subjects actually chose. Recall that their choices cannot be explained by differences in utility level, as subjects were asked (and repeatedly reminded) to equate the utility of the alternatives. Table 2.5 shows the frequency with which each category was chosen over each other category.

If subjects were choosing their alternatives randomly with respect to the category of the objects, we would expect to find approximately equal numbers of elements in the top and bottom diagonal sections of Table 2.5. We rejected this hypothesis using a quasi-symmetry model ($p < .0001$), suggesting that the category combinations influence the choice of object. Follow-up analyses revealed that subjects had a significant tendency to choose noncommodities over commodities and currencies and to choose commodities over currencies. The estimated utilities based on

Table 2.5. *Choices by Category Combination in Experiment 2*

Pooled	Currency	Commodity	Noncommodity	Totals
Currency	—	282	191	473
		.13	.09	.22
Commodity	422	—	217	639
	.20		.10	.30
Noncommodity	513	487	—	1000
	.24	.23		.47
Totals	935	769	408	2112

Note: Rows show the chosen alternatives. The upper value in each cell is choice frequency; the lower value is choice proportion.

Luce's choice model for currencies, commodities, and noncommodities are −21.9, −6.1, and 28, respectively. (There are no significance levels for these analyses, which are based on confidence intervals that are two standard deviations below and above the estimated value of the parameter. If this interval does not contain zero, we can reject the null hypothesis in each case [Luce & Suppes, 1965].)

Discussion

The results of Experiment 2 supported all the hypotheses stated previously. It appears that the lack of specificity of attribute level in Experiment 1 caused the currencies to be rated most difficult to trade off. When the utility levels in Experiment 2 were equated, this artifact disappeared, revealing that noncommodities were the most difficult to trade off, followed by commodities and then by currencies. We also tested the effects of category membership on behavior and found that the difficult tradeoffs took longer. Category membership was also related to choice: Noncommodities were chosen most often, followed by commodities and then by currencies, presumably due to the difference in rated importance accorded to each category. This is consistent with the findings of Slovic (1975).

Consistent with Experiment 1, gender differences were found, with women showing greater dimensionality in their similarity judgments than men. Again, women also appeared to treat objects of sentimental value as noncommodities, whereas these appeared more similar to the commodities for men. Interestingly, this did not affect the proportion of objects in each category chosen by men and women (as no interaction of gender with category chosen was found). In general, when resolving a tie in value, people seem to have a tendency to choose noncommodities, then commodities, and then currencies. Subjects may use the heuristic "Pick the alternative with the highest value on the most important dimension" suggested by Slovic (1975). The correlation between rated importance for men and women was very high; thus this heuristic would result in no interaction of gender with object chosen.

In Experiments 1 and 2 we found the hypothesized categories useful in predicting tradeoff difficulty, the object that will be chosen, and the amount of time taken to choose. However, two issues still remain: To what extent do these categories have defining features beyond rated importance? And can our findings generalize beyond the small number of items in each category we have examined? These questions were pursued in Experiment 3.

Experiment 3

Experiments 1 and 2 induced category membership from subjects' similarity judgments using MDS and clustering analyses, which provided considerable support for the distinction between noncommodities and other goods. In Experiment 3 we examined the category structure further by asking subjects direct questions concerning the properties of the items. Based on Schwartz's (1986) definitions, we formed the following hypotheses:

> *Hypothesis 7:* Noncommodities will be rated as more important, less tradable, intrinsically more valuable, and less concrete than commodities and currencies.
>
> *Hypothesis 8:* Commodities will be rated as more concrete and more intrinsically valuable than currencies.

Method

Subjects. Subjects were 22 students at the University of Chicago, solicited by advertisements and paid $8 per hour.

Stimuli. The stimuli were the 12 items used in Experiment 2.

Procedure. Each stimulus was presented by the computer in random order to the subject, who was asked to rate it on a scale from −20 to 0 (neutral) to +20 on the following questions:

1. How important is the item to you?
2. To what extent can the item be appropriately traded?
3. To what extent does the item have intrinsic value?
4. To what extent is the item concrete?

Subjects were also asked to assign each item to one of the three categories in a forced-choice paradigm. The categories were defined as follows. The term *commodities* was avoided because of its special meaning concerning the commodities market. *Untradables* was thought to be clearer in this context than *noncommodities*.

A. *Consumer goods:* Items that can be bought and sold appropriately.
B. *Currencies:* Items that can act as stand-ins for the value of other objects.
C. *Untradables:* Items that either cannot be traded in markets or that lose some of their value by being bought and sold.

For each object displayed, subjects were asked to type in the category (A, B, C) that they felt best described it. They were told that there were no right or wrong answers, just opinions. They were free to assign any number of items to any category.

Results

The results from four ratings questions for each item, grouped by category, are shown in Table 2.6. (We added 20 to each rating to make all ratings positive.) One subject missed one rating on the categorization task, so $N = 21$ for this task. (Unfortunately, gender information was not collected. This experiment was done before we were aware of its potential importance.)

Overall the three categories (commodities, currencies, and noncommodities) received differential ratings on the four questions (importance, tradability, intrinsic value, and concreteness) ($F(2,273) = 9.49$, $p < .0001$, $MSE = 108.69$). Noncommodities were rated as significantly more important and less tradable than both commodities and currencies; commodities and noncommodities had more intrinsic value than currencies; and noncommodities were significantly less concrete than

Table 2.6. *Mean Ratings on Each Question for All Items, Grouped by Category, in Experiment 3*

Category	Item	Imp	Trade	Intr	Conc
Noncommodities	Pain	24.157	12.065	22.582	15.679
	OSV	26.739	8.995	22.527	15.707
	Promotion	25.299	13.614	23.641	16.413
	Grade	28.614	9.294	15.435	14.054
	Mean	26.203	10.992	21.046	15.463
Commodities	Computer	20.109	34.701	23.614	34.185
	Clothes	21.685	33.261	22.364	33.723
	Vacation	20.897	26.929	25.082	20.707
	Apartment	25.824	31.165	23.921	33.949
	Mean	22.129	31.514	23.745	30.641
Currencies	Mall	6.984	34.674	8.071	29.783
	Grocery	13.261	33.288	8.071	29.022
	Time	30.540	17.926	29.631	12.813
	Money	27.908	34.891	16.603	25.190
	Mean	19.673	30.195	15.594	24.202

Imp = rated importance, Trade = tradability, Intr = intrinsic value, Conc = concreteness.

currencies, which were less concrete than commodities (Bonferroni tests; all differences were significant at $p < .05$). No other significant differences were found (Bonferroni tests). Interestingly, objects of sentimental value were rated as not concrete, despite being, in some sense, physical objects. Currencies had low intrinsic value (being socially defined, with the exception of "time").

The results of the forced-choice classification are shown in Table 2.7. The correct choices (as hypothesized a priori) are shown in boldface. It is clear that the overwhelming majority of responses (202 of 264) classified the items correctly. For each item, with the exception of "time," the modal response is the correct one. In some cases, almost all subjects chose the correct category (e.g., for "computer," "money," and "pain"). It is noteworthy that the one poorly classified item in the forced-choice procedure ("time") was also the item that did not fit well into the results of the four questions listed earlier. Examining the MDS plots (Figures 2.1 and 2.2) from Experiments 1 and 2 also supports this conclusion:

Table 2.7. *Frequency of Category Assignment for Each Item from Forced-Choice Procedure in Experiment 3 (Correct Assignment in Bold Type)*

Correct Category	Item	Noncomm	Comm	Curr
Noncommodity	Pain	**21**	1	0
	OSV	**18**	1	4
	Promotion	**12**	2	8
	Grade	**17**	0	5
Commodity	Computer	0	**21**	1
	Clothes	1	**20**	2
	Vacation	4	**12**	6
	Apartment	0	**20**	2
Currency	Mall	0	10	**12**
	Grocery	0	8	**14**
	Time	14	1	**7**
	Money	0	2	**20**

"Time" is placed in a different category from all the other currencies in almost all cases.

Discussion

Experiment 3 was designed to directly expose possible distinctions between categories in light of the results of the first two experiments. The results indicate that noncommodities, commodities, and currencies have different properties (importance, intrinsic value, concreteness, and tradability). The categories seemed to be intuitive to our subjects, as they were mostly able to assign the items to the categories correctly with minimal instruction or category definition. As in the previous experiments, the currencies and commodities were not clearly distinguished from each other. However, the key to this lack of separation may lie with the ratings for "time." Whereas the remaining items all received similar ratings on all questions, "time" stands out as clearly different. It was rated as the most important member of the category, as the only item that was not tradable, as the only item with high intrinsic value, and as the only item that is not concrete. These results clarify the situation in the previous experiments, in which the currencies were not classified together or well separated from the commodities. The remaining items (money, mall, and grocery coupons) appear to have more in common and may be differentiated from the commodities.

Further research is needed to elucidate the role of currencies and commodities and to classify "time" correctly. We should also note that our studies have examined only 14 items in total; ideally, a much broader range of goods would be needed to see whether the category structure proposed holds for other members. (Obviously, resource limitations made this difficult.) In an attempt to examine more items, we conducted an informal study in which we asked 12 subjects to list out five commodities and five noncommodities (with no further instructions). A vast range of items were generated, making formal classification or clustering difficult. However, there was a notable separation of categories: Only one item (artwork) was listed by two different subjects as belonging to different categories. Several of the items that we used in our experiments appeared in subjects' spontaneous lists (e.g., camera, clothes, health, objects of sentimental value). Only one item that we used was cross-classified: One subject generated a "vacation": It can be either a commodity that can be purchased in a travel agency or a social experience with a friend (and thus a noncommodity). A final observation about the items generated by the subjects was that the commodities list was quite homogeneous, with the goods listed being objects that can be bought in a store. The noncommodities, however, seemed to to consist of several rather different subgroups: for example, environmental goods (e.g., fresh air), relationships (e.g., friends), and informational goods (e.g., wisdom, knowledge). Further research can establish whether there are differences in tradability between these possible subcategories.

General Discussion

The research presented in this chapter suggests that there are large differences in the ease with which different kinds of attributes can be compared and decided between, and that there are clear regularities governing when tradeoffs will be difficult and when indifference and indecision will result. The key to these issues appears to be the categories to which the alternatives in the tradeoffs belong. The MDS and clustering analyses point to the existence of well-defined psychological categories of objects: The separation between noncommodities and other objects (commodities and currencies) seems particularly clear. Evidence for the categories came from a variety of different sources: similarity judgments (Experiments 1 and 2), choices and reaction times (Experiment 2), forced-choice classifications, direct judgments of hypothesized defining features of the categories, and spontaneous generation of items (Experiment 3). The clustering analyses suggest that the objects studied form distinct categories, but that these categories are arrayed along the continua of importance and personalness (for women) derived from the MDS analyses.

Our results complement a growing body of social psychological work in the social constructionist tradition examining the definition of the self through material goods. We found that men and women do not differ greatly in the alternatives that they view as important (dimension 1 of the MDS analysis). Similarly, Dittmar (1989) found that men and women listed similar kinds of possessions when asked to name their five most important things. However, Dittmar also found that the *reasons* that possessions were viewed as important differed markedly between men and women. Women attended not only to the usefulness of an object but also to its role as a symbol of personal and emotional attachment. Men concentrated more on the relationship of the objects to leisure and activity. Similar distinctions have been made by other investigators: for example, Csikszentmihalyi and Rochberg-Halton's (1981) distinction between men valuing objects of action and women valuing objects of contemplation concerned with relationships, and Prentice's (1987) distinction between instrumental and symbolic objects. Of particular interest in our studies was the differential treatment by men and women of objects of sentimental value. In Experiments 1 and 2, women apparently treated them as noncommodities, whereas (contrary to our hypothesis) men regarded them as similar to other concrete objects (commodities). We tentatively conclude from this finding that men on average attach less sentimental value to objects than women and view objects more in terms of their usefulness than their symbolic or relational value. Why this should be so is beyond the scope of this chapter.

The other striking difference between men and women lay in the dimensionality of the categorizations. Our results were similar to those of Dittmar (1989) in that women's categorizations were bidimensional (importance and relationship-oriented), whereas men were more concerned with importance (usefulness) alone. For women, then, choice may involve tradeoffs between the two dimensions and may thus be more problematic. Men may merely choose on the basis of unidimensional considerations, at least for the stimuli we examined. We do not, however, wish to conclude from our results that women's judgments are *generally* more complex that men's. For example, Barlas and Bockenholt (1992) studied subjects' judgments of contraceptive devices. Men's judgments were characterized by two dimensions (risk and pleasure), whereas women provided a unidimensional solution based on risk alone. We predict an interaction of dimensionality with gender based on the specific stimuli used and the goals of the subjects involved.

Relation of the Findings to Public Policy

In addition to implications for individual decision making, our results may be informative to those making public policy. We have demonstrated that some decisions are more difficult than others and that this difficulty can be partially explained by classification of the attributes involved. In particular, decisions involving tradeoffs between noncommodities are the most difficult. This difficulty may lead policymakers to shy away from such decisions, showing decision aversion (Beattie et al., 1993). The public may also prefer their elected representatives to pretend that no tradeoffs are made between difficult-to-trade items. In a resource-limited world such tradeoffs must be made, and it is questionable whether the public good is served by hiding the decision process. Yet in cases where lawmakers have had the courage to make explicit the tradeoffs involved to allow a democratic debate, there has been public outrage. For example, in the early 1990s, the State of Oregon held public meetings to help decide which medical procedures should be covered by Medicaid and which should not. Such decisions obviously involve tradeoffs between many important (noncommodity) considerations, such as level of pain and length of life, and also involve trading of these attributes against money. Rather than congratulating politicians for their candidness in allowing the debate to take place, members of the public expressed abhorrence at the idea of making such tradeoffs, apparently preferring to pretend that such decisions need not be made.

A second area in which our results relate to public policy issues is in the definition of legally allowable markets. Most societies place bans on the free exchange of certain goods, even if the parties involved all wish the transaction to take place. For example, prostitution is illegal in many countries, even between consenting parties. Similarly, it is illegal to sell one's children, or even oneself, into slavery. Some economists argue that universal commodification should be allowed, whereas the polar opposite is a Marxist universal noncommodification (see Radin, 1987, for a discussion of these issues). The commodities and currencies we used in our studies seemed to our subjects to be appropriately traded in markets, whereas they seemed to have clear intuitions that the noncommodities either cannot or should not be traded. From time to time, however, cases arise for which we do not have such strong and unconflicting intuitions, suggesting perhaps that there are gray areas between noncommodities and commodities.

Legal economists and medical ethicists are currently wrangling over the ramifications of recent advances in reproductive technologies. For example, the debate concerning the legality of surrogate mothering centers on the right of a woman to sell her reproductive services to another couple (Arneson, 1992; Satz, 1992). Recent court cases have highlighted the issue of the ownership and usage of frozen human embryos following the death or divorce of the parents. The crux of the debate is whether the embryos are commodities (in which case they may be divided as other property is in probate or divorce settlements) or whether they are subject to different laws as noncommodities (Corea, 1988). The resolution of these arguments will change our commonsense views of what defines a person, a child, and a parent.

Schwartz (1986) refers to the confusion of market considerations with social and moral considerations as *economic imperialism*. Such a confusion amounts to regarding all goods as market tradable (i.e., commodities). Schwartz argues that once an item has become viewed by society as an economic good (commodity), it is no longer possible for people individually to treat the good as a noncommodity even if they wish to. For example, one might believe that education is a basic right that should be accorded to all, regardless of ability to pay. However, once society brings education into the realm of the market, this point of view cannot be acted on: There may be no educational institutions for poor people to attend. Thus the market serves to erode nonmarket goods. As Schwartz (1986) writes, "Freedom and democracy in the market may undercut freedom and democracy in society as a whole" (p. 283). In considering the role and desirability of political action committees, the U.S. Congress is acknowledging that there is a fine line between contributing to a congressperson whom you hope endorses your views and buying votes. When citizens can buy votes, votes have changed from noncommodities to commodities, and democracy has suffered as a direct result.

Relation to Decision Aiding

Decision aids are increasingly used in many different domains (nuclear power plant siting, medical diagnosis, and personnel selection, to name just a few; see, e.g., Kaufman and Thomas, 1977; von Winterfeldt and Edwards, 1986). Decision aids are cost effective only when the decision under consideration is both difficult to make and important for the client. They are also useful only if they lead to superior (and therefore different) choices than those that would be made on the basis of intuition alone. Yet, paradoxically, it is for difficult, important decisions that clients are *least* likely to want to trust a decision aid that they may feel they do not understand, and that advises them to take a different course of action from the one that they would choose. We therefore see applications of our research to decision analysis.

It is clear that decision difficulty relates to category membership and other decision features, particularly attribute importance. A decision analyst should be able to look at the client's decision and predict whether the decision is likely to involve tradeoffs that are difficult for the client to make. As noted earlier, difficult tradeoffs may be those that show the most unreliability (e.g., intransitivities) in the judgments. Thus additional consistency checks may be required to satisfy both the client and the analyst that the judgments are valid. We hope to test this hypothesis directly in future research. Alternatively, the reaction time and choice data from Experiment 2 suggest that some kinds of attributes (noncommodities) may lead people to use lexical decision rules. Such rules cannot be captured within the framework of compensatory decision aids. A decision must then be made on whether the client really intends to act lexicographically, or whether a compensatory model will force him or her to make judgments that do not really accord with his or her true preferences.

Textbook examples of decision problems usually involve simple decisions trading off commodities and currencies. A favorite example is the apartment selection task, which has well-specified dimensions like "rent," "distance from campus," and "size." These kinds of problems are probably well suited to a compensatory, MAUT-style analysis. However, our research suggests that there may be difficulties in extending the types of problems considered to those that also include noncommodity attributes, at least for some subjects. For example, comparing apartment size and rent may seem very different from comparing longevity and degree of pain when deciding between different courses of medical treatment. Different technologies may be needed to elicit meaningful judgments that clients believe reflect their underlying preferences.

Our concern is not to criticize multiattribute decision aids. Given the limited information processing capacity of humans and the many judgmental errors that we habitually make, decision aids should be extremely useful in a wide variety of problem applications. We wish merely to question whether the same technologies used for commodities and currencies should also be extended to noncommodities, or whether we should look at new technologies to aid people in making what are potentially difficult and painful decisions.

References

Anderberg, M. R. (1973). *Cluster analysis for applications*. New York: Academic Press.

Arneson, R. J. (1992). Commodification and commercial surrogacy. *Philosophy and Public Affairs, 21*, 132–164.

Barlas, S., & Bockenholt, U. (1992). Multi-dimensional evaluation of importance. Manuscript: Center for Decision Research, University of Chicago.

Beattie, J. (1988). Perceived differences in tradeoff difficulty. Unpublished Ph.D. dissertation, Department of Psychology, University of Pennsylvania, Philadelphia.

Beattie, J., & Barlas, S. (October 1990). Decision difficulty and the nature of utility. Paper presented to the Operations Research Society of American/The Institute of Management Science Conference, Philadelphia.

Beattie, J., & Barlas, S. (August 1991). Predicting decision difficulty from attribute classification. Paper presented to the Thirteenth Research Conference of Subjective Probability, Utility and Decision Making, Fribourg, Switzerland.

Beattie, J., & Baron, J. (1991). Investigating the effect of stimulus range on attribute weight. *Journal of Experimental Psychology: Human Perception and Performance, 17*, 571–585.

Beattie, J., Baron, J., Hershey, J. C., & Spranca, M. D. (1994). Psychological determinants of decision attitude. *Journal of Behavioral Decision Making, 7*, 129–144.

Bettman, J. R., & Sujan, M. (1987). Effects of framing on evaluation of comparable and noncomparable alternatives by expert and novice consumers. *Journal of Consumer Research, 14*, 141–154.

Butler, D. B., & Loomes, G. (1988). Decision difficulty and imprecise preferences. *Acta Psychologica, 68*, 183–196.

Corea, G. (1988). *The mother machine: Reproductive technologies from artificial insemination to artificial wombs*. London: The Women's Press.

Csikszentmihalyi, M., & Rochberg-Halton, E. (1981). *The meaning of things: Domestic symbols and the self*. Cambridge: Cambridge University Press.

Dittmar, H. (1989). Gender identity–related meanings of personal possessions. *British Journal of Social Psychology, 28*, 159–171.

Dittmar, H. (1992). *The social psychology of material possessions: To have is to be*. London: Harvester Wheatsheaf.

Ebbesen, E. B., & Konecni, V. J. (1980). On the external validity of decision-making research: What do we know about the decisions in the real world? In T. S.

Wallsten (Ed.), *Cognitive processes in choice and decision making behavior* (pp. 21–46). Hillsdale, NJ: Erlbaum.

Fischhoff, B., Slovic, P., & Lichtenstein, S. (1980). Knowing what you want: Measuring labile values. In T. S. Wallsten (Ed.), *Cognitive processes in choice and decision making behavior* (pp. 117–142). Hillsdale, NJ: Erlbaum.

Foa, U. G., & Foa, E. B. (1974). *Societal structures of the mind.* Springfield, IL: Thomas.

Frisch, D., Jones, K. T., & O'Brien, M. (1992). What makes decisions difficult? Manuscript: Department of Psychology, University of Oregon, Eugene.

Goldstein, W. M., & Beattie, J. (1991). Judgments of relative importance in decision making: The importance of interpretation and the interpretation of importance. In D. R. Brown and J. E. K. Smith (Eds.), *Frontiers in mathematical psychology* (pp. 110–137). New York and Berlin: Springer-Verlag.

Isen, A. M., & Geva, N. (1987). The influence of positive affect on acceptable level of risk and thoughts about losing: The person with a large canoe has the largest worry. *Organizational Behavior and Human Decision Processes, 39,* 145–154.

Johnson, E., & Tversky, A. (1983). Affect, generalization, and the perception of risk. *Journal of Personality and Social Psychology, 45,* 20–31.

Johnson, M. D. (1984). Consumer choice and strategies for comparing noncomparable alternatives. *Journal of Consumer Research, 11,* 741–753.

Johnson, M. D. (1986). Modeling choice strategies for noncomparable alternatives. *Marketing Science, 5,* 37–54.

Kaufman, G. M., & Thomas, H. (Eds.). (1977). *Modern decision analysis: Selected readings.* Harmondsworth, Middlesex, England: Penguin Books.

Keeney, R. L., & Raiffa, H. (1976). *Decisions with multiple objectives.* New York: Wiley.

Luce, R. D., & Suppes, P. (1965). Preference, utility, and subjective probability. In R. D. Luce, R. R. Bush, and E. Galanter (Eds.), *Handbook of mathematical psychology* (pp. 107–123). New York: Wiley.

Mano, H. (1992). Judgments under distress: Assessing the role of unpleasantness and arousal in judgment formation. *Organizational Behavior and Human Decision Processes, 52,* 216–245.

Parducci, A. (1965). Category judgment: A range-frequency model. *Psychological Review, 72,* 407–418.

Prentice, D. A. (1987). Psychological correspondence of possessions, attitudes, and values. *Journal of Personality and Social Psychology, 53,* 993–1003.

Radin, M. J. (1987). Market-inalienability. *Harvard Law Review, 100,* 1849–1937.

Ross, R. T. (1934). Optimum orders for the presentation of pairs in the method of paired comparisons. *Journal of Educational Psychology, 25,* 375–382.

Satz, D. (1992). Markets in women's reproductive labor. *Philosophy and Public Affairs, 21,* 107–131.

Savage, L. J. (1954). *The foundation of statistics.* New York: Wiley.

Schneider, S. L. (1992). Framing and conflict: Aspiration level contingency, the status quo, and current theories of risky choice. *Journal of Experimental Psychology: Learning, Memory, and Cognition, 18,* 1040–1057.

Schwartz, B. (1986). *The battle for human nature.* New York: Norton.

Schweitzer, S., & Scalzi, C. (1981). The cost effectiveness of bone marrow transplant therapy and its policy implications. In *The implications of cost-effectiveness analysis of medical technologies: Background paper no. 2: Case studies of medical technology* (pp. 43–75). Washington, DC: Government Printing Office.

Shafer, G. (1986). Savage revisited. *Statistical Science, 1,* 463–501 (with commentary).

Shepard, R. N. (1964). Attention and the metric structure of the stimulus space. *Journal of Mathematical Psychology, 1,* 54–87.

Shepard, R. N., Romney, A. K., & Nerlove, S. B. (Eds.). (1972). *Multidimensional scaling. Theory and applications in the behavioral sciences* (Vols. I and II). New York: Seminar Press.

Slovic, P. (1975). Choice between equally valued alternatives. *Journal of Experimental Psychology: Human Perception and Performance, 1,* 280–287.

Stevens, S. S. (1975). *Psychophysics. Introduction to its perceptual, neural, and social prospects.* New York: Wiley.

Teghtsoonian, R. (1971). On the exponents in Steven's Law and the constant in Ekman's Law. *Psychological Review, 78,* 71–80.

Tetlock, P. E. (1986). A value pluralism model of ideological reasoning. *Journal of Personality and Social Psychology, 50,* 819–827.

Turner, J. L., Foa, E. B., & Foa, U. G. (1971). Interpersonal reinforcers: Classification, interrelationship, and some differential properties. *Journal of Personality and Social Psychology, 19,* 168–180.

Tversky, A. (1972). Elimination by aspects: A theory of choice. *Psychological Review, 79,* 281–299.

Tversky, A., Sattath, S., & Slovic, P. (1988). Contingent weighting in judgment and choice. *Psychological Review, 95,* 371–384.

Von Winterfeldt, D., & Edwards, W. (1986). *Decision analysis and behavioral research.* New York: Cambridge University Press.

Walzer, M. (1983). *Spheres of justice.* Oxford: Blackwell.

3 The Enhancement of Feature Salience in Dichotomous Choice Dilemmas

David A. Houston, Deborah Sherrill-Mittleman,
and Matthew Weeks

Much of the work on choice models has focused on how aspects of a choice dilemma, independent of rational assessments of the relative value of the choice alternatives, can systematically bias decision makers. Often, these aspects work by selectively directing individuals' attention to certain features of the alternatives, thereby affecting the assessments of the alternatives (Tversky & Kahneman, 1974, 1981). Research has looked at biases stemming from prior ownership of one of the choice alternatives (Kahneman & Tversky, 1979), differentially framing choices in terms of gains versus losses (Kahneman & Tversky, 1984; Smith & Petty, 1996), the use of compensatory or noncompensatory decision strategies (Sanbonmatsu, Kardes, & Gibson, 1991), and the introduction of an additional alternative to the set of choice options (e.g., asymmetric dominance and compromise effects; Baron, 1994).

Investigators in our laboratory have examined a number of such aspects that affect the resolution of choice dilemmas by systematically *enhancing the salience* of some categories of features at the expense of other categories (e.g., enhancing the salience of the good features of a pair of alternatives at the expense of the bad features). Such differences in feature salience can, in turn, affect which features contribute disproportionately to a judgment. This chapter focuses on a specific set of these aspects: (1) the *cancellation-and-focus model* of comparison for choice and its enhancement of the unique rather than the shared features of paired alternatives (Houston & Sherman, 1995; Houston, Sherman, & Baker, 1991) and the unique features of the starting point of the comparison relative to the unique features of the target of the comparison (Houston, Sherman, & Baker, 1989), (2) *negative versus positive political advertising* and their enhancement of the bad versus good features, respectively, of a pair of political candidates (Houston, Doan, & Roskos-Ewoldsen,

1999; Houston & Roskos-Ewoldsen, 1998), and (3) instructions to resolve a choice dilemma as either a *preference or a rejection judgment*, and the resulting enhancement of the good or the bad features, respectively (Houston & Weeks, 1998). Finally, we discuss the possibility of more than one of these factors combining to produce a compound form of feature salience enhancement. Specifically, we present some preliminary examinations of the combined feature salience effects of the cancellation-and-focus model and instructions to resolve a choice dilemma as either a preference judgment or a rejection judgment.

The Cancellation-and-Focus Model: The Feature Mapping Model of Comparison for Choice

Observed asymmetries in similarity judgments led Tversky (1977) to propose a feature matching model for comparison for judgments of similarity. When comparing two objects, the comparison process itself can affect the recruiting and weighting of the features of those paired objects. Tversky's feature matching model of the comparison process stresses the importance of specifying which object is made the starting point, or *Subject*, of the comparison and which is the target, or *Referent*, of the comparison. When the Subject is used as the starting point in the comparison, the features of the Referent are recruited in reference to those of the Subject. Accordingly, because the Subject's features are used as a kind of checklist, features *unique* to the Subject will be made especially salient, whereas features *unique* to the Referent will be neglected in the comparison process. The importance of the unique features of the Subject has been demonstrated in many judgment domains, including similarity judgments (Srull & Gaelick, 1983; Tversky, 1977), the use of analogies (Read, 1987), and the detection and identification of change (Agostinelli, Sherman, Fazio, & Hearst, 1986).

The *purpose* for which the comparison is being made can also affect which features of the compared items are used or emphasized in that comparison. For example, whereas shared features are important to similarity judgments (Srull & Gaelick, 1983; Tversky, 1977), they provide no distinguishing information for preference judgments (Houston et al., 1989, 1991). Regardless of which item the individual chooses, he or she will end up with an item that possesses the shared features. Accordingly, Houston et al. (1989, 1991) proposed a *feature matching model of comparison for choice* that involved two components: (1) the *cancellation* of features *shared* by the alternatives and (2) *focus* on the remaining *unique* features, especially those of the alternative that serves as the Subject of comparison. The cancellation component of the model is derived from the nature of a choice task itself, whereas the focus component is derived in part from the nature of choice tasks and in part from the emphasis placed on the unique features of the Subject (Houston et al., 1989; Tversky, 1977).

Now, in comparisons for some judgments, participants can be induced to use *either* the first or the second alternative of a pair of items as the Subject of comparison (e.g., similarity judgments; Srull & Gaelick, 1986). However, in comparisons for choice, the unique versus the shared features of paired alternatives are treated very differently. Only the unique features are relevant for judgments of choice; shared features have no role in such judgments. Accordingly, knowledge of which features are shared and which are unique is of great importance to choice judgments. In turn, features become either unique or shared for a given pair of alternatives only when the *second* item of the pair is encountered. So when this important piece of information is learned, the second item of the pair is present, whereas the first item must be retrieved from memory. Thus, for choice judgments, use of the second item of the pair as the Subject of the comparison is strongly dictated by the nature of such judgments. All experimental efforts to have participants use the first alternative of a pair as the Subject of comparison have failed; and for comparisons for choice, the second alternative is *always* the Subject and the first alternative is *always* the Referent (for a full discussion of the problem of shifting the Subject in comparisons for choice, see Houston et al., 1989).

Because both processes of the cancellation-and-focus model enhance the salience of the unique features of the paired alternatives at the expense of their shared features, the predominant *valence* of the pair's unique features emerges as an important aspect of the choice pair. Thus, *unique-good pairs* are those that share all or most of the same bad features while having all or mostly unique good features (see the paired automobiles in the top panels in Table 3.1). Conversely, *unique-bad pairs* are those that share all or most of the same good features while having all or mostly unique bad features (see the paired automobiles in the bottom panels in Table 3.1). The predominant valence of the pair's unique features has been demonstrated to have an effect on a number of stages in the choice process, including perceptions of *choice conflict* (Houston & Doan, 1996; Houston & Sherman, 1995) and systematic *choice reversals*, dependent on which item is the Subject and which is the Referent for a

Table 3.1. *The Cancellation-and-Focus Model of Comparison for Choice*

A. Choice Conflict: Unique-Good Pair of Choice Alternatives

Automobile A		Automobile B
Rarely needs repairs	←	Good financing
Stereo included	←	Consumer guide
Prestigious model	←	Good acceleration
Air conditioning	←	Friend recommends
Hard-to-find service	←	*Hard-to-find service*
Poor warranty	←	*Poor warranty*
Poor mileage	←	*Poor mileage*
Overpriced	←	*Overpriced*

When *either* alternative becomes the focus of attention:

1. The shared-bad features (in italics) will cancel out as irrelevant to the choice, and its unique-good features will be emphasized.
2. The result is effectively an *approach-approach conflict* with little vacillation and quick decisions.
3. There is *high* postchoice satisfaction with the choice and *high* postchoice evaluation of both alternatives.

B. Choice Conflict: Unique-Bad Pair of Choice Alternatives

Automobile C		Automobile B
Good financing	←	*Good financing*
Consumer guide	←	*Consumer guide*
Good acceleration	←	*Good acceleration*
Friend recommends	←	*Friend recommends*
High insurance	←	Hard-to-find service
Many recalls	←	Poor warranty
Few colors	←	Poor mileage
Hard to get parts	←	Overpriced

When *either* alternative becomes the focus of attention:

1. The shared-good features (in italics) will cancel out as irrelevant to the choice, and its unique-bad features will be emphasized, so focus switches to other alternative.
2. Now *its* unique-bad features will be emphasized, so focus switches back to other alternative.
3. The result is effectively an *avoidance-avoidance conflict* with much vacillation and slow decisions.
4. There is low postchoice satisfaction with the choice and low postchoice evaluation of the alternatives.

given comparison (Houston & Roskos-Ewoldsen, 1998; Houston et al., 1989; Houston & Weeks, 1998).

Choice Conflict

Choice conflict refers to the internal conflict that an individual experiences when making a choice between competing alternatives. The nature of such a conflict has typically been viewed as arising out of an individual's evaluation of the features of the choice alternatives themselves. That is, if the evaluation of the features is primarily positive, thereby creating a conflict between two desirable goals, then there is an *approach-approach conflict*. If the evaluation of the features is primarily negative, thereby creating a conflict between two undesirable goals, then there is an *avoidance-avoidance conflict* (Lewin, 1933, 1951; Miller, 1944). Approach-approach choices are characterized by an attraction to the focal item, finding its good features appealing and choosing it for its merits. Accordingly, making a choice between two items in which the positive features are prominent is relatively easy and psychologically pleasant. In contrast, when a choice is experienced as an avoidance-avoidance conflict, it is characterized by eliminating one item on the basis of its detriments and choosing the remaining alternative by default. Such a choice process is difficult and feels psychologically unpleasant (Houston & Doan, 1996).

Consider again the unique-good pair of automobiles depicted in the top panel of Table 3.1. In this case, the shared bad features provide no differentiating information on which a choice could be based and will cancel each other. Because both items' unique features are primarily positive, once the individual begins to focus primarily on one of the items, that item should be favored. Thus, the decision process should be fast, with little vacillation between the alternatives. However, now consider the unique-bad pair of automobiles depicted in the bottom panel of Table 3.1. In this case, as the person focuses on either item, its unique-bad features should become especially prominent and the item should become increasingly less appealing. This emphasis on the unique-bad features of the current focus of the comparison should turn the individual toward the alternative. But once the individual's attention is switched to the alternative, the alternative's unique-bad features become especially salient and it, too, becomes increasingly less appealing. The result is a slow decision process, with much vacillation between the alternatives. In this analysis, it is not the overall values of the alternatives that establish the nature of the conflict. Rather, it is the valence of the unique features of the alternatives as *made salient* by the comparison process.

Thus, Automobile B, present in *both* pairs in Table 3.1, selected against evaluatively equivalent items in the two situations, should be rated very differently. This difference would reflect the cancellation component of the model, which involves disregarding some features while emphasizing others. For unique-good choices, the bad features of Automobile B would become irrelevant and the good features would be highlighted. For unique-bad choices, the good features of Automobile B would become irrelevant and the bad features would be highlighted. In this way, the evaluation of an item depends not on its objective features, but on the alternatives to which it is compared.

Accordingly, choices between unique-bad alternatives are likely to invoke conflict of an avoidance-avoidance nature, involving the "hesitancy, tension, vacillation, or complete blocking" that Miller (1944) spoke of. In line with this reasoning, Houston et al. (1991, Experiment 1) found such greater "hesitancy," in the form of longer decision times, for unique-bad pairs (avoidance-avoidance conflicts) than for unique-good pairs (approach-approach conflicts).

Postdecision regret may be invoked by the unique negative features of the chosen item and/or the unique positive features of the rejected item (Festinger, 1957, 1964; Gerard & Orive, 1987). After a choice between items with unique-good features, the features that invoke negative feelings (i.e., the unique good features of the rejected alternative) are easy to avoid. Once an alternative is rejected, its good features are removed from sight. This is not the case, however, with a choice between items with unique-bad features. After such a choice, the features of the choice that are likely to produce anxiety (i.e., the unique-bad features of the accepted item) are present. The high level of anxiety and discomfort that accompanies avoidance-avoidance choice should carry over into low levels of satisfaction after the choice is made. As expected, when the participant's attention was on the chosen item, choices between unique-bad pairs produced much lower levels of postchoice satisfaction than did choices between unique-good pairs (Houston et al., 1991, Experiment 2; Houston & Sherman, 1995, Experiment 2). Note also that people tend to be "regret averse" when making choices (i.e., prefer to make regret-minimizing choices; Beattie, Baron, Hershey, & Spranca, 1994; Zeelenburg & Beattie, 1997). The nature of unique-bad pairs makes such a strategy extremely difficult.

Another implication of the cancellation aspect of the model concerns postchoice evaluations of both the chosen and rejected alternatives. In a choice between unique-good items, the shared negative features are irrelevant and cancel out, leaving a choice between one set of good features and a different set of good features. It is the good features of the chosen item (and to some extent of the rejected item) that are made salient in the choice process. The psychological situation is different when the choice is between unique-bad items. It is the shared positive features that are irrelevant and cancel out, leaving a choice between one set of bad features and a different set of bad features. It is the bad features of the alternatives that are made salient in the choice process.

Accordingly, two individuals could choose the identical item, and yet have very different psychological experiences in arriving at that choice and very different feelings about the chosen item. When that item is chosen in a unique-good context, it should be evaluated more positively. Because the focus of the choice was on the items' good features, even the rejected alternative should be evaluated relatively positively. However, if the same item is chosen in a unique-bad context, the focus on the bad features should lead to a relatively poor evaluation of both the chosen and rejected alternatives. Houston and Sherman (1995) found that in postchoice evaluations of the alternatives, items that were part of unique-bad pairs were rated lower than identical items encountered as part of unique-good pairs. This difference resulted from simply varying the pairing of the alternatives to produce cancellation of the good or the bad features of a pair.

Choice Reversals

Returning to the unique-good pair of automobiles at the top of Table 3.1, in addition to the *cancellation* of the shared features (effectively producing an approach-approach conflict), the *focus* component of the model (based, in part, on the importance of the direction of comparison; Tversky, 1977) makes the unique features of the alternative that serves as the *Subject* of comparison especially salient. Accordingly, when making comparisons between roughly equivalent items, people should be more likely to focus on the unique features of the Subject and less likely to take into account the Referent's unique features. Thus, for unique-good pairs, the enhanced salience of the Subject's unique good features and the relative neglect of the unique good features of the Referent should make the *Subject* the relatively preferred alternative. The reverse should occur for unique-bad pairs (the automobiles at the bottom of Table 3.1). In this case, the unique-bad features of the Subject should predominate in the comparison process, and the *Referent* should be relatively preferred. Therefore, keeping the two items of a choice dilemma constant, for unique-good pairs, the Subject should be favored, *regardless* of which of the paired items is the Subject, whereas for unique-bad pairs, the Referent should be favored, *regardless* of which is the Referent. Such choice reversals have been demonstrated for choice dilemmas resolved either as preference judgments (Houston et al., 1989) or as rejection judgments (Houston & Weeks, 1998).

To summarize, the cancellation-and-focus model of comparison for choice specifies an enhanced role for the unique features of choice alternatives at the expense of the shared features. Accordingly, the nature of the choice conflict experienced by the decision maker will depend on the predominant *valence* of the unique features of the paired alternatives, with unique-good pairs producing approach-approach conflicts and unique-bad pairs producing avoidance-avoidance conflicts. Further, the enhanced salience of the Subject of comparison's unique features, relative to those of the Referent, produces systematic choice reversals for roughly equivalent alternatives, with the Subject, regardless of which alternative is the Subject, being favored for unique-good pairs and the Referent, regardless of which alternative is the Referent, being favored for unique-bad pairs.

The cancellation-and-focus model predicts differences in relative feature salience that result from the comparison for choice process. Other forms of enhancing feature salience can depend on which information about the choice alternatives is emphasized by advocates of the competing alternatives themselves. Further, the emphasis placed by one competing alternative will also be affected by its interaction with its competitor's emphasis.

Comparing the Candidates and the Role of Negative and Positive Political Advertising

Political campaigns often consist of a mix of positive and negative advertisements. *Positive advertisements* focus on the positive personal or character features of the favored candidate rather than on the weaknesses of the opponent. In contrast, *negative advertisements* focus on the negative personal or character features of the opponent rather than on the strengths of the favored candidate (Ansolobehere & Iyengar, 1995;

Budesheim, Houston, & DePaola, 1996; Johnson-Cartee & Copeland, 1991). Nonetheless, a given candidate will often favor the use of predominantly positive or negative appeals in his or her campaign, thereby allowing the campaign as a whole to be characterized as positive or negative.

Consider voters' comparisons of competing candidates. These candidates have a number of features relevant to their qualifications and appeal for office (e.g., previous public service, relevant experience, ideologies, issue positions). Their qualities are a mix of positive (e.g., a successful lobbying effort to get a major manufacturer to build a new factory in the state, bringing with it hundreds of new jobs) and negative (e.g., an admission of marital infidelity) characteristics.

However, the characteristics people deem relevant to making a choice between competing candidates will be affected by which of those characteristics the opposing political campaigns choose to emphasize. Thus the public perception of each candidate's image is constructed by the interaction of the candidate's own campaign with that of his or her opponent (Houston et al., 1999; Johnson-Cartee & Copeland, 1991). Competing campaigns create a synergy between them; if the campaigns in tandem focus primarily on negative features, then the entire atmosphere of the campaign takes on a negative tone that can lower voters' evaluations of both candidates (Ansolobehere & Iyengar, 1995). It would seem to follow, conversely, that if the campaigns in tandem emphasize positive advertising, voters' evaluation of both candidates should improve, as well as evaluations of the choice itself.

In this manner, *joint negative campaigns*, by making the bad features of the choice alternatives salient in the choice process, produce what is effectively an avoidance-avoidance conflict. As noted earlier, avoidance-avoidance choices are characterized by a number of difficulties. They produce unpleasant prechoice conflict and low levels of postchoice satisfaction. Further, Lewin (1933) pointed out that the preferred alternative when faced with an avoidance-avoidance conflict is to simply refuse to choose (in the case of a political campaign, not to vote). Thus, both candidates should be more negatively evaluated, and the choice itself should produce more negative evaluations. Because of the focus on the bad features, even the candidate selected is also evaluated relatively negatively. However, by the same reasoning, *joint positive campaigns* produce what is effectively an approach-approach conflict by making the good features of the choice alternatives salient in the choice process. Accordingly, both candidates should be more positively evaluated, and the choice itself should produce more positive evaluations. Because of the focus on the good features, even the candidate rejected is also evaluated relatively positively.

Houston et al. (1999) had subjects evaluate two candidates for the U. S. Senate. All subjects first read the same two candidate biographies, which consisted of a mix of positive and negative characteristics pretested to be approximately equivalent. One candidate was a self-described "liberal," the other a "conservative." The candidates' positions on five issues were also reported, with the liberal taking consistently liberal positions and the conservative taking consistently conservative positions. On the basis of these self-reports, subjects were classified as either liberals or conservatives. For liberal subjects, the liberal candidate was considered the "shared-ideology" candidate and the conservative candidate was considered the "opposing-ideology" candidate. For conservative subjects, the conservative candidate was classified as the shared-ideology candidate and the liberal candidate was classified as the opposing-ideology candidate. After reading the biographies, subjects read advertisements supposedly produced by the candidates' campaigns. Each candidate engaged in either a positive or a negative campaign. The positive and negative campaigns of shared- and opposing-ideology candidates were fully crossed, creating a 2 × 2 design.

Although both positive-positive and negative-negative paired campaigns narrowed the difference between the ideologically opposed candidates, they did so for very different reasons. The positive-positive campaign produced relatively *high* ratings for both candidates, whereas the negative-negative campaign produced relatively *low* ratings for both candidates. That is, when each campaign focused on the positive characteristics of its own candidate, *both* candidates were perceived as desirable alternatives, creating an approach-approach conflict. When both campaigns focused on the negative characteristics of their opponent, *both* candidates were perceived as undesirable alternatives, creating an avoidance-avoidance conflict. In line with this interpretation, subjects said they were less likely to vote in the negative-negative condition. They also expressed lower levels of confidence in their voting choice in the negative-negative condition (Houston et al., 1999).

Of particular importance, in contrast to notions that people will excuse replying to negative attacks in kind, the assessments of the shared-ideology candidate were downgraded for using a negative campaign *only* when the opposing-ideology candidate also used a negative campaign. Assessments of the opposing-ideology candidate were upgraded by using a positive campaign *only* when the shared-ideology candidate was also using a positive campaign. Accordingly, only when the paired campaigns *joined* in making *either* the positive *or* the negative features particularly salient to the decision makers did the transformation of identical pairs of candidates resolve itself as an approach-approach or an avoidance-avoidance conflict, respectively.

Competing advocacy campaigns are not the only way to focus decision makers' attention on either the postive or negative features of paired alternatives. Instructions on *how* to consider and resolve a choice dilemma can also produce such effects, and we turn now to one such situation.

Preference and Rejection Judgments in Choice Dilemmas

Any dichotomous choice dilemma may be characterized in two distinctly different ways. The individual making the judgment may construe the dilemma as deciding which of the two paired alternatives he or she *prefers* and select that alternative. However, the individual may also construe that same choice dilemma as deciding which of two paired alternatives he or she *rejects*, thus leaving the remaining alternative as the one received by default (Houston et al., 1991).

These two different characterizations of a choice dilemma can, in turn, influence how the choice process unfolds. A preference judgment entails deciding which of the two alternatives is better *liked*. In turn, judgments of liking should rely primarily on the attractiveness of the alternatives. Judging the relative attractiveness of paired items encourages the individual to determine which item has the more *desirable* features and then to select it on the basis of these merits. Thus, if one's goal is to decide which of two alternatives is preferred, the *good* features of the alternatives should be more salient than the *bad* features during the decision process.

A judgment of rejection, however, entails deciding which of the two alternatives is more *disliked*. Such judgments of disliking should, in turn, rely mostly on the unattractiveness of the alternatives. Judging the relative unattractiveness of paired items encourages determining which item has the more *undesirable* features and then rejecting it on the basis of these detriments. Thus, when the goal is to decide which alternative to reject, the *bad* features of the alternatives should be more salient than the *good* features during the decision process.

Shafir (1993) demonstrated that an *enriched* option (i.e., an option with extremely good and extremely bad features) will be both more preferred *and* more rejected than an *impoverished* option (i.e., an option with only moderately good and moderately bad features). Shafir argued that because decision makers seek to justify their choice, the differential instructions on how to resolve the choice dilemma trigger different *response modes* – that is, preference instructions encourage justification by citing positive features, whereas rejection instruction encourage justification by citing negative features (see also Ganzach & Schul, 1995, and Wedell, 1997, for further discussion of the differences between preference and rejection judgments).

Houston and Weeks (1998) reasoned that if instructions to resolve a choice dilemma either as a preference judgment or as a rejection judgment directly enhance the salience of the good features or the bad features, respectively, of the paired alternatives, then people should rate good features as more important to their decisions when making preference judgments but should rate bad features as more important to their decisions when making rejection judgments.

In three separate studies, Houston and Weeks (1998) had participants designate which features of the alternatives were most important to their decisions. In all three studies, each participant was instructed to resolve six choice dilemmas by making either a preference judgment or a rejection judgment. Three different methods of indicating feature importance were used: (1) following completion of *all* six choices, participants *checked off* which features were most important to their judgments on lists reinstating all of the features of the alternatives; (2) immediately after *each* judgment, participants *listed* from memory which features were important to their judgments; and (3) participants *tagged*, on line, which features they wished to review *prior* to making their judgments. Note that participants in both the preference and rejection judgment conditions made judgments about the same pairs of alternatives. Thus, the differential attention given good and bad features rests entirely on the characterizations of the choice dilemmas as judgments of preference or rejection.

For both the *check-off* and *listing* studies, participants resolved the choice dilemmas by making *preference* judgments designated more *good* than *bad* features as important, whereas participants resolving the choice dilemmas by making *rejection* judgments designated more *bad* than *good* features. In the on-line *tagging* study, although those participants making preference judgments tagged more *good* than *bad* features, those making rejection judgments tagged an *equal* number of good and bad features. Overall, then, the greater salience of good features in preference judgments was pronounced, emerging in some form in all three studies, using three different methods of designating feature importance. Although the greater designation of bad features in rejection judgments emerged in only two of the three studies, in all three studies the *interaction* of judgment type and features designated was statistically significant.

We turn now to some preliminary thoughts on combining factors that selectively enhance feature salience. Specifically, we examine the mitigation of the cancellation-and-focus model's pattern of choice reversals when instructions to resolve the choice dilemma either as a preference judgment or as a rejection judgment enhance the good or bad features, respectively, of the target of the comparison.

Interacting Patterns of Feature Salience: The Cancellation-and-Focus Model and Preference/Rejection Judgments

Instructions to resolve a choice dilemma as a preference judgment appear to heighten the salience of the good features of paired items, whereas instructions to resolve a choice dilemma as a rejection judgment appear to heighten the salience of the bad features of the items. The cancellation-and-focus process also makes unique features more salient than shared features for both types of judgment. However, as noted earlier, features become unique or shared only when the *second item of each pair (the Subject)* is encountered. Accordingly, when the participant is assessing the *first* member of a pair of alternatives (and recall that the first member of a pair is always the *Referent* for choice judgments), the extent to which her attention will be drawn to a particular subset of the Referent's features should depend primarily on whether she is making a preference judgment or a rejection judgment, with the former encouraging concentration on the good features of the Referent and the latter encouraging concentration on its bad features.

What are the implications of increasing the salience of a subset of the *Referent's* features for the cancellation-and-focus model? Consider again the situation with a unique-good, shared-bad pair of alternatives (the pair of automobiles in the top panels of Table 3.1). When the individual encounters the second of the automobiles, she will cancel the shared bad features and resolve the choice dilemma on the basis of the competing unique-good features. For an individual resolving the choice dilemma as a *rejection* judgment, the initial salience of the *bad* features of the first auto (the Referent) should have little or no effect because the bad features of both items will cancel out. However, if an individual is resolving the dilemma as a *preference* judgment, the Referent's *good features* will be salient. Thus, when the latter individual encounters the second auto (the Subject), her initial emphasis on the Referent's good features could, at least partially, reduce the neglect of the Referent's unique-good features and, accordingly, *lessen* the relative advantage in choice enjoyed by the *Subject* of *unique-good pairs*.

Once again, the situation is different for a unique-bad, shared-good pair of alternatives (the pair of automobiles in the bottom panel of Table 3.1). For an individual resolving the choice dilemma as a *preference* judgment, the initial salience of the *good* features of the first auto (the Referent) should have little or no effect because the good features of both items will cancel out during the choice process. However, if an individual is resolving the dilemma as a *rejection* judgment, the Referent's *bad features* will be salient. Thus, when the latter individual encounters the second auto (the Subject), his initial emphasis on the Referent's bad features could, at least partially, reduce the neglect of the Referent's unique-bad features and, accordingly, *lessen* the relative advantage enjoyed by the *Referent* of *unique-bad pairs*.

To summarize, for *unique-good* pairs, *the advantage of the Subject* should be *mitigated or lessened* by the salience given the *good* features of the Referent by *preference* judgment instructions. However, for *unique-bad* pairs, *the advantage of the Referent* should be *mitigated or lessened* by the salience given the *bad* features of the Referent by *rejection* judgment instructions.

Some support for these predictions can be seen in the previous comparison for choice studies of Houston and his colleagues (Houston & Roskos-Ewoldsen, 1998; Houston & Sherman, 1995; Houston et al., 1989, 1991). In all of these studies, the choice dilemmas were exclusively resolved as preference judgments. Accordingly, we would expect to see a mitigation of the Subject's advantage for unique-good pairs relative to the Referent's advantage for unique-bad pairs. In the six studies in these papers that used the standard cancellation-and-focus paradigm, the unique-bad mean is significantly *below* the midpoint of the scale (i.e., 6.50 on a 12-point, forced-choice scale, which is the expected value for equivalent pairs) in all six of these studies. However, the unique-good mean did *not* significantly differ from the midpoint in five of these studies (Houston & Roskos-Ewoldsen, 1998; Houston & Sherman, 1995, Experiment 1; Houston et al., 1989, Experiments 1 and 3; Houston et al.,

1991, Experiment 2). Indeed, in one of these studies (Houston et al., 1989, Experiment 1), the unique-good mean, although significantly higher than the unique-bad mean, was itself (6.32) below the midpoint of the scale. In only one of these six studies (Houston et al., 1989, Experiment 2) was the unique-good mean significantly above the scale midpoint.

A quantitative analysis was conducted to confirm these consistent findings across the six studies. Because these studies employed a common metric, the means were tested against the midpoint using a t-test for paired samples; as expected, the overall departure from the midpoint was significant for the unique-bad scores ($t(5) = 8.08$, $p < .0001$), whereas the unique-good scores did not differ reliably from the midpoint ($p = .221$). Two possible limitations inherent in this particular analysis involve assumptions of equal sample size and homogeneity of variance across studies. The sample sizes ranged from $N = 50$ to $N = 93$, but sample size differences are generally considered problematic only when the variation exceeds a 2 to 1 ratio (Kish, 1965). Finally, the size of the t value indicates that the effect could withstand any potential heterogeneity of variance.

We further examined this possibility by having participants resolve six dichotomous choice dilemmas, using the standard cancellation-and-focus paradigm but having half of the participants select which alternative they preferred (i.e., making preference judgments) and half select which alternative they rejected (i.e., making rejection judgments). For each participant, three dilemmas involved unique-good pairs and three involved unique-bad pairs. We expected that rejection judgment instructions would lessen the advantage of the Referent in unique-bad pairs, whereas preference judgment instructions would lessen the advantage of the Subject in unique-good pairs.

Method

Participants. Participants were 103 undergraduates at the University of Memphis who participated for course credit and were run in groups of 4 to 16. Fifteen participants were dropped from the analyses for failure to follow directions, leaving a total of 88 participants (45 making a preference judgment and 43 making a rejection judgment).

Materials and Procedure

The descriptive feature lists used were for four categories of objects (apartments, automobiles, vacation spots, and college courses in the participant's major) and for two categories of persons (a work partner of the same gender and a blind date). The feature lists were the same as those used in Houston et al. (1989, 1991). Participants were randomly assigned to make either a preference judgment or a rejection judgment for six categories, three with unique-good pairs and three with unique-bad pairs. The assignment of both versions of each pair was counterbalanced across orders, as was the order of presentation of the two descriptions within each version. Each participant received a booklet containing descriptions of a pair of items from each of the six categories. For each category, the feature list for each item was presented on its own page with a category label. Participants could take as long as needed to read each page, but once a page was turned, they could not turn back to it. After reading the second feature list, the participant completed a 12-point, forced-judgment scale. Participants repeated this procedure for all six categories.

Results and Discussion

Choice rating scales were reversed for participants making rejection judgments. Thus, for all participants, lower numbers (1–6) indicate that the Referent held the favored position (i.e., *preferred* or *not rejected*), whereas higher numbers (7–12) indicate that the Subject held the favored position (i.e., *preferred* or *not rejected*). After reversal of the scales for participants making rejection judgments, unique-good and unique-bad mean scores were again produced for each participant. A 2 (*judgment pair*: unique-good vs. unique-bad) × 2 (*judgment type*: preference or rejection) mixed factors analysis of variance was then performed, with judgment pair as the within-participants factor and judgment type as the between-participants factor.

Judgment Reversals for Unique-Good and Unique-Bad Pairs. There was a significant main effect for judgment pair, $F(1, 86) = 22.53$, $p < .001$, with the mean for unique-good pairs ($M = 7.58$, $SD = 2.10$) significantly higher than the mean for unique-bad pairs ($M = 5.91$, $SD = 2.22$). Therefore, both preference reversals *and* rejection reversals were again replicated.

Initial Choices: Preference and Rejection Judgments. As noted, the expected value for equivalent choice alternatives is the rating scale's midpoint (6.50). Accordingly, the cancellation-and-focus model expects that the means for unique-good pairs will be *above* 6.50 (because of the Subject's advantage in unique-good pairs), whereas the means for unique-bad pairs will be *below* 6.50 (because of the Referent's advantage in unique-bad pairs). Further, we predicted that preference judgment instructions would lessen (but not eliminate) the relative advantage of the Subject for unique-good pairs, whereas rejection judgment instructions would lessen (but not eliminate) the relative advantage of the Referent for unique-bad pairs.

We expected that preference judgment instructions would *reduce* the Subject's advantage for unique-good pairs (i.e., the mean for unique-good/preference pairs would be *lower* than the mean for unique-good/rejection pairs). Further, we expected that rejection judgment instructions would reduce the Referent's advantage for unique-good pairs (i.e., the mean for unique-bad/preference pairs would also be *lower* than the mean for unique-bad/rejection pairs). Thus, for *both* unique-good and unique-bad pairs, the values for *rejection* judgments were predicted to be *higher* than the values for *preference* judgments. Accordingly, we expected that the rejection judgment mean would be higher than the preference judgment mean.

A 2 (*judgment pair*: unique-good vs. unique-bad) × 2 (*judgment type*: preference or rejection) mixed factors analysis of variance was performed on this transformed scale, with judgment pair as the within-participants factor and judgment type as the between-participants factor. As predicted, there was a significant main effect for judgment type, $F(1, 86) = 4.21$, $p < .05$, with the mean for rejection judgments ($M = 7.05$, $SD = .215$) significantly higher than the mean for preference judgments ($M = 5.93$, $SD = .210$). Further, an examination of Table 3.2 shows that this main effect rests on *both* the predicted reduction of the Subject's advantage in unique-good pairs under preference judgment instructions (i.e., the unique-good/preference judgment mean is less than the unique-good/rejection judgment mean) *and* the predicted reduction of the Referent's advantage in unique-bad pairs under rejection judgment instructions (i.e., the unique-bad/rejection judgment mean is higher than the unique-bad/preference judgment mean).

The differential emphsis placed on good versus bad features, based on the characterization of the choice dilemma as a preference or a rejection judgment, modified the standard resolutions of the choice dilemmas predicatedby the cancellation-and-focus model. The emphasis placed on the good features of the Referent by preference (as opposed to rejection) judgment instructions lessened the relative advantage of the Subject in

Table 3.2. *Initial Judgment*

Judgment Type	Judgment Pair		
	Unique Good	*Unique Bad*	
Preference judgment	**7.30**	**5.57**	6.43
Rejection judgment	**7.83**	**6.27**	7.05
	7.58	5.91	

Notes: Judgment pair   F(1, 86) = 22.53; $p < .001$
Judgment type   F(1, 86) = 4.21; $p < .05$
Scale: (1–12)-6.50
Higher numbers = subject is favored (preferred or not rejected).
Lower numbers = referent is favored (preferred or not rejected).

unique-good pairs. However, the emphasis placed on the bad features of the Referent by rejection (as opposed to preference) judgment instructions lessened the relative advantage of the Referent in unique-bad pairs.

Thus, in this study the choice judgments between approximately equivalent items showed effects of both the cancellation-and-focus model (i.e., whether the alternatives consisted of unique-good or unique-bad pairs) and the judgment type (i.e., whether the choice dilemmas were resolved as preference or rejection judgments). The basic pattern predicted by the cancellation-and-focus model, based on the enhanced salience of the unique features of the Subject (i.e., the Subject holding the favored position [preferred or not rejected] for unique-good pairs and the Referent holding the favored position [preferred or not rejected] for unique-bad pairs), was maintained under *both* preference and rejection judgment instructions. However, judgment type did *modify* this basic pattern, reducing the Subject's advantage in unique-good pairs under preference judgment instructions and the Referent's advantage in unique-bad pairs under rejection judgment instructions.

The study presented here represents an initial effort to look at interactions of salience-enhancing aspects in the choice process. An individual resolving a choice dilemma as a *rejection* judgment places his or her initial emphasis on the bad features of the Referent. For unique-good pairs, this enhancement of the salience of the bad features of the Referent is rendered moot by the cancellation of the shared-bad features. But for unique-bad pairs, the enhancement of the salience of the bad features of the Referent does affect the eventual judgment, reducing the Referent's advantage. Similarly, an individual resolving a choice dilemma as a *preference* judgment places his or her initial emphasis on the good features of the Referent. For unique-bad pairs, this enhancement of the salience of the good features of the Referent is rendered moot by the cancellation of the shared-good features. But for unique-good pairs, the enhancement of the salience of the good features of the Referent does affect the eventual judgment, reducing the Subject's advantage.

Conclusion

We have reviewed three aspects of the choice process that affect the resolution of choice dilemmas by systematically enhancing the salience of either the good or the bad features of choice alternatives. Because practically all possible choice alternatives consist of a mix of relatively positive and relatively negative features, aspects of the choice process that systematically concentrate the decision maker's attention on one of these categories of features at the expense of the other can bias estimates of the value of the alternatives. Indeed, the identical item will be differentially evaluated simply by embedding it in different choice contexts that enhance the salience of a different set of the item's features (e.g., the cancellation of a different set of "shared features" leads Automobile B in Table 3.1 to be more positively evaluated when compared for choice to Automobile A than when compared to Automobile C).

The feature salience factors reviewed here have led to important applied as well as theoretical advances. The cancellation-and-focus model has helped to clarify decision making in the area of consumer behavior (Dhar & Sherman, 1996; Sanbonmatsu et al., 1991), and both that model and the model of the synergistic effects of negative and positive advertising have contributed to the understanding of political choices (Hodges, 1997; Houston et al., 1999; Houston & Roskos-Ewoldsen, 1998). Both choices and the feeling of satisfaction or regret engendered by those choices in these important applied areas have been demonstrated to be affected by these factors.

Finally, interactions of such salience-enhancing aspects should produce complex salience effects. We presented a preliminary look at one such interaction – the mitigation of the cancellation-and-focus model's pattern of choice reversals by instructions to resolve a choice dilemma either as a preference judgment or as a rejection judgment. Research is needed to examine when and under what conditions such aspects will combine to form interacting patterns of salience enhancement.

References

Agostinelli, G., Sherman, S. J., Fazio, R. H., & Hearst, E. S. (1986). Detecting and identifying change: Additions versus deletions. *Journal of Experimental Psychology: Human Perception and Performance, 12*, 445–454.

Ansolobehere, S., & Iyengar, S. (1995). *Going negative: How attack ads shrink and polarize the electorate.* New York: Free Press.

Baron, J. (1994). *Thinking and deciding (2nd ed.).* New York: Cambridge University Press.

Beattie, J., Baron, J., Hershey, J. C., & Spranca, M. D. (1994). Psychological determinants of decision attitude. *Journal of Behavioral Decision Making, 7*, 129–144.

Budesheim, T. L., Houston, D. A., & DePaola, S. J. (1996). The persuasiveness of in-group and out-group political messages: The case of negative political campaigning. *Journal of Personality and Social Psychology, 70*, 523–534.

Dhar, R., & Sherman, S. J. (1996). The effects of common and unique features in consumer choice. *Journal of Consumer Research, 23*, 193–203.

Festinger, L. (1957). *A theory of cognitive dissonance.* Stanford, CA: Stanford University Press.

Festinger, L. (1964). *Conflict, decision, and dissonance.* Stanford, CA: Stanford University Press.

Ganzach, Y., & Schul, Y. (1995). The influence of quantity of information and goal framing on decision. *Acta Psychologica, 89*, 23–36.

Gerard, H. B., & Orive, R. (1987). The dynamics of opinion formation. In L. Berkowitz (Ed.), *Advances in experimental social psychology* (Vol. 20, pp. 171–202). San Diego, CA: Academic Press.

Gilbert, D. T., Pelham, B. W., & Krull, D. S. (1988). On cognitive busyness: When persons perceivers meet persons perceived. *Journal of Personality and Social Psychology, 54*, 733–740.

Hastie, R., & Park, B. (1986). The relationship between memory and judgment depends on whether the judgment task is memory-based or on-line. *Psychological Review, 93*, 258–268.

Hodges, S. D. (1997). When matching up features messes up decisions: The role of feature matching in successive choices. *Journal of Personality and Social Psychology, 72*, 1310–1321.

Houston, D. A., & Doan, K. A. (1996). Comparison of paired choice alternatives and choice conflict. *Applied Cognitive Psychology, 10*, 125–135.

Houston, D. A., Doan, K. A., & Roskos-Ewoldsen, D. (1999). Negative political advertising and choice conflict. *Journal of Experimental Psychology: Applied, 5*, 3–16.

Houston, D. A., & Roskos-Ewoldsen, D. (1998). Cancellation-and-focus model of choice and preferences for political candidates. *Basic and Applied Social Psychology, 20*, 305–312.

Houston, D. A., & Sherman, S. J. (1995). Cancellation and focus: The role of shared and unique features in the choice process. *Journal of Experimental Social Psychology, 31*, 357–378.

Houston, D. A., Sherman, S. J., & Baker, S. M. (1989). The influence of unique features and direction of comparison on preferences. *Journal of Experimental Social Psychology, 25*, 121–141.

Houston, D. A., Sherman, S. J., & Baker, S. M. (1991). Feature matching, unique features, and the dynamics of the choice process: Predecision conflict and post-decision satisfaction. *Journal of Experimental Social Psychology, 27*, 411–430.

Houston, D. A., & Weeks, M. (1998). Should I decide which alternative I *prefer* . . . or which alternative I *reject*? Feature salience in choice dilemmas. Working paper, University of Memphis.

Johnson-Cartee, K. S., & Copeland, G. A. (1991). *Negative political advertising: Coming of age.* Hillsdale, NJ: Erlbaum.

Kahneman, D., & Tversky, A. (1979). Prospect theory: An analysis of decision under risk. *Econometrica, 47*, 263–291.

Kahneman, D., & Tversky, A. (1984). Choices, values and frames. *American Psychologist, 39*, 341–350.

Kish, L. (1965). *Survey sampling.* New York: Wiley.

Lewin, K. (1933). Environmental forces. In C. Murchison (Ed.), *A handbook of child psychology* (pp. 590–625). Worcester, MA: Clark University Press.

Lewin, K. (1951). *Field theory in social science.* New York: Harper.

Miller, N. E. (1944). Experimental studies of conflict. In J. M. Hunt (Ed.), *Personality and the behavior disorders* (Vol. 1, pp. 431–465). New York: Roland Press.

Read, S. J. (1987). Similarity and causality in the use of social analogies. *Journal of Experimental Social Psychology, 23*, 189–207.

Sanbonmatsu, D. M., Kardes, F. R., & Gibson, B. D. (1991). The role of attribute knowledge and overall evaluations in comparative judgment. *Organizational Behavior and Human Decision Processes, 48*, 131–146.

Shafir, E. (1993). Choosing versus rejecting: Why some options are both better and worse than others. *Memory & Cognition, 21*, 546–556.

Smith, S. M., & Petty, R. E. (1996). Message framing and persuasion: A message processing analysis. *Personality and Social Psychology Bulletin, 22*, 257–268.

Srull, T. K., & Gaelick, L. (1983). General principles and individual differences in the self as a habitual reference point: An examination of self-other judgments of similarity. *Social Cognition, 2*, 108–121.

Tversky, A. (1977). Features of similarity. *Psychological Review, 84*, 327–352.

Tversky, A., & Gati, I. (1978). Studies of similarity. In E. Rosch & B. Lloyd (Eds.), *Cognition and categorization* (pp. 81–98). Hillsdale, NJ: Erlbaum.

Tversky, A., & Gati, I. (1982). Similarity, separability, and the triangle inequality. *Psychological Review, 89*, 123–154.

Tversky, A., & Kahneman, D. (1974). Judgment under uncertainty: Heuristics and biases. *Science, 185*, 1124–1131.

Tversky, A., & Kahneman, D. (1981). The framing of decisions and the rationality of choice. *Science, 221*, 453–458.

Uleman, J. S., Newman, L. S., & Winter, L. (1992). Can personality traits be inferred automatically? Spontaneous inferences require cognitive capacity at encoding. *Consciousness and Cognition, 1*, 77–90.

Wedell, D. H. (1997). Another look at reasons for choosing and rejecting. *Memory & Cognition, 25*, 873–887.

Zeelenberg, M., & Beattie, J. (1997). Consequences of regret aversion 2: Additional evidence for effects of feedback on decision making. *Organizational Behavior and Human Decision Processes, 72*, 63–78.

4 The Impact of Emotional Tradeoff Difficulty on Decision Behavior

Mary Frances Luce, John W. Payne,
and James R. Bettman

Introduction

Tradeoffs are clearly a fundamental aspect of choice. Unless a choice is trivial (e.g., a dominating alternative exists), decision makers must accept less of one choice attribute in order to get more of another. Thus, it is not surprising that much of behavioral decision research has focused on when and how people make tradeoffs (see Bettman, Luce & Payne 1998 for a recent review). Much applied research assessing individual preferences and values (e.g., decision analysis, marketing research) also has at its core explicit or implicit tradeoff elicitation. For example, conjoint methodologies assess consumer tradeoffs in order to gain insight into issues such as the relative importance of attributes like price or safety to car buyers (e.g., Green & Srinivasan 1990).

Over the past several years, we have conducted a program of research concerned with how emotional tradeoff difficulty influences decision behavior. This chapter outlines our research stream addressing the effects of emotional sources of tradeoff difficulty on decision processing patterns and choice outcomes. The research stream began a few years after Jane Beattie completed her dissertation on difficult tradeoffs, and we have had the benefit of her insights regarding tradeoff difficulty (see Beattie 1988; Beattie & Barlas 1993). In her work, Jane considered various sources of tradeoff difficulty, with the emotional nature of tradeoffs as one such factor. We have focused on this aspect of tradeoff difficulty, investigating both the antecedents and the consequences of emotional tradeoff difficulty across several empirical studies.

The body of empirical work that we review in this chapter has caused us to expand our theoretical framework for understanding decision strategy selection (i.e., understanding how people decide how to decide). Across a large number of studies, decision processing behavior, measured by tracking information acquisition, can be understood as a result of the decision maker trading off the accuracy provided by various possible decision strategies with the effort required by these strategies (e.g., Payne, Bettman & Johnson 1993). Decision makers appear to respond to environmental characteristics in an adaptive manner if one postulates that they are making effort-accuracy tradeoffs. Thus, for instance, when aspects of the environment increase the relative accuracy advantage of more normative decision strategies over more heuristic strategies, decision makers tend to shift their processing behavior toward patterns that are consistent with normative strategies. Conversely, when environmental factors increase the relative effort cost of normative over heuristic strategies, decision makers tend to shift toward more heuristic processing patterns. Most of the research conducted within this framework utilizes decision contexts and manipulations that are likely to be associated with low levels of emotion – for instance, choice among alternative gambles offering small, positive monetary payments. As we will argue, we believe that the effort-accuracy framework must be expanded in order to explain decision behavior in more consequential decision contexts (see Bettman et al. 1998). Specifically, we believe that it is necessary to add the meta-goal of coping with negative emotion to the meta-goals involving accuracy and effort in order to predict and explain decision strategy selection in potentially threatening decision environments. We argue that this is an important extension of the effort-accuracy framework because decisions that matter more (to both the decision maker and society) are, almost by definition, more threatening and therefore more likely to be influenced by coping goals.

Conceptualizations of Tradeoff Difficulty

The standard economic view of decision behavior assumes that "a tradeoff is a tradeoff is a tradeoff." Rational choice theories assume that individuals have well-articulated preferences for attributes and therefore can readily calculate *exchange rates* between various attributes (see Lucas 1986, McFadden 1997, and Plott 1996 for recent views). That is, these theories assume that decision makers not only can compute their value for various attribute levels, but that they can weight relative advantages and disadvantages appropriately across differing attributes. The economic view may acknowledge lack of information as a factor complicating some tradeoffs. However, this view does not generally acknowledge that some tradeoffs may be avoided on principle or because of emotional considerations. Along with others (e.g., Hogarth 1987; Shepard 1964), we believe that decision makers may specifically respond to the emotional distress associated with tradeoffs. Although cognitive effort explanations for tradeoff difficulty are well documented in the decision theory literature (e.g., Payne et al. 1993), we believe that emotional sources of tradeoff difficulty are an important and relatively overlooked additional source of influence on choice.

We define emotional tradeoff difficulty as the level of subjective threat associated with an explicit between-attribute tradeoff within the context of a particular choice. We believe that emotional tradeoff difficulty is defined at the level of specific attribute pairs. For instance, trading off safety and purchase price in the context of an automobile purchase decision may be more threatening than trading off comfort and purchase price within the context of the same automobile purchase. Further, we believe that emotional tradeoff difficulty is sensitive to the direction of contemplated tradeoffs. For instance, completing a tradeoff that sacrifices safety for money may be more threatening than completing a tradeoff that sacrifices money for safety.

By defining emotional tradeoff difficulty as the level of subjective threat, we distinguish this concept from the *emotion experienced* during a choice. We make this distinction because we believe that decision makers often recognize the emotional potential of choice tradeoffs and engage in coping strategies that forestall experienced emotion. For instance, a parent who anticipates that it will be very emotion-laden to trade off decreases in the quality of her child's health care with monetary savings can avoid the negative emotion inherent in that tradeoff by taking actions that maximize her child's health, even if at great expense. In such a situation, the opportunity to engage in an effective coping strategy may result in decision behavior being influenced by emotion-relevant considerations, even though negative emotion resulting from decision tradeoffs is not actually experienced. Thus, our framework differs from research, notably the case studies reported by Janis and Mann (1977), that focuses on decision making under conditions of extreme experienced stress. We take a more general perspective, noting that the desire to minimize or cope with negative emotion may sometimes act as a meta-goal influencing decision strategy selection and therefore influencing many aspects of decision behavior.

Chapter Organization and Scope

In this chapter, we discuss a series of experiments investigating the effects of emotional tradeoff difficulty on decision behavior, specifically decision processing patterns and decision outcomes. Before doing so, we briefly discuss Lazarus's (1991) theory of emotion elicitation, which we used as a theoretical point of departure. In order to develop manipulations of emotional tradeoff difficulty and make predictions about the effects of emotional tradeoff difficulty on decision behavior, we applied this general theory to choice environments specifically.

Theoretical Development

Background: Lazarus's Theory of Emotion Elicitation

We use Lazarus's (1991) model of emotion elicitation as a starting point for understanding the generation of emotional tradeoff difficulty in decision making. Lazarus argues that emotion results from a set of cognitive appraisals. Primary appraisal addresses the stakes one has in the outcome of an encounter and has three components. *Goal relevance* assesses whether there is anything at stake in an encounter, that is, whether the encounter has any potential relevance for valued goals and therefore any potential for emotion. *Goal congruence* assesses whether the encounter is expected to involve positive or negative outcomes and therefore determines whether emotions will be positive or negative. Situations associated with anticipated negative outcomes are characterized as threats and generally lead to negative emotions. Because we are concerned in this chapter with decision situations involving threats to valued goals, we will use the terms *threatening* and *(negatively) emotion-laden* interchangeably. Finally, *goal content* assesses the particular goals that are at stake, influencing the exact form of the emotional experience (e.g., whether guilt versus shame is felt).

Secondary appraisal addresses one's options and prospects for coping. Specifically, secondary appraisals address whether the individual believes she or he can improve the relevant situation, whether future outcomes are expected to worsen, and whether blame or credit for oneself or another is warranted. The inclusion of secondary appraisal as a major proposed component of emotion elicitation reflects Lazarus's view that emotion and coping enter into a dynamic process involving bidirectional causality.

Appraisals of actual or potential negative emotion elicit coping behaviors that Lazarus (1991) classifies as either problem focused or emotion focused. Problem-focused coping involves attempts to solve the environmental problem leading to emotion, whereas emotion-focused coping involves attempts to alter experienced emotion directly without altering the underlying situation. Emotion-focused coping is further classified into avoidance and changing the meaning of a situation. Much research indicates that *both* problem-focused and emotion-focused coping efforts are typically brought to bear on any individual stressful episode (e.g., Folkman & Lazarus 1988).

In summary, Lazarus defines primary appraisals of stakes and secondary appraisals of coping options as the major components of emotion elicitation. He further classifies coping behaviors into problem-focused and emotion-focused forms. In the following section, we outline several general propositions regarding emotional tradeoff difficulty and decision behavior. These propositions are a direct result of our adaptation of Lazarus's general emotion theory to the specific context of decision behavior.

Major Propositions of Our Tradeoff Difficulty Model

Our theoretical framework for understanding the effects of emotional tradeoff difficulty on decision behavior is associated with three main sets of propositions. First, decision characteristics (e.g., attribute identities and values) can generate decision-related emotions in general and emotional tradeoff difficulty in particular. Second, emotional tradeoff difficulty may influence patterns of information processing during choice deliberation. Third, emotional tradeoff difficulty may influence choice outcomes. In this section, we briefly outline our rationale for each set of propositions. In the following section, we outline the empirical support that we have generated to date for these propositions.

Propositions Regarding Emotional Tradeoff Difficulty. Within the specific context of a decision task, we argue that attribute identities and attribute values are two major factors influencing emotional tradeoff difficulty by altering decision makers' primary appraisals. First, because attributes determine the goals that are implicated in a decision, we believe that attribute identities have a major impact on assessments of goal relevance and goal content during primary appraisal. That is, decision attributes define the outcomes associated with, and therefore the goals implicated in, a decision. For instance, the attribute "automobile safety" may implicate goals associated with personal survival, whereas the attribute "automobile styling" may implicate goals associated with personal expression, and these differing goals may be associated with differing assessments of stakes by a particular decision maker. Thus, attribute identities should influence emotional tradeoff difficulty.

Second, the relative or absolute values of choice alternatives on the relevant attribute(s) should influence primary appraisal by determining the degree to which the goals implied by each attribute are appraised as likely to remain satisfied or unsatisfied. Thus, we believe that attribute values have a major impact on assessments of goal congruence during primary appraisal. For example, choosing between a very safe car and an extremely safe car is likely to involve a more positive primary appraisal than would choosing between a very unsafe car and an extremely unsafe car. Both conflict among attribute values (the degree to which one attribute has to be sacrificed for another to be maximized) and the valence of attribute values (whether alternatives are seen as generally good or bad) are therefore likely to influence appraisals of goal content, potentially contributing to emotional tradeoff difficulty. By direct extension, the framing of attribute values (e.g., whether the decision maker's reference point results in a particular set of attribute values being experienced as gains or losses) should influence secondary appraisal by altering the subjective valence of attribute values. Reference points that are external to a decision can generate these loss-versus-gain frames. Alternatively, decision conflict can generate frames within a decision; for instance, the better value of one alternative on an attribute may be used as a reference point against which the worse value of another alternative on that same attribute is considered.

Because appraisals of both goal relevance and goal incongruence are thought necessary to generate negative emotion, we believe that attribute identities and values interact to determine emotional tradeoff difficulty. Specifically, emotional tradeoff difficulty is expected when attribute identities implicate valued goals and attribute values indicate that these goals may be blocked. Thus, our Decision Threat Proposition, stated here, lays out general conditions under which we expect a decision task to be characterized by threat, potentially eliciting negative emotion:

> *Decision Threat Proposition:* The potential for negative emotion will be associated with decision tasks involving poor values on attributes with links to valued goals.

We predict that decision situations characterized by potential losses on highly desired attributes are high in emotional tradeoff difficulty and will often generate negative emotion during decision processing. However, secondary appraisals identifying readily available coping options may mitigate primary appraisals associated with negative emotions, consistent with Lazarus's (1991) notion of secondary appraisals of coping options potentially mitigating emotions associated with primary appraisals of the stakes associated with an encounter. We recognize this aspect of emotion elicitation in our theoretical framework for emotional tradeoff difficulty. We argue that avenues for coping, such as the ability to avoid a choice or delegate the choice to another responsible party, will mitigate the negative emotion associated with the threat of having to accept poor values on one or more highly desired attribute(s), as proposed here.

> *Coping-Opportunity Proposition:* An available option for coping will mitigate feelings of negative emotion associated with the potential necessity of accepting poor values on attributes with links to valued goals.

Thus, our Decision Threat Proposition and our Coping-Opportunity Proposition jointly specify how decision characteristics can affect negative emotion during choice. In the following section, we develop two propositions addressing how motivations to cope with these negative emotions can alter decision processing patterns.

Propositions Regarding Decision Processing. Once emotional tradeoff difficulty is generated through attribute identities and/or values, we expect decision makers to engage in problem- and emotion-focused coping efforts. We believe that the major form of problem-focused coping relevant to choice behavior is the motivation to work harder in order to do a good job of solving the choice problem with which one is confronted (e.g., see the discussion in Janis & Mann 1977 of vigilant decision making). Because effort feedback (rather than feedback regarding the normative accuracy of a particular decision strategy or outcome) is both available to the decision maker and often relatively observable by others, we expect increased processing effort to be the major result of motivations to engage in problem-focused coping in decision situations.

> *Processing-Effort Proposition:* Problem-focused coping concerns will lead to increased effort in processing under increased emotional tradeoff difficulty.

The Processing-Effort Proposition involves a proposed reaction to negative emotion that overlaps with an observed reaction to accuracy-maximization goals (e.g., Payne, Bettman & Luce 1996). That is, both an increased desire to maximize decision accuracy and an increased desire to cope with negative emotion are expected to cause increased decision effort. Thus, the Processing-Effort Proposition does not by itself require a theoretical expansion of the effort-accuracy framework, as one could simply postulate that coping considerations cause an increased focus on accuracy goals. However, as is argued next, we believe that coping behavior may simultaneously involve problem-focused and emotion-focused efforts, and therefore increased effort in reaction to negative emotion will occur simultaneously with shifts in decision processing that are inconsistent with reactions to accuracy goals.

We believe that the major form of emotion-focused coping relevant to decision processing is a desire to avoid particularly distressing explicit tradeoffs between attributes (e.g., Hogarth 1987; Shepard 1964). That is, if tradeoff difficulty is elicited by the perception that valued goals must be given up, then the decision maker should try either to avoid these sacrifices altogether or, at least, to make them implicit (rather than explicit). For instance, a decision maker threatened by the possibility of giving up quality of medical care in choosing employee benefits may shield herself from the problematic tradeoff between medical care and money by considering only plans she can afford (screening on money) and by considering quality of care only for affordable or possible plans. By considering attributes sequentially rather than simultaneously, this strategy makes the tradeoff between medical care and money implicit in that the decision maker never confronts the (perhaps higher) level of care she could have obtained by spending more money. Thus, we believe that decision makers will adjust their patterns of decision processing to accommodate emotion-focused coping concerns.

> *Processing-Pattern Proposition:* Emotion-focused coping concerns will lead to decision processing patterns that avoid explicit between-attribute tradeoffs.

As is discussed further in the context of our empirical work, we operationalize our Processing-Pattern Proposition by measuring which information is considered by a decision maker and in what order.

Consideration of emotion-focused coping behaviors, which lead to our Processing-Pattern Proposition, is the primary reason that we argue for an expansion of the effort-accuracy framework to incorporate emotion-minimization goals. That is, although problem-focused coping behaviors are likely to mirror accuracy-maximization behaviors, we expect emotion-focused coping to be undertaken simultaneously with problem-focused coping. These emotion-focused coping behaviors are similar to effort-minimization behaviors in that they are expected to involve avoidance of particularly emotion-laden or threatening processing operations. However, emotion-focused coping and effort minimization are likely to diverge in that the specific processing operations that are most cognitively taxing (and are therefore avoided in the pursuit of effort minimization) are not necessarily the operations that are most emotionally taxing.

Summarizing the preceding two propositions, we believe that problem-focused and emotion-focused coping motivations will influence the extent and the pattern of decision processing, respectively. Thus, we expect that tasks with greater potential for negative emotion will simultaneously lead to more extensive decision processing and more processing that avoids tradeoffs (attribute-based decision processing). This joint prediction regarding decision processing runs counter to much work in less emotion-laden contexts, where environmental aspects that encourage more extensive processing typically also encourage more compensatory (alternative-based) processing (e.g., Payne et al. 1993). We also believe that coping motivations will influence final choice outcomes, as discussed in the following section.

Propositions Regarding Choice Outcomes. We stated previously that decision makers will engage in emotion-focused coping through avoidance by altering the form of their decision processing. In certain decision situations, it may also be possible to engage in avoidance by making particular choices. For instance, the employee making the problematic health care decision could engage in coping by considering little or no choice information and accepting a default or previously chosen option. We define an *avoidant option* as a choice recommended by some objective reason or label independent of value-based tradeoffs. Such reasons could include a status-quo position or the endorsement of another person. Choice of these options may satisfy emotion-focused coping motivations to avoid distressing choice operations, as such choices can be made without engaging in difficult explicit tradeoffs. Thus, we believe that the choice share of these avoidant options will increase as tradeoffs become more emotionally difficult.

Avoidant-Choice Proposition: Emotion-focused coping considerations will lead to increased choice of avoidant options under increased emotional tradeoff difficulty.

In some decision situations, the directional nature of emotional tradeoff difficulty may also provide some opportunities to engage in emotion-focused coping through avoidance of distressing choice operations. For instance, an individual who is threatened by the potential of giving up medical care in order to save money (versus the prospect of giving up money in order to gain medical care) could engage in coping by choosing a health plan that maximizes perceived quality of care despite the potential cost. Of course, the coping option of avoiding emotionally difficult tradeoffs by making a lexicographic choice (i.e., a choice that maximizes one attribute) will be attractive only for decision situations involving one attribute that is particularly emotionally difficult to trade.

Lexicographic-Choice Proposition: Emotion-focused coping considerations will lead to increased use of lexicographic choice based on an emotionally difficult-to-trade attribute.

Thus, we propose that particular decision outcomes will increase in attractiveness in more emotion-laden situations. Specifically, choosing either an avoidant option or an option that maximizes a particularly difficult-to-trade attribute may provide emotion-focused coping benefits by allowing the decision maker to avoid troubling explicit tradeoffs. This prediction is consistent with our general notion that decision makers may seek to minimize negative emotion in their choice behavior, as well as seeking to maximize decision accuracy while minimizing cognitive effort.

Summary of Propositions. In summary, we make six basic propositions regarding emotional tradeoff difficulty by adapting Lazarus's (1991) emotion framework to the particular situation of decision making. We predict that choice situations will generate negative emotions when they require potential acceptance of low values on highly desired attributes (Decision Threat Proposition). We further predict that this negative emotion will be mitigated by easily available coping options (Coping-Opportunity Proposition). We expect emotional tradeoff difficulty to influence decision processing patterns by motivating more extensive processing that avoids explicit between-attribute tradeoffs (Processing-Effort and Processing-Pattern Propositions). We further expect emotional tradeoff difficulty to motivate increased choice of avoidant options where available (Avoidant-Choice Proposition) and to motivate lexicographic choices maximizing a particularly difficult to trade attribute where feasible (Lexicographic-Choice Proposition). We have generated empirical support for all six of these propositions, as outlined in the following section.

Empirical Evidence

In this section, we outline research from three papers addressing the effects of emotional tradeoff difficulty on choice behavior. One of these papers (Luce, Bettman & Payne 1997) focuses on decision processing patterns. The two remaining papers (Luce 1998; Luce, Payne, & Bettman 1999) focus on choice outcomes, considering avoidant choice and lexicographic choice, respectively. Both the Luce et al. (1997) and Luce (1998) papers contain measures of the negative emotion associated with various decision situations, primarily as manipulation checks. Thus, these papers address propositions regarding the generation of negative emotion as well. We discuss the effects of tradeoff difficulty on decision processing behavior, and then we discuss effects on choice outcomes. In each of these sections, we address the impact of decision characteristics on the negative emotion experienced during choice.

Decision Processing Behavior

In order to measure the effects of tradeoff difficulty on decision processing patterns, it is necessary to have both a theoretical framework for understanding decision processing and a methodology for measuring it. As discussed in the Introduction, we advocate a broad choice goals framework for understanding decision processing patterns (see Bettman et al. 1998). That is, we expect decision makers to decide how to decide based on tradeoffs between meta-goals. We believe that minimizing negative emotion is an important meta-goal; we also believe that emotion-minimizing goals are activated within a larger context of tradeoffs between the goals of maximizing decision accuracy and minimizing cognitive effort. Thus, we have extended Payne et al.'s (1993) effort-accuracy framework for predicting decision processing patterns by adding an emotion-minimization meta-goal to that framework.

Payne et al.'s work on decision processing also provides a well-developed methodology for observing and describing individuals' decision processing patterns using the Mouselab software system. This methodology typically involves providing choice information to subjects on a computer screen in matrix form, with the piece of information in each cell hidden. For instance, research participants may be presented with a choice matrix for which decision attributes (e.g., safety, price, and styling within an automobile-choice context) define columns and decision alternatives (e.g., Car A, Car B) define rows. Each cell of this matrix is a covered box providing a specific piece of decision information when opened with the mouse-controlled pointer; for instance, the cell associated with the price attribute for Car A may read "$16,000." Subjects undertake decision processing by using a mouse-controlled cursor to open boxes one at a time, and the Mouselab program records the order and timing of information acquisitions. These data are used to construct dependent variables that characterize decision processing patterns.

Within the Mouselab methodology, three main dependent measures capture much of the variance in decision processing. The first measure is simply how much information is processed, assessed using a count of total acquisitions (typically counting reacquisitions) during choice and/or the overall response time of the choice. The second measure is whether information is processed selectively across either attributes or alternatives (i.e., different amounts of information are processed for each attribute or alternative) or consistently (i.e., the same amount of information is processed for each attribute or alternative). The third measure is the pattern of decision processing. Processing may be organized more by alternative, in which multiple attributes of one alternative are considered before information about another alternative is processed. Alternatively, a decision may be processed more by attribute, in which the values of several alternatives on a single attribute are processed before information about another attribute is considered. Generally, compensatory decision rules, that is, rules involving explicit tradeoffs between decision attributes, are associated with less selective and more alternative-based decision processing (e.g., Payne 1976).

Extensive research has established theoretical links between these dependent variables and underlying decision strategies (Payne et al. 1993). For instance, the weighted adding strategy (i.e., expected-utility maximization) is typically taken as the normative standard for decision accuracy and is associated with alternative-based, extensive, and consistent decision processing. Payne et al. (1996) found that decision makers given the explicit goal of maximizing decision accuracy in the context of choices among simple monetary gambles display more extensive, less selective, and more alternative-based processing patterns than do subjects given the effort-minimization goal (see also Creyer, Bettman, & Payne 1990). Further, these aspects of processing (i.e., extensive, consistent, and alternative-based processing) are significantly correlated with the tendency to choose the expected-value-maximizing alternative, whereas the opposite processing patterns are correlated with choice of the lexicographic alternative (i.e., the alternative that is best on the most important attribute).

Research utilizing the effort-accuracy paradigm typically finds relatively stable relationships among the three aspects of decision processing identified earlier. One way to summarize prior results is to note that many of the environmental characteristics studied within the effort-accuracy framework influence the general tradeoff between effortful, alternative-based normative decision strategies and less effortful, more attribute-based heuristic strategies (e.g., Payne et al. 1993). For instance, increasing attribute conflict and decreasing time pressure both increase the relative accuracy advantage of normative over heuristic strategies (leading to more normative processing), whereas increased decision problem size increases the relative effort disadvantage of normative strategies (leading to more heuristic processing). Thus, environmental characteristics that elicit more effortful processing also typically elicit more alternative-based and consistent processing. However, prior work on decision processing patterns typically measured decision processing within the context of decision tasks with low potential for eliciting negative emotion. As is discussed next, the environmental characteristic of increased emotional threat appears to provide an exception to this general pattern.

In Luce et al. (1997), we manipulated decision-related threat in two different ways across two main experiments. First, within the decision context of choosing a child to support through a charity, we manipulated negative emotion by altering the stated expected rate of support for nonchosen children (at 10% or 90%). This manipulation of negative emotion is not consistent with our Decision Threat Proposition; however, it is interesting to note that it had effects on emotion and decision processing analogous to the effects of manipulations constructed to be consistent with that proposition and described next.

In a second experiment, using the decision context of choosing a job to take after graduation, we crossed manipulations regarding both attribute identity (low versus high emotion) and attribute value (low versus high conflict) in order to generate emotional tradeoff difficulty.

The within-subjects manipulation of attribute identity involved presenting each subject with two decisions composed of five hypothetical jobs, each defined across four attributes. The identity of two of the four attributes was manipulated on an individualized basis between the two decision tasks each subject completed. Specific attributes were chosen on the basis of a preliminary, separate experimental session during which each subject responded to multiple measures of both importance and loss aversion for a set of 15 potential attributes. Going from the low-emotion to the high-emotion attribute identity condition, we attempted to hold attribute importance measures constant while replacing attributes relatively low in loss aversion with attributes relatively high in loss aversion. Consider an example subject who rated the attributes "yearly salary" and "job security" as equally important but who also associated "job security" with higher levels of loss aversion. For that subject, the low-emotion decision task would involve alternative jobs defined in terms of differing levels of job security, whereas the high-emotion task would involve alternatives defined in terms of yearly salary. A second attribute would be altered across high- versus low-emotion attribute identity conditions in the analogous manner, and finally, each decision display would be filled out with two other attributes (held constant across attribute-identity conditions). The rationale behind using measures of loss aversion to operationalize our attribute identity manipulation was that trading off attributes involves accepting more of one for less of another, so that negative emotion generated by attribute tradeoffs may be predicted by levels of loss aversion, especially when attribute importance is held constant. A second, between-subjects manipulation of conflict in attribute values altered the average correlation between values on different attributes within the decision matrix, therefore altering the degree to which one attribute had to be sacrificed in order for another to be maximized. Both high-conflict and high-emotion attribute identity, and particularly their combination, resulted in more self-reported negative emotion, supporting our Decision Threat Proposition. That is, more loss-averse attributes were generally associated with more negative emotion, but this effect was stronger in the higher (versus the lower) conflict group.

Recall that our Processing Effort Proposition predicts increased decision effort in more threatening decision environments. We tested this proposition using standard measures of decision effort (i.e., total information acquisition and response times) discussed earlier. Consistent with our reasoning regarding problem-focused coping in choice, we found increased response times and more total acquisitions in conditions associated with increased decision-generated negative emotion.

Our Processing Pattern Proposition hypothesizes that, under increasing emotional tradeoff difficulty, decision makers will engage in emotion-focused coping by considering different attributes sequentially rather than simultaneously, thereby keeping necessary tradeoffs implicit rather than explicit. We tested this proposition by considering the pattern of subjects' decision processing. As expected, we found that more threatening decision environments were associated with more attribute-based patterns of processing. Thus, overall, decision behavior became *both* increasingly effortful and increasingly attribute based as decision threat was increased through higher loss aversion in attribute identities and/or higher conflict in attribute values.

A complicating issue is that many different underlying decision strategies could result in attribute- versus alternative-based patterns of processing, and processing pattern is unlikely to have a one-to-one mapping with tradeoff completion versus avoidance. For instance, an alternative-based decision strategy involving the construction of global evaluations of each alternative may also avoid direct comparison of changes across multiple alternatives on one attribute with changes on another. Thus, although the construction of global evaluations involves weighting various attributes (implying some aspect of between-attributes compromise), it does not necessarily involve explicit consideration of the specific losses associated with choosing one alternative over another. Conversely, an additive difference decision strategy (e.g., Tversky 1969) is associated with both attribute-based processing and explicit tradeoffs. This strategy evaluates the differences in subjective value between two alternatives on an attribute-by-attribute basis, aggregating differences for each pair of considered alternatives and retaining the favored alternative in each pair for further evaluation. Thus, although our processing-pattern proposition is stated in terms of the relatively straightforward measurement of attribute- versus alternative-based processing, we also conducted supplementary analyses. These analyses demonstrate that the increase in attribute-based processing for the higher threat decision tasks tended to be driven by particularly long (e.g., involving approximately four pieces of information) attribute-based processing sequences located at the beginning of decision processing. Thus, it appears that subjects in the more threatening task environments were more likely to approach decision processing initially by considering attributes sequentially, looking across the alternatives but within an attribute.

As discussed previously, selectivity in decision processing is a third general characteristic of decision processing patterns, often measured in concert with effort and processing pattern. In general, we did not find effects on selectivity in the Luce et al. (1997) experiments, perhaps because increasingly effortful processing is generally associated with decreased selectivity, whereas increasingly attribute-based processing is generally associated with increased selectivity.

A self-reported negative emotion measure, taken immediately after each choice, partially mediated these effects on processing effort and pattern. Thus it supported our theoretical framework by indicating that the observed processing changes were motivated by the desire to cope with decision-generated negative emotion.

The results reported by Luce et al. (1997) indicate that a negatively emotional decision context appears to alter the pattern of relationships between aspects of decision processing when compared to less emotional environments. More specifically, in Bettman et al. (1993), we manipulated attribute conflict in the context of low-emotion attributes (small, positive monetary winnings for risky choices) and found that increased conflict was associated with more extensive and more *alternative*-based processing. However, in Luce et al. (1997), we found that increased conflict was associated with more extensive and more *attribute*-based processing, as outlined previously.[1] Thus, decision makers responded to increased conflict in attribute values in a different manner when those values were related to relatively low-emotion attributes (in Bettman et al. 1993) versus potentially threatening attributes (in Luce et al. 1997).

Choice Outcomes

Although we were able to make some relatively general predictions regarding decision processing patterns under emotional tradeoff difficulty, our theory regarding the effects of tradeoff difficulty on choice is dependent on specific aspects of the available choice alternatives. In general, we predict that some choices will have particular features that satisfy the emotion-focused coping goal of avoiding explicit tradeoffs and that these choices will be increasingly attractive under increasing emotional tradeoff difficulty. Our Avoidant Choice Proposition predicts increased choice of avoidant options, and our Lexicographic Choice

Proposition predicts more lexicographic choice patterns in potentially emotion-laden decision situations. We addressed these two propositions in two different papers focused on choice outcomes. In the first of these papers, we also addressed our Coping-Opportunity Proposition regarding the mitigating effects of a coping option (specifically, the opportunity to choose an avoidant option) on experienced negative emotion.

Choice of Avoidant Options. Luce (1998) investigated the effect of emotional tradeoff difficulty on choice shares of three different avoidant options within a hypothetical multiattribute purchase decision that involved choosing one of four available automobiles. Two between-subjects manipulations addressed decision threat and the presence of avoidant options, respectively. First, attributes describing the automobiles were manipulated on the basis of a pretest using a separate sample of subjects such that decisions involved attributes associated with either higher or lower degrees of loss aversion, on average. We expected the presence of more loss-averse attributes to generate increased decision threat because the relevant choice task was characterized by substantial conflict between attribute values. Second, a manipulation of subjects' response options was crossed with the attribute identity manipulation. One group, the control group, simply indicated a choice among the available alternatives. A second group of subjects was given the opportunity to indicate that they would maintain the status quo by choosing a previously chosen alternative, that is, one alternative in the overall choice set was associated with a status quo label. Luce (1998) hypothesized that choosing the status quo was an avoidant option, satisfying emotion-focused coping goals, because it allowed the decision maker to explain and justify her choice (to herself and others) in terms of the status quo label, which was independent of specific attribute weights or tradeoffs. A second avoidant option was the opportunity to report that the subject would prolong the search instead of committing to one of the available options. Again, such a choice can be explained without the necessity of considering the relative merits of various alternatives, and therefore without a focus on specific attribute weights and tradeoffs. A third avoidant option was the opportunity to choose an alternative that dominated a second alternative in the choice set. This alternative may satisfy emotion-focused coping goals in that the dominance relationship provides an objective justification for one's choice that does not rely on tradeoffs (e.g., Simonson 1989). Choice shares of all three avoidant options increased when the decision task was defined in terms of more (versus less) loss-averse attributes. These choice findings are consistent with our prediction that emotion-focused coping considerations would motivate increased choice of avoidant options (see our Avoidant Choice Proposition).

The previously described choice effects could be explained using the standard effort-accuracy framework, if one assumes that considering more loss-averse attributes is more cognitively demanding, leading to avoidant choice as a mechanism for minimizing effort. However, emotion and response time measures reported in Luce (1998) suggest the necessity of considering emotion minimization as a goal motivating avoidant choice. First, emotion ratings taken across both the experiment described previously and a second, related experiment allow some conclusions to be made regarding the direct relationships between avoidant choice and experienced emotion. In the first experiment, negative emotionality was assessed immediately after decision processing by asking subjects to report their expectations regarding the emotionality of the decision task if they were to repeat this same decision in the real world. For this measure, the control group showed a significant increase in negative emotion with more loss-averse attributes. However, emotion ratings in all three (noncontrol) avoidant option groups were insensitive to the attribute identity manipulation. Further, mediation analyses indicated that subjects who actually chose an avoidant alternative were driving this lessened reactivity to attribute identity. That is, choice of an avoidant option (versus choice of another option) resulted in less assessed emotionality in loss-averse-attribute conditions. This finding is consistent with Lazarus's argument that primary appraisals of decision threat (which we propose are elicited by the manipulation of attribute identity) are moderated by secondary appraisals of anticipated coping opportunities (which we propose include the opportunity to choose an avoidant option). More specifically, subjects who chose an avoidant option may have felt that they would repeat this choice if they made the decision again, so this repeat decision was assessed as likely to be relatively nonthreatening. This pattern of emotional results supports our Coping-Opportunity Proposition in that the presence, and particularly the choice, of an avoidant option appears to mitigate feelings of negative emotion elicited by the presence of loss-averse attributes.

A second experiment in Luce (1998) measured negative emotion during decision processing, using a design crossing high versus low loss aversion in attribute identities with the presence or absence of a status quo alternative. Once again, tradeoff difficulty resulted in increased choice of the status quo alternative. Further, in this experiment, an initial phase of processing was carried out (and evaluated by each subject in regard as to current emotionality) before the avoidant option (if relevant) was presented. Subjects who rated this initial processing phase as more emotion-laden were more likely to choose a status quo alternative if it became available. Thus, although it is certainly not surprising that subjects presented with more loss-averse attributes were more likely to indicate that they would choose the status quo, the mediation of this choice effect by self-reported negative emotion provides a unique theoretical basis explaining status quo effects. These findings support our argument that the choice of avoidant alternatives can be motivated by a desire to cope with the threats posed by emotionally difficult choice tradeoffs.

In addition, the results of the two experiments just outlined appear to illustrate the dynamic relationship between emotion and coping proposed by Lazarus (1991). Specifically, decision makers who feel more negative emotion initially are more likely to choose an avoidant option once it becomes available, but decision makers who choose such an option estimate lower levels of later emotion. We believe this divergence in emotion patterns is a direct result of subjects' learning that an avoidant choice is an effective mechanism for coping.

A second reason for considering emotion minimization as a meta-goal arises from analyzing response times. Response time measures collected as part of Luce's second experiment cast further doubt on effort minimization as an explanation of the avoidant choices we observed in reaction to higher tradeoff difficulty. In particular, mediation analyses indicate that choice of the status quo alternative follows *increased* decision response times. Therefore, it does not seem that avoidant choices are made to decrease cognitive effort. This provides further evidence for the necessity of expanding effort-accuracy frameworks to incorporate effects of emotional tradeoff difficulty.

Lexicographic Choice. In Luce et al. (1999), we investigated emotion-focused coping through a specific form of lexicographic choice. In particular, we investigated the choice between higher quality and lower price in a highly simplified, two-attribute, two-alternative decision set. For example, a subject in this experiment may have been asked to choose between renting Apartment A, characterized by $500 in monthly rent and a 25% yearly chance of being a crime victim, and Apartment B, characterized by $1,000 in rent but only an 11% chance of being a crime victim. Thus, we used specific quality attributes (apartment safety, apartment condition, etc.) in order to construct price–quality tradeoffs in choice. In order to focus on difficult, value-revealing tradeoffs, we tailored the choice stimuli to each subject based on his or her earlier response to a matching-task question. This question asked each subject to set a price for the high-quality alternative in the relevant stimulus pair (e.g., setting a rent for Apartment B) such that he or she would be indifferent between that alternative and a lower-quality alternative (e.g., Apartment A). Either three or five individually tailored choice stimuli per alternative pair were then created for each subject such that the price of the high-quality alternative would be systematically arrayed around his or her earlier matching-task response.

In general, in the Luce et al. (1999) studies, we found that incorporating emotional tradeoff difficulty into models predicting responses in these difficult choice environments added precision to these models. In the first experiment, we measured several attribute characteristics and developed estimates of relative (quality versus price) attribute importance and emotionality. The emotionality measure significantly added to the prediction of choice patterns, even after controlling for the importance measure. In particular, because the quality attribute was rated as relatively more emotion-laden, decision makers appeared to cope with potential tradeoff difficulty by choosing the option that was better on that attribute, even at prices significantly higher than the stated matching price at which the subject reported that he or she would be indifferent between higher and lower quality.[2]

In this paper, we also considered a second variable related to emotional tradeoff difficulty in choice in addition to measured attribute emotionality. In particular, we found that providing subjects with a reference point framing quality attribute values as *losses* (versus gains) was associated with increased choice of the high-quality alternative, even in situations where such choice was inconsistent with earlier matching-task responses. Importantly, these findings did not generalize to losses involving attributes stated in currency terms (i.e., the purchase price for a car and the commute time for an apartment). Thus, decision makers appeared to cope with the emotional threat of quality-attribute losses by choosing the high-quality alternative, even at prices significantly higher than their stated matching price, but they did not show analogous behavior for price-attribute or time-attribute losses. This provides a further indication that attribute values (here, subjective values in terms of gains or losses) interact with attribute identities to influence potential coping behavior. We believe that currency attributes (in our experiments, attributes expressed as dollars or time) do not show the same pattern of reference point effects because these attributes are associated with relatively mundane goals and therefore do not tend to elicit negative emotion as easily as the noncurrency, quality attributes we considered. Similarly, currency attributes may generate less negative emotion in choice because decision makers are used to giving up these attributes in return for other benefits. We did not measure negative emotion in the context of these choices because we were concerned with creating demand effects by focusing subjects on the emotional nature of their choice task. However, a separate set of subjects responding to scenario questions rated scenarios involving losses (versus gains) on quality attributes as particularly emotion-laden.

Summary of Choice Outcome Effects. Our research to date indicates that consideration of emotional tradeoff difficulty improves our ability to predict and explain choice patterns. Specifically, certain types of choices appear to provide an advantage in terms of emotion-focused coping by allowing a choice to be identified independently of explicit between-attribute tradeoffs. Avoidant options offer this advantage by providing a reason or label independent of attribute values, whereas lexicographic choices offer this advantage in situations where the problematic tradeoff involves (only) sacrifices on a particular attribute. We find that both sorts of choices increase under emotional tradeoff difficulty.

Conclusions and Implications

We believe that an important lesson provided by our work on tradeoff difficulty is that "a tradeoff is not just a tradeoff." More generally, when people talk about what is "important" to them, they may mean many different things. For example, various notions of importance may include relative weight in specific tradeoffs, willingness to pay, or emotional threat associated with giving up an attribute. In order to understand decision behavior fully, we believe that it is crucial to understand *and distinguish among* these different dimensions along which individuals respond to decision attributes. Thus, we agree with Jane Beattie's proposition that an important decision-making issue is the content of decision tradeoffs in general and the difficulty of these tradeoffs in particular.

We also believe that coping with or minimizing experienced and anticipated negative emotion is a meta-goal with significant influence on decision behavior. Thus, we have extended Payne et al.'s

(1993) effort-accuracy decision framework in order to incorporate emotion-minimization goals. It appears that the relevance of emotion-minimization considerations alters decision behavior and complicates the interpretation of existing relationships between processing characteristics and effort minimization or accuracy maximization.

Much remains to be learned regarding the causes and consequences of emotional tradeoff difficulty in choice, and there are several application areas for this new knowledge. First, different measurement techniques (e.g., choice versus pricing) may be more or less strongly influenced by emotional tradeoff difficulty. Thus, considerations of emotional tradeoff difficulty provide one potentially important source of explanation for preference reversals across response modes such as those found between matching and choice in Luce et al. (1999). Of course, such preference reversals can have important implications for areas of applied research that attempt to distill community values or predict marketplace behavior. For instance, survey methods attempting to measure individuals' values concerning publicly held environmental goods (i.e., contingent valuation techniques) are frequently criticized (Hausman 1993). We view such contingent valuation tasks as a major subset of high-tradeoff-difficulty tasks and argue that these tasks are strongly influenced by concerns for coping with emotional tradeoff difficulty. For instance, the widely noted problem of protest responses in contingent evaluation may sometimes involve subjects' refusal to calculate and report the relevant tradeoffs explicitly.

One important caveat is that the studies reported in this chapter all used hypothetical decision scenarios and therefore did not confront decision makers with the substantial goal threats associated with many real-world decisions (e.g., the real possibility of being robbed after renting an apartment in an unsafe neighborhood). However, there are at least two possible sources for the variance in emotion ratings in our studies. First, subjects may have been reporting their naive or lay theories of emotion, expressing how they believed they would feel and cope if actually presented with the relevant decisions. Second, subjects may have felt real threats to their self-esteem as decision makers, even in the absence of any real threats from decision consequences (see Janis & Mann 1977 on this distinction). We believe that our results are clearly suggestive of emotion effects in choice, but we also believe that there are major opportunities for future research in this domain. For instance, medical, insurance, and major consumer purchase decisions are all associated with severe potential losses and therefore with potential emotional threats. Given the importance of this topic, we believe that it would be useful to generalize our work to real-world decision situations with real emotional implications.

Notes

1 We found these conflict effects within both the high and low tradeoff difficulty groups. However, note that even the low tradeoff difficulty group was probably considering attributes with great potential for emotion elicitation, given the nature of the overall decision task (i.e., choosing a job).
2 Of course, the attribute prominence effect also predicts a tendency to choose the high-quality alternative at above-matching values, but only *if* quality is more important than price. Thus, we controlled for the attribute prominence effect both by controlling statistically for measured importance weights and by demonstrating that our tradeoff difficulty results were found even for the substantial subset of our data within which the price attribute was rated as more important than the quality attribute.

References

Beattie, Jane (1988), *Perceived Differences in Tradeoff Difficulty*. Unpublished doctoral dissertation. University of Pennsylvania, Philadelphia.

Beattie, Jane and S. Barlas (1993), "Predicting Perceived Differences in Trade-off Difficulty." Working Paper. University of Sussex, Falmer, England.

Bettman, James R., Mary Frances Luce and John W. Payne (1998), "Constructive Consumer Choice Processes." *Journal of Consumer Research*, 25, 187–217.

Bettman, James R., Eric J. Johnson, Mary Frances Luce and John W. Payne (1993), "Correlation, Conflict, and Choice," *Journal of Experimental Psychology: Learning, Memory and Cognition*, 19, 931–951.

Creyer, Elizabeth H., James R. Bettman and John W. Payne (1990), "The Impact of Accuracy and Effort Feedback and Goals on Adaptive Decision Behavior," *Journal of Behavioral Decision Making*, 3, 1–16.

Folkman, Susan and Richard S. Lazarus (1988), "Coping as a Mediator of Emotion," *Journal of Personality and Social Psychology*, 54, 466–475.

Green, Paul E. and V. Srinivasan (1990), "Conjoint Analysis in Marketing: New Developments with Implications for Research and Practice," *Journal of Marketing*, 54, 3–19.

Hausman, J. A. (1993), *Contingent Valuation: A Critical Assessment*. Amsterdam: North Holland.

Hogarth, Robin M. (1987), *Judgment and Choice* (2nd ed.). New York: Wiley.

Janis, Irving L. and Leon Mann (1977), *Decision Making: A Psychological Analysis of Conflict, Choice, and Commitment*. New York: Free Press.

Lazarus, Richard S. (1991), "Progress on a Cognitive-Motivational-Relational Theory of Emotion," *American Psychologist*, 46, 819–834.

Lucas, Robert E., Jr. (1986), "Adaptive Behavior and Economic Theory," *Journal of Business*, 59, S401–S426.

Luce, Mary Frances (1998), "Choosing to Avoid: Coping with Negatively Emotion-Laden Consumer Decisions," *Journal of Consumer Research*, 24, 409–433.

Luce, Mary Frances, James R. Bettman and John W. Payne (1997), "Choice Processing in Emotionally Difficult Decisions," *Journal of Experimental Psychology: Learning, Memory and Cognition, 23,* 384–405.

Luce, Mary Frances, John W. Payne and James R. Bettman (1999), "Emotional Trade-off Difficulty and Choice," *Journal of Marketing Research, 36,* 143–159.

McFadden, Daniel (1997), "Rationality for Economists." Working Paper, Department of Economics, University of California, Berkeley.

Payne, John W. (1976). Task Complexity and Contingent Processing in Decision Making: An Information Search and Protocol Analysis. *Organizational Behavior and Human Performance, 16,* 366–387.

Payne, John W., James R. Bettman and Eric J. Johnson (1993), *The Adaptive Decision Maker.* Cambridge: Cambridge University Press.

Payne, John W., James R. Bettman and Mary Frances Luce (1996), "When Time Is Money: Decision Behavior Under Opportunity Cost Time Pressure," *Organizational Behavior and Human Decision Processes, 66,* 131–152.

Plott, Charles R. (1996), "Rational Individual Behavior in Markets and Social Choice Processes: The Discovered Preference Hypothesis," in *The Rational Foundations of Economic Behavior,* ed. Kenneth J. Arrow et al. New York: St Martin's, 225–250.

Shepard, R. N. (1964), "On Subjectively Optimum Selection among Multiattribute Alternatives," in *Human Judgments and Optimality,* ed. M. W. Shelley and G. L. Bryan. New York: Wiley, 257–281.

Simonson, Itamar (1989), "Choice Based on Reasons: The Case of Attraction and Compromise Effects," *Journal of Consumer Research, 16,* 158–174.

Tversky, A. (1969). Intransitivity of Preferences. *Psychological Review, 76,* 31–48.

5 Impulse Buying in Ordinary and "Compulsive" Consumers

Helga Dittmar

Impulse Buying: Nonrational Consumer Decision Making on the Increase?

Impulse buying relates to this book's theme because it creates internal conflict in decision making. Consumers often experience conflict between wanting particular consumer goods *now*, on the spur of the moment, and wanting to spend their money sensibly on objects from which they can be sure to derive more long-term satisfaction. If this conflict does not happen simultaneously, it can happen sequentially when consumers follow their impulse to buy and then come to regret their bad decision sooner or later (although not invariably). This chapter explores what drives people toward this apparently nonrational form of consumer decision making by conceptualizing impulse buying as consumers attempt to deal with discrepancies between the way they see themselves (actual self) and the way they would like to be (ideal self). As will be argued, this process requires a particular cultural context of mass consumption, and the kind of impulse buying dealt with in this chapter may therefore be specific to Western, economically developed countries.

The research reported in this chapter was supported by Economic and Social Research Council Grant L122251012 as part of the Economic Beliefs and Behaviour Programme. Special thanks go to Susanne Friese, who worked as research assistant on the project; to Rod Bond for his help with the discounting data analysis; and to Peter Taylor-Gooby for his support and help as Programme Director.

This chapter is dedicated to Jane Beattie, who worked with me on all aspects of the research reported until her tragic death shortly before the project ended. The loss of both her inspiring collaboration as a colleague and her company as a friend was very great, and I still miss her. Jane was wonderful to work with and enriched my life in more ways than one.

Traditional approaches to economics, decision making, and consumer behavior theories assume a rational, discerning, thoughtful consumer who gathers information strategically and buys goods according to functional cost-benefit tradeoffs. This rational consumer also – supposedly – holds stable, well-defined preferences and makes choices consistent with these preferences. Impulsive buying flies in the face of these assumptions because it refers to the purchase of goods without careful deliberation, perhaps with insufficient information, and without prior intent. Impulsive purchases are quite often those that one would not, following rational reflection, wish to have made (e.g., Hoch & Loewenstein, 1991). Buying behavior has also been considered from an impulse control perspective in psychology (e.g., Christenson, Faber, de Zwaan, & Raymond, 1994), but more with an intention to understand the excessive buying of compulsive consumers.

Thus, impulsive and excessive buying are of interest because they challenge rational choice models. Moreover, there are good reasons for proposing that these forms of nonrational buying have increased dramatically over the last two decades. Linked economic, social, and cultural changes in advanced economies have created a climate in which individuals make consumer decisions. Personal disposable incomes have increased markedly, and credit facilities have mushroomed. Taking the United Kingdom as an example, personal disposable income has risen by about 75% after adjusting for inflation (*Social Trends*, 1994), and the number of credit cards in use has more than quadrupled (Rowlingson & Kempson, 1994). Along with these developments in modern consumer spending are important shifts in the psychological, social, and cultural significance of buying consumer goods, which have come to play an increasingly strong role in people's lives. It seems that this dimension of our lives is now so complex that people are liable to make choices in a fashion altogether different from that of the putative rational, consistent decision maker.

Consumer goods can and do function as material symbols of who a person is and who he or she would like to be. The practice of buying provisions to satisfy the physical needs of oneself and one's family has shifted to using consumer goods as a modern means of acquiring and expressing a sense of self-identity (e.g., Dittmar, 1992), regulating emotions (e.g., Elliott, 1994), or gaining social status (e.g., McCracken, 1990). This shift is captured by the stereotype of modern consumerism: "I shop, therefore I am." Buying goods in order to bolster one's self-image is probably a motivation that plays some role in most buying behavior, but it may be particularly important when people engage in nonplanned, spur-of-the-moment purchases that are then regretted.

Although most people experience an occasional lapse of judgment in purchasing, in an extreme form it can result in excessive buying behavior.[1] Empirical studies on shopping addiction or compulsive buying have been carried out recently in the United States (Hanley & Wilhelm, 1992; O'Guinn & Faber, 1989), Canada (Valence, d'Astous, & Fortier, 1988), Germany (Scherhorn, Reisch, & Raab, 1990), Belgium (Vlerick, 1998), and the United Kingdom (Elliott, 1994). None of these are prevalence studies, but their findings suggest that such extreme buying behavior is on the increase, affecting an estimated 2 to 5% of adults in developed Western economies. This affliction can leave sufferers severely distressed and financially crippled. Turning these percentages into actual numbers, these estimates imply that – for instance – up to half a million adults could be affected in the United Kingdom and possibly more than 10 million adults in the United States.

Previous Explanatory Models and a New Social Psychological Perspective

Models of impulsive and excessive buying in economics, consumer research, and psychology are disjointed theoretically and methodologically and have enjoyed little cross-fertilization (Dittmar, Beattie, & Friese, 1995, 1996). Moreover, *impulse buying* has had different meanings to different theoretical perspectives. Presumably there is a considerable difference between *reminder impulse buying* (in which a shopper remembers the need for an essential item on seeing it in the shop) and *pure impulse buying* (a novelty or escape purchase that breaks the normal buying pattern). Consumer behaviorists have tended to regard any unplanned purchase as impulse buying, whereas economists and psychologists have generally studied the (possibly irrational) aspects of pure impulse buying. We define impulse buying as a spur-of-the-moment decision in the shop, similar to Stern's (1962) pure impulse buying, and contrast it with planned purchasing, in which the buyer intended to purchase a particular good before reaching the shop.

Economics and Decision Making

The backbone of standard microeconomic theory is the assumption that economic agents have well-articulated, internally coherent, and consistent preferences. Impulse buying presents a problem for this rational choice model because such purchases may be associated with a high degree of postpurchase regret. A recent study found that 80% of impulse buyers reported negative consequences from their purchases (Rook, 1987), and even if not all impulse purchases are regretted (e.g., Rook & Fisher, 1995), it is clear that excessive buyers would prefer not to have carried out many of their purchases after a shopping binge. This suggests that the preference at the point of purchase (to buy the object) is inconsistent with the later preference (regret at having bought it). Various modifications of economic theory have been proposed to account for impulsive buying (and other time-inconsistent preferences), all of which remain within the utility framework. The standard explanation is the discounting model (e.g., Strotz, 1956) or more recent variations of it. Essentially, these models assume that impulse buyers discount the future at too rapid a rate, where the benefits of the desired object at the point of imminent purchase outweigh the (future) problem of paying the bill. Their major weakness is that they do not provide an explanation for the mistake itself, that is, why discounting rates should be disproportionately high or why and how people shift between short-term and long-term preferences. The most recent and most sophisticated theory of time-inconsistent preferences is Hoch and Loewenstein's (1991) reference point model, in which losses loom larger than gains. Consumers are assumed to adapt partially (imaginatively) to owning the good before they actually purchase it: Hence, forgoing the purchase would be experienced as a loss (forcing the consumer toward the purchase). The authors propose a number of factors assumed to increase the probability of a *reference shift* (and hence impulse buying), which apply regardless of the type of consumer good in question. This application of economic theory to consumer research partially addresses the limitations of the earlier models by highlighting the importance of consumers' *perceptions and evaluations* of goods as crucial to understanding impulsive buying. Although all of these economic models explain some aspects of impulsive buying, they fail to account for one of the most striking aspects of the behavior: why certain goods (such as fashionable clothes) are bought impulsively and excessively, whereas others (such as basic kitchen equipment) commonly are not.

Consumer Behavior and Marketing

Perhaps surprisingly, the consumer behavior and marketing literatures have also neglected this aspect of impulse buying. The mainstream approach has been concerned with identifying general factors that increase unplanned purchasing, such as exposure to in-store stimuli (e.g., shelf location; Abratt & Goodey, 1990), or with developing atheoretical lists of those foods and drinks that are most likely to be bought impulsively (e.g., Bellenger, Robertson, & Hirschman, 1978). This information may be useful for choosing goods for sales promotions, but it does not explain underlying motivations or predict beyond the particular goods studied. Moreover, these studies tend to use purely behavioral definitions of impulse buying, such as regarding a purchase as impulsive if it was not on the buyer's original shopping list (e.g., Kollat & Willet, 1967). However, this situation may be starting to change; one recent study examines psychological precursors of impulse buying (Beattie & Ferrell, 1998).

Psychological Perspectives

These perspectives have fallen into two categories: cognitive and clinical. The cognitive approach places impulsive shopping within the framework of impulse control in general (e.g., Mischel, 1961). This work has shown that impulse control improves with developmental stage, and can be used as an individual difference parameter to predict performance on certain cognitive tasks (e.g., Baron, Badgio, & Gaskins, 1986). Like the economic and consumer behavior approaches, the cognitive literature assumes a rational decision maker. In contrast, the clinical literature has been concerned with the excessive buying of compulsive shoppers, and the main perspectives to date have been clinical psychological or psychiatric models. Although not listed (as yet) as a psychiatric disorder in its own right in the current diagnostic manual, DSM-IV (American Psychiatric Association, 1994), excessive buying is treated as a specific manifestation of one or more general psychiatric disorders, including impulse control, compulsions, and addictions (e.g., Black, Repertinger, Gaffney, & Gabel, 1998; McElroy, Keck, Harrison, Pope, Smith, & Strakowski, 1994). A recent American clinical study reports that 95.8% of sufferers described buying that resembled an impulse control disorder (Christenson et al., 1994), and work in Germany proposes that the "shopping high" reported by sufferers can be better understood in an addiction framework (e.g., Scherhorn et al., 1990). Other clinical research argues that excessive buying has a compulsive component (e.g., Black, 1998). In more phenomenologically oriented research, compulsive shopping is described as an "inability to control an overpowering impulse to buy" (O'Guinn & Faber, 1989) or as "excessive impulsive consumption" (Faber, O'Guinn, & Krych, 1987). This approach assumes that excessive impulsive buying is a deviant activity, qualitatively distinct from ordinary consumer behavior, without considering that there may be underlying social psychological mechanisms centered on consumers' self-concept that play a role in *both* ordinary and excessive impulse buying. In common with the other models, it cannot explain why only certain goods are bought impulsively and excessively.

A New Social Psychological Model

Taking into account the changed context of buying behavior and the social psychological functions consumer goods fulfill for people leads to a new perspective in which goods are linked to consumers' self-concept because they function as important material symbols of personal and social identity (Dittmar, 1992, 1996). Symbolic self-completion theory (Wicklund & Gollwitzer, 1982) proposes that perceiving shortcomings in one's self-concept produces a motivation to compensate. Among diverse strategies, this can involve acquiring and using material symbols that are relevant to those aspects of the self felt to be lacking. In order to determine whether an individual uses consumption as a symbolic self-completion strategy – rather than sports, say – we drew on Richins and Dawson's (1992) conceptualization of materialism as an individual value orientation in which the acquisition of material goods is a central life goal, a prime indicator of success, and a key to happiness and self-definition. Finally, we used Higgins's (1987) conceptualization of self-discrepancies between actual self (how an individual sees the self) and ideal self (how the individual would ideally wish to be). Our research is the first application of self-discrepancies to buying behavior, and we designed our own measure for the project. A corollary of our theory is that consumers will differ in the goods that they buy impulsively along the lines of the social categories to which they belong because such categories are powerful determinants of a person's sense of self (e.g., Tajfel, 1984). We examined gender as a particularly pervasive social category.

Our theoretical model is described in more detail elsewhere (Dittmar, Beattie & Friese, 1996; Dittmar & Beattie, 1998), but it is presented schematically in Figure 5.1, where arrows represent causal links. In other words, people who are high in self-discrepancies *and* who are prone to use material goods as compensation should buy a lot on impulse, should be motivated by mood and self-image buying considerations, and should have excessive buying tendencies. It is important to

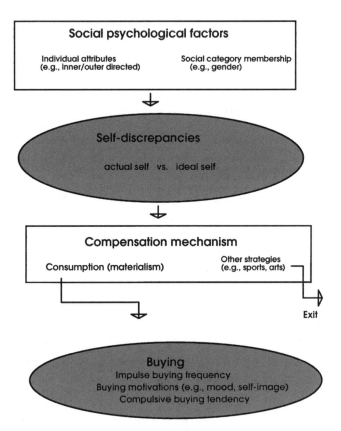

Figure 5.1. Social psychological model of impulsive and excessive buying.
Source: Dittmar, Beattie, and Friese (1996).

emphasize at this point that we do not propose that self-discrepancies are the *only* reason for impulsive and excessive buying; rather, this practice is multidetermined. However, we do propose that the conjunction of high self-discrepancies and materialism will lead to such buying behavior.

The main objective of the research project was to develop and test a social psychological model of impulse buying behavior in ordinary and excessive (compulsive) shoppers that proposes that buying consumer goods can be understood as an attempt to bolster self-image and personal identity. Several general hypotheses can be derived from this model for empirical study:

- Some consumer goods make more likely impulse buys than others.

- Self-image concerns are a particularly important decision consideration in impulsive and excessive buying.
- Systematic differences exist between excessive and ordinary consumers in impulse buying, self-concept, and consumption values, and buying behavior can be predicted from a person's self-discrepancies if he or she has materialistic values.

A Multimethod Approach

These hypotheses were tested in three linked studies that drew on different methodological approaches. A mail survey was used to collect questionnaire measures of planned and impulsive buying behavior, buying motivations, shopping attitudes, and self-concept. Using experimental decision-making methodology, we developed a computer-run study on *discount rates* for different consumer goods. Finally, we carried out qualitative research on the process of, and reasons for, impulse buying using in-depth interviews and shopping diaries. These quantitative and qualitative methods should produce convergent data on the hypotheses under consideration.

Mail Survey

Forty mature students participated in a preliminary mail study aimed at refining measures (Dittmar, Beattie, & Friese, 1995). The final sample of the survey consisted of 331 respondents, who were classified as either ordinary ($n = 236$) or excessive ($n = 95$) buyers. Our strategy of contacting respondents was aimed explicitly at producing a sample for the purpose of testing our theoretical model rather than a sample that could be considered representative (hence the overrepresentation of excessive shoppers, who comprised 29% of the sample). The sample consisted mainly of two groups: respondents who had been in contact with a shopping addiction self-help organization and a larger group of respondents whose addresses were selected so that they residentially matched (by town and street) those of the self-help group. Further addresses were obtained through radio and newspaper appeals, as well as through *snowballing* – asking respondents to indicate on the questionnaire whether they knew of somebody who might have problems with shopping and might be interested in participating in the survey. The overall response rate for this postal questionnaire was 56%, which compares favorably with standard rates of around 30–40%. Female shoppers were overrepresented in the sample, and the number of excessive male shoppers was regrettably low.[2] There were no systematic differences between ordinary and excessive buyers apart from a slight age difference,[3] which confirms that the two groups can be considered matched on economic and sociological indicators (e.g., educational qualifications, occupation, income, and number of credit cards used). The questionnaire consisted of seven main parts:

- A compulsive shopping scale, which measured the tendency toward compulsive shopping and was used as a screen to divide the sample into excessive and ordinary shoppers (d'Astous, Maltais, & Roberge, 1990).
- A rated frequency of buying nine types of durable consumer goods as planned purchases (including, e.g., clothes or kitchen equipment).
- Buying motivations for planned purchases (including functional, mood-related, and self-image motivations).
- A self-discrepancy measure (developed for this project). This consisted of respondents completing the sentence "I am ... but I would like to be. . . " repeatedly and then rating the size and salience of each self-discrepancy.
- Frequency of buying the same nine types of goods as impulse purchases.
- Motivations for impulse purchases.
- A materialism scale used as a proxy measure for the extent to which an individual uses consumption as a compensation strategy (Richins & Dawson, 1992). An example item is "Some of the most important achievements in life include acquiring material possessions."

Respondents in the mail survey were asked whether they were willing to participate in follow-up studies, and the final sample for the experimental and qualitative studies consisted of 61 respondents. The number of compulsive male shoppers in these follow-up studies was so small that they had to be excluded from statistical analysis. Comparisons were therefore made between three shopper groups: excessive female shoppers, ordinary female shoppers, and ordinary male shoppers.

Computer-Run Experiment on Discounting Rates

Discount rates measure the subjective cost of delaying immediate gratification, and in the standard matching paradigm of intertemporal choice methodology (e.g., Benzion, Rapoport, & Yagil, 1989), respondents match the utility of a good to be consumed now (e.g., £100) with a (larger) delayed good of the same type in the future (e.g., £X 1 year from now) by setting X such that they are indifferent between the two choices. An annual discount rate of 50% means that a person demanded £150 as the *compensation price* to wait a year rather than receive £100 immediately. By using vouchers for different types of shops as stimuli (e.g., selling clothing or body care products), discount rates for different types of consumer goods could be investigated.

The discounting experiment was also run in a separate, additional study with 100 students, as well as with the respondents from the mail survey. Slightly different sets of consumer goods were examined in the two studies, but in both samples clothes were included as a typical high-impulse good and body care products as a typical low-impulse good. The voucher amounts were £10, £50, and £200, and delays ranged from 1 day to 2 years. The computer-run program started by explaining the task and presenting two examples to train respondents in entering their compensation prices for waiting. The items were presented in blocks (all amount and delay combinations for one particular type of good), which were randomized to counteract order and fatigue effects.

Qualitative Studies

These studies consisted of having respondents keep a shopping diary and interviewing them in depth. In the diary, they recorded each impulse purchase of durable consumer goods over a period of 4 weeks, including information about:

- the good bought
- a global evaluation of how good or bad they felt about themselves during three phases of their shopping trip (just before the purchase, just afterward, and after getting home)
- their thoughts and feelings during the same three phases

The format for reporting thoughts and feelings was unstructured, chosen with the explicit rationale that respondents would be more likely to record those concerns most salient to them than when prompted by constructs developed by the researchers. In-depth interviews were carried out with respondents when the completed shopping diary was collected.[4] Respondents were asked to comment on their experience of the diary and discounting experiment. Ten interviews each with ordinary female and male shoppers and 10 interviews with female excessive buyers were selected for in-depth thematic analysis (reported in more detail in Dittmar & Drury, 2000). The following four themes were central:

- Commonsense definitions of impulse and planned buying
- Prevalence and meanings of regret about impulsive and planned purchases
- Features of a typical impulse-buying episode
- Relation of shopping to the self

Main Findings

The main findings of the research project are presented here under four headings, drawing on these linked studies as a whole rather than discussing results from each study in turn.

Types of Consumer Goods and Impulsive Behavior

When examining whether some types of consumer goods make more likely impulse purchases than others, it is important to take into account not only how often a good is bought on impulse, but also how often it is bought as a planned purchase. For instance, if a good is bought very frequently – but even more so as a planned than as an impulse purchase – taking only the raw impulse buying frequency would be misleading. From the buying frequencies reported in the mail survey, we therefore constructed an *impulsivity index*, which allows us to ascertain which goods are most likely to be bought on impulse relative to their planned purchasing frequency. It can vary between -1 (the good is always bought in a planned fashion and never on impulse) and $+1$ (the good is always bought on impulse and is never planned). If a good is bought equally frequently both on impulse and by plan, then the impulsivity index is zero, independent of the absolute buying frequencies.

The types of goods that make the two most likely impulse buys – clothes and jewelry – seem closely linked to self-image and appearance, in contrast with the two types of good that are least likely to be bought on impulse – practical footwear and body care products. Means for ordinary and excessive shoppers are shown in Figure 5.2. With one exception they are negative, indicating that goods are bought slightly more often by plan than on impulse, but there are clear relative differences

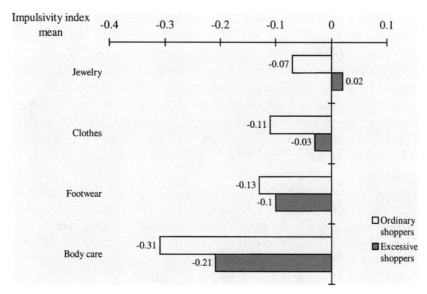

Figure 5.2. Excessive and ordinary shoppers' impulse buying of four types of goods (two highest and two lowest on impulsivity index).

between types of consumer goods. Excessive shoppers do more (proportional) impulse buying than ordinary shoppers overall, but the difference is greater on the high-impulse goods – clothes and jewelry – than the low-impulse goods.

In addition to differences between ordinary and excessive shoppers there were gender differences, confirming that this social category influences which types of goods are bought on impulse (cf. Dittmar & Beattie, 1998).

However, the approach taken in the mail survey – asking respondents to report buying frequencies (as well as decision considerations) separately when purchasing goods by plan and on impulse – assumes, first, that consumers are able to draw a clear distinction between planned and impulse buying and, second, that their behavior is organized in terms of these two distinct modes of buying. The question arises of whether these two types of buying are, in fact, distinct activities for consumers and can be meaningfully contrasted in terms of underlying motivations – as we assumed – or whether most purchase decisions involve both planning and impulse to some extent.[5] For instance, the decision to go through the stores to buy oneself an appearance booster (such as clothes or jewelry) involves an intention to purchase a particular category of consumer good, although the exact item or store is not planned in advance. The in-depth interviews were used to check the validity of our approach by eliciting spontaneous commonsense definitions of impulse versus planned buying. Responses in the interviews confirmed a consensus among both ordinary and excessive shoppers that planned buying is clearly distinguished from impulse buying: Consumers act like rational decision makers; they shop around and choose the best value for money within their financial limits. Definitions of impulse buying were more diverse but were characterized by little deliberation and by psychological motivations – desire, wanting, treat, thrill – overtaking financial considerations. Women emphasize emotional aspects of impulse buying more than men, and the lack of regard for financial consequences becomes extreme for excessive shoppers who find the urge to buy irresistible. This is clearly a far cry from the definitions of planned buying, validating the conceptualization of pure impulse and pure planned buying as opposite extremes of consumer behavior.

The shopping diaries enabled a comparison between the self-report ratings in the mail survey and actual impulse buying behavior. Clothes and accessories (e.g., a handbag) were the most frequent impulse buys, constituting more than a third of all reported purchases. In contrast, kitchen items were hardly reported at all. Although the impulsivity rank order of consumer goods in the diary study does not map exactly on the impulsivity index derived from the mail survey, there is considerable agreement on which items make impulse purchases more and less likely. Impulse buying frequency differed between the shopper groups: Excessive female buyers reported a mean of 5.3 impulse purchases per month, which is higher than the mean of 4.1 purchases given by ordinary shoppers. Thus, the diary findings replicate and support the results of the mail survey.

The finding that some goods are bought more frequently on impulse than others challenges standard economic and psychological accounts, which tend to see impulsive behavior as a general (i.e., object-independent) overweighing of short-term gratification ("I want that good now") relative to longer-term concerns ("I will have to pay the bill later, and I am already in debt"). The proposal that impulsivity differs according to type of consumer good was also supported by the experimental study, which elicited discount rates. However, discount rates are difficult to grasp intuitively. For this reason, the main findings presented here give the raw money amount respondents entered: their compensation price for waiting rather than receiving a voucher immediately. In

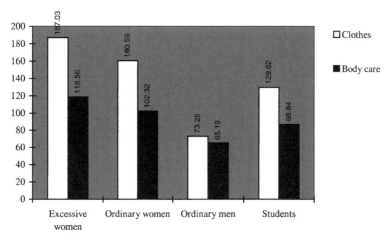

Figure 5.3. Mean compensation price (in £s) for different shopper groups for waiting instead of receiving a £50 voucher now for clothes and body care products (averaged across delay).

the student sample, the mean compensation price in pounds (and the discount rate) was significantly higher for clothes than for body care goods. Findings for the mail survey sample give an even stronger indication that compensation prices were significantly higher for clothes than for the other types of consumer goods for all voucher amounts, including body care products. Thus, the overweighing of short-term benefits is dependent on the type of consumer good, and clothes – as the most typical impulse good – had the highest compensation price for waiting compared to body care products, which had the lowest.

Even more important, the expectation derived from the standard account that excessive consumers should simply have higher purchase rates, regardless of the consumer good, was not confirmed. Instead, it was found that excessive shoppers have particularly high *compensation prices* (or discount rates) for goods typically bought on impulse. As an example, findings comparing compensation prices for clothes and body care products (with £50 as the voucher amount) are shown in Figure 5.3, with the means for the student sample included for illustrative purposes.

Regret in Impulse and Planned Buying

Although there is a substantial body of research on regret in decision making (e.g., Loomes & Sugden, 1982; Starmer & Sugden, 1998), the extent of regret in impulse buying specifically has received hardly any empirical attention. A study by Rook (1987) found that 80% of impulse buyers reported some negative consequences from their purchases, but regret was not specifically singled out. A later follow-up study found that regret for impulse buying depends somewhat on the situation (Rook & Fisher, 1995). In our diary study, which focused on explicitly stated regret rather than on negative consequences more generally, the experience of regret after impulse purchases was common: Over half of the respondents (55%) reported regret at least once. Excessive female shoppers tended to report regret more frequently after getting home than did ordinary shoppers. This finding fits well with the global self-evaluation results, which showed that excessive female shoppers felt worse about themselves after getting home with the purchase than just after they bought it. These shoppers were significantly more likely than ordinary shoppers to experience at least occasional regret, with 82% reporting regret at least once compared to 53% of ordinary female shoppers and 33% of male shoppers.

Thus regret about impulse purchases is common but by no means ubiquitous. Men appear to experience regret less often than women. However, this leaves two important questions unaddressed: Are impulse purchases more likely to be regretted than planned buys? and How do consumers experience regret, and does its meaning fit with a conceptualization of *time-inconsistent preferences*? Both questions were examined in the in-depth interviews.

With respect to the first question, there was considerable agreement among the different shopper groups that regret is more likely to occur after impulse purchases because planned buys are better "thought through." The following excerpt typifies this viewpoint:

Yes, absolutely, you are more likely to. If you plan something, you think about it longer and you know what kind of thing and quality you are looking for. (Ordinary male buyer)

As in the diary study, regret for an impulse purchase was by no means ubiquitous. A good number of interviewees did express regret, but others were pleased with what they had bought or did not regret their buys as long as they were inexpensive, even if they no longer wanted the good concerned. Discourses about regret were more elaborated and sophisticated among female shoppers, particularly excessive buyers, than among men. It became clear that regret has complex meanings for people and that it can include diverse dimensions of impulse buying. Five themes were mentioned prominently, which are described subsequently and illustrated with a typical quote each. In terms of differences between the three shopper groups studied, male shoppers tended more toward the first theme, while the second and third were discourses mentioned most by excessive female buyers. Female shoppers – both ordinary and excessive – mentioned the last two themes more prominently.

Theme 1

The actual good bought is regretted because it turns out to be unsatisfactory in some way, such as low in quality, bad value for the money, or unsuited for the buyer's purpose (e.g., clothes that are too short).

The ones I regret most, and most often, are when you buy something and you think it is a good buy 'cos it's cheap or it looks cheap, and you think that must be good value for money, and then the quality is such that you can't really use it. I have some [items of clothing] upstairs which are too short and I was told they were long. [ ] Yeah, you regret having bought that type of thing. (Ordinary male buyer)

Theme 2

Consumers expressed regret about the money they had spent on the purchase, or regret for their spending patterns more generally, but not for the actual items bought, which they were still happy to have.

You don't regret buying it. It's just when you can't pay for it, that's [laughs] what you regret. Especially if it's on credit cards. (Excessive female buyer)

Theme 3

A version of *anticipated regret* or of the dual-self model proposed by Shefrin and Thaler (1988) seems to be captured in the descriptions some excessive consumers gave of internal conflict, of being torn between the desire for short-term gratification and the "ought" of more rational long-term planning.

I'll check that I've got my credit cards and I'll be saying to myself. . . it's like having a split personality. Go away, walk away, get on a bus, get a taxi home even. Get a taxi, go straight home, think about it. [ ] Well, one side of me's saying, so what, it's only money, it's my money, I can spend it as I wish, I've got no other pleasures. I don't go out, I don't mix with people, I don't drink, I don't smoke.

And then the rational side of me'll be saying no, don't spend it, but save it until next week and you'll have twice as much to spend. (Excessive female buyer)

Theme 4

A discourse mainly of female buyers focused on feeling guilty if the impulse buy was for themselves because the money could have been spent better for others, thus judging the entitlements of others to be greater than those of the self.

I can go out and buy things that are nice, but because I've bought them for him or the children I don't feel guilty. So, I think sometimes if you go out and spend on yourself, you do, normally think "Oh perhaps, you know, shouldn't really have spent that." But if you've spent it on the others, it doesn't matter, does it? (Ordinary female buyer)

Theme 5

Some respondents said that they later wished they had not bought particular goods because the goods were disappointing in terms of expected psychological benefits; they did not cheer the person up or they did not bring the person closer to his or her ideal self-image.

It [item of clothing] isn't quite my shape. It didn't look as attractive as I thought it would, maybe because, I am short waisted, it wasn't for my type of body. Occasionally I take it back. (Ordinary female buyer)

The theme that the aim of improving the self-image is not always achieved is also one that emerged in the shopping diaries. Reported self-image gains were coded both as a motivation before purchase and as a descriptor afterward (with the criterion that self-image had been stated for at least a quarter of the purchases). Patterns over time are especially interesting here. Only 18% of excessive female shoppers reported self-image gains after getting the purchase home, whereas self-image gains were clearly a strong motivation before the purchase, stated by almost half of them (46%).

Given the exploratory nature of the qualitative studies, these findings can only be regarded as suggestive. However, taken together, buyers' accounts seem to demonstrate that regret cannot be captured by the one-dimensional concept of time-inconsistent preferences. Rather, regret is a multidimensional construct both psychologically and socially. For instance, the same impulse purchase can simultaneously be regretted on one dimension (e.g., money spent) and not regretted on another (e.g., the actual good bought).

Decision Considerations in Impulse Buying

Findings from the mail survey confirm that high-impulse goods (such as clothes and jewelry) are bought for different reasons than low-impulse goods (such as footwear and body care products). For low-impulse goods, functional motivations[6] are rated most important; consumers are concerned with whether the purchase is good value for money and whether it is practical or useful. In other words, they behave like rational decision makers. For high-impulse goods, however, psychological buying motivations become more powerful than price and usefulness; consumers buy because the purchase "puts me in a better mood," "makes me feel more like the person I want to be," and "expresses what is unique about me." Thus, intending to bolster one's self-image and mood are rated as particularly salient in impulse buying.

The importance of self-image gains was confirmed in the open-ended accounts of impulse purchases given in the shopping diaries. Four different buying motivations were mentioned often enough to be coded[7] – mood improvement, self-image gain, usefulness, and good value for money. These motivations are not mutually exclusive, as respondents could, and often did, state more than one motivation for an impulse purchase. In order to assess which motivations are consistently important in impulse buying, respondents were classified as stating a motivation explicitly only if they reported it for at least a quarter of their impulse buys. Of the respondents who did report consistent motivations, more than half referred to self-image gains (52%) and to good value for money (52%). Just under half described their purchases as useful (48%), and a fifth stated that they bought on impulse to improve their mood (20%). Thus, although functional concerns (usefulness and price) clearly were important decision considerations in impulse buying, self-image gains were reported to play an equally strong role as an anticipated benefit. Mood change appeared comparatively less important.

In the survey, the differences between decision considerations for goods often bought on impulse compared to goods hardly ever bought on impulse were similar for ordinary and excessive shoppers: Functional concerns decreased and psychological concerns increased. However, the relative importance of decision considerations diverged for these

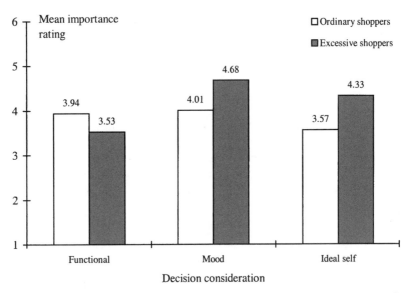

Figure 5.4. Excessive and ordinary shoppers' decision considerations when buying high-impulse goods.

two different groups of consumers. Referring to high-impulse goods, Figure 5.4 shows these differences for three types of decision considerations: functional ("good value for money," "useful"), mood ("puts me in a better mood"), and ideal self ("makes me feel more like the person I want to be").

Differences between the two shopper groups are significant for each of these decision considerations. Functional buying considerations are relatively less important for excessive shoppers than for ordinary shoppers, and psychological decision considerations are more central. The largest difference occurs for excessive shoppers who are motivated to buy in order to feel "more like the person I want to be," that is to move closer to their ideal self.

Predicting Impulsive and Excessive Buying from Consumers' Self-Concept

In our model, we propose that impulsive and excessive buying can be predicted from a person's self-discrepancies – gaps between actual and ideal selves – if he or she has highly materialistic values. In other words, these shoppers need to believe that material goods help them compensate by bringing them closer to their ideal selves. Those with large self-discrepancies but low materialistic tendencies might instead turn to alcoholism, eating disorders, or sports addiction as compensation strategies.

In support of this model, excessive shoppers reported that buying in order to bolster their self-image was a more important consideration than it was for ordinary shoppers (as described in the previous section). Moreover, they held stronger materialistic values. In the survey, the mean rating of ordinary shoppers (3.15) fell below the midpoint of the materialism scale (3.50), whereas the mean rating of excessive shoppers (3.90) fell above the midpoint. Thus, it seems that excessive shoppers believe much more strongly than ordinary shoppers that acquiring consumer goods is an important route to success, happiness, and a sense of identity.

In terms of discrepancies in consumers' self-concept, we constructed a single quantitative index for each of the respondents on the basis of their indications for each self-discrepancy of how far away they felt they were from their ideal self (size of discrepancy) and how much they worried about it (importance of discrepancy) (see Dittmar et al., 1996). The extent and salience of self-discrepancies were measured separately because they can be independent of each other. For instance, there may be a large discrepancy between a person wanting to be thin rather than heavily overweight, but the person may never worry about it. This approach was informed by Jane Beattie's work on multiattribute decision making. The possible range of the *self-discrepancy index* is 1–36, and excessive shoppers had a much higher mean score (16.0) than ordinary shoppers (10.5). Thus, excessive shoppers reported greater and more psychologically salient self-discrepancies than did ordinary shoppers.

One of the most central concerns of the research project was whether impulsive and excessive buying can be predicted directly from an individual's self-discrepancies and materialistic values. Hierarchical multiple regression analyses were carried out in order to address this question, for which individuals were classified as either low or high in materialism, whereas the *self-discrepancy index* was treated as a continuous variable.[8]

One of the most important variables to be predicted was an individual's tendency toward compulsive buying, as measured by the screener questionnaire developed by d'Astous et al. (1990). Self-discrepancies should be linked to excessive buying tendencies *only* when consumers use consumption as a compensatory strategy. Thus, our model predicts that the relationship between self-discrepancy and tendency toward

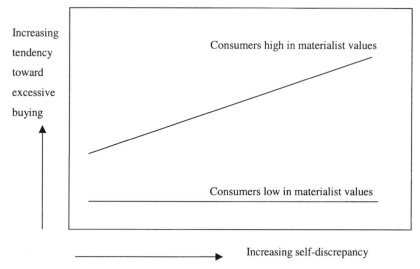

Figure 5.5. The relationship between self-discrepancy and excessive buying tendency as a function of materialist values. Source: Dittmar and Beattie (1998).

excessive buying should be small or absent when a person's materialism is low, but that this relationship should be present when materialism is high. Figure 5.5 gives a schematic outline of this proposition.

The model found strong support from the data for female shoppers, for whom large self-discrepancies in combination with materialistic values were a powerful predictor of the tendency to become an excessive buyer. There was no relationship between the self-discrepancy index and an excessive buying tendency for women low in materialist values ($r = 0.16$; nonsignificant). In contrast, for women high in materialist values, this relationship was strong ($r = 0.49$; $p < .001$). The predictions did not work as well for male consumers, which may in part reflect the small sample of excessive male buyers. Alternatively, the fact that links were stronger for women than for men might suggest that shopping still constitutes a more culturally available and socially acceptable activity for women. This does not mean that men do not engage in self-image enhancement through buying, but they might be more likely to focus on very occasional, expensive objects, such as a sports car, a computer, or a boat. Moreover, there may well be other compensation strategies, which are more available and socially sanctioned for men. For instance, in the United Kingdom, men seem more likely to engage in excessive sports or go to a pub to drink with their friends. These interpretations are strengthened by the finding that a respondent classified as an excessive shopper in the mail survey was over two and a half times as likely to be a woman rather than a man, as well as by our difficulties in finding male excessive shoppers to take part in the project.

It is important to emphasize that this gender explanation should not be misunderstood as an essentialist account of differences between male and female consumers.[9] Rather, we are putting forward the argument that shopping will remain gendered in the way described only as long as cultural norms and social representations (e.g., Moscovici, 1988) continue to frame shopping as closely linked to women's social, personal, and gender identities. In addition, there may be social constraints that may make shopping a more likely compensation strategy for women than for men, who might have better opportunities for engaging in diverse sports or leisure activities. For instance, primary caregivers and homemakers – who are still predominantly women – may be able to bring their children along on shopping trips but not on excursions to the gym. However, with changes in the occupational and domestic roles of women and men, as well as the recent increasing emphasis on appearance, body image, and consumption of goods for men as well (e.g., Dittmar & Morse, 1997), it seems likely that excessive buying may become more common in men.

Conclusion and Implications

The reported findings suggest a theoretical basis for therapeutic intervention, given that self-discrepancies have been identified as one important underlying motivation for excessive buying. Self-help organizations for shopping addiction and counseling services for debt management tend to concentrate on helping clients develop realistic budget plans and strategies for long-term debt reduction. Their clients' concerns with self-image remain unaddressed. Current medical treatment for compulsive buying often entails the use of antidepressant drugs (e.g., Black, Monahan, & Gabel, 1997) such as Prozac or behavioral therapies. These forms of treatment reduce the number of shopping episodes, but buying tends to increase again after the end of treatment. From the perspective developed in this chapter, this implies that treatment should focus on changing the underlying motivations for shopping rather than on alleviating the symptoms. The issues of self-discrepancies and materialism need to be addressed, either by helping clients to change aspects of their self-concept or by finding different, more positive avenues for self-completion that are less costly. We do not claim that compulsive buyers are *only*, or even *mainly*, excessive impulse purchasers who are propelled by strong self-discrepancies, but it appears that they constitute at least one subpopulation of compulsive buyers. Psychiatric studies have tended to focus on patients who are hospitalized or in treatment for diverse clinical conditions, and it is therefore not surprising that they have found that individuals who buy excessively also have other psychiatric conditions, such as eating disorders (e.g., Faber, Christenson, de Zwaan, & Mitchell, 1995) or pathological gambling (e.g., Black & Moyer, 1998). But it seems likely that other excessive shoppers lead fairly normal and reasonably successful lives, apart from their buying behavior. It is probably safest to conclude at this stage that excessive buyers are not a homogeneous group, but rather a collection of subpopulations with different pathways into shopping addiction. This argument is in line with a recent paper offering different typologies of compulsive buying behavior with different drivers (DeSarbo & Edwards, 1996).

Moreover, there are further theoretical and practical reasons why a better understanding of impulsive and excessive buying behavior is important to researchers and policymakers in the fields of economics, consumer behavior, and psychology. Because impulse purchases represent a significant percentage of personal resource allocation decisions, reductions (increases) in impulse purchase rates should lead to higher (lower) aggregate savings rates (Thaler & Shefrin, 1981). Encouragement (discouragement) of impulse purchasing is realistic only when its basis is better understood. The demonstration that individuals' discount rates are good-specific raises some interesting issues for economic models of individual choice. However, our aim is to complement – rather than challenge outright – existing rational choice models in economics and consumer research by predicating impulsive and excessive buying as based – at least in part – on the social psychological motivation of bolstering aspects of the self-concept.

Notes

1   The term *excessive buying* is used in this chapter because it seems preferable to the terms *compulsive buying* or *shopping addiction*, which is used more commonly. It avoids the assumption built into *compulsive* that consumers experience shopping as an activity over which they have absolutely no control and that has only negative aspects, and it circumvents controversies about whether to conceive of excessive buying as an addiction instead, because consumers also experience an emotional "high" while shopping.

2   Of the 95 excessive shoppers in the mail survey, only 16 were men, i.e., less than 20%, despite considerable efforts to recruit them through radio appeals, flyers, and advertisements in magazines.

3 On average, compulsive shoppers were slightly younger than ordinary shoppers, which is consistent with the claim that excessive buying is a recent phenomenon more likely to be found among younger consumers. Age was not consistently related to any of the dependent variables of interest.

4 For some of respondents farthest away from the southeast, shopping diaries were returned by mail and the interview was carried out by telephone to eliminate traveling costs.

5 I am grateful to Folke Ölander, who alerted us to definitional issues around impulse buying in his review of our first paper from the project (Ölander, 1995).

6 In contrast to buying behavior, where the ratio between planned and impulse buying frequency differs according to type of consumer good, decision considerations for a type of good are similar regardless of whether it is bought by plan or on impulse. Thus, ratings for buying motivations were averaged across planned and impulse purchases.

7 The coding system developed for the diaries showed excellent interrater reliability: The mean agreement per category was 93%.

8 Interaction variables were created by multiplying personal self-discrepancies with (a) level of materialism, (b) gender, and (c) both gender and materialism. The first part of this analysis consisted of a main-effects-only model, where level of materialism, gender, and self-discrepancy were entered as predictors. In the second step, the two-way interaction terms were added as further predictors, and the three-way interaction term in a third step to assess the presence, strength, and nature of any interactions between materialism, self-discrepancy, and possibly gender.

9 We are grateful to Nick Pidgeon for alerting us to this possible misinterpretation.

References

Abratt, R. & Goodey, S. D. (1990). Unplanned buying and in-store stimuli in supermarkets. *Managerial and Decision Economics, 11*, 111–121.

American Psychiatric Association. (1994). *Diagnostic and Statistical Manual for Mental Disorders (DSM-IV) (4th ed.)*. Washington, DC: American Psychiatric Association.

Baron, J., Badgio, P. & Gaskins, I. W. (1986). Cognitive style and its improvement: A normative approach. In R. J. Sternberg (ed.), *Advances in the Psychology of Human Intelligence* (Vol. 3, pp. 173–220. Hillsdale, NJ: Erlbaum.

Beattie, S. E. & Ferrell, M. E. (1998). Impulse buying: Modeling its precursors. *Journal of Retailing, 74*, 169–191.

Bellenger, D. N., Robertson, D. H., & Hirschman, E. C. (1978). Impulse buying varies by product. *Journal of Advertising Research, 18*, 15–18.

Benzion, U., Rapoport, A. & Yagil, J. (1989). Discount rates inferred from decisions: An experimental study. *Management Science, 35*, 270–284.

Black, D. W. (1998). Recognition and treatment of obsessive-compulsive spectrum disorders. In R. P. Swinson, M. M. Antony, & P. L. Baer (eds.), *Obsessive-Compulsive Disorder: Theory, Research and Treatment*, pp. 426–457. New York: Guilford.

Black, D. W., Monahan, P. & Gabel, J. (1997). Fluvoxamine in the treatment of compulsive buying. *Journal of Clinical Psychiatry, 58*, 159–163.

Black, D. W. & Moyer, T. (1998). Clinical features and psychiatric comorbidity of subjects with pathological gambling behavior. *Psychiatric Services, 49*, 1434–1439.

Black, D. W., Repertinger, S., Gaffney, G. R. & Gabel, J. (1998). Family history and psychiatric comorbidity in persons with compulsive buying. *American Journal of Psychiatry, 155*, 960–963.

Christenson, G. A., Faber, R. J., de Zwaan, M. & Raymond, N. C. (1994). Compulsive buying: Descriptive characteristics and psychiatric co-morbidity. *Journal of Clinical Psychiatry, 55*, 5–11.

d'Astous, A., Maltais, J. & Roberge, C. (1990). Compulsive buying tendencies of adolescent consumers. *Advances in Consumer Research, 17*, 306–313.

DeSarbo, W. S. & Edwards, E. A. (1996). Typologies of compulsive buying behavior: A constrained clusterwise regression approach. *Journal of Consumer Psychology, 5*, 231–262.

Dittmar, H. (1992). *The Social Psychology of Material Possessions: To Have Is To Be.* Hemel Hempstead, U.K.: Harvester Wheatsheaf, and New York: St. Martin's Press.

Dittmar, H. (1996). The social psychology of economic and consumer behavior. In G. R. Semin & K. Fiedler (eds.), *Applied Social Psychology*, pp. 145–172. London: Sage.

Dittmar, H. & Beattie, J., 1998. Impulsive and excessive buying behavior. In P. Taylor-Gooby (ed.), *Choice and Public Policy: Limits of Welfare Markets*, pp. 123–144. London: Macmillan.

Dittmar, H., Beattie, J. & Friese, S. (1995). Gender identity and material symbols: Objects and decision considerations in impulse purchases. *Journal of Economic Psychology, 16*, 491–511. (Also available on the World Wide Web: at http://www.ukc.ac.uk/ESRC/).

Dittmar, H., Beattie, J. & Friese, S. (1996). Objects, decision considerations and self-image in men's and women's impulse purchases. *Acta Psychologica, 93*, 187–206. Special issue on Decision Making and Emotions. (Also available on the World Wide Web: http://www.ukc.ac.uk/ESRC/).

Dittmar, H. & Drury, J. (2000). Self-image – is it in the bag? A qualitative comparison between "ordinary" and "excessive" consumers. *Journal of Economic and Consumer Psychology, 21*, 109–142.

Dittmar, H. & Morse, E. (1997). The effect of exposure to attractive male media images on the self- and body-esteem of young hetero- and homosexual men. Paper presented at the British Psychological Association Social Section Conference, Brighton.

Elliott, R. (1994). Addictive consumption: Function and fragmentation in postmodernity. *Journal of Consumer Policy, 17*, 159–179.

Faber, R. J., Christenson, G. A., de Zwaan, M. & Mitchell, J. (1995). Two forms of compulsive consumption: Comorbidity of compulsive buying and binge eating. *Journal of Consumer Research, 22*, 296–304.

Faber, R. J., O'Guinn, T. C. & Krych, R. (1987). Compulsive consumption. *Advances in Consumer Research, 14*, 132–135.

Hanley, A. & Wilhelm, M. S. (1992). Compulsive buying: An exploration into self-esteem and money attitudes. *Journal of Economic Psychology, 13*, 5–18.

Higgins, T. (1987). Self-discrepancy: A theory relating self to affect. *Psychological Review, 94*, 319–340.

Hoch, S. J. & Loewenstein, G. F. (1991). Time-inconsistent preferences and consumer self-control. *Journal of Consumer Research, 17*, 1–16.

Kollat, D. T. & Willet, R. P. (1967). Is impulse purchasing really a useful concept for marketing decisions? *Journal of Marketing, 33*, 79–83.

Loomes, G. & Sugden, R. (1982). Regret theory: An alternative theory of rational choice under uncertainty. *Economic Journal, 92*, 805–824.

McCracken, G. (1990). *Culture and Consumption*. Indianapolis: Indiana University Press.

McElroy, S. L., Keck, P. E., Harrison, G., Pope, M. D., Smith, M. R. & Strakowski, S. M. (1994). Compulsive buying: A report of 20 cases. *Journal of Clinical Psychiatry, 55*, 242–248.

Mischel, W. (1961). Preference for delayed reinforcement and social responsibility. *Journal of Abnormal and Social Psychology, 62*, 1–7.

Moscovici, S. (1988). Some notes on social representations. *European Journal of Social Psychology, 18*, 211–250.

O'Guinn, T. C. & Faber, R. J. (1989). Compulsive buying: A phenomenological exploration. *Journal of Consumer Research, 16*, 147–157.

Ölander, F. (1995). In search of missing links: Comments on three papers on spending and consumption. *Journal of Economic Psychology, 16*, 531–539.

Richins, M. & Dawson, S. (1992). Materialism as a consumer value: Measure development and validation. *Journal of Consumer Research, 19*, 303–316.

Rook, D. W. (1987). The buying impulse. *Journal of Consumer Research, 14*, 189–199.

Rook, D. W. & Fisher, R. J. (1995). Normative influence on impulsive buying behavior. *Journal of Consumer Research, 22*, 305–313.

Rowlingson, K. & Kempson, E. (1994). *Paying with Plastic: A Study of Credit Card Debt*. London: Policy Studies Institute.

Scherhorn, G., Reisch, L. A. & Raab, L. A. (1990). Addictive buying in West Germany: An empirical investigation. *Journal of Consumer Policy, 13*, 155–189.

Shefrin, H. & Thaler, R. (1988). The behavioral life cycle hypothesis. *Economic Enquiry, 26*, 609–643.

Social Trends (1994). Volume 25 Government Statistical Service Publications. London: Her Majesty's Stationery Office.

Starmer, C. & Sugden, R. (1998). Testing alternative explanations of cyclical choices. *Economica, 65*, 347–361.

Stern, A. (1962). The significance of impulse buying today. *Journal of Marketing, 26*, 59–62.

Strotz, R. H. (1956). Myopia and inconsistency in dynamic utility maximization. *Review of Economic Studies, 23*, 165–180.

Tajfel, H. (ed.) (1984). *The Social Dimension*, Vols. 1 and 2. Cambridge: Cambridge University Press.

Thaler, R. H. & Shefrin, H. M. (1981). An economic theory of self-control. *Journal of Political Economy, 89*, 392–410.

Valence, G., d'Astous, A. & Fortier, L. (1988). Compulsive buying: Concept and measurement. *Journal of Consumer Policy, 11*, 419–433.

Vlerick, P. (1998). Personal communication at the IAREP Qualitative Methods Workshop, May, Exeter, UK.

Wicklund, R. A. & Gollwitzer, P. M. (1982). *Symbolic Self-Completion*. Hillsdale, NJ: Erlbaum.

6　What We Do When Decisions Go Awry: Behavioral Consequences of Experienced Regret

Marcel Zeelenberg, J. Jeffrey Inman,
and Rik G. M. Pieters

> Let us consider some of the consequences to be expected if there does,
> indeed, exist such immediate post-decision salience of dissonance.
> Phenomenally, such salience of dissonance might be experienced as a
> feeling of regret, something that most of us have felt, probably, at one
> time or another. A person, for example, may shop around for an
> automobile to buy, investigate several kinds, and finally decide on
> which to purchase. As soon as the purchase is accomplished and
> final, he may well be assailed by a sudden feeling of "Oh, my, what
> have I done!"
>
> (Festinger, 1964, p. 99)

Any book on the subject of conflict and tradeoffs in decision making
would be incomplete without a discussion regarding a major component of such conflict – regret. The possibility of regret associated with
postchoice conflict was acknowledged by Festinger (1964) in his theory
of cognitive dissonance, as indicated by the chapter-opening quotation.
Regret is a negative, cognitively based emotion that we experience when
realizing or imagining that our present situation would have been better
had we acted differently. It is a nasty feeling associated with self-blame,
the wish to undo the regretted event, and the tendency to kick oneself. The basis of regret is cognitive in the sense that one needs to think
about one's decision, both the chosen option and the rejected options,
in order to experience it. In this chapter we argue that besides being
unpleasant – or, perhaps more plausible, as a consequence of it – regret

We thank Elke Weber, Jon Baron, Gideon Keren, and Lisa Abendroth for helpful comments
on an earlier version of this chapter. The writing of this chapter was supported by a
grant from the Netherlands Organization for Scientific Research (NWO/MAG 400-73-
040) awarded to Marcel Zeelenberg.

is a strong motivating force that may exert a significant impact on our day-to-day behavior. For example, when we regret not having purchased a ticket for the last gig of the Rolling Stones, we may be more likely to buy one the next time they go on their "final" tour.

According to Festinger, none of us is likely to be a stranger to regret. Landman (1993, p. 110) has also argued that "regret is a common, if not universal, experience." Moreover, some have claimed that particular decisions will always produce regret (Humberstone, 1980). Betting on the outcome of a soccer tournament is an example of such a decision. Imagine that you place a bet of 100 euros on the Dutch team winning the European Soccer Championship in the year 2000, and they lose. You probably regret wasting the money. If they win, however, you may end up regretting not having placed more money on this outcome. Thus, either way, you may end up with regret. Fortunately, regret is not always unavoidable. Nevertheless, there is also empirical evidence underscoring Festinger and Landman's claims that regret is frequently experienced. For example, in a study of verbal communication of emotions, Shimanoff (1984) found that regret was the most frequently named negative emotion. Thus, in spite of our efforts to avoid regret when deciding between different courses of action, regret is a frequently felt emotion. It may be experienced in purely individual settings, as well as in social or interpersonal settings. The experience of regret may therefore have behavioral implications in many different situations, and these implications are our current concerns.

Regret may also affect many of our decisions when it is not yet experienced, as described by regret theory (Bell, 1982; Loomes & Sugden, 1982). That is, people may anticipate future regrets and make tradeoffs in their decision making to avoid or minimize them. For example, we may decide to buy a particular insurance policy that is much too expensive (e.g., bicycle theft insurance) only because we want to avoid the (rather unprobable) regret that results from needing it but not having bought it (i.e., if the bicycle is stolen). Several researchers have reported such anticipated regret effects (e.g., Beattie, Baron, Hershey, & Spranca, 1994; Inman & McAlister, 1994; Ritov; 1996; Zeelenberg, Beattie, van der Pligt, & de Vries, 1996; for an overview, see Zeelenberg, 1999). However, this chapter does not deal with the effects of anticipated regret or its psychological consequences, but focuses instead on the effects of the experience of this emotion on future behavior. Other researchers have demonstrated the psychological consequences of the experience of regret, such as effects on goal setting (Lecci, Okun, & Karoly, 1994) and rumination (Handgraaf, Zeelenberg, & Manstead, 1997; Savitsky, Medvec, & Gilovich, 1997). On a theoretical level, the behavioral implications of regret were also noticed by Festinger (1964), who argued that

post-decision regret is simply the manifestation of the fact that the dissonance has suddenly become salient. . . . [I]t would seem reasonable for him [the decision maker] to feel regret and to think that perhaps he did something wrong. . . . [I]f during the period when dissonance is salient, a person were given the opportunity to reconsider, he should show some inclination to reverse his decision. (pp. 99, 100)

In spite of these early theoretical insights, no systematic empirical research has addressed these behavioral consequences of regret. In the remainder of this chapter, we attempt to shed some light on this issue by attempting to answer the question "What do we *do* when we experience regret?" That is, what are its behavioral implications? We first address the nature of regret: When and how is it felt? We then pose the following specific questions: "Does experienced regret influence subsequent decisions?", "Are the effects of regret direct effects, or do they occur through the effect of regret on satisfaction with the decision outcome?", "Are these effects regret specific, or can they be explained by other emotions as well?", and finally, "Do regrets stemming from actions have different behavioral effects than regrets stemming from inaction?" Because of the limited attention to these behavioral effects of experienced regret in the literature, we draw almost exclusively on our own research program to address these questions. Although considerable work remains to be done in this area, we hope that the results provided here will convince the reader that regret has significant, direct, and typical behavioral responses that merit investigation.

Video Games, Lottery Tickets, and Television Shows

Regret is evoked when an obtained outcome compares unfavorably with an outcome that could have been obtained had we chosen differently, and it typically occurs in instances where decision makers perceive themselves to be responsible for this outcome. Hence, the experience of regret focuses attention on one's own role in the occurrence of a regretted outcome. It motivates one to think about how this event could have happened and how one could either change it or prevent its future occurrence. Research on the phenomenology of regret has shown that it is accompanied by the feeling that one should have known better and by a sinking feeling, by thoughts about the mistake one has made and the opportunities lost, by a tendency to kick oneself and to correct one's mistake, and by wanting to undo the event and to get a second chance (Roseman, Wiest, & Swartz 1994; Zeelenberg, van Dijk, Manstead, & van der Pligt, 1998c). This suggests that regret, as well as being a rather unpleasant state, may carry some clear benefits for the individual (Landman, 1993). These benefits obviously stem from the impact of regret on the subsequent behavior of people. Let us now consider what this behavioral impact of regret may be and how it may take place.

An example of what we may do when experiencing regret is provided by Loftus and Loftus (1985). In their book about the psychology of video games, they argue that the experience of regret may be an important factor in the decision to continue playing video games:

In most situations regret is something that you just have to live with. But that is not true with video games. Often when playing a video game, the game ends because you've made a mistake, and you immediately know exactly what you've done wrong. "If only I hadn't eaten the energizer in this game before trying to grab that cherry," you say to yourself. "I knew it was the wrong thing to do, and I did it anyway." But now you don't have to sit there being annoyed and frustrated. Instead you can play the game again and correct the mistake. So in goes another quarter. But in the process of playing again, you make another mistake. And spend another quarter to correct it. And so it goes. (p. 30)

As this example demonstrates, the experience of regret may motivate one to undo the regretted outcome. Although we agree with Loftus and Loftus that these games provide clear-cut opportunities to undo your regrets, we disagree with their conclusion that in most other cases you just have to live with the regret. To the contrary, the experience of regret is often accompanied by opportunities to correct your decision or somehow try to alter the consequences. Moreover, the phenomenology of regret evokes behavioral consequences directed at fighting the regret, making it disappear, undoing it, or reducing it (Zeelenberg et al., 1998c), and this often prompts us to search actively for possibilities of reparative action. A familiar example of the impact of regret is regretting having purchased a particular consumer good (e.g., an extravagant blouse that does not quite fit your style). This regret may motivate you to try to get the money back, change the item for something else (a more modest piece of clothing), sell the good to someone else, or maybe use it as a present (for an extravagant friend).

Regrets vary in intensity and severity, and so do their behavioral consequences. An extreme, tragic example of the impact of regret took place in April 1995 when a middle-aged inhabitant of Liverpool, in the United Kingdom, took his own life after missing out on a £2 million prize in the National Lottery. He did so after discovering that the numbers he always selected, 14, 17, 22, 24, 42, and 47, were that week's winning combination. On this occasion, however, he had forgotten to renew his 5-week ticket on time; it had expired the previous Saturday. When reading about this unfortunate event, thoughts like "If only he had renewed his ticket on time, as he usually did..." are evoked almost automatically. It seems that this person was bothered by similar thoughts and that these thoughts, coupled with the extreme accompanying regret, may have played a role in his decision to end his life.

Other effects of the experience of regret, luckily less dramatic, can be seen on television. For the past few years, people in the Netherlands have had the opportunity to undo their interpersonal regrets during a nationwide broadcast television program called *I Am Sorry*. Fox Television has been broadcasting a very similar show in the United States since June 1997 under the name *Forgive or Forget* (Ockhuysen, 1998). A variety of interpersonal regrets is depicted in this show, ranging from someone who regrets not helping a friend who has been going through a difficult time, to someone who regrets having said something bad about a deceased person at his funeral, to someone who regrets having slapped his best friend in the face. In this television show, regretters are provided with the opportunity to apologize and offer a bunch of flowers to the person who is the target of their regrets.

These examples not only reveal that the experience of regret is quite common and may take different forms, mild or intense and interpersonal as well as individual, but also that there are clear behavioral consequences of these experiences for our future behavior. Unfortunately, the examples we have provided are mere demonstrations of what we may do when decisions go awry. At present there is little systematic insight into the behavioral implications of the experience of regret. As Oliver (1997, p. 228) says, "researchers have investigated the occurrence of regret, rather than its consequences."

Does Experienced Regret Influence Subsequent Decisions?

The first evidence concerning the effects of regret on subsequent decisions can be found in a study by Festinger and Walster (1964). The purpose of this study was not to show the effects of regret, but rather to demonstrate that the mere act of choosing produces regret. Regret itself, however, was not assessed, but was inferred from the fact that participants showed decision reversal, a behavioral consequence. Festinger and Walster had participants rank several different haircuts on attractiveness. Half of the participants, the prior choice participants, knew in advance that they could have the most attractive haircut for free. The no prior choice participants were unaware of this. Since this task implied a choice for the prior choice participants, it was expected to produce some dissonance, and hence regret. For the no prior choice participants, ranking did not imply a choice, and hence dissonance and the accompanying regret were not expected. When all participants were finally asked to choose a coupon for a free haircut, the prior choice participants showed more decision reversals than the no prior choice participants. This decision reversal may be interpreted as a consequence of the regret stemming from dissonance.

Thus, the Festinger and Walster study provides some support for the idea that the experience of regret has behavioral consequences. However, a direct relation between the experience of regret and behavior could not be tested because regret was not measured. A study that allowed us to test for the effects of regret on subsequent behavior more directly is reported in Zeelenberg and Beattie (1997, Experiment 3).

In this experiment we studied the effects of regret in a bargaining experiment and measured the intensity of the experienced regret. A repeated ultimatum game was used to manipulate the experience of regret experimentally in order to investigate its consequences for subsequent decisions. In brief, we had participants make a decision and provided them with feedback that could or could not evoke regret. The intensity of their regret was assessed; then they had to make a second, similar decision. In this way, we were able to test whether the regret over the first decision influenced their second decision. This was indeed the case. We now describe the experiment, and the paradigm used, in somewhat more detail.

The ultimatum game is a simple bargaining game with two players, a proposer and a responder (Güth, Schmittberger, & Schwarze, 1982). The players are given a sum of money, say 100 guilders, and the proposer may offer a division of this money to the responder (e.g., 25 guilders for you, 75 guilders for me). The responder can then either accept this offer or reject it, in which case neither player receives any money.

In the Zeelenberg and Beattie experiment, we focused on the decision of the proposer (i.e., how much to offer to the responder). Hence,

Table 6.1. *Means for First Offer, Regret, and Second Offer for Both Feedback Conditions*

| | Feedback Condition | | | |
	2 Guilders Too Much	10 Guilders Too Much	$F(1,44)$	$p <$
First offer	35.69	30.43	2.79	n.s.
Regret	1.30	2.09	11.02	.003
Second offer	34.69	26.34	8.41	.006

Note: These data are from Zeelenberg and Beattie (1997, Experiment 3). The first and second offers are the proposers' mean offer to the responders of a 100-guilder fixed pie. The regret score is the mean regret over the first offer indicated by the proposer on a 7-point scale, with higher scores indicating more regret.

all players were proposers; although they thought they were interacting with other players, they were in fact playing against a computer program. Proposers can end up either regretting offering too little in cases where their offer is rejected or regretting offering too much in cases where their offer is accepted. Research has shown that proposers tend to make offers in the area of 30–40%, and often a 50-50 split, and that responders tend to reject offers of less then 20% (for a review, see Camerer & Thaler, 1995). Thus, because proposers generally offer much more than 20%, regret stemming from offering too little will occur less often than regret stemming from offering too much. We therefore focused on the impact of this last type of regret and studied how it may affect decisions about what to offer in a second round of the game.

The procedure was as follows: Participants made their offer and learned that it had been accepted. They also received feedback on how much less they could have offered (10 guilders or 2 guilders) and still had their offer accepted. After this information was given, the intensity of their regret was assessed. The results are depicted in Table 6.1. Participants who could have offered 10 guilders less experienced more regret than did participants who could have offered only 2 guilders less.

When participants were asked to play a second round of the ultimatum game (against another responder), their offers were clearly influenced by the regret experienced over the first offer. First of all, those who had offered 10 guilders too much (who experienced the greatest regret) lowered their offers substantially in the second round of the game, whereas those who had offered 2 guilders too much (who experienced less regret) lowered their offers very little in the second round. Interestingly, these differences between the two conditions disappeared when we controlled statistically for the intensity of the experienced regret in an analysis of covariance. We concluded that not the manipulation alone, but also the experience of regret resulting from it, was responsible for the effects on subsequent decisions. Hence, the behavior of the participants could be described as *regret management*: They behaved in such a way that their currently experienced regret would be lessened or that future regret would be minimized.

As far as we know, this is the only published experimental demonstration of effects of regret on subsequent decisions. Hence, there is still a lot to be learned about how this influence takes place. Are these effects direct consequences of the experience of regret or does the experience of regret influence overall satisfaction with decision outcomes (e.g., utility), which in turn drives future decisions? The latter would be consistent with ideas in regret theory. As Loomes (1988, p. 464) argued: "The psychological intuition behind regret theory is that if an individual chooses A (and therefore rejects B) and state j occurs, the overall level of satisfaction he experiences will depend not simply upon x_{Aj} but also upon how x_{Aj} compares with x_{Bj}. If what he gets is worse than what he might have had, it is suggested that the satisfaction associated with x_{Aj} will be reduced by a decrement of utility due to regret." Alternatively, the behavioral effects could well be direct consequences of the experience of regret, as suggested by research in emotion theory (e.g., Frijda & Zeelenberg, 2000). The issue of the causal path from regret to behavioral consequences is addressed next.

Are the Effects of Experienced Regret Mediated by Satisfaction?

The question of whether the effects of experienced regret are mediated by more general outcome satisfaction is based on the findings of two recent studies by Inman, Dyer, and Jia (1997) and Taylor (1997). In these studies it is shown that regret – manipulated as information about a forgone option that appeared to produce a better outcome than the chosen option – has an impact on satisfaction or, more broadly speaking, on postchoice valuation. Inman et al. (1997) developed a generalized utility model of choice that incorporates regret effects. This model asserts that regret influences satisfaction. Taylor (1997) studied consumer satisfaction with movies and arrived at the similar prediction that expectations concerning forgone alternatives can influence satisfaction with the chosen film. In short, both studies found that the valuation of an obtained decision outcome was influenced both by how the outcome of the chosen option compared to the previously held expectations and by how it compared to the outcome of the unchosen option (a proxy for regret). It may well be that regret alters subsequent behavior only indirectly through its impact on satisfaction. Recently we (Inman & Zeelenberg, 1998) reported an experiment that tested whether regret might also have direct effects in addition to the effects that may occur via its influence on satisfaction.

The setup of the study was as follows (for details, see Inman & Zeelenberg, 1998): Participants in a consumer decision-making study were asked to choose between two brands of writing instruments and were allowed to keep the chosen one. Next, they read a *Consumer Reports* evaluation of both writing instruments. Participants in the *regret condition* read that the forgone pen was evaluated more favorably than the chosen pen. The reverse was true in the *rejoicing condition* (i.e., the chosen pen was evaluated more positively than the forgone alternative). In the *neutral condition*, the two pens were evaluated as being quite similar to one another. Next, satisfaction and repurchase intentions were assessed.

The results concerning satisfaction were in line with the findings by Inman et al. (1997) and Taylor (1997). Regret participants were less satisfied with their writing instrument than neutral participants, who were less satisfied than rejoicing participants. The same was found for repurchase intentions. Regret participants were less likely to repurchase the writing instrument than neutral participants, who were less likely to repurchase it than rejoicing participants. These results are depicted in Table 6.2. Next, we tested whether satisfaction mediated the effects of the regret manipulation on repurchase intentions. We found that although satisfaction and repurchase intention were strongly related, satisfaction only partially mediated the effect on repurchase intentions. Our regret manipulation still had a significant effect on repurchase intention after the impact via satisfaction was statistically controlled for. Thus it seems

Table 6.2. *Mean Satisfaction and Repurchase Intention in the Three Conditions*

	Regret ($n = 25$)	Neutral ($n = 25$)	Rejoicing ($n = 24$)	F(2,67)	$p <$
Satisfaction	7.0	8.2	9.6	7.90	.001
Repurchase intention	4.9	8.7	10.8	16.38	.001

Note: These data are from Inman and Zeelenberg (1998, Experiment 1). The satisfaction measure is composed of a rating for satisfaction with the chosen alternative and a rating for the overall evaluation of the chosen alternative ($\alpha = 0.90$). The repurchase intention was measured by asking participants to indicate the likelihood that they would make the same selection given what they had learned about the writing instruments. All ratings were made on 12-point scales.

that the effects of regret on subsequent behavior do not occur via its effects on satisfaction alone; regret also has direct behavioral consequences.

Note that in this study regret was not assessed, although it was manipulated. A study in which regret was assessed produced essentially the same results (Zeelenberg & Pieters, 1999). Here we focused on the behavioral consequences of consumer dissatisfaction with services. Regret, satisfaction, and several behavioral responses were measured. This study also found that regret has direct behavioral consequences over and above the influence of (dis)satisfaction. We will discuss this study in more detail shortly because this study also allowed us to compare the behavioral consequences of regret with those of the related emotion of disappointment. This is relevant for the question addressed next.

Are These Effects Regret Specific?

Regret and disappointment have in common the fact that they are experienced when the outcome of a decision is unfavorable. Both are negative emotions that originate in a comparison process in which the outcome obtained is compared to an outcome that might have been. However, there are also some clear differences between these emotions (for a review, see Zeelenberg, van Dijk, Manstead, & van der Pligt, 2000). For example, regret is associated with internal attributions, whereas disappointment is more often associated with external attributions. This difference in responsibility is consistent with the assumptions in regret theory (Bell, 1982; Loomes & Sugden, 1982) and disappointment theory (Bell, 1985; Loomes & Sugden, 1984). These assumptions specify that regret stems from a comparison of the obtained outcome with an outcome that would have been obtained had a different choice been made (*wrong decisions*) and that disappointment stems from a comparison of the obtained outcome with an outcome that would have been obtained had things that were not under the decision maker's control been different (*disconfirmed expectancies*). The Zeelenberg and Pieters study (1999) shows that the effects of regret are emotion-specific effects and that they are not caused by other specific negative emotions, such as disappointment, or by general negative affect, such as dissatisfaction.

The specific details of the study were as follows: We asked participants to report on experiences in which they were dissatisfied with a service they had purchased. In order to obtain a sample of experiences in which both regret and disappointment would be present, we included two instructions in our study. The first asked about dissatisfaction caused by the fact that, in retrospect, the consumer would have liked to have chosen a different service provider. The second instruction probed for experiences of dissatisfaction caused by the fact that the obtained service was worse than expected. The amounts of experienced regret and disappointment were assessed, together with the overall dissatisfaction with the service and the service provider and behavioral responses in which the consumers engaged. The behavioral responses were regressed on the experiences of regret and disappointment and the satisfaction measures. The results showed that the experience of disappointment significantly predicted the extent to which the consumers engaged in word-of-mouth (how much they talked to others about the bad experience). In contrast, the experience of regret predicted the extent to which the consumers were likely to switch to another service provider. Moreover, there was a small negative relationship between regret and word-of-mouth: The more regret consumers experienced, the less likely they were to share their experience with others. This makes sense, considering that we want to kick ourselves when we experience regret. We don't want to communicate to others that we want to kick ourselves, at least most of us. In addition, regret in this case also implies a sense of embarrassment about having chosen the wrong course of action, which may also contribute to talking less to others about the experience. These results were obtained when the impact of dissatisfaction was already accounted for in the regression analyses. Thus, they again show that the experience of regret has implications for future behavior and that these implications are regret specific.

Another study supports these findings in a very different context (Zeelenberg, Keren, & Gerritsen, 1997). This study was set up to test for effects of experienced regret on subsequent decisions using a more traditional gamble paradigm. A procedure developed by Denes-Raj and Epstein (1994) was used. In this task, participants are offered an opportunity to win money by drawing a red marble out of an urn that contains both white and red marbles. In our experiment, one urn contained 1 red and 9 white marbles, whereas the other urn contained 9 red and 91 white marbles. Denes-Raj and Epstein showed that participants may sometimes prefer to draw from the urn with nine red marbles (a 9% change of winning), although the urn with only one red marbles is objectively better (a 10% change of winning). They reported that participants informed them that although they *knew* that the probabilities in the 1 in 10 case were better, they *felt* they had a better chance in the 9 in 100 case. Because of this internal conflict in the participants' preferences, we thought that this task could be used to induce regret.

The procedure was straightforward. Participants were given a questionnaire describing the two urns and were asked to choose one. Then, on a subsequent page, they were informed that they had picked a white marble out of the chosen urn and therefore had not won any money. They were also informed that in order to see what would have occurred, they would also choose a marble form the rejected urn. This appeared to be a red marble (indicating that they would have won had they chosen the other option). Next, they were asked to indicate to what extent the following statements applied to them now that they know the outcome of the game: "I regret my choice," "I am disappointed in the outcome," and "I would like to undo what happened." They could do this on 9-point scales with endpoints labeled *does not apply at all* (1) and *does apply very well* (9). Finally, they were informed that they could play the game once more and were asked from which urn they would draw this time.

Out of the 135 students who participated in this study, 103 chose the 1 in 10 urn and 32 chose the 9 in 100 urn. Twelve participants (six from each group) decided to switch to the other urn in the second choice. Table 6.3 shows the means on the three dependent variables for those who switched and those who did not switch. As can be seen, these two groups differed only with respect to the regret experienced over the first

Table 6.3. *Levels of Regret and Disappointment and Desire to Undo the Outcome for Switchers and Nonswitchers*

	Switch ($n = 12$)	Nonswitch ($n = 123$)	$t(133)$	$p <$
Regret	6.00	3.73	2.94	.005
Disappointment	6.50	6.19	0.48	n.s.
Undoing	5.67	4.60	1.30	n.s.

Source: Data from Zeelenberg et al. (1997).

choice. It seems that high levels of regret promote switching, whereas high levels of disappointment do not, a conclusion supported by the correlations between the dependent variables depicted in Table 6.4. Regret, but not disappointment, correlates significantly with switching. At the same time, both regret and disappointment correlate with the desire to undo the outcome, suggesting that both emotions may express dissatisfaction with the unfavorable outcome.

These findings are consistent with those reported by Zeelenberg and Pieters (1999). Both studies show that regret strongly promotes the

Table 6.4. *Correlations Between Regret, Disappointment, Desired Undoing, and Actual Switching*

	Regret	Disappointment	Undoing	Switching
Regret	—			
Disappointment	.22*	—		
Undoing	.33[†]	.32[‡]	—	
Switching	.25[‡]	.04	.11	—

* $n = 135$.
[†] $p < .05$.
[‡] $p < .005$.
Source: Data from Zeelenberg et al. (1997).

tendency to switch to another option or behavioral alternative and that this effect is driven by regret. This last study also shows that both regret and disappointment are associated with the wish or tendency to undo the negative outcome. This finding was also reported in Zeelenberg et al. (1998c), and this study showed that the wish to undo the regretted outcome was significantly more profound in the case of regret. On the basis of the these findings, we conclude that some of the effects observed (i.e., switching and undoing) are indeed regret specific.

Do Action Regrets Have Different Effects Than Inaction Regrets?

Now that we have established that regret has direct idiosyncratic effects on behavior, the question becomes "Does regret always have the same consequences, regardless of what the specific causes of regret were?" That is, "Does the process that led to regret impact on the intensity or type of behavioral consequences of regret?"

In the literature, a distinction is often made between regret that stems from decisions to act and regret that stems from decisions not to act. Research has shown that action regrets are often more painful than inaction regrets (e.g., Baron & Ritov, 1994; Connolly, Ordóñez, & Coughlan, 1997; Kahneman & Tversky, 1982; Landman, 1987; Ritov & Baron, 1990; Zeelenberg et al., 1998b). Gilovich and Medvec (1994, 1995; see also Gilovich, Medvec, & Kahneman, 1998) showed in a number of studies that this pattern is reversed for long-term regrets. That is, when we look back on the thing we regret most, we typically think about things we could have done but did not do.

One of the explanations that Gilovich and Medvec (1994, 1995) offered for this temporal pattern of regret is that action regret promotes reparative action more than inaction regret. This may occur simply because action regret is more intense in the short run, but it may also be the result of some characteristic difference between action regret and inaction regret. Action regret typically refers to a decision that took place at one moment in time. Inaction regret, is different. For example, the inaction regret of not having had enough education (one of the most frequent regrets; see Landman, 1993) is most likely not the result of a single decision, but rather a retrospective realization that one wasted an opportunity. Therefore, in general, it takes us longer to realize that we regret not having acted than it takes us to realize that we regret an action. A recent series of studies reported in Zeelenberg, van der Pligt, and Manstead (1998a) tested whether there was indeed differential undoing behavior after action and inaction regrets. This research is described next.

In this research, the undoing of interpersonal regrets was studied by analyzing cases from the television program *I Am Sorry*, described earlier (for details, see Zeelenberg et al., 1998a). The typical behavioral response in interpersonal regrets is to apologize to the person who is affected by the regretted decision. We analyzed a total of 64 cases drawn from 18 different television shows and found that action regrets resulted in behavioral undoing more often. Approximately 70% of the cases represented action regrets. Consistent with this finding, we also found that there was much more time between the occurrence of the regretted event and the behavioral undoing for inaction regrets (median time elapsed, approximately 3.5 years for inaction regrets compared to 1 year for action regrets). These results were replicated in a follow-up survey using a representative sample of the Dutch population.

These results suggest that the behavioral consequences may depend on the nature of a specific regret experience. It was found that action regret occurs more quickly and results more often in behavioral undoing than does inaction regret. It is not yet clear whether this difference is attributable solely to the differences in intensity between the two regrets. Moreover, as demonstrated throughout this chapter, regret motivates people to undo the regret or the regretted outcome, or at least engage in reparative action to alleviate the painful experience by remedying its causes. Importantly, this motivation does not prescribe the particular type of undoing in which the individual should engage. Rather, it seems to be guided by both the characteristics of the situation and personal characteristics (e.g., the stubbornness of the individual). Thus, regret promotes undoing, but whether this results in apologies depends on whether the regret is individually based (e.g., a consumer purchase) or more interpersonally based (e.g., an argument with a friend). Further, whether an individual engages in apologies depends on the nature of the regret (i.e., action or inaction) and the predicted effect of the apology.

The answer to the question of whether regrets have different effects seems to be dependent on the level of abstraction. On the one hand, when we are very specific, different regrets seem to promote very different behaviors. An interpersonal regret promotes apologies, whereas a consumer regret may evoke a tendency to change the purchased good. On the other hand, at a higher level of abstraction, both behaviors can be qualified as undoing behaviors. This leads us to conclude that different regrets lead to the similar desire to undertake reparative action, but that the specific manifestation of the action depends on the idiosyncrasies pertaining to the regretted event.

What Is the Normative Status of These Effects?

What we have seen in this chapter is that experienced regret not only affects well-being (i.e., makes you feel bad) but also gives direction to future behavior. Some have argued that this is an unwanted effect. Howard (1992, p. 38), for example, stated: "My preferences must be based on prospects – the futures I face. Regret is a bad thought that arises when I think about futures I might have received instead of the future I did receive." The point here seems to be that experienced regret can be considered a sunk cost. Sunk costs are costs incurred at an earlier time, and because our decision should be based only on the costs and outcomes that will occur in the future, honoring sunk costs is irrational (Arkes & Blumer, 1985). Thus, one might argue that it is irrational to be influenced by the experience of regret.

Alternatively, if one considers rational behavior to mean acting in a way that is intended and perceived as wanted by the individual (Aarts, 1996), then these regret effects are *not* irrational or dysfunctional per se. To the contrary, we maintain that regret can be a very functional emotion (Landman, 1993). Because experienced regret is informative about one's concerns – we typically feel regret over bad decisions that have some significance to us – it may help us to achieve our goals more effectively in the future (Frijda, 1986; Frijda & Zeelenberg, 2000). For example, regret can promote undoing behavior in order to repair what went wrong.

Regret may shape our future choices in order to prevent us from making the same regrettable mistakes in the future. Experienced regret, because it makes mistakes more painful, helps us to learn from them (e.g., it may prompt us to switch to a better alternative). It also makes mistakes more salient and therefore easier to remember. As Shefrin and Statman (1986, p. 57) argued, "both the unpleasant pain of regret and the pleasurable glow of pride can lead to learning. They help us to remember clearly both bad and good choices." A similar argument was put forward by Farnsworth in his recent book on regretted decision in the context of contract law. He writes, "If you sometimes had "past Regrets" because of unexpected difficulties in performing, you could allay your "future Fears" by including in your agreement a force majeure clause, excusing you from performing should such difficulties arise" (1998, p. 19).

Moreover, as we have seen in this chapter, when we experience regret, we are motivated to undo the cause of the regret. For example, after buying a product that proves to be suboptimal, regret can motivate us to ask for our money back, or it may result in apologies in the case of interpersonal regrets. In both instances, regret protects us from wasting money and helps us to maintain good social relationships.

Final Thoughts

Decisions, by their very nature, involve intrapersonal conflict of interests. The tradeoff between various goals and the choice of one behavioral alternative over others lead to tensions that people try to deal with and regret that they try to avoid or minimize by taking specific courses of action. Hence regret has specific behavioral consequences. Although there are many examples of regret effects on behavior in our daily lives, there is a paucity of research addressing them. We have presented some preliminary evidence from our own research to show that regret does affect our behavior, and that these behavioral consequences of regret are not attributable to other factors, such as dissatisfaction or disappointment. Of course, much remains to be known about the effects of regret on behavior. For example, in addition to the effect discussed in this chapter, regret may have other influences on future behavior. Previous research (Beattie et al., 1994) and theorizing (Janis & Mann, 1977) indicated that anticipated regret produces a tendency to delay decision making. One reason for this delay is that people want to gather extra information in order to make a better decision and thereby prevent regret (e.g., Ordóñez, Benson, & Beach, 1999). Similar delay effects can be expected for experienced regret. Regret is related to thinking about what went wrong and wanting a better outcome in the future, and it should motivate people to think more carefully about alternative courses of action to reduce future conflict. To our knowledge, this prediction has not yet been tested.

One might also predict that future risk-taking is influenced by the experience of regret. Unfortunately, the effects of experienced regret on risk-taking are not straightforward. Decision makers can regret taking a risk (when the risky option results in a bad outcome), but they can also regret not taking a risk (when one learns that the risky option would have resulted in a better outcome). In general, we would predict that those who regret having taken a risk will be more cautious (i.e., risk averse) in the future, but those who regret not having taken a risk will prefer a riskier option in the future. Thus, we expect no single effect of regret on risk-taking. Rather, the effects of the experience of regret on risk-taking can only be predicted when the source of regret is known. Clearly, although it is an important topic, much more research is needed to gain a complete understanding of what we do when decisions go awry.

References

Aarts, H. (1996). *Habit and decision making: The case of travel mode choice.* Ph.D. dissertation, University of Nijmegen.

Arkes, H. R., & Blumer, C. (1985). The psychology of sunk cost. *Organizational Behavior and Human Decision Processes, 35*, 124–140.

Baron, J., & Ritov, I. (1994). Reference points and omission bias. *Organizational Behavior and Human Decision Processes, 59*, 475–498.

Beattie, J., Baron, J., Hershey, J. C., & Spranca, M. D. (1994). Psychological determinants of decision attitude. *Journal of Behavioral Decision Making, 7*, 129–144.

Bell, D. E. (1982). Regret in decision making under uncertainty. *Operations Research, 30*, 961–981.

Bell, D. E. (1985). Disappointment in decision making under uncertainty. *Operations Research, 33*, 1–27.

Camerer, C., & Thaler, R. H. (1995). Ultimatums, dictators and manners. *Journal of Economic Perspectives, 2*, 209–219.

Connolly, T., Ordóñez, L. D., & Coughlan, R. (1997). Regret and responsibility in the evaluation of decision outcomes. *Organizational Behavior and Human Decision Processes, 70*, 73–85.

Denes-Raj, V., & Epstein, S. (1994). Conflict between intuitive and rational processing: When people behave against their better judgment. *Journal of Personality and Social Psychology, 66*, 819–829.

Farnsworth, E. A. (1998). *Changing your mind: The law of regretted decisions.* New Haven: Yale University Press.

Festinger, L. (1964), The post-decision process. In L. Festinger (Ed.), *Conflict, decision, and dissonance* (pp. 97–100). Stanford, CA: Stanford University Press.

Festinger, L., & Walster, E. (1964). Post-decision regret and decision reversal. In L. Festinger (Ed.), *Conflict, decision, and dissonance* (pp. 100–112). Stanford, CA: Stanford University Press.

Frijda, N. H. (1986). *The emotions.* Cambridge: Cambridge University Press.

Frijda, N. H., & Zeelenberg, M. (2000). Appraisal: What is the dependent? In K. R. Scherer, A. Schorr, & T. Johnstone (Eds.). *Appraisal processes in emotion: Theory, methods, research.* New York: Oxford University Press.

Gilovich, T., & Medvec, V. H. (1994). The temporal pattern to the experience of regret. *Journal of Personality and Social Psychology, 67*, 357–365.

Gilovich, T., & Medvec, V. H. (1995). The experience of regret: What, when, and why. *Psychological Review, 102*, 379–395.

Gilovich, T., Medvec, V. H., & Kahneman, D. (1998). Varieties of regret: A debate and partial resolution. *Psychological Review, 105*, 602–605.

Güth, W., Schmittberger, R., & Schwarze, B. (1982). An experimental analysis of ultimatum bargaining. *Journal of Economic Behavior and Organization, 3*, 367–388.

Handgraaf, M., Zeelenberg, M., & Manstead, A. S. R. (1997, November). *Piekeren en het sociaal delen van emoties* [*Rumination and social sharing of emotions*]. Paper presented at the 12th Dutch Association for Social Psychological Research Conference, Enschede, the Netherlands.

Howard, R. (1992). In praise of the old time religion. In W. Edwards (Ed.), *Utility theories: Measurements and applications* (pp. 27–56). Boston: Kluwer Academic.

Humberstone, I. L. (1980). You'll regret it. *Analysis, 40,* 175–176.

Inman, J. J., Dyer, J. S., & Jia, J. (1997). A generalized utility model of disappointment and regret effects on post-choice valuation. *Marketing Science, 16,* 97–111.

Inman, J. J., & McAlister, L. (1994). Do coupon expiration dates influence consumer behavior? *Journal of Marketing Research, 31,* 423–428.

Inman, J. J., & Zeelenberg, M. (1998). *"Wow, I could've had a V8!": The role of regret in consumer choice.* Center Discussion Paper No. 9879, Center for Economic Research, Tilburg University, the Netherlands.

Janis, I. L., & Mann, L. (1977). *Decision making: A psychological analysis of conflict, choice, and commitment.* New York: Free Press.

Kahneman, D., & Tversky, A. (1982). The simulation heuristic. In D. Kahneman, P. Slovic, & A. Tversky (Eds.), *Judgment under uncertainty: Heuristics and biases* (pp. 201–208). New York: Cambridge University Press.

Landman, J. (1987). Regret and elation following action and inaction. *Personality and Social Psychology Bulletin, 13,* 524–536.

Landman, J. (1993). *Regret: The persistence of the possible.* New York: Oxford University Press.

Lecci, L., Okun, M. A., & Karoly, P. (1994). Life regrets and current goals as predictors of psychological adjustment. *Journal of Personality and Social Psychology, 66,* 731–741

Loftus, G., & Loftus, E. F. (1985). *Mind in play.* New York: Basic Books.

Loomes, G. (1988). When actions speak louder than prospects. *American Economic Review, 78,* 463–470.

Loomes, G., & Sugden, R. (1982). Regret theory: An alternative theory of rational choice under uncertainty. *Economic Journal, 92,* 805–824.

Loomes, G., & Sugden, R. (1984). The importance of what might have been. In O. Hagen & F. Wenstrøp (Eds.), *Progress in utility and risk theory* (pp. 219–235). Dordrecht: D. Reidel.

Ockhuysen, R. (1998, January 22). Endemol weert zich tegen diefstal televisie-idee [Endemol defends itself against theft of television idea]. *De Volkskrant,* p. 1.

Oliver, R. L. (1997). *Satisfaction: A behavioral perspective on the consumer.* New York: McGraw-Hill.

Ordóñez, L. D., Benson, L., III, & Beach, L. R. (1999). Testing the compatibility test: How instructions, accountability and anticipated regret affect prechoice screening of options. *Organizational Behavior and Human Decision Processes, 78,* 63–80.

Ritov, I. (1996). Probability of regret: Anticipation of uncertainty resolution in choice. *Organizational Behavior and Human Decision Processes, 66,* 228–236.

Ritov, I., & Baron, J. (1990). Reluctance to vaccinate: Omission bias and ambiguity. *Journal of Behavioral Decision Making, 3,* 263–277.

Roseman, I. J., Wiest, C., & Swartz, T. S. (1994). Phenomenology, behaviors, and goals differentiate discrete emotions. *Journal of Personality and Social Psychology, 67,* 206–211.

Savitsky, K., Medvec, V. H., & Gilovich, T. (1997). Remembering and regretting: The Zeigarnik effect and the cognitive availability of regrettable actions and inactions. *Personality and Social Psychology Bulletin, 23*, 248–257.

Shefrin, H. M., & Statman, M. (1986). How not to make money in the stock market. *Psychology Today, February*, 52–57.

Shimanoff, S. B. (1984). Commonly named emotions in everyday conversations. *Perceptual and Motor Skills, 58*, 514.

Taylor, K. A. (1997). A regret theory approach to assessing consumer satisfaction. *Marketing Letters, 8*, 229–238.

Zeelenberg, M. (1999). Anticipated regret, expected feedback and behavioral decision-making. *Journal of Behavioral Decision Making, 12*, 93–106.

Zeelenberg, M., & Beattie, J. (1997). Consequences of regret aversion: 2. Additional evidence for effects of feedback on decision making. *Organizational Behavior and Human Decision Processes, 72*, 63–78.

Zeelenberg, M., Beattie, J., van der Pligt, J., & de Vries, N. K. (1996). Consequences of regret aversion: Effects of expected feedback on risky decision making. *Organizational Behavior and Human Decision Processes, 65*, 148–158.

Zeelenberg, M., Keren, G., & Gerritsen, L. E. M. (1997). *Effects of experienced regret on future decisions*. Unpublished manuscript.

Zeelenberg, M., & Pieters, R. (1999). Comparing service delivery to what might have been: Behavioral responses to regret and disappointment. *Journal of Service Research, 2*, 86–97.

Zeelenberg, M., van der Pligt, J., & Manstead, A. S. R. (1998a). Undoing regret on Dutch television: Apologizing for interpersonal regrets involving actions and inactions. *Personality and Social Psychology Bulletin, 24*, 1113–1119.

Zeelenberg, M., van Dijk, W. W., & Manstead, A. S. R. (1998b). Reconsidering the relation between regret and responsibility. *Organizational Behavior and Human Decision Processes, 74*, 254–272.

Zeelenberg, M., van Dijk, W. W., Manstead, A. S. R., & van der Pligt, J. (1998c). The experience of regret and disappointment. *Cognition and Emotion, 12*, 221–230.

Zeelenberg, M., van Dijk, W. W., Manstead, A. S. R., & van der Pligt, J. (2000). On bad decisions and disconfirmed expectancies: The psychology of regret and disappointment. *Cognition and Emotion, 14*, 521–541.

7   Decisions About Prenatal Screening

Rosemary Murray and Jane Beattie

Introduction

Research on decision making has shown that a number of emotional factors can influence the choices that people make. Decisions are often not made simply on the basis of factors that will lead to the greatest subjective expected utility. Other important influences on decision making include the anticipation of regretting a decision if it turns out badly (Bell, 1982; Loomes & Sugden, 1982), an aversion to making certain kinds of decisions (Beattie, Baron, Hershey, & Spranca, 1994), and a bias against choosing to take actions that could lead to a bad outcome as opposed to allowing the same outcome to occur by inaction (Ritov and Baron, 1990; Spranca, Minsk, & Baron, 1991). These interrelated factors have been shown to be important in laboratory studies of decision making, and one aim of this study was to investigate the role of these factors in a real-life decision regarding prenatal testing. Forty pregnant women took part in structured interviews about how they decided whether or not to have the Triple Test.

Background to the Triple Test

The Triple Test is a maternal blood test that provides a pregnant woman with an estimate of the risk that her fetus has Down syndrome and an estimate of the risk that it has a neural tube defect (e.g., anencephaly or spina bifida). The test measures levels of three chemical "markers" in the woman's blood. Raised levels of unconjugated oestriol and human chorionic gonadotrophin and low levels of alphafetoprotein in the mother's blood are associated with an increased risk of Down syndrome.

A raised level of alpha-fetoprotein is associated with an increased risk of a neural tube defect.

The test can be carried out from the 16th week of pregnancy, and results are available within 7 days. No definite diagnosis can be based on the Triple Test, but it gives a more accurate estimate of the risk of the baby's having Down syndrome or a neural tube defect. The test detects two out of three cases of Down syndrome and four out of five cases of severe spina bifida. If the risk was estimated to be less than 1 in 250, the result would be presented as *screen negative* and the woman could be reassured that there was very little chance of her baby's being affected by either condition. If the risk was greater than 1 in 250, she would be told that the result was *screen positive*, and she would be offered further tests such as amniocentesis for Down syndrome or ultrasound scanning for spina bifida, in order to gain a definite diagnosis. The amniocentesis test causes a miscarriage in approximately 1 in 100 women tested. There are no problems known to be associated with ultrasound scans.

The incidence of Down syndrome (about 1 in 700 births in the United Kingdom) is known to increase with the age of the pregnant woman, from about 1 in 1,000 in mothers who are 28 years of age to 1 in 200 in mothers who are 38 years of age (Cuckle, 1993). This led to the practice of screening for Down syndrome on the basis of maternal age. Amniocentesis was routinely offered to women who would be 36 or older at the time of delivery. The risk of spina bifida does not increase with maternal age, but it occurs in approximately 1 in 400 births. A raised level of alphafetoprotein in the mother's blood (MSAFP) is associated with an increased risk of the fetus having a neural tube defect such as spina bifida. If a raised level of MSAFP is detected, then the woman would be offered a detailed ultrasound scan in order to give a more definite diagnosis.

On the basis of screening by age-related risk for Down syndrome alone, approximately 9% of women were offered amniocentesis. Seventy percent of babies with Down syndrome are born to women under 35 years of age (because over 90% of pregnant women are younger than 36). Therefore, the maximum percentage of Down syndrome pregnancies detected with amniocentesis was 30%. In fact, Wald et al. (1988) report that only 15% are detected prenatally with this test. By using the information from the Triple Test combined with the age-related risk of Down syndrome to give a revised risk figure, the accuracy of the screening can be greatly improved. Results of the Triple Test trials reported by

Wald et al. (1992) suggest that 55–60% of Down syndrome pregnancies can be detected in this way (depending on the uptake of the Triple Test and the subsequent uptake of amniocentesis). If all the women who get a screen positive result (an estimated risk greater than 1 in 250) have amniocentesis, higher rates of detection can be achieved with approximately the same number of amniocentesis tests (Wenstrom, Williamson, Grant, Hudson, and Getchell, 1993).

Serum screening tests such as the Triple Test provide information about the fetus and enable further tests to be offered to women shown to be at higher risk for carrying fetuses with Down syndrome or spina bifida. Thus, these tests present younger pregnant women with choices about testing that they would not previously have had to make.

This chapter reports findings from an interview study of 40 pregnant women, examining how they decided whether to accept the Triple Test. Psychological factors such as decision aversion, regret, and omission bias have been shown to be important in laboratory studies of decision making. We investigated whether these factors were also influential in this real-life decision.

The first two factors, decision aversion and regret, have been discussed in the introduction to this book. The third factor, omission bias, concerns the distinction between acts and omissions (Ritov & Baron, 1990; Spranca, Minsk, & Baron, 1991). Harm is an act, but failing to prevent harm is an omission. People are more tolerant of harmful omissions than of harmful acts. For example, many people think that it is wrong to vaccinate a child against a fatal disease if the vaccine also causes fatalities, even if the fatalities from the disease greatly exceed those from the vaccine (Ritov & Baron, 1990; Meszaros et al., 1996). Omission bias is related to regret: Regret is greater for harmful acts than for harmful omissions (Kahneman & Tversky, 1982), and part of the bias toward harmful omissions over harmful acts is a result of this anticipated regret (Ritov & Baron, 1995). The omission option can be defined as the default, that is, what happens if you do nothing to prevent it or simply accept what you are offered (Schweitzer, 1994).

Recruitment of Participants for the Study

The Triple Test was offered free of charge to all pregnant women in the Brighton area where the study took place. At the first visit to her doctor at the start of pregnancy, each woman in the area was routinely given a leaflet explaining the Triple Test. The leaflet included a consent form that she was asked to complete by checking the "yes" or the "no" box to indicate whether she wanted to have the Triple Test.

Women were told about the study in a letter that they received together with the Triple Test leaflet from their doctor. Their contact details were then passed on to the researcher (by the general practitioner or midwife) so that they could be contacted by telephone and invited to take part. In the initial telephone call, it was made clear to the women that their participation in the study was entirely voluntary and that it would not affect the care they would receive from their doctors and midwives. Forty-eight women were referred in this way and were contacted by telephone. Forty agreed to take part in the study. Those who declined to take part were not asked to give any reasons for declining. The interviews were arranged to take place during the 12th week of pregnancy, 2 or 3 days before the women were due to return the consent form to the midwife indicating their decision about the test. Interviews were all carried out in the participants' homes.

Demographic Details

Women older than 35 were not invited to take part because they would normally be offered amniocentesis on the basis of their greater age-related risk for carrying a fetus with Down syndrome. Deciding whether or not to have the Triple Test would therefore be different for the older women in comparison to the younger women. The extra information from the Triple Test results might help them choose not to have amniocentesis. If the Triple Test showed a much lower risk of Down syndrome compared with their age-related risk, then they might refuse amniocentesis and avoid the associated risk of miscarriage. In contrast, younger women would previously have considered themselves to be at low risk for Down syndrome and would not have been offered any tests routinely for it. For these younger women, the offer of the Triple Test would make them consider the possibility of having a baby with Down syndrome. The mean age of participants (at the time of the first interview) was 29 years.

Information

At the time of the study, the usual practice was for women to be given an information leaflet when they first sought medical care at the start of pregnancy and then to be asked for a decision about the Triple Test at their first meeting with the midwife. Therefore, the leaflet was the main source of information. The participants in the study were asked in the first interview, "Have you discussed the test with your midwife or general practitioner?"; 35 out of the 40 had not had an opportunity to do so. They were expecting to have a chance to ask the midwife about the test a few days later at the "booking visit," when they would hand in the consent form.

Previous studies had shown that pregnant women often had very little knowledge about the tests they were given, sometimes not even knowing that they had been given a particular test (Marteau, Johnston, Plenicar, Shaw, & Slack, 1988; Statham & Green, 1993). In order to find out whether the participants in this study were well informed about basic aspects of the Triple Test, they were asked the following questions:

> "What can you remember about when and how the test is done?" (from the 16th week of pregnancy [1 point]; it is a blood test [1 point])
>
> "What can you remember about what the test is for?" (It tests for Down syndrome [1 point] and spina bifida [1 point])
>
> "What do you think a screen positive result means?" (greater/ raised risk of either spina bifida or Down syndrome [1 point])
>
> "What do you think a screen negative result means?" (low risk of spina bifida and Down syndrome [1 point])

The answers were scored by two independent markers, with 1 point given for each complete and correct answer (as shown). There was a maximum possible score of 6 points. The mean score of the women in the study was 5.2 points. Some aspects of the test were remembered better than others. All the women said that the test screened for Down syndrome, and 38 out of the 40 said that it screened for spina bifida. The timing of the test was not remembered so well, with only 27 out of the 40 giving the correct answer. All but one patient correctly said that it was a blood test. Thirty-eight of the women correctly said that a screen positive result meant that they were in the group at greater risk, but only 31 said that a screen negative result indicated a low risk. The others said that screen negative result meant either that there was no risk of the baby having either Down syndrome or spina bifida or that the baby was definitely healthy.

The information leaflet from the hospital gave probability information for some of the possible outcomes. For example, it gave figures for the risk of having a baby with Down syndrome or spina bifida. There was a short description of the common problems associated with each of the conditions being tested for and of the additional tests that would be offered if the test result was screen positive. The risk of miscarriage caused by amniocentesis was given in the leaflet as "about 1 in every 100" and was also referred to as "a very slight risk."

The leaflet stated that approximately 1 in 20 women would get a screen positive result. It gave some information about the accuracy (sensitivity and specificity) of the test. It explained the level of sensitivity as follows: "The test cannot predict all cases of Down syndrome or severe spina bifida. No test can do this. . . . It does help to detect two out of three cases of Down syndrome and four out of five cases of severe spina bifida." The specificity was described in the following way: "Over 90% of women with this screen positive result will have a normal healthy baby."

The cutoff level for a screen positive result was a revised risk of 1 in 250 or greater, but this figure was not mentioned in the leaflet. It simply said that women with a screen positive result were in the group with a "greater risk." Marteau, Plenicar, and Kidd (1993) criticized the inaccuracy of such terms, and described how the risk of Down syndrome was referred to as "high risk" and the risk of miscarriage following amniocentesis was referred to as "low risk" in circumstances in which the probability of each was actually the same.

The leaflet appeared to have been written on the assumption that the various risks or probabilities would be important to women when deciding about the test. Not all the probability figures that would be needed to calculate the subjective expected utility of accepting or declining the Triple Test were provided, but most were given. For example, the probability of getting a screen positive result was given as 1 in 20, but it would have been different for each of the conditions being tested for, and this might be particularly important to those women who felt that they would act differently in response to a screen positive result for each condition. In order to find out what they believed the various probabilities to be, based on the information in the leaflet, the participants were asked to say what they thought the probabilities were for 13 possible outcomes.

The women significantly overestimated the risk that they were carrying a baby with Down syndrome ($F = 7.337$, $p = .02$). Each woman's approximate age-related risk of Down syndrome was obtained from a published table (Wald, 1984), and this was compared to their own risk estimate. The mean probability was 0.13%, and the mean subjective probability was 2.26%. There was a similar overestimation of the risk of spina bifida. The probability of carrying a baby with spina bifida was 0.25% and the mean subjective probability was 2.77%. The participants overestimated the probability of getting a screen positive result. The probability was 5%, but the mean subjective probability was 22.63% ($F = 16.882$, $p = .002$). The women overestimated the specificity of the test and underestimated its sensitivity. The leaflet stated that over 90% of women with a screen positive result would have a normal, healthy baby, but the mean subjective probability of having a normal baby, given a screen positive result, was 76.95% ($F = 11.884$, $p = .005$). The mean risk of having a Down syndrome baby, given a screen negative result, was 0.03% and the risk of having a baby with spina bifida, given a screen negative result, was 0.05%, but the mean subjective probabilities were 3.04% and 2.97%, respectively. The participants accurately remembered the risk of miscarriage after amniocentesis as 1%.

To try to determine whether the risk information was important to the women in making their decision, the degree of correlation between the risks and their rating about having the test was calculated. None of the risks, either subjective or documented, predicted the women's ratings about having the Triple Test. For example, the correlation between the subjective risk of carrying a baby with Down syndrome and the rating about having the test was 0.1970, and the correlation between the subjective risk of carrying a baby with spina bifida and the rating about having the test was 0.0895. This contrasts with findings by Marteau et al. (1991), which showed that the perceived risk of abnormality (but not the objective probability) may be particularly important in predicting decisions about testing. A number of the women in this study commented that they could not remember the risk information very well but that they did not think the figures were at all important to them.

Reasons for Accepting or Declining the Triple Test

One of the first questions asked in the interview was what the participant planned to do regarding the Triple Test. They were asked to indicate the point on a rating scale that best represented how they felt.

At the moment how do you feel about having the Triple Test?

(Please mark the point on the line that best represents your feelings)

I have decided not to have it.	I probably won't have it, but I might.	I am really not sure what I'll do.	I probably will have it, but I might not.	I have decided to have it.

This showed that 18 of the women had decided to have the test, 2 had decided not to have it, and the other 20 were undecided. When they made a final decision about the test, 34 accepted it and 6 declined it.

After giving their rating on the scale, the women were asked for their reasons and were allowed talk about them as long as they wished. All the women offered at least one reason for their decision to accept or decline the test (or for their indecision about it), giving a total of 55 reasons. Some of the reasons were given by more than one person, so the number of women giving a particular reason is given in parentheses.

The following reasons were given by participants to explain why they were probably or definitely going to accept the Triple Test:

> "For peace of mind" (7)
> "It's a harmless blood test, there's no reason not to" (7)
> "To be able to have a termination if something is wrong" (6)
> "To be prepared for the birth of a handicapped child" (6)
> "I want as much information as possible" (5)
> "It will give us an option if things are wrong" (5)
> "Simply because it is there" (2)
> "For research purposes – for the benefit of the medical profession" (1)
> "The doctors and midwives seem to advise having it" (1)
> "Because it's for your benefit" (1)
> "Because it's free" (1)

These reasons were given by women who felt they would either probably or definitely decline the Triple Test:

> "There is no point, as I wouldn't have a termination" (2)
> "I don't want the worry of it all. I'd rather have a happy pregnancy" (2)

> "I would rather not know than be faced with choosing whether to have a termination at 24 weeks" (2)
>
> "I just don't want it" (1)
>
> "I might be forced into a decision that I'm not happy about making" (1)
>
> "I am not sure I want to sit around for three weeks waiting for an amnio result and then not be able to make up my mind" (1)

Some women were completely undecided about the test at the time of the interview, and they gave the following reasons for being uncertain:

> "It seems so unreliable, with no clear-cut answers" (1)
>
> "The medical culture seems to push people toward accepting treatment. You perceive it as treatment or something that you should really go through and do" (1)
>
> "I wouldn't know whether or not to have an abortion. I wouldn't want an abortion *or* a handicapped child" (1)
>
> "The tests wouldn't show how severe the handicap would be" (1)

The reasons that women gave for their intention to accept the test were sometimes the same as the ones given by other women for making the opposite decision. For example, some women intended to have the test because they would then have a choice about termination, whereas others intended to decline it in order to avoid being faced with that choice. Some felt that because they would not have a termination there was no point in having the test, but others felt that they wanted the test because they were certain that they would not have a termination but would need to have time to prepare for the baby. One woman saw the fact that the test was being promoted by doctors and midwives as a reason to have it, whereas another woman gave that as a reason for her uncertainty about it. One woman was going to decline the test to avoid worry and have a happy pregnancy, but seven others were intending to accept the test for the same reason, to be reassured and not worry. Farrant (1985) described the desire for reassurance as a strong motivating factor for pregnant women to accept prenatal tests and contrasted this with the obstetricians' reason for encouraging testing: the detection of abnormality. In this study, seven women said they were having the test for reassurance, but a large number of the participants also intended to have the test in order to be able to detect abnormality and to have a choice about termination.

Several participants mentioned the later decisions as being very important, and there was a significant correlation between women's ratings about having the Triple Test and their ratings about having amniocentesis ($r = 0.5991$, $p = .002$). There was also a correlation between ratings about having the Triple Test and ratings about choosing termination ($r = 0.4893$, $p = .015$). Most of the women who intended to have the Triple Test also intended to have amniocentesis if they got a screen positive result, and slightly fewer intended to terminate their pregnancy if Down syndrome or spina bifida was diagnosed.

Prediction of Future Preferences

Many of the women based their decision to accept or decline the Triple Test on their intended decisions about later tests and termination. Anecdotal evidence from the local hospital suggested that women were not always able to predict their future preferences about termination. Women who had felt certain that they would not choose termination if tests revealed that their baby would be handicapped decided to terminate the pregnancy when they were actually given that information. A study of attitudes toward prenatal testing in a group of people at high risk for Huntington's disease also showed a difference between hypothetical decisions and actual behavior (Adam et al., 1993). Forty-three percent said they would have tests if they were pregnant, but only 18% actually did. The extent to which the women in this study were able to predict their future preferences about further tests was examined. In a sample of this size, it was not possible to determine whether the participants actually did what they had planned to do when faced with a "screen positive" result because only 2 of the 40 women got a screen positive result. However, the longitudinal aspect of the study enabled a comparison of how women felt about possible later decisions at different stages of pregnancy. This showed that most women consistently expressed an intention to have an ultrasound scan in the event of a screen positive result for spina bifida but that many of the women felt less certain about having amniocentesis and termination of pregnancy when they were asked about these decisions later in their pregnancy compared with their feelings at the first interview. Several said that they had not initially realized that the pregnancy would be so far advanced by the time the definite diagnosis and possible termination would take place. This showed that it was difficult for many of the participants in the study to predict, when deciding whether or not to have the Triple Test, how they might feel later about subsequent decisions. It is not clear whether any of their ratings about hypothetical choices accurately indicated what they would have chosen if faced with the real decisions, but the fact that these ratings changed over time suggests that pregnant women find it very difficult to predict their future feelings about such decisions.

Decision Difficulty

On the face of it, the decision on whether or not to have the Triple Test is a simple one. A venous blood sample is taken from the pregnant woman in the usual way, normally at the same time as blood would be taken for other routine tests. Therefore, information about the health of the baby can be gained at very little inconvenience to the mother and at no risk to the pregnancy. Anecdotal evidence suggested that many women found the decision to be a difficult one. To examine this issue, the participants in the study were asked to mark the point on a rating scale that they felt best represented how easy or difficult they found the decision. Twenty-seven of the women rated the decision as easy, 2 rated it as not easy or difficult, and 11 rated it as difficult.

Decision Aversion

People have been shown to dislike having to make certain kinds of decisions, preferring to arrive at the same outcomes without having to decide. The study by Beattie et al. (1994) showed that people do not like having to consider certain kinds of choices. They would rather not know what they would do. The decision on whether to have amniocentesis, which might itself harm the fetus and which might yield a positive result, leading to a choice between terminating the pregnancy or raising a handicapped child, was hypothesized to be one that many pregnant women would dislike. If women felt that in order to decide whether to have the Triple Test they needed to decide whether to have further tests and possibly a pregnancy termination, then this may have led to decision aversion regarding the initial screening test.

Some women spontaneously mentioned not wanting to have to make decisions about later tests as their reason for rejecting the Triple Test when asked at the start of the interview. A number of further questions were asked in order to discover whether this possibility of future decision making influenced their feelings about the Triple Test. The participants were asked to indicate which of the three following statements most closely reflected their feelings:

- The fact that it could lead to an additional decision about amniocentesis is something that I like about the Triple Test.
- The fact that it could lead to an additional decision about amniocentesis does not affect my feelings about the Triple Test one way or the other.
- The fact that it could lead to an additional decision about amniocentesis is something that I dislike about the Triple Test.

A similar set of three statements asking about ultrasound was presented, as well as a set of statements about termination. "The fact that it could lead to an additional decision about amniocentesis is something that I dislike about the Triple Test" was chosen by 28% of the women. One explained her dislike of it as follows:

"Because of leading you into something where you could lose your baby and it might be absolutely fine all the time. But then it would feel like such a gamble to just ignore it and you'd worry all the way through if you didn't have the test, the amnio I mean."

Another said:

"Because I didn't want to have to make a decision . . . it was to do with having to think about it so much and make a decision on something."

When the same options were presented but were related to a decision about termination, 35% chose the "dislike" option. One woman said:

"I hate the thought of being in this dilemma. The thought of that decision just makes me feel sick."

Another said:

"I suppose I dislike it because I dislike the thought of making a decision like that."

None of the participants said that they disliked the Triple Test because it could lead to a decision about ultrasound. They were not worried about making a decision about ultrasound because it would not harm the baby in any way.

Two people independently scored the transcripts of the interviews for the number of certain types of comments contained in them. Twenty-five out of the 40 women made one or more comments showing decision aversion. These comments supported the idea that some of the women were upset by the prospect of the decisions to which the Triple Test decision might lead.

Regret

When people look back on decisions they have made, there is often an element of regret in their evaluation. One knows the outcome of the chosen option and can sometimes know what an alternative choice would have brought about. When the chosen option results in a worse outcome than the unchosen option, regret may be felt, and when the chosen option produces a better result, the opposite feeling of elation may be experienced. It has been proposed (Bell, 1982; Fishburn, 1982; Loomes & Sugden, 1982; Sugden, 1985) that these feelings not only play a part in the evaluation of decisions already made, but also that anticipation of regret can play an important part in the decision-making process itself. Tymstra (1989) proposed that anticipated decision regret could be an important influence in decision making about medical testing. People would make a particular choice partly in order to avoid regret in the future due to not having made that choice. The Triple Test decision could lead to outcomes that might later cause women to regret their decision, and the anticipation of such regret might be a powerful motivating factor.

Conflict may arise because both a decision to accept the test and a decision to decline it could potentially lead to regret. If a woman declined testing and then gave birth to a severely handicapped baby, she would know that she could have chosen to find out about the handicap during the pregnancy and could have chosen termination. She may imagine this scenario when she is deciding whether to have the test and may imagine regretting her decision to decline the test if this was the outcome. Similarly, if a woman took the screening test and had a screen positive result (suggesting a high risk of Down syndrome) leading to an amniocentesis test that caused her to miscarry a healthy baby, she would be aware that if she had not chosen to have the tests, she would probably have given birth to a healthy baby. When deciding whether to have the Triple Test, she may anticipate the regret she would feel if events unfolded in this way. It was hypothesized that those women who could vividly imagine not only situations in which they would regret accepting the test, but also situations in which they would regret declining it, would experience considerable conflict over the decision.

To examine the influence of regret, we specifically asked, "Can you imagine at any point in the testing program regretting any of the choices you had made and wishing that you had made a different choice? How?" The number of comments showing regret, both in response to this question and at other points in the interview, were counted to produce *regret scores* for the participants. Twenty-eight out of the 40 participants mentioned at least one situation in which they could imagine regretting their decision. The number of times that women mentioned anticipated regret varied from no mention at all (by 12 of the participants) to 11 comments from 1 woman. There were 18 comments about regretting a decision not to have the test. Most women were anticipating regret if they then had a handicapped baby, but some also imagined regretting missing out on the reassurance that the test would probably have given them, for example:

"It would have been hard not knowing, for all those months, after the leaflet has sort of got you thinking about possible handicaps right from the start of your pregnancy."

There were 17 regret comments about having the Triple Test, 7 simply saying that the women might feel they had made the wrong choice afterward and 10 saying that they would regret having the test if they got a screen positive result. Some felt that the worry involved in having amniocentesis and waiting for the result would cause them to regret having the Triple Test, and some felt that the fact that it would require more decisions would make them regret having the test. One woman said:

"I understand that you don't have to go forward for the amniocentesis and that you can, you know, not. But I think it would obviously be worrying to know that you are positive, and it would leave you with a nagging feeling that you should go and find out."

Twenty-nine comments were made about regret following an amniocentesis test that caused a miscarriage. Most women felt they would regret this if the baby would have been healthy, and some felt that they would regret having the amniocentesis if it caused a miscarriage, regardless of the health of the baby. Anticipated regret about termination of pregnancy was mentioned in 36 comments. Five comments were made about anticipated regret if the tests did not detect a handicap.

Regret does appear to have been an important motivating force for many of the women in the study, and it was the source of decision difficulty particularly in those who could imagine regretting both accepting and declining the Triple Test. Many women explained their feelings about the Triple Test in terms of anticipated regret. The number of comments made by each woman showing anticipated regret was significantly correlated with their ratings about how difficult they found the Triple Test decision ($r = 0.5056$, $p = .001$) and with their state anxiety score at the initial interview ($r = 0.4361$, $p = .020$).

Omission Bias

The issue of bias against taking actions that could lead to harm rather than omissions that could lead to the same outcome was also examined. It was thought that if women felt that they were making the routine or expected choice about testing, they would feel less responsible and would anticipate less regret and guilt if it turned out badly than if they felt they were going against the norm. Therefore, if they felt that they were expected to have the test as a matter of routine, then they might feel more anxious about declining the test than they would if the test was not routinely offered but was available to women who particularly asked to have it. The effect of presenting the test in these alternative ways could not be directly compared because all women in the local area were being offered the test in the same way, but women were asked how they would have preferred the test to be presented to them and were asked to give reasons for their preferences.

The decision on whether or not to have the Triple Test was presented as a straightforward choice: "yes" or "no." The women were given the following instructions on the form: "Please [check] the box below and sign your name once you have decided whether or not you want the blood test. There were two boxes respectively labeled "No, thank you" and "Yes, please." To find out whether the women in the study perceived the presentation of the test in this way, they were asked to indicate one of the following options to show how the test had been described to them:

- I have to have the test.
- I will get the test unless I say I don't want it.
- I just have a choice (by [checking] "yes" or "no").
- I will not get the test unless I ask for it.
- I can't have the test even if I want it.
- I'm not sure.

Most of the women (36 out of 40) chose "I just have a choice (by [checking] either 'yes' or 'no'), but 3 chose "I will get the test unless I say I don't want it" and 1 chose "I will not have the test unless I ask for it." Some women commented that although they were given a free choice, they still felt that they were expected to have the test. One woman who declined the test said that she had been asked to explain why she didn't want it and was called "a silly girl" for declining it.

To see whether the participants welcomed the decision about the test being presented as a straight choice, they were asked to say which of the following was the way they would have liked the Triple Test to have been presented to themselves out of the following options:

- To have been given the Triple Test without being told about it unless further tests were needed.
- To have been given the Triple Test and to know it.
- To have been given the Triple Test unless I said I didn't want it.
- To have just been given a choice about the Triple Test: (e.g., by [checking] either "yes" or "no").
- Not to have been given the Triple Test unless I said I wanted it.
- Not to have been offered the Triple Test, but to have been offered amniocentesis.
- For the Triple Test not to have been available at all.

The presentation "To have just been given a choice about the Triple Test (e.g., by [checking] 'yes' or 'no')" was chosen by 25 out of the 40 women. The women who wanted this presentation all said that they wanted to be able to make the choice themselves. Some acknowledged that having the choice might be difficult, but they still would rather have it. For example, two women gave these reasons for liking that presentation:

"Because then it is completely your choice. Some of the others, they sort of do it and not tell you they are doing it or just to be given it regardless, and I think some people would rather not know and would just rather put it to the back of their minds and not have to worry about it. But no, I think it is better to be given the choice, definitely."

"Because I believe it is a choice and a lot of the other ones take the choice away from you, and I would rather have the choice at the end of the day, even though it is harder."

Fifteen of the women would have preferred a less straightforward choice for themselves because it would have saved them the necessity of deciding. These were the women who had rated the decision as difficult or as "not easy or difficult." All of them would have liked to have avoided the worry that they felt the decision had caused them. The following reasons were offered by women who would rather have just been given the test:

"Because then you don't have any decisions to make . . . it is just a little blood test and you haven't got any decisions to make."

"You wouldn't need to think about it unless something was wrong . . . if I hadn't been given that leaflet, I wouldn't even be considering having a Down's or a spina bifida child because I would just think, well, it's not going to happen to me. So if it had just been done on me, that would have been fine."

"Because . . . it would save you from having to make a decision until . . . until it was much more likely . . . that you really had to choose to do something at that stage."

"I suppose it's because having a baby is a bit worrying, anyway, because you keep wondering about it, and it would just be less to worry about because you might not even ever have a problem."

All the participants were then asked which was the best way to decide who gets the test, choosing from among these options:

- For everyone to be given the Triple Test without being told about it unless further tests were needed.
- For everyone to be given the Triple Test and to know it.
- For everyone to get the Triple Test unless they say they don't want it.
- For everyone just to have a choice about the Triple Test: (e.g., by [checking] either "yes" or "no").
- For no one to get the Triple Test unless they ask for it.
- For no one to be offered the Triple Test, but all women to be offered amniocentesis.
- For no one to be offered the Triple Test, but all women to be offered ultrasound.
- For no one to be offered the Triple Test, but all women over 36 to be offered amniocentesis.
- For the Triple Test not to be available at all.

Thirty-one of the women chose the maximum-choice option for everyone. Therefore, some of the women who wanted to have less choice and responsibility themselves still felt that everyone else should have a free choice. This was a typical explanation:

"Simply because it's a personal view about what I'm prepared to do or not, and I don't feel I have any right to, I mean, I have a strong view that other people should be given the choice to do what they want."

Conclusions

For many of the women in the study, anticipated regret was an important influence on their decision about accepting or declining the Triple Test. Some would have preferred not to have had to decide about the test because they found the decision difficult and worrying. These women were made to face choices and possible outcomes that they would rather have not had to consider. The preference of some of the women to have been given the test without being told about it clearly suggests that decision aversion and omission bias were influential. The comments about anticipated regret suggest that this was a source of concern for a great many of them.

References

Adam, S., Wiggins, S., Whyte, P., Block, M., Shokeir, M. H. K., Soltan, H., Meschino, W., Summers, A., Suchowersky, O., Welch, J. P., Huggins, M. H., Theilmann, J., & Hayden, M. R. (1993). Five year study of prenatal testing for Huntington's disease: Demand, attitudes and psychological assessment. *Journal of Medical Genetics, 30*, 549–556.

Beattie, J., Baron, J., Hershey, J. C., & Spranca, M. D. (1994). Psychological determinants of decision attitude. *Journal of Behavioral Decision Making, 7*, 129–144.

Bell, D. E. (1982). Regret in decision making under uncertainty. *Operations Research, 30*, 961–981.

Cuckle, H. S. (1993). *Antenatal screening.* London: Department of Environmental and Preventive Medicine, St Bartholomew's Hospital Medical College.

Farrant, W. (1985). "Who's for amniocentesis?" The politics of prenatal screening. In H. Homans (ed.), *The Sexual Politics of Reproduction.* London: Gower.

Fishburn, P. C. (1982). Nontransitive measurable utility. *Journal of Mathematical Psychology, 26*, 31–67.

Johnson, E. J., Hershey, J. C., Mesaros, J., & Kunreuther, H. (1993). Framing, probability distortions, and insurance decisions. *Journal of Risk and Uncertainty, 7*, 35–51.

Kahneman, D., & Tversky, A. (1982). The psychology of preferences. *Scientific American, 246*, 160–173.

Loomes, G., & Sugden, R. (1982). Regret theory: An alternative theory of rational choice under uncertainty. *Economic Journal, 92*, 805–824.

Marteau, T. M., Johnston, M., Plenicar, M., Shaw, R. W., & Slack, J. (1988). Development of a self-administered questionnaire to measure women's knowledge of prenatal screening and diagnostic tests. *Journal of Psychosomatic Research, 32,* 403–408

Marteau, T. M., Kidd, J., Cook, R., Michie, S., Johnston, M., Slack, J., & Shaw, R. W. (1991). Perceived risk not actual risk predicts uptake of amniocentesis. *British Journal of Obstetrics and Gynaecology, 98,* 282–286.

Marteau, T. M., Plenicar, M., & Kidd, J. (1993). Obstetricians presenting amniocentesis to pregnant women: Practice observed. *Journal of Reproductive and Infant Psychology, 11,* 3–10.

Meszaros, J. R., Asch, D. A., Baron, J., Hershey, J. C., Kunreuther, H., & Schwartz-Buzaglo, J. (1996). Cognitive processes and the decisions of some parents to forego pertussis vaccination for their children. *Journal of Clinical Epidemiology, 49,* 697–703.

Ritov, I., & Baron, J. (1990). Reluctance to vaccinate: Omission bias and ambiguity. *Journal of Behavioral Decision Making, 3,* 263–277.

Ritov, I., & Baron, J. (1995). Outcome knowledge, regret, and omission bias. *Organizational Behavior and Human Decision Processes, 64,* 119–127.

Schweitzer, M. (1994). Disentangling status quo and omission effects: Experimental evidence. *Organizational Behavior and Human Decision Processes, 58,* 457–476.

Spranca, M., Minsk, E., & Baron, J. (1991). Omission and commission in judgment and choice. *Journal of Experimental Social Psychology, 27,* 76–105.

Statham, H. & Green, J., (1993). Serum screening for Down's syndrome: Some women's experiences. *British Medical Journal, 307,* 174–176.

Sugden, R. (1985). Regret, recrimination and rationality. *Theory and Decision, 19,* 77–99.

Tymstra, T. (1989). The imperative character of medical technology and the meaning of anticipated decision regret. *International Journal of Technology Assessment in Health Care, 5,* 207–213.

Wald, N. J. (ed.). (1984). *Antenatal and Neonatal Screening.* Oxford: Oxford University Press.

Wald, N. J., Cuckle, H. S., Densem, J. W., Nanchahal, K., Royston, P., Chard, T., Haddow, J. E., Knight, G. J., Palomaki, G. E., & Canick, J. A. (1988). Maternal serum screening for Down's syndrome in early pregnancy. *British Medical Journal, 297,* 883–887.

Wald, N. J., Kennard, A., Densem, J. W., Cuckle, H. S., Chard, T., & Butler, L. (1992). Antenatal maternal serum screening for Down's syndrome: Results of a demonstration project. *British Medical Journal, 305,* 391–394.

Wenstrom, K. D., Williamson, R. A., Grant, S. S., Hudson, J. D., & Getchell, J. P. (1993). Evaluation of multiple-marker screening for Down's syndrome in a statewide population. *American Journal of Obstetrics and Gynecology, 159,* 793–797.

8 Talk About Tradeoffs: Judgments of Relative Importance and Contingent Decision Behavior

William M. Goldstein, Sema Barlas, and Jane Beattie

Life is full of choices, and choices are full of tradeoffs. Hardly ever is one lucky enough to find an alternative that is superior in every way to other alternatives. Almost always, a course of action that has an advantage in some sense also has a disadvantage in some other sense. As a result, people have developed ways of thinking about and discussing the senses in which choice alternatives can vary. Alternatives are said to possess different features or to vary along different attributes. Moreover, two salient facts are as apparent to decision makers as they are to decision researchers. First, it is obvious that not all differences between choice alternatives are equally deserving of attention and concern. Some differences hardly make a difference, whereas others are extremely important and deserve to be influential in choices between alternatives. Second, it is clear that people often disagree about which attributes are the relatively important ones. Consequently, discussions about "relative importance" and "priorities" are common. Relative importance judgments are made spontaneously in ordinary conversation, and the ordering of priorities is often central in policy statements by groups and organizations.

It would be of enormous practical value if people's preferences could be inferred easily from their statements of relative importance. Such statements are frequently made when people, as principals, must delegate decision-making responsibility to others, to agents who will act on the principals' behalf and try to decide as the principals would prefer.

This research was supported by National Science Foundation Grant SES 89-22156 to William M. Goldstein and Jane Beattie. The experiments reported in this chapter were planned and conducted in collaboration with Jane, and it is therefore appropriate for her to be included as a coauthor. That Jane died in the midst of several ongoing collaborative research projects underscores the tragedy of her young death and the magnitude of our collective loss.

However, it is not established that relative importance statements do or even can communicate this information. A better understanding of relative importance judgments would shed light on this issue and may facilitate clear communication between principals and agents.[1] There is also potential for practical benefit in the area of negotiations. Parties in negotiation have special opportunities to resolve their differences in a mutually satisfying way when they disagree about the relative importance of the issues to be settled. Specifically, each party can concede something on an issue he or she considers to be relatively unimportant and receive a concession on an important issue. The magnitudes of appropriate concessions, however, depend on the degree of importance and the relation between importance and preference, and this relation is not well understood.

In addition to its potential practical benefits, the study of relative importance judgments can advance our theoretical understanding of decision making. Judgments of relative importance can provide a window onto the metacognition of decision making, in that people often characterize their own and other people's decision making in these terms. If we understood exactly what information people intended their relative importance judgments to convey, we could assess the correctness of their judgments and thereby assess people's insight into their own decision processes. Moreover, importance judgments seem likely to bear on a largely neglected aspect of decision making, namely, its experiential qualities, such as the conflict and difficulty that decision makers often experience. Finally, it is noteworthy that the concept of relative importance has already found its way into theoretical explanations of certain decision anomalies (Tversky, Sattath, & Slovic, 1988). A fuller understanding of the psychology of relative importance will deepen our understanding of these decision anomalies.

Contingent Decision Behavior and Communication Via Relative Importance Judgments

Two Relationships Between Relative Importance Judgments and Decisions

Imagine a principal who is instructing an agent how to make decisions on the principal's behalf when the set of alternatives cannot be foreseen perfectly. Casual observation suggests, and a pilot study we conducted confirms, that people spontaneously talk about the relative importance of the attributes of the alternatives that might be encountered. How can this information be useful to the agent? In order for agents to infer principals' decisions from their relative importance statements, two things must occur: Principals' relative importance judgments must *encode* the required information, and agents must *decode* the information properly. For encoding to take place, the *actual* correspondence between principals' relative importance judgments and their decisions must be well behaved and systematic. For decoding to take place, agents must have accurate *beliefs* about the correspondence between principals' relative importance judgments and their decisions. In sum, drawing valid inferences from a principal's relative importance judgment requires that there be a coincidence of two potentially distinct relationships between the principal's relative importance judgments and decisions: the actual relation and the relation that the agent believes to obtain. Our research addressed both of these relations, attempting to shed light on the components of principal–agent communication via relative importance judgments.

In the studies to be described, respondents reported their *own* decisions and relative importance judgments. This provided us with the information to study the actual relation between the two. In addition, we asked respondents to draw *inferences* about a hypothetical target person, inferring the target person's relative importance judgments from her decisions. These inferences provided us with the information to study people's beliefs about the relation that obtains between decisions and relative importance judgments. By requiring respondents to consider whether and how they would make use of information that we manipulated, the inference task provided us with a more incisive tool for examining respondents' cognitive processes in interpreting and using relative importance information than we could obtain otherwise.

Interpretations of Relative Importance

The actual relation between decisions and relative importance judgments seems likely to depend on at least two factors. First, there is the insight possessed by the decision maker. To the extent that decision makers are unaware of the factors that affect them, it is hard to see how decision makers could use relative importance judgments (or any other deliberate reports) to encode information that would vary systematically with their preferences. Second, in addition to insight, the relation between decisions and relative importance judgments presumably depends on what the decision maker understands *relative importance* to mean, that is, the decision maker's *interpretation* of this term. In fact, the decision maker's interpretation of relative importance becomes more crucial to the extent that people *do* have insight, for it is especially the insightful decision maker whose relative importance judgment can be relied on to encode whatever it is he or she means by relative importance.

The interpretation of relative importance is also central to an understanding of people's beliefs about the relation between decisions and relative importance judgments. Presumably, it is their interpretation, their understanding of the *meaning* of relative importance, that provides the grounds for people to have beliefs about this relation at all. Although people may understand relative importance to have additional implications beyond the relation between decisions and relative importance judgments, their beliefs about this relation are a fundamental part of their interpretations – the part that is relevant to principal–agent communication.

Putting this together, there are two sources of miscommunication about decision making via relative importance judgments, and the interpretation of relative importance figures heavily in both. First, the principal could be wrong in the sense of lacking insight. That is, the principal's relative importance judgment could fail to reflect his or her own intended interpretation of relative importance. Second, the principal could be misunderstood if the principal and agent have different interpretations of relative importance. Because people's interpretations of relative importance seem basic to an understanding of principal–agent communication, impinging on both the encoding of information and the decoding of information, we chose to emphasize this aspect in our research. The inferences that people drew about the target person reveal people's beliefs about the relation between decisions and relative importance judgments and are a direct reflection of their interpretations. These data, therefore, were central to our analysis. We used these data, in turn, to inform our analysis of the actual relation between decisions and relative importance judgments.

Contingent Decision Behavior and Judgments of Relative Importance

Decision researchers have devoted a good deal of attention in recent years to factors whose manipulation can change people's decisions among a fixed set of alternatives. As a result, there are numerous task and contextual manipulations that are known to affect people's decisions. If people's relative importance judgments summarize their decisions (or their decision-making strategies), such manipulations might affect people's relative importance judgments as well.

Specifically regarding communication via relative importance judgments, two questions arise. First, in addition to their effect on decisions, do such task and contextual manipulations affect principals' relative importance judgments? Second, are agents sufficiently attuned to these effects on principals' decisions (and possibly on principals' relative importance judgments) that the inferences they draw about the principals' behavior shift appropriately? In the studies to be described, we addressed these questions with respect to a particular set of task effects, called the *preference reversal* phenomena, whereby people's reported preference orderings depend on the response mode used to elicit the preferences (e.g., attractiveness ratings, minimum selling prices, paired comparison orderings; see, e.g., Goldstein & Einhorn, 1987; Tversky et al., 1988).

We were particularly interested in a specific way in which the preference-response mode might affect the (actual or inferred) relation between decisions and relative importance judgments. That is, we thought that a shift in response modes (rank orders versus minimum selling prices) might induce a shift in the respondents' interpretation of relative importance. Specifically, we hypothesized that a ranking response mode, because it focuses on the comparative advantages and disadvantages of the stimuli, would encourage the use of a relative sensitivity interpretation. By contrast, we thought that a pricing response mode, because it is a single-stimulus evaluation of overall desirability, would suggest the use of a relative impact interpretation. These particular interpretations of relative importance are elaborated next.

Relative Sensitivity and Relative Impact

In earlier work (Goldstein & Beattie, 1991), we distinguished three categories of interpretation of relative importance, two of which are relevant here: relative sensitivity and relative impact. These categories are not mutually exclusive (see Goldstein & Beattie, 1991, footnote 6), so it may not be possible to determine definitively that people endorse one category and reject the other. Nevertheless, the core ideas underlying the categories are quite different, and we can contrast prototypical members of each category.

Notions of relative sensitivity relate changes in the attribute levels of a stimulus to changes in its desirability. The key idea is that a change in a relatively important attribute produces a greater change in stimulus desirability than a similar change in a relatively unimportant attribute. The prototypical example of a relative sensitivity measure is marginal rate of substitution (MRS). If preferences can be described by a linear model, MRS reduces to ratios of the linear coefficients. By contrast, notions of relative impact are not so focused on stimulus change. Rather, they assess the proportion of a stimulus's desirability that is due to each attribute. Again, when preferences can be described by a linear model, the prototypical example is what Shanteau (1980) calls *impact* and what Anderson and Zalinski (1988) call *part-worth*, that is, the part of the sum that is associated with a particular attribute.

To illustrate the difference between interpretations and to introduce our experimental setting, consider three sets of prizes that might be offered, for example, in a game show. All the prizes consist of vacations at a Florida beach resort, with travel, hotel, and meal expenses covered, but they vary along two attributes: the duration of the vacation and the amount of cash in an expense account available for other expenses. (Respondents were informed that any money left unspent in the expense account would be forfeit at the end of the vacation.) In Set A, the prizes factorially combine durations of 3, 7, 10, and 14 days with cash amounts of $100, $200, $300, and $400, to form 16 prizes in all. (See Figure 8.1) In Set B, the same durations (3, 7, 10, and 14 days) are combined with cash amounts of $600, $700, $800, and $900, and in Set C the same durations are combined with cash amounts of $1,100, $1,200, $1,300, and $1,400. Of course, people would rather have more money than less, and we presume that people would prefer longer vacations to shorter vacations (within this range). The question is how people will view the relative importance of time and money in determining their preferences within each set.

For most people, an increment of $100 increases the desirability of a small monetary gift more than it increases the desirability of a large monetary gift. Therefore, preferences among the prizes of Set C should show less sensitivity to (changes in) the monetary amounts than do preferences among the prizes of the other stimulus sets. If people are interpreting relative importance in terms of relative sensitivity, they should judge the relative importance of the expense account to be smallest in Set C and largest in Set A. On the other hand, consider the overall magnitude of desirability rather than changes in it. It is by virtue of the larger expense accounts that the prizes in Set C are more desirable than

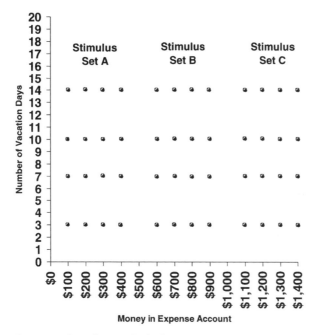

Figure 8.1. Stimulus sets for both experiments (vacation packages).

corresponding prizes in the other sets. That is, the expense accounts in Set C contribute more to the magnitude of desirability of these prizes (absolutely and relative to the durations of the vacations) than the expense accounts in Sets A or B contribute to the desirability of those prizes. Therefore, if people interpret relative importance in terms of relative impact, they should judge the relative importance of the expense account to be largest in Set C and smallest in Set A. In the experiments to be described, we used stimuli of just this type and just this logic to see if people favored one interpretation of relative importance over the other and to see if the preference-response mode affected people's interpretations.

Experiments 1 and 2

Experimental Design

Experiments 1 and 2 were similar in a number of ways. In each experiment, respondents considered Stimulus Sets A, B, and C, composed of vacation packages as described previously and displayed in Figure 8.1. Also, each experiment consisted of three parts. In part 1, respondents received instructions and engaged in practice trials that familiarized them with the stimuli, the response modes, and the tasks. In part 2, respondents considered each stimulus set in turn, first responding according to their own preferences and then dividing 100 points to indicate the relative importance of the expense account and the vacation duration in their own judgment. In part 3, respondents inferred the relative importance judgments of a target person ("Sue") from her preferences among the prizes in the three stimulus sets. Finally, both experiments involved the same pair of preference-response modes: preferential ranking of the vacation packages and the setting of minimum selling prices for each vacation package.

The two experiments differed as follows. In Experiment 1, response mode was a within-subject factor. All respondents used both response modes in giving their own preferences, and they inferred Sue's relative importance judgments from both her ranks and her prices. We constructed prices for Sue so that they would be additive and would exhibit decreasing marginal utility for both duration and money. We determined Sue's preference ranking from the rank ordering of her prices. Thus, these two orderings of the stimuli were the same. That is, the hypothetical Sue did not exhibit any preference reversals between minimum selling price and preferential ranking. Figure 8.2 shows Sue's minimum

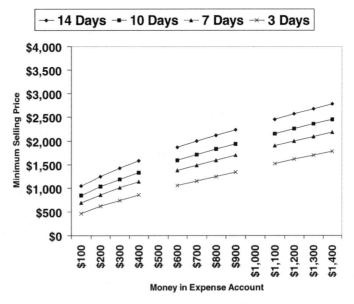

Figure 8.2. Minimum selling prices of hypothetical target person in Experiment 1.

selling prices for the vacation packages in the three stimulus sets. (Of course, respondents were given this information numerically, not graphically, and for only one stimulus set at a time.) The only between-subjects factor for Experiment 1 was the order in which respondents used the two response modes. Thus, to summarize the design of Experiment 1, there were two within-subject factors (Stimulus Set and Response Mode) and one between-subjects factor (Task Order). Twenty respondents were assigned to each task order, for a total of 40 respondents in Experiment 1.

By contrast, in Experiment 2, response mode was a between-subjects factor. Respondents either gave their own preferential ranking and drew inferences from Sue's ranks, or they gave their own prices and drew inferences from Sue's prices. Moreover, we used four different pricing groups, which differed from each other only in the numerical values that they saw for Sue's prices. (Figures showing Sue's prices will appear later.) The rank order of the prices was the same for all groups (and the same as Sue's rank order shown to the ranking group). This manipulation was designed to test whether people would be responsive to the magnitudes of Sue's prices, apart from the rank order of these prices. Twenty or 21 respondents were assigned to each of the five groups in Experiment 2, for a total of 102 respondents.

Results of Experiment 1

Beliefs About the Relation Between Decisions and Relative Importance Judgments. The inferences that respondents drew about Sue's relative importance judgment from her ranking or prices provided us with the information to study people's beliefs about the relation between decisions and relative importance judgments. These beliefs reflect people's interpretations of relative importance, which presumably guide the ways that agents decode principals' statements, as well as the ways that principals encode the information in the first place. Because the interpretation of relative importance is central to both encoding and decoding of relative importance information, we start with this issue.

Do Interpretations of Relative Importance Depend on the Preference-Response Mode? We had hypothesized that the interpretation of relative importance might depend on the response mode of the decisions, with rankings encouraging a relative sensitivity interpretation and minimum selling prices encouraging a relative impact interpretation. To test for this, we had constructed Sue's decisions so that the money in the

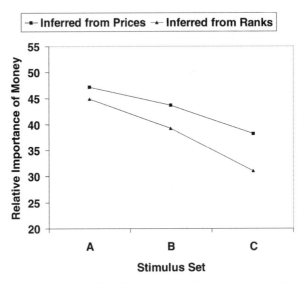

Figure 8.3. Respondents' inferences of relative importance of money displayed separately for each preference-response mode of target person.

expense account was increasing in relative importance from Stimulus Set A to B to C, in the sense of relative impact, and it was decreasing from Stimulus Set A to B to C, in the sense of relative sensitivity. In fact, when respondents inferred Sue's relative importance judgments from her preferences, there was a significant interaction between Response Mode and Stimulus Set ($F(2,76) = 4.87$, $p = .0102$). The form of this interaction, however, gave only a measure of partial support to our hypothesis that the pricing response mode would encourage a relative impact interpretation. (See Figure 8.3.) Specifically, in splitting 100 points between duration and money, the points that respondents assigned to money produced means that decreased more rapidly across the stimulus sets when inferred from Sue's ranks (means of 44.9, 39.3, and 31.1 for Stimulus Sets A, B, and C, respectively) than when inferred from Sue's prices (means of 47.2, 43.7, and 38.2 for A, B, and C, respectively). Although a relative impact interpretation would have produced increasing means across the stimulus sets, the fact that the means decreased more slowly when inferences were drawn from prices suggests that some respondents may have switched interpretations or tried to compromise between interpretations.

In any case, quite apart from our specific hypothesis about the interpretations of relative importance that would be induced by the preference-response modes, the results contradict the response-mode-independent use of *any* interpretation of relative importance that depends only on the preference order. In particular, the results contradict the (response-mode-independent) use of marginal rate of substitution, the most prominent of the relative sensitivity interpretations among decision researchers. This is because Sue's minimum selling prices had the same rank order as her ranks. If respondents were attentive only to the rank order information, the Response Mode factor would show neither main effects nor interaction effects with any other factor. However, in addition to the significant interaction already discussed between Response Mode and Stimulus Set, the main effect of Response Mode was significant ($F(1,38) = 22.56$, $p = .0001$). The mean relative importance of money was 43.0 when inferred from Sue's minimum selling prices compared to a mean of 38.4 when inferred from Sue's ranks.

Resistance to Switching Interpretations. To our surprise, Task Order produced a significant main effect ($F(1,38) = 12.35$, $p = .0012$), with the mean relative importance of money inferred to be higher among respondents who first drew inferences from Sue's prices (mean $= 46.3$) than among respondents who first drew inferences from her ranks (mean $= 35.1$). Moreover, there were marginally significant interactions with Task Order: the two-way interaction between Task Order and Stimulus Set ($F(2,76) = 3.10$, $p = .0507$), and the three-way interactions between Task Order, Stimulus Set, and Response Mode ($F(2,76) = 2.81$, $p = .0666$).

These interactions are consistent with a process in which respondents' interpretations of relative importance are influenced by the response mode they see first, with some subsequent "stickiness" in switching away from the initial interpretation. To see this, consider the two-way interaction. (See Figure 8.4.) Among respondents who first drew inferences from Sue's ranks (which we hypothesized to reinforce the relative sensitivity interpretation, leading to a decrease across the stimulus sets), the mean relative importance of money decreased more rapidly across the stimulus sets (means of 42.1, 35.4, and 27.9) than among respondents who first drew inferences from Sue's prices (means of 50.0, 47.6, and 41.4).

The structure of the three-way interaction has an analogous form. (See Figure 8.5.) Within each Task Order (i.e., comparing the top two curves of Figure 8.5 and comparing the bottom two curves), respondents' inferences from Sue's prices decreased more slowly across the stimulus

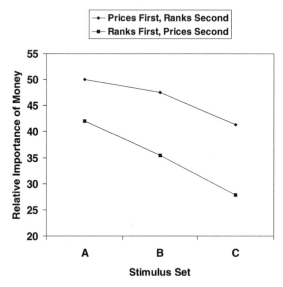

Figure 8.4. Respondents' inferences of relative importance of money displayed separately for each task order.

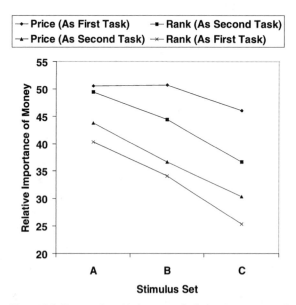

Figure 8.5. Respondents' inferences of relative importance of money displayed separately for each task order and preference-response mode of target person.

sets than their inferences from Sue's ranks.[2] Note, however, that when a task was performed second (i.e., the middle two curves of Figure 8.5), the decrease of the means across the stimulus sets did not match that of the same task when performed first (i.e., the two extreme curves of Figure 8.5). Specifically, the third curve from the top represents respondents' inferences from Sue's prices after inferences were drawn from her ranks. That curve drops 13.4 points, far more than the 4.5-point drop shown by respondents whose first task was to draw inferences from Sue's prices (i.e., the top curve). Apparently, these respondents were still largely under the influence of their first task (i.e., the bottom curve, where the drop is 15.0 points). Similarly, the second curve from the top represents respondents' inferences from Sue's ranks after inferences were drawn from her prices. That curve drops 12.7 points, not quite enough to match the 15-point drop exhibited by respondents whose first task was to draw inferences from Sue's ranks (i.e., the bottom curve). Apparently, these respondents were still somewhat under the influence of their first task (i.e., the top curve, where the drop is only 4.5 points). Thus, the interaction is consistent with a sort of primacy effect, and evidently there is greater "stickiness" in shifting from ranks to prices than in shifting from prices to ranks.

Actual Relation Between Decisions and Relative Importance Judgments. With the respondents' own preferences and relative importance judgments, we can study the relation that actually obtains between these variables and, in particular, whether and how information about one's preferences is encoded into one's relative importance judgments. In this section, we address the following questions: (1) Is the actual relation between decisions and relative importance judgments well behaved and systematic? (2) Does the response mode with which preferences are reported affect the relative importance judgments as well as the preferences themselves? (3) Do the response modes affect the interpretation of relative importance?

Is the Relation Well Behaved and Systematic? To address this question, we needed an objective characterization of respondents' preference orders that could be compared to their subjective relative importance judgments. To obtain an objective index of the relative importance of the stimulus attributes, we computed rank-order correlations between respondents' preferences and the stimulus attributes (expense account value and duration of vacation).[3] These correlations were computed

Table 8.1. *Correlations Between Objective Measures of Importance and Subjective Judgments of Relative Importance*

Response Mode	Stimulus Set A	Stimulus Set B	Stimulus Set C
Preferential ranking	.82	.75	.74
Minimum selling price	.59	.57	.64

separately for each respondent, stimulus set, and response mode (i.e., minimum selling price and preferential ranking). (Hereafter, we refer to these correlations as the *objective measures*.) Next, we compared these objective measures to the respondents' relative importance judgments. Separately for each stimulus set and response mode, we computed the correlation (across respondents) between the objective measure and the judged relative importance of the expense account. The means of these correlations are shown in Table 8.1.

As shown by the generally high values of the correlations, especially for the ranking response mode, the respondents were able to encode information into their relative importance judgments that is indicative of the way their preferences differed from those of their peers. We suspect that the generally higher values found for the ranking response mode are due to three facts. First, our objective measure captures only one sense of relative importance, namely, relative sensitivity; moreover, it does so in a way that is sensitive only to the preference order. Second, the evidence reviewed earlier contradicts the response-mode-independent use of any interpretation of relative importance that depends only on the preference order. Third, as reviewed earlier, we found partial support for our hypothesis that rankings induce respondents to interpret relative importance as relative sensitivity and prices induce them to interpret it as relative impact. In sum, we suspect that our objective measures happened to correspond more closely to what respondents *meant* by relative importance when they were ranking than when they were pricing the stimuli. In any case, the generally high correlations show that respondents' relative importance judgments encoded a remarkable amount of information concerning individual differences. The relation between preferences and relative importance judgments does indeed appear to be well behaved and systematic.

Does the Preference-Response Mode Affect the Relative Importance Judgments as Well as the Preferences Themselves? From previous research on preference reversal phenomena, we expected that the ranking and pricing tasks would elicit different preferences, and in fact they did. One way to see this is to compare the means of our objective measures across the two response modes. The mean rank order correlations between respondents' preferential ranks and the stimulus attributes were .474 and .574 for expense account value and vacation duration, respectively. The mean rank order correlations between respondents' prices and the stimulus attributes were .404 and .721 for expense account value and vacation duration, respectively. The differential relative importance of the two attributes (expense account and vacation duration) under the two response modes (ranking and pricing) produced a significant interaction between the Attribute and Response Mode factors in a repeated-measures analysis of variance of the Fisher-Z transformed correlations ($F(1, 36) = 4.77$, $p = .0355$). Thus, respondents evaluated the same vacation packages somewhat differently under the two response modes, placing more relative emphasis on vacation duration in the pricing task than in the ranking task. Put another way, tradeoffs between shorter-but-richer and longer-but-poorer vacations tended to favor the longer-but-poorer vacations more often in the pricing task than in the ranking task.

To examine the response mode effect more directly, we considered pairs of vacations that were ordered differently under the two response modes. For such pairs, either the pricing task favors the longer-but-poorer vacation whereas the ranking task favors the shorter-but-richer vacation, producing a preference reversal in one direction, or the other situation occurs, producing a preference reversal in the opposite direction. We classified each respondent as to whether he or she had a predominant direction of reversal, producing reversals more often in one direction than in the other. As shown in Table 8.2, for each stimulus set, the modal respondent was one whose predominant direction of reversal was to favor longer-but-poorer vacations in pricing and to favor shorter-but-richer vacations in ranking. Moreover, for Stimulus Sets A and B, the modal respondent was significantly more frequent than respondents who reversed predominantly in the opposite direction (loglinear analysis yields $z = 2.54$, $p < .01$ for Stimulus Set A; $z = 1.94$, $p < .05$ for Stimulus Set B; and $z = .189$, $p < .84$ for Stimulus Set C).

The finding that response mode affects preferences is not new. (However, we were surprised by the predominant pattern of the reversals we observed. We will elaborate this point in the General Discussion

Table 8.2. *Number of Subjects Exhibiting Preference Reversals Predominantly in One Direction*

Predominant Direction of Reversal	Stimulus Set A	Stimulus Set B	Stimulus Set C
Pricing favors longer but poorer, and ranking favors shorter but richer	23	17	14
Ranking favors longer but poorer, and pricing favors shorter but richer	8	7	13
Both directions are equally frequent	9	16	13
Total (number of subjects)	40	40	40

section.) The question that is new is whether respondents' relative importance judgments are correspondingly sensitive to the response mode by which the preferences are expressed. To assess this, we subjected the relative importance judgments to a repeated-measures analysis of variance with three factors (Task Order, Stimulus Set, and Response Mode). (The means are shown in Figure 8.6.) We found only one

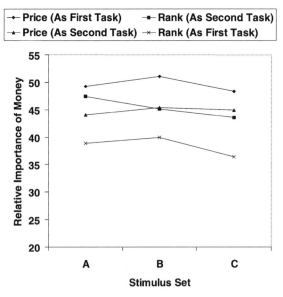

Figure 8.6. Respondents' own judgments of relative importance of money displayed separately for each task order and preference-response mode.

significant effect. There was a significant main effect of Response Mode ($F(1,38) = 5.35$, $p = .0263$), with the mean relative importance of the expense account judged to be 41.9 in the ranking task and 47.1 in the pricing task. At some level, it is encouraging that respondents' relative importance judgments were sensitive to a task manipulation that affected their preferences. However, the relative importance judgments appear to have shifted in the *wrong direction* if we compare them to our objective measures. Respondents judged the relative importance of the expense account to be greater in the pricing task, where, in fact, their preferences more often favored the longer-but-poorer vacations. Although this result appears to indicate a profound lack of insight on the part of the respondents, we maintain that a proper evaluation of the result depends on whether respondents had the same interpretation of relative importance under the two response modes. We will return to this issue in the General Discussion section.

Do the Preference-Response Modes Affect the Interpretation of Relative Importance? We addressed this question earlier by examining respondents' inferences from a hypothetical target person's ranks and prices for the vacation packages. That analysis indicated that respondents could not be using (exclusively and consistently) any interpretation of relative importance that depends only on the preference order. We also found partial support for our hypothesis that the ranking task elicits a relative sensitivity interpretation of importance, whereas the pricing task elicits a relative impact interpretation. Although respondents' inferences from the target person's preferences provide our primary data for considering whether preference-response modes affect the interpretation of importance, we also examined this issue in the context of the respondents' own preferences and relative importance judgments.

One indication that the relationship between respondents' preferences and relative importance judgments may depend on the preference-response mode appeared in the earlier analyses of the correlations between our objective measures and the relative importance judgments. (See Table 8.1.) There we found that the relative importance judgment correlated well with the objective measure for the preferential ranking task but somewhat less well for the pricing task. Because our objective measure is in fact a relative sensitivity measure of importance, this result suggests that respondents may have interpreted relative importance in a manner more akin to relative sensitivity in the ranking task than in the pricing task, and we now pursue this possibility.

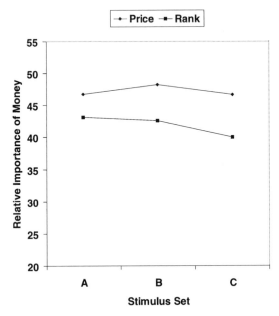

Figure 8.7. Respondents' own judgments of relative importance of money displayed separately for each preference-response mode.

Unlike the preferences that we constructed for the hypothetical Sue, we could not guarantee in advance that respondents would provide ranks and prices whose relative sensitivity to the money in the expense account decreased from Stimulus Set A to B to C, whereas the relative impact of the expense account increased from Stimulus Set A to B to C. If respondents' ranks and prices did have this property, then relative importance judgments that switched from monotonically decreasing across the stimulus sets to monotonically increasing would indicate a switch in interpretation from relative sensitivity to relative impact.

We will spare readers the details of verifying that respondents' preferences did have the desired property because an examination of their relative importance judgments showed no significant change in pattern across the stimulus sets. (See Figure 8.7.) The monotonically decreasing means in the ranking task suggest the relative sensitivity interpretation of relative importance, whereas the nonmonotonic means of the pricing task do not. However, the interaction between Stimulus Set and Response Mode was not significant ($F(2,76) = 1.30$, $p = .2773$). In fact, as mentioned earlier, a repeated-measures analysis of variance of the three factors (Task Order, Stimulus Set, and Response Mode) revealed only one significant effect: a significant main effect of Response Mode. Although this finding may appear to conflict with our earlier analyses of respondents' inferences about Sue, we should emphasize an important difference between the present analyses and the earlier ones. In the case of Sue, all respondents confronted the same preferential ranking and minimum selling prices and had to draw inferences about the relative importance of the attributes. In the case of the respondents' own judgments, the heterogeneity of the respondents' preferences can be expected to translate into heterogeneity of their relative importance judgments, with the result that we expect much less statistical power in these analyses than in the earlier ones.

Results of Experiment 2

In Experiment 1, we found that respondents inferred relative importance judgments for Sue that contradicted the response-mode-independent use of any interpretation of relative importance that depends only on the preference order (e.g., marginal rate of substitution). We conducted Experiment 2 to explore this finding further. In particular, we wanted to know whether respondents inferred different relative importance judgments because of the shift in preference-response mode per se, or because they were sensitive to information present in Sue's prices other than the rank order of the prices, that is, the magnitudes of the prices. Recall that Experiment 2 employed the same Stimulus Sets A, B, and C, composed of vacation packages, as in Experiment 1. Also, as in Experiment 1, respondents gave responses to all three stimulus sets according to their own preferences and relative importance judgments, after which they inferred the relative importance judgments of a target person (Sue) from her judgments of the three stimulus sets. In addition, Experiment 2 involved the same pair of response modes as before: preferential ranking of the vacation packages and the setting of a minimum selling price for each vacation package. Unlike Experiment 1, Response Mode was a between-subjects factor in Experiment 2. Respondents either gave their own preferential ranking and drew inferences from Sue's ranks, or they gave their own prices and drew inferences from Sue's prices. Four different pricing groups were included, which differed from each other only in the numerical values that they saw for Sue's prices. (See Figures 8.8 to 8.11 for the prices shown to

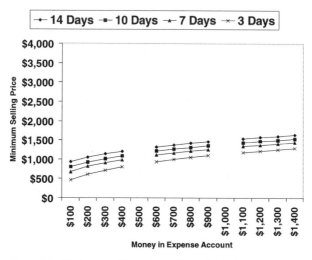

Figure 8.8. Minimum selling prices of hypothetical target person in Experiment 2: prices low and compressed.

the different groups.) The rank order of the prices was the same for all groups (and the same as Sue's rank order shown to the ranking group). This manipulation allowed us to test whether people are responsive to the magnitudes of Sue's prices, and not merely to the rank order of these prices.

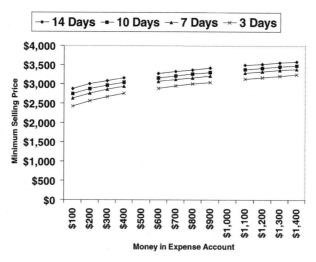

Figure 8.9. Minimum selling prices of hypothetical target person in Experiment 2: prices high and compressed.

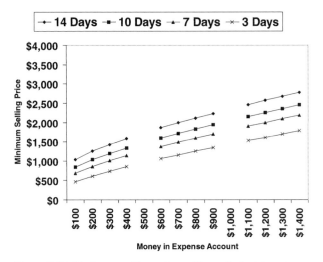

Figure 8.10. Minimum selling prices of hypothetical target person in Experiment 2: prices low and dispersed.

Beliefs About the Relation Between Decisions and Relative Importance Judgments. Our main results concern the inferences that respondents drew about Sue's relative importance judgment from her ranking or prices. Replicating the results of Experiment 1, the pricing groups inferred greater importance for money than did the ranking groups,

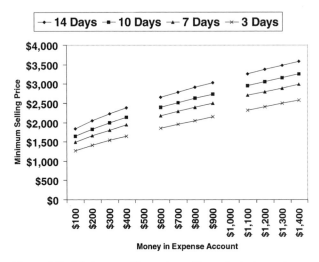

Figure 8.11. Minimum selling prices of hypothetical target person in Experiment 2: prices high and dispersed.

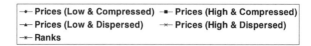

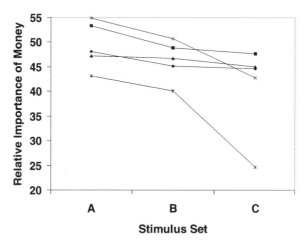

Figure 8.12. Respondents' inferences of relative importance of money displayed separately for each group.

producing a significant main effect for the Group factor ($F(4, 97) = 3.28$, $p = .0145$). (The means are shown in Figure 8.12.) This result again contradicted the response-mode-independent use of any interpretation of relative importance that depends only on the preference order because all five groups drew inferences from preferences (i.e., ranks or prices) that had the same rank order.

Moreover, there was again partial support for our hypothesis that relative importance would be interpreted as relative sensitivity when inferences were drawn from ranks and as relative impact when inferences were drawn from prices. There was a significant interaction between Group and Stimulus Set ($F(8, 194) = 2.81$, $p = .0057$) such that the relative importance inferred from ranks decreased more rapidly across the stimulus sets than did the relative importance inferred from prices. Thus, again, although a relative impact interpretation for prices would have produced increasing means, the fact that these means decreased more slowly suggests that some respondents may have adopted the relative impact interpretation or tried to compromise between interpretations.

Our new result is that respondents were *not* sensitive to the magnitudes of the prices from which they were inferring relative importance judgments. When the four pricing groups were analyzed by themselves, only the main effect of the Stimulus Set was significant

($F(2,156) = 8.21$, $p = .0004$). The main effect of Group was not significant ($F(3,78) = .64$, $p = .59$), nor was the interaction between Group and Stimulus Set significant ($F(6,156) = 1.39$, $p = .22$). Nevertheless, the interaction described earlier (when all five groups were analyzed together) indicates that the effect of the preference-response mode was not merely a response bias, that is, a tendency to report uniformly greater importance for money when drawing inferences from prices instead of ranks. Rather, the evidence suggests that the pricing and ranking response modes did induce respondents to adopt different interpretations of relative importance, but that each interpretation was sensitive only to the rank order of the preferences.

Actual Relation Between Decisions and Relative Importance Judgments. As in Experiment 1, respondents reported greater relative importance for money when they were pricing the vacation packages (mean $= 49.2$) than when they were ranking them (mean $= 35.2$). Unlike Experiment 1, however, this seemed to reflect insight rather than the lack of it: Respondents in the pricing groups had preferences that produced higher rank order correlations with the expense account in the vacation packages (mean $= .454$) than did respondents in the ranking group (mean $= .398$). (In Experiment 2, we couldn't directly compare respondents' relative importance judgments with the direction of preference reversals because the response mode was varied between subjects.)

An anomalous result was that respondents' relative importance judgments increased across the stimulus sets ($F(2,194) = 4.63$, $p = .0109$; see Figure 8.13), suggesting a relative impact interpretation of relative importance, despite the fact that their inferences from Sue's prices and ranks suggested a relative sensitivity interpretation. We had no reason to anticipate that respondents might interpret relative importance differently when reporting their own views than when inferring importance from someone else's preferences. Further research should pursue this possibility.

General Discussion

At the beginning of this chapter, we offered several reasons for being interested in a detailed account of people's statements about the relative importance of attributes. Among them, the interest that has most guided us here is the desire to understand and improve communication about decision making (e.g., between a principal and an agent). Consideration of what is involved in a principal's encoding of information

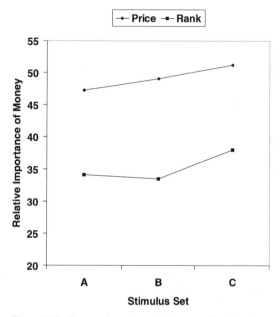

Figure 8.13. Respondents' own judgments of relative importance of money displayed separately for each preference-response mode.

into a relative importance judgment, and in an agent's decoding of that information, led us to focus primarily on people's interpretations of relative importance and the factors that might affect that interpretation (e.g., the response mode by which preferences are expressed). In this section, we will briefly summarize what our experiments have yielded on this matter and then go on to comment on implications for some other issues where light could be shed by a greater understanding of people's relative importance judgments. Specifically, we will comment on people's insight into their own decision making and on the family of decision anomalies known as *preference reversal phenomena*.

Principals and Agents

Although we didn't arrange our respondents into pairs to play the roles of principals and agents, we believe that our experiments are relevant to communication between people in such roles because they investigated the relationship(s) between preferences and statements about relative importance. These relationships may not exhaust what people mean by relative importance, but we believe that they are a crucial part of people's interpretations of the term, and in particular that they are the part that is most central to the information that a principal needs to convey to an agent.

We had hypothesized that interpretations of relative importance might depend in a particular way on the response mode by which preferences are reported. Specifically, we had thought that rankings would encourage a relative sensitivity interpretation and that minimum selling prices would suggest a relative impact interpretation. This hypothesis received only partial support in two experiments. Nevertheless, both experiments supported the more general notion that interpretations of relative importance are affected by the response mode. Not only did inferences from Sue's prices, as opposed to her ranks, elicit greater importance judgments for money, despite the fact that her prices and ranks had the same rank order. In addition, the inferred relative importance values decreased more rapidly from Stimulus Set A to B to C when inferences were drawn from Sue's ranks rather than from her prices. Put differently, the relationship between (Sue's) preferences and (respondents' inferred) relative importance judgments depended on the response mode by which (Sue's) preferences were reported. We take this relationship to be indicative of respondents' interpretation of relative importance and so a shift in the relationship indicates a shift in interpretation.

The implication of this finding is that interpretations of importance are labile. Therefore, for both theoretical and practical reasons, it is important to conduct research to map out the variety of interpretations that people employ and the conditions that influence their selection and use. Among the practical implications of the present results, agents should regard principals' statements about relative importance with caution: The relationship between these statements and the principals' preferences depends on the preference-response mode that the principals have in mind. Further research must determine this dependence more precisely and explore other factors that may affect the relationship between relative importance and preference.

Insight

One theoretical issue that depends on an understanding of people's interpretations of relative importance is the determination of whether or to what extent people's statements about relative importance exhibit insight. We saw in Experiment 1 that respondents judged the relative importance of the expense account to be greater to them in the pricing task than in the ranking task. Yet, at the same time, our objective measures of relative importance indicated that respondents' preferences accorded greater relative importance to the expense account in the ranking task than in the pricing task. One possible conclusion is that respondents don't really know how the expense account and the vacation duration affect their preferences; their reports reflect their lay theories about the influences of these factors rather than any introspective awareness of their decision processes (cf. Nisbett & Wilson, 1977). Certainly, people are not always aware of the factors that affect them or of how the effect is brought about.

However, in this instance, we hesitate to draw the pessimistic conclusion that people lack insight. After all, respondents' judgments of relative importance corresponded well enough to our objective measures to yield substantial correlations. (See Table 8.1.) One might reply to this that the correlations capture individual differences. Perhaps the respondents have some gross information about how they differ from others but lack subtle information about the impact of the preference-response mode. We hesitate to accept even this position. In our opinion, it is premature to reject the possibility that respondents applied different interpretations of relative importance when they responded to the two preference-response modes. The reports of relative importance may have been intended to convey one thing in connection with the rank ordering task (e.g., relative sensitivity) and another thing in connection with the minimum selling price task (e.g., relative impact). If so, the fact that respondents' preferences actually accorded greater importance to money (in the sense of relative sensitivity) in the ranking task than in the pricing task can be reconciled with the fact that they judged money to be more important in the pricing task than in the ranking task, without implying a lack of insight.

The evidence for such a possibility is not definitive, but it is suggestive enough to leave the possibility open for now. We failed to obtain clear evidence from respondents' own preferences and relative importance judgments that their interpretations of relative importance were affected by the response mode. This lack of clear evidence for a response-mode-induced shift in interpretation suggests that respondents' apparent lack of insight should be regarded as just that. On the other hand, we did obtain support for response-mode-dependent interpretations when we analyzed respondents' inferences about Sue, and as we mentioned earlier, this analysis gives us more statistical power. In particular, the data strongly rejected the hypothesis that respondents employ an interpretation of relative importance that is sensitive only to the preference *order*, and that that interpretation is applied independent of the preference-response mode. Our objective measure, on the other hand, had exactly these properties. Therefore, we think it would be a mistake to infer from a lack of correspondence between the subjective and objective measures that the respondents lacked insight. This conclusion, if it comes to that, must wait for further research to pin down more definitively what people intend their reports of relative importance to convey. If people's reports fail to live up to their own intentions, then they do indeed lack insight, but this has not yet been established.

Preference Reversals

One of the reasons that we were interested in investigating relative importance judgments in the context of shifting preference-response modes is that preference reversal phenomena (i.e., dependence of the preference order on the preference-response mode) have been attributed to changes in the relative weight of attributes as a function of the preference-response mode (Tversky et al., 1988). If *weight* is understood as subjectively perceived relative importance, then our data suggest that the situation is more complicated in that the interpretation, and not merely the magnitude, of relative importance may be shifting across preference-response modes. If respondents were employing a single interpretation, it cannot have been MRS (which is usually what decision researchers mean by weight) because MRS is sensitive only to the preference *order*, and the data rejected any such interpretation. On the other hand, weight might be understood as a technical term not necessarily related to subjectively perceived relative importance. In this case, weight must be elaborated and measured in terms of psychological process, and not merely computed as a summary statistic from the preferences (e.g., as a regression coefficient) in order for it to be explanatory, and not just descriptive, of changes in the preference order across response modes.

In either case, we were surprised to find that Experiment 1 produced preference reversals that conflict with the pattern that the contingent-weighting model was designed to explain.[4] Specifically, Tversky et al. (1988) proposed that work by Fitts and Seeger (1953) on stimulus-response compatibility effects could be applied to preference reversal phenomena. According to the compatibility hypothesis, "the weight of any input component is enhanced by its compatibility with the output"

(Tversky et al., 1988, p. 376). As Fischer and Hawkins (1993) pointed out, Tversky et al. (1988) applied this hypothesis in two different ways to form two compatibility hypotheses: a scale-compatibility hypothesis and a strategy-compatibility hypothesis. The scale-compatibility hypothesis asserts that a stimulus attribute should loom larger when the response mode is compatible with the attribute in the sense of being expressed on a similar scale. In our case, because minimum selling prices and expense account values are both expressed in dollars, the scale-compatibility hypothesis predicts that the expense account should loom larger in the pricing task than in the ranking task. However, the opposite was true of our data. As shown by the predominant direction of reversals (see Table 8.2), respondents' preferences placed more relative weight on the expense account when ranking, rather than pricing, the vacation packages. The strategy-compatibility hypothesis asserts that choice and ranking tasks, as compared with matching, pricing, and rating tasks, are more likely to elicit the use of a lexicographic strategy (which favors the alternative that is better on the most important attribute for which the stimuli are discriminable). Therefore, the more "prominent" (i.e., important) attribute is predicted to loom larger in a ranking task than in a pricing task. Again, however, the opposite was true in our data. Both subjective and objective measures indicated that vacation duration was more important to our respondents than the expense account. Yet Table 8.2 shows that this more important attribute loomed larger in the pricing task than in the ranking task.[5]

We have no explanation to offer for why our data did not conform to the commonly observed pattern. If this anomalous pattern is found to replicate, it indicates that there are still some new wrinkles to be found regarding preference reversals.

General Conclusion

A better understanding of the variety of interpretations of relative importance that people employ, and the conditions that influence their selection and use, would have both theoretical and practical implications. In addition to the possibility of improving people's communication about their preferences, we argue that such an understanding should inform our account of people's insight into their own decision processes (or the lack thereof) and may shed light on the explanation of preference reversals. More broadly, we think that the study of people's relative importance judgments can inform us about the metacognition of decision making and about experiential aspects of decision making that have been largely neglected in the literature.

Notes

1 Our concern here should not be confused with economists' *principal–agent problem*, i.e., the problem of motivating agents to act in the interests of principals. Rather, we are concerned with the ability of principals to *communicate* their interests to well-intentioned agents with the use of statements about relative importance.

2 For respondents who saw Sue's prices first, i.e., the top two curves of Figure 8.5, the means were 50.6, 50.7, and 46.1, for a drop in 4.5 points, for inferences drawn from Sue's prices, and means of 49.4, 44.4, and 36.7, for a drop of 12.7 points, for inferences drawn from Sue's ranks. For respondents who saw Sue's ranks first, i.e., the bottom two curves of Figure 8.5, the means were 43.8, 36.7, and 30.4, for a drop of 13.4 points, for inferences drawn from Sue's prices, and means of 40.4, 34.2, and 25.4, for a drop of 15.0 points, for inferences drawn from Sue's ranks.

3 We chose to use these rank-order correlations as our objective indices of relative importance for three reasons. First, they depend only on the rank order of the preference response, and not on its magnitude. This permitted us to compute the indices for both of the preference-response modes used here (i.e., minimum selling price and preferential ranking) and to compare them across these response modes without making any assumptions about the relation between preferential ranks and the magnitude of preference. Second, unlike the estimated values of model parameters (e.g., the coefficients of linear models), the interpretation of the rank-order correlations is not conditional on the correctness or fit of a model. Third, using the rank-order correlations provided comparability with some of our other work in this area (Goldstein, 1990; Goldstein & Mitzel, 1992).

4 In Experiment 2, the preference-response mode was manipulated as a between-subjects factor, so we couldn't examine the data for preference reversals.

5 In terms of subjective importance, if not in terms of our objective measures, respondents did conform to the compatibility hypothesis in both of its forms. Respondents reported the subjective importance of the monetary attribute to loom larger in the (scale-compatible) pricing task than in the ranking task. Also, they reported the more important attribute (i.e., vacation duration) to loom larger in the (strategy-compatible) ranking task than in the pricing task.

References

Anderson, N. H., & Zalinski, J. (1988). Functional measurement approach to self-estimation in multiattribute evaluation. *Journal of Behavioral Decision Making, 1*, 191–221.

Fischer, G. W., & Hawkins, S. A. (1993). Strategy compatibility, scale compatibility, and the prominence effect. *Journal of Experimental Psychology: Human Perception and Performance, 19*, 580–597.

Fitts, P. M., & Seeger, C. M. (1953). S–R compatibility: Spatial characteristics of stimulus and response codes. *Journal of Experimental Psychology, 46*, 199–210.

Goldstein, W. M. (1990). Judgments of relative importance decision making: Global vs. local interpretations of subjective weight. *Organizational Behavior and Human Decision Processes, 47*, 313–336.

Goldstein, W. M., & Beattie, J. (1991). Judgments of relative importance in decision making: The importance of interpretation and the interpretation of importance. In D. R. Brown & J. E. K. Smith (Eds.), *Frontiers in mathematical psychology* (pp. 110–137). New York and Berlin: Springer-Verlag.

Goldstein, W. M., & Einhorn, H. J. (1987). Expression theory and the preference reversal phenomena. *Psychological Review, 94*, 236–254.

Goldstein, W. M., & Mitzel, H. C. (1992). The relative importance of relative importance: Inferring other people's preferences from relative importance ratings and previous decisions. *Organizational Behavior and Human Decision Processes, 51*, 382–415.

Nisbett, R. E., & Wilson, T. D. (1977). Telling more than we can know: Verbal reports on mental processes. *Psychological Review, 84*, 231–259.

Shanteau, J. (1980). The concept of weight in judgment and decision making: A review and some unifying proposals. (Tech. Rep. No. 228). Boulder, CO: University of Colorado, Center for Research on Judgment and Policy, Institute of Behavioral Science.

Tversky, A., Sattath, S., & Slovic, P. (1988). Contingent weighting in judgment and choice. *Psychological Review, 95*, 371–384.

9   Private Values and Public Policy

Michael Jones-Lee and Graham Loomes

The Basic Question

There are many ways in which governments and their agencies can promote greater health and safety. They may undertake projects themselves, using taxpayers' money, or they may introduce new regulations or laws that impose costs more or less indirectly on some or all members of the population. But because nearly all such measures consume resources that might otherwise have been used to produce other desirable goods or services, the question governments must address is: What balance should be struck between health and safety benefits and the costs of providing them? In practical terms, this amounts to asking: What monetary value should be attached to any health and safety improvement in order to weigh it appropriately against the opportunity costs of bringing it about?

In principle, this is not such a difficult question to answer – at least, not as far as standard welfare economics and conventional decision theory are concerned. Economic theory assumes that people can weigh improvements in their health and/or safety along with all of the other goods and services they consume, and can judge which combination of

Much of the work reported in this chapter has been conducted in collaboration with a large number of others, including Jane Beattie, Trevor Carthy, Sue Chilton, Judith Covey, Paul Dolan, Richard Dubourg, Jagadish Guria, Lorraine Hopkins, Peter Philips, Nick Pidgeon, Angela Robinson, and Anne Spencer. Funding for the research in question has come from the Department of Transport, the Economic and Social Research Council, London Underground Limited, the Ministry of Agriculture, Fisheries and Food, the New Zealand Land Transport Safety Authority, and a consortium comprising the Health & Safety Executive, the Department of Environment, Transport and the Regions, the Home Office, and Her Majesty's Treasury. However, the views expressed in this chapter do not necessarily represent those of any of the individuals or organizations listed here.

safety and other goods will maximize their welfare (subject to whatever budget constraints they may face). On this basis, the task facing applied researchers in this field is to construct a set of questions that will reveal the extent to which respondents are prepared to forgo other goods (and thus release some of their current wealth) in order to pay for some particular health or safety benefit.

If people can respond to such questions with considered answers that reveal their tradeoff, at the margin, between wealth and safety, it is then straightforward to calculate people's collective willingness to pay (WTP) for reductions in the risks of death or injury, which is the measure that most economists would regard as the appropriate one for governments to use as the basis for valuing those benefits.

For example, suppose that we consider a region with a population of 1 million people, and suppose that a program of road safety improvements in that region is expected to reduce the number of road accident deaths by 10 each year. (Clearly, it is likely that a rather larger number of nonfatal injuries will also be prevented by such a measure; but for the moment, to keep things simple, let us focus just on fatalities.) Such a program would not benefit every member of the population equally; but on average, it would reduce the annual risk of dying in a road accident by 1 in 100,000 for each person in the region. In most regions of the United Kingdom, that would constitute a reduction of about 20% of the baseline risk, so it is not a negligible improvement.

Introspection (and experience) suggests that if a representative household were asked to consider the prospect of reducing each household member's risk of death on the roads by 20%, and were told that the cost of implementing the necessary measures would work out at an extra £1 per head per year, the great majority would have no hesitation in agreeing that this would be good – indeed, excellent – value for money. In other words, the population of the region would, collectively, be willing to spend at least £1 million each year to reduce the number of road deaths by 10: Thus we could be fairly sure that using a figure of £100,000 to represent the public's valuation of the benefit of preventing a road fatality would be a considerable understatement.

On the other hand, if the average household were told that implementing the necessary measures would raise the cost of living by £500 per year for every man, woman, and child, it seems highly unlikely that they would be willing to forgo all the other things they could get for that money in order to reduce the average individual risk by 1 in 100,000. In other words, a value of £50 million for each road death prevented would almost certainly greatly overstate the weight most people would attach to that benefit relative to the opportunity costs of achieving it.

We might therefore feel quite confident in saying that the monetary value to be assigned to the benefit side of any measure expected, on average, to prevent one road fatality in the United Kingdom lies somewhere between £100,000 and £50 million. Thus even casual introspection establishes that this value – which has come to be known as the *value of statistical life (VOSL)* or, alternatively, the *value of preventing a fatality (VPF)* – has finite upper and lower bounds. Moreover, this reasoning is not limited to the prevention of premature death: Very similar principles can also be applied to reductions in the risks of a broad spectrum of nonfatal injuries or illnesses.

However, for most practical policy purposes, such casual introspection is not sufficient: If cost-benefit analysis is to be used to inform the allocation of scarce resources between a large number of competing projects involving a wide variety of safety and nonsafety benefits, we need far more precise estimates of the values of preventing deaths and injuries, and we need to be able to show that any such values are securely rooted in the expressed preferences of the affected population. In recent years, a number of studies have been undertaken to provide the kinds of figures required. The remainder of this chapter will consider the principles and practicalities involved in a selection of such studies, the problems encountered, the results generated, and the possible implications for theory and policy in this important area.

Principles, Practicalities ... and Problems

Viewed from the perspective of mathematicians, economists, and statisticians such as von Neumann and Morgenstern (1944) and Savage (1954), it might seem to be a matter of elementary logic that if the average individual strictly prefers a 1 in 100,000 reduction in the annual risk of death to anything else she can buy for £1, but strictly prefers what she can buy for £500 to that same annual reduction in risk, there must be a value somewhere between £1 and £500 at which she is indifferent between the money and the risk reduction. By standard logic, there cannot be more than one such value, and thus preferences ought in principle to be capable of being mapped with great precision. This assumption underpins conventional economic theory, and it has been the basis for much empirical work that supposes that so long as researchers can devise sufficiently clear and carefully targeted questions, they will tap into people's ready-made and highly articulated preferences and elicit the precise, robust, and internally consistent responses needed for policy purposes.

It may be worth noting in passing that neither von Neumann and Morgenstern nor Savage actually subscribed to this characterization of human preferences as a *descriptive* model, but rather proposed their theories of choice under uncertainty as *normative* prescriptions for prudent decision making. In fact, von Neumann and Morgenstern specifically refer to real decision making as taking place in "a sphere of considerable haziness" (1944, p. 20), and Savage acknowledges that "real people frequently and flagrantly behave in disaccord with the utility theory, and ... behavior of that sort is not at all typically considered abnormal or irrational" (1954, p. 100).

Indeed, the reality is that most people find it difficult to state with any great confidence a point estimate value for even relatively uncomplicated items, such as simple lotteries involving straightforward chances of winning modest and familiar sums of money (see, e.g., Butler and Loomes, 1988). If people find it hard to make precise, accurate judgments in such *relatively* simple cases, how much more imprecise are their judgments likely to be when they try to weigh small reductions in already small probabilities of unfamiliar health states on the one hand against sums of money on the other?

One way of allowing for such imprecision – and trying to get some indication of its magnitude – is to ask questions that invite respondents to begin by identifying amounts of money they believe they definitely *would* be willing to pay, and also amounts they believe they definitely would *not* be willing to pay, for some given reduction in the risk of death or injury. If there is a gap between the largest amount a respondent states she definitely would pay (labeled the *Min*) and the smallest amount she says she definitely would not pay (the *Max*), she can then be asked to identify the point within that *band of imprecision* where it is most difficult to decide whether or not to pay – this point being taken to be the *Best* estimate of the respondent's valuation of the risk reduction.

That was the thinking behind the procedure adopted during piloting for a study commissioned by the U.K. Department of Transport to elicit values for preventing nonfatal road injuries relative to the value for preventing fatalities. Values were sought for reductions in the risks of death and four typical nonfatal road injuries. Descriptions of each of the nonfatal injuries were printed on cards and labeled R, S, X, and W. These descriptions, together with the wording on the card representing a fatality – coded K – are reproduced in Figure 9.1.

K

Injuries resulting in death

R

In hospital
- Several weeks, possibly several months
- Moderate to severe pain

After hospital
- Continuing pain/discomfort for the rest of your life, possibly requiring frequent medication
- Substantial and permanent restrictions on work and leisure activities

S

In hospital
- 1–4 weeks
- Moderate to severe pain

After hospital
- Some pain, gradually reducing, but may recur when you take part in some activities
- Some restrictions on leisure and possibly some work activities for the rest of your life

W

In hospital
- 2–7 days
- Slight to moderate pain

After hospital
- Some pain/discomfort for several weeks
- Some restrictions on work and/or leisure activities for several weeks/months
- After 3–4 months, return to normal health with no permanent disability

X

In hospital
- 1–4 weeks
- Slight to moderate pain

After hospital
- Some pain/discomfort, gradually reducing
- Some restrictions on work and leisure activities, steadily reducing
- After 1–3 years, return to normal health with no permanent disability

Figure 9.1. Injury descriptions.

Respondents were presented with a series of questions in which they were asked to consider what they would be willing to pay annually to have a safety feature fitted to their vehicle that would reduce their baseline risk of each injury in turn by 50%, that is, by 4, 6, 12, 18, and 10 in 100,000 per annum for K, R, S, X, and W, respectively.

Values were elicited by an iterative procedure using a plain white disc in which a small window was cut to reveal just one amount at a time. Respondents were asked whether they would be prepared to pay the amount displayed in the window. They could give one of three responses: "definitely yes," "definitely no," or "not sure." Depending on their answer, the amount displayed was adjusted – increased if they said "definitely yes" and decreased if they said "definitely no"; when they became unsure, it was moved up and down until the interviewers were able to identify the Min and the Max. Then respondents were asked to identify the sum at which they would find the decision about whether or not to pay most finely balanced, that is, their Best estimate.

We had been warned that one possible problem with this procedure was that respondents might be unduly influenced by the first amount of money they saw displayed in the window. Of course, standard economic theory assumes that an individual with stable, well-formed preferences will be uninfluenced by the starting point in an iterative bidding process. However, in order to check for any impact, we allocated respondents at random to one of two subsamples: In one, the first amount displayed was always £25; in the other, it was £75. We had hoped that, at worst, any *starting point effect* might be limited to influencing the choice of just where within the band of imprecision the Best estimate fell, with no substantial effect on the Min and Max values – which were, after all, amounts that respondents had asserted they were quite definite about.

With the benefit of hindsight, those initial expectations now seem a little naive. There is, it has to be admitted, something paradoxical about the idea that people have rather hazy and ill-formed preferences, and yet can still be expected to state with reasonable precision their personal Min and Max values. Arguably, it would be more logical to suppose that if people are hazy about their preferences, they are also likely to be hazy about the extent of their haziness – which is exactly what the evidence suggested.

Table 9.1 reports the subsample mean Min, Max, and Best estimates for each of the five risk reductions. The data reveal strong starting point effects: The mean Best responses elicited from the subsample presented with a starting point of £75 are 89% to 166% higher than those their

Table 9.1. *Starting Point Effects*

	£25 Starting Value		£75 Starting Value	
Reduction in annual	Min	87	Min	232
risk of death by	Best	113	Best	265
4 in 100,000	Max	149	Max	350
Reduction in annual	Min	94	Min	222
risk of injury R by	Best	121	Best	258
6 in 100,000	Max	144	Max	308
Reduction in annual	Min	102	Min	196
risk of injury S by	Best	117	Best	221
12 in 100,000	Max	145	Max	267
Reduction in annual	Min	82	Min	170
risk of injury X by	Best	90	Best	194
18 in 100,000	Max	110	Max	233
Reduction in annual	Min	61	Min	158
risk of injury W by	Best	66	Best	174
10 in 100,000	Max	81	Max	218

counterparts elicited from the subsample presented with a £25 starting point. This is not simply a matter of one or two outliers influencing the subsample means in a particular way: An analysis of the median responses largely replicates the result, with the ratios of median responses ranging from 1.50:1 to 2.35:1.

Moreover, this result could not be attributed simply to the starting value shifting the position of the best estimate within otherwise reasonably stable bands of imprecision. As indicated by the summary statistics in Table 9.1 and as discussed more fully in Dubourg et al. (1997), there is no tendency for the £75 starting value to push the Best estimate relatively higher in the interval between Min and Max than the £25 starting value; indeed, if anything, the reverse is true. On the other hand, what we do find is that the initial value presented to respondents not only influences the mean and median Best estimates, but also affects the absolute magnitude of the intervals between Min and Max, which for the most part work out at between 30% and 50% of their respective best estimates. Given that Min and Max are supposed to represent the lower and upper bounds that respondents feel sure about, the fact that the distance between them can be altered by a factor of between 1.65 (Injury S) and 3 (Injury W) is unsettling.

An even more disturbing feature of Table 9.1 is that in *every one* of the five comparisons between the mean Min values elicited from a £75 starting point and the corresponding mean Max values elicited from a £25 starting point, the former are 35% to 94% higher than the latter (with the medians once again telling much the same story). In other words, there was not a single case in which the comparable bands of imprecision overlapped to any extent. Something that economic theory would consider to be as unimportant as the starting point in an iterative bidding process turned out to shift the Min, Max, and Best estimates to such an extent that, if two clones were allocated to different subsamples, one would be liable to state amounts she definitely *would* pay that are significantly higher than some of the amounts the other clone claims she definitely would *not* pay, for no other reason than being presented with different figures at the beginning of the iterative elicitation procedure.

A clear implication of this finding is that respondents' preferences may be considerably more imprecise and vulnerable to cues and biases than the Min–Max intervals would suggest: Given the lack of overlap between intervals, a better estimate of the true band of imprecision might be the difference between the *higher* of the two Max values and the *lower* of the two Min values. On this basis, the bands of imprecision for this dataset would be as big as or bigger than their respective *Best* estimates. What is more, even that may be an underestimate: Had we used starting points of £10 and £100, it seems probable that we would have produced even wider bands. And although intuition of the kind used at the start of this chapter suggests that there must be *some* limit to the width of such bands, it is clear that the haziness of people's preferences is a significant feature, and one that we must try to understand better if we intend to elicit responses for the purpose of informing and influencing public policy.

Oversensitivity to Things That Shouldn't Matter

The starting point effects just described are merely one manifestation (albeit a very striking one) of a more widespread problem that challenges researchers working in this area: namely, a tendency for many respondents to be oversensitive to features that, from the standpoint of conventional theory, should be irrelevant. Indeed, there is now an extensive literature documenting violations of the *invariance principle*, which requires that stated values/preferences should not vary with inessential changes in the description of the options or with the particular procedures used to elicit them. Slovic (1995) has provided a concise history of a number of the best-known violations of both description invariance and procedure invariance, often, but not exclusively, involving lotteries of various kinds. In this subsection, the list is extended to include several examples drawn from the health and safety field.

In light of the starting point effects just described, a further phase of piloting replaced the disc mechanism with a *payment card* on which respondents were asked to check each amount they were sure they would pay, put a cross next to each amount they were sure they would not pay, and put an asterisk next to the amount at which they would find it most difficult to decide. In this case, the issue was whether the *range* of values presented on the payment cards – from £0 to £500 for one subsample and from £0 to £1,500 for the other subsample – would affect responses in the same way that the starting point had done. Although the effect here was somewhat less dramatic, there was still a significant unwelcome influence. Moreover, as described more fully in Dubourg et al. (1997), there were sufficient other disquieting patterns in the data to cause us to be wary of relying exclusively on WTP questions.

Thus, in the subsequent main study intended to establish appropriate relativities between preventing fatalities and preventing different degrees of nonfatal injury (as described more fully in Jones-Lee et al., 1995a), half of the sample were asked WTP questions of the kind described previously, but the other half were asked *standard gamble* (SG) questions of the following form (where Q denotes the particular injury description being evaluated relative to normal health and death):

Suppose you were in a road accident and you were taken to a hospital. The doctors tell you that if you are treated in the usual way, you will certainly experience the consequences shown below on card Q. However, they also tell you that there is a different treatment available, but its outcome is not certain. If it succeeds, you will be restored to your normal state of health. But if it fails, you will die.

On the facing page of the questionnaire there were two columns, one showing the chances of success of the risky treatment and the other showing the corresponding chances of failure. A procedure analogous to that used for the WTP questions was deployed to identify Min and Max values. Respondents were then asked for the balance of probabilities that would make it hardest to decide which treatment to choose – this being treated as their Best estimate. Since the WTP and SG procedures are

Table 9.2. *Weights for Preventing Nonfatal Injuries*

Injury	WTP-Based Weight	SG-Based Weight
R	0.875	0.233
S(4)	0.640	
		0.151
S(12)	0.262	
X	0.232	0.055
W	0.210	0.020

Note: S(4) and S(12) are the weights for Injury S estimated, respectively, on the basis of risk reductions of 4 in 100,000 and 12 in 100,000 per annum. As can be seen, using the smaller risk reduction in WTP questions results in Injury S appearing nearly two and a half times worse than when the larger risk reduction is used.

both built on the same theoretical foundation, they should, in principle, produce a broadly similar pattern of results.

Using the Best estimates obtained from the WTP and SG questions, Table 9.2 shows the mean weights for preventing the various nonfatal injuries (as described in Figure 9.1) relative to preventing a fatality.

It can be seen that the WTP questions generated estimates that were 3.75 to 10.5 times greater than those produced by the SG questions. And although not reported here, examination of Min and Max responses shows that *in every case* the mean Max figure elicited by the SG procedure is strictly lower than the corresponding Min figure elicited via WTP. So here too we observe massive discrepancies (including shifts of the Min–Max intervals to the extent that they do not overlap at all) between two sets of measures generated by procedures that, according to standard economic theory, should be approximately equivalent.

Such disparities are easy to reproduce, even with small samples of people with mathematical skills well above average. In subsequent work with such respondents, we explored the thinking that lies behind people's responses, and it is clear that the two types of questions encourage respondents to focus on several quite different factors and/or to view the same factors from rather different perspectives (see Jones-Lee et al., 1995b).

In two other studies – Dolan et al. (1995) and Covey et al. (1995) – SG was compared with another theoretically equivalent procedure involving *Risk-Risk (RR)* tradeoffs, as developed by Viscusi et al. (1991). The essence of the RR question is to present respondents with the prospect of reducing one risk while increasing another and to establish the marginal tradeoff that respondents consider would leave them just as well off as they are now. Thus in the Dolan et al. study, respondents were asked to consider a Y in a million increase in the risk of a nonfatal injury and then, at the end of a Min–Max iterative procedure, identify what reduction in the risk of death would best offset that increase. To enable comparisons with other studies, the risk increases for injuries R, S, X, and W were set at 60, 120, 180, and 100 in a million, respectively.

Once again, the two procedures produced systematically different results, with both means and medians elicited via RR suggesting that all injuries were substantially more severe than when measures were elicited via SG questions. Thus, although RR questions may be theoretically equivalent to SG questions under standard assumptions, their greater complexity, combined with respondents' insensitivity to different magnitudes of small changes in risk, casts serious doubts on their usefulness as a means of collecting individual preference data that can reliably be incorporated into public policy decisions.

From what has been said so far in this subsection, it might appear that the SG procedure is being promoted, if not as the gold standard, then at least as the procedure that has fewest obvious warts. To some extent that is the case, but that is not to say that there are no grounds for concern about the SG procedure, too.

One practical problem encountered during the kind of work just discussed has been the difficulty of using SG questions to obtain direct links between fatalities and relatively minor/temporary injuries, such as W and X. In the main study reported in Jones-Lee et al. (1995a), 75% of respondents said that they definitely would not accept even a 0.01 risk of death in order to be "instantly cured" of Injury X; and on the basis of piloting, we did not even attempt a direct SG question for Injury W. Instead, we had to arrive at a value by "chaining" two responses, one from the question linking Injury S to death and the other presenting respondents with a choice between the certainty of W or a risky treatment where the consequence of failure was S rather than death.

Of course, such chaining procedures are not unproblematic. It has long been known that the utility indices derived from SG questions may vary according to which *reference states* are used. For example, Llewellyn-

Thomas et al. (1982) showed how manipulations of these reference states could produce systematically different sets of utility indices, and in a subsequent paper they concluded that "it may be naive to think of any state of health as possessing a single utility or value" (Llewellyn-Thomas et al., 1984, p. 550). However, given that no procedure is likely to be completely free from blemish, we decided to explore further the scope – and limitations – of other variants of the approach using chained SG questions. The results of this exploration are reported in the later sections of this chapter. But first, in order to put this more recent work in proper perspective, the next subsection considers another discomforting pattern emerging from earlier studies: an apparent tendency on the part of many respondents to take little or no account of factors that standard theory predicts *should* have a significant impact on their responses.

Undersensitivity to Things That Should Matter

Earlier, when discussing the results presented in Table 9.1, the emphasis was on the disturbingly strong between-sample impact of the amount that happened to be chosen as the starting point for the iterative bidding procedure. However, those data also bear witness to another phenomenon that threatens to undermine the whole value elicitation enterprise: namely, the insensitivity respondents often display to information about the nature and size of the risk changes involved.

Consider the mean responses for the last two questions reported in Table 9.1. Respondents were asked to state their willingness to pay for an 18 in 100,000 reduction in their risk of Injury X, and then immediately afterward were asked their WTP for a 10 in 100,000 reduction in their risk of Injury W.

In a preliminary ranking and rating exercise, nearly all respondents had, as expected, ranked W (from which they would recover completely in 3–4 months) as less serious than X (whose effects would last for 1–3 years), and on a scale where 100 represented normal health and 0 represented death, they had given W an average score of 80 and X an average score of 64. We should therefore expect that when asked their WTP for a smaller reduction in the risk of an injury they recognized as clearly less serious, they would give a strictly lower figure than in the previous question, where both the severity of the injury and the size of the risk reduction were greater.

Yet the fact was that a number of respondents stated *exactly the same* WTP in both questions, and nearly all of the others gave a response that, although *somewhat* lower, did not fall by enough even to take full account of the smaller risk reduction, let alone the lesser severity of the injury. The consequence was that when their responses were converted into WTP per 1 in 100,000 reduction in risk, no fewer than 55 out of 63 respondents appeared to be willing to pay strictly more per 1 in 100,000 reduction in the risk of the injury they had explicitly rated as less severe. Thus the preference ordering over X and W inferred by processing their WTP responses in the standard way was, for more than five out of six members of this sample, the complete opposite of the ordering they had given just a few minutes earlier in the ranking and rating exercise (which, we can be fairly sure, would be the ordering they would wish to see reflected in road safety policy).

Unfortunately, such insensitivity in WTP responses is all too easy to replicate even when the problem is simplified or when the question concerns goods with which respondents are more familiar. A number of examples are given in Jones-Lee et al. (1995a). In one case, the injury description (Injury S) was held constant across an adjacent pair of questions while the risk reduction was varied by a factor of 3: Yet only 180 (45.5%) of the 395 respondents gave a strictly lower WTP for the smaller risk reduction, whereas almost as many (178, or 45.1%) gave exactly the same response to both questions. Thus the value of preventing Injury S inferred from one question was nearly two and a half times greater than the value of preventing the same injury inferred from the other question. In two other cases, the risk reduction was held constant and the severity of the injury was varied between adjacent questions: Yet even so, between 35% and 40% of respondents stated the same WTP from one question to the next.

Notice that all of the examples given demonstrate *within-respondent* insensitivity to changes in *adjacent questions*. That is, the conditions seemed to us at the time to be about as conducive to appropriate discrimination as we could make them. But in light of that experience, a subsequent design, conducted as part of piloting for a study for the U.K. Health and Safety Executive (HSE) and several government departments, and reported more fully in Beattie et al. (1998), went to even greater lengths to encourage respondents to be sensitive to the magnitude of the safety improvement under consideration.

It had been suggested to us that one source of difficulty might be many respondents' lack of familiarity with small probabilities. So we used scenarios similar to the one given toward the beginning of this chapter, where people were asked to consider two program of road safety improvements in their region (whose boundaries were set to encompass a population of about 1 million people, or 400,000 households). One program would reduce the number of road deaths in the region by 5 per year, whereas a more extensive program would reduce the number of deaths by 15 per year. This was the Annual (A) treatment, to which half of the sample were allocated at random. The other half were assigned to the Five-Year (F) treatment, where the reductions were presented as 25 or 75 deaths prevented during the next 5 years.

Rather than go directly to a one-to-one interview, respondents were brought together in small focus groups (typically five or six people in each) and were taken through the scenarios to which they had been assigned. They were given stylized (but essentially accurate) information about the baseline number of road deaths each year in their region, were asked to think how they and other household members' risks stood relative to the average person in the region, and were invited to consider how much both the 5-per-year and the 15-per-year program were worth to their household. Overcoming our fear of insulting people's intelligence, we even went as far as to ask people which program they thought would be of greater benefit/worth to their household: As might be expected, respondents generally considered it obvious that the program that prevented three times more deaths provided the greater benefit.

In the subsequent individual interviews (typically conducted within a few days of the initial focus group meeting), respondents were taken through an elicitation procedure of the Min–Max kind to get a figure for their estimate of what each program would be worth to their household. They were asked to record this estimate as a provisional one, on the understanding that if they wished, they could revise the figure in light of any further consideration. We then embarked on a discussion of people's provisional responses with the following "prompt":

"In the past, we've found that some people say that preventing 15 (75) deaths on the roads is worth three times as much to them as preventing 5 (25) deaths on the roads; but other people don't give this answer. Can you say a bit about why you gave the answers you gave?"

Despite this prompt (which might be regarded by some as verging on "leading" respondents), despite the fact that we were using numbers of deaths prevented rather than small probability changes, and despite the almost universal agreement that the larger program was more beneficial than the smaller one, 22 of the 56 respondents placed the same nonzero value on both programs, and only 11 gave a value for the larger program that was more than double the value they placed on the smaller program. Overall, then, the mean (median) value placed on the 15-per-year reduction was just 33% (41%) higher than the corresponding value placed on the 5-per-year reduction. Thus even our somewhat blatant attempt to encourage greater sensitivity to the magnitude of the benefit appears to have failed. Moreover, the A form of question produced a significantly different distribution of values from those generated by the F form of question. The net result was that the implied VPFs varied by as much as a factor of 4 (between £2.56 million and £11.07 million), depending on the size of the program and the form of the question.

One possible explanation for the insensitivity to the magnitude of the benefit displayed in the preceding study may be that, to a large extent, people valued both programs as "good causes," where the essential goodness of the cause is not simply and strictly proportional to the number of deaths prevented, but where the "warm glow" or "moral satisfaction" element is a substantial and invariant component of people's valuation (see, e.g., Kahneman and Knetsch, 1992). From what people said in the groups, there was some support for this conclusion – but to an extent that would constitute no more than a partial explanation. Another possible interpretation is that people compartmentalize their expenditure judgments into *mental accounts* (Thaler, 1985), one of which might entail a *safety budget* that is exhausted by their valuation of the smaller program, so that there is no scope to give a higher value for the larger program. And again, we have found some support for this notion in terms of people saying that "they gave what they could afford" for each of two benefits, so that their response did not vary with the magnitude of the benefit.

However, although both of these explanations undoubtedly work in some circumstances, there is much evidence that they cannot readily accommodate. For example, instead of (or as well as) asking what people are willing to *pay* for some risk reduction or other benefit, they may (also) be asked what they would be willing to *accept* (WTA) as compensation for some increase in risk or some other disbenefit. Here there is no budget constraint, either mental or real (and arguably precious little warm glow or moral satisfaction), and yet, as Dubourg et al. (1994) and Baron and Greene (1996) have reported, WTA responses show no greater sensitivity to magnitude than do WTP responses. More recently still, Frederick and Fischhoff (1997) have reported a series of studies showing that respondents exhibit considerable insensitivity into quantity even for a range of reasonably familiar market goods.

A review of 28 health and/or safety valuation studies (Beattie et al., 1996, Appendix A) shows just how pervasive and persistent such insensitivity appears to be. The picture that emerged from that survey was one of a strong inverse relationship between the size of the risk reduction(s) that researchers presented to respondents and the VPFs derived: When it was calculated on the basis of a 2 in 1,000 reduction in the risk of death, the VPF might be as low as £70,000 in 1994 prices (Acton, 1973), whereas when it was calculated on the basis of a reduction of 1 in 6,000,000, a VPF of more than £40 million could be generated (Covey et al., 1995). In light of this review, we considered – and not altogether in jest – writing a paper with the title "The Answer Is £50: Now, What Is the Question?" to convey in a slightly (but not greatly) exaggerated way the extent to which responses to WTP questions appear to ignore, or at best underweight, information about the quality and quantity of the goods that theory supposes to be of central concern.

How Should We React to the Evidence?

In the face of what might appear to be a depressingly long list (which could easily have been made much longer) of examples demonstrating the difficulty of eliciting anything like robust and reliable values for health and safety benefits, how should we react?

One possible reaction would be to declare that the whole enterprise of eliciting people's preferences in this area is simply doomed to fail, so that we should call off the search and rely instead on the existing sociopolitical processes to handle these decisions. However, this would be to forget that one of the factors motivating researchers to embark on this enterprise was the evidence that politicians and/or their expert advisers had little or no knowledge about the values of the population whose health and safety were being affected and whose money was being spent. Worse still, the evidence suggested that the political process itself was vulnerable to a number of influences – politicians' short-term interests and personal/ideological prejudices, interest group pressures, media attention, and a variety of other factors that tended to greatly amplify some risks while downplaying others (see Kasperson, 1992, for more on this) – and that this led to the enactment of policies that *implicitly* entailed VPFs that might vary from one case or one context to another by factors of tens, if not hundreds, for which little or no basis or justification in terms of people's welfare could be found.

A second reaction, observed among a number of researchers with a longstanding commitment to and/or a strong vested interest in the use of WTP methods, especially in relation to environmental policy, is to assert the normative power of conventional assumptions and attribute many of the apparent limitations in the empirical data to defects of wording and/or study design. Thus while trying to refine (and define for others) what they consider to be best practice, such researchers may also include one or two *internal consistency checks*, on which basis they may exclude irrational individuals' responses from the analysis, supposing that what is left is, in essence, a reflection of true preferences plus well-behaved white noise.

In such studies, it is not atypical to find that something between a quarter and a half (and sometimes more) of all data are excluded from the analysis due to the failure of respondents to pass whatever consistency tests have been incorporated. However, there is often a disquieting degree of arbitrariness about this process because there appear to be no objective criteria for deciding how many and what kinds of consistency tests should be used. Thus there are grounds for concern that, had different tests been substituted for those actually used, a substantial number of those passed as rational by the tests actually used might have been excluded by the alternative tests, and a good proportion of those excluded by the actual tests might have been admitted by the alternative tests. Furthermore, if the different tests had been *added* rather than substituted, the effect might well have been to exclude many more members of the sample from the analysis. Some studies (e.g., Miller and Guria, 1991) that have excluded a substantial proportion of their respondents have also reported that on other key questions there was no significant difference between the pattern of responses of those ruled out compared with those ruled in. This may be a further indication of the arbitrariness of the inclusion/exclusion process and may reinforce the concern that, despite the superficial rigor of the procedures, the data being used for analysis may really provide no sounder basis for public policy than the data excluded as suspect.

A third reaction to the evidence is to accept that people do not have ready-made, well-articulated true preferences for the kinds of health and safety goods that have been the focus of this chapter. Rather, when presented with questions of the kind discussed earlier, people are forced to construct their response(s). Moreover, bearing in mind that many surveys require them to produce their answers either immediately or after only rather limited opportunities for reflection, respondents are liable to use whatever simplifying strategies come most readily to hand, picking up on available (though unintended) cues, attending to simpler items of information, and neglecting or underweighting more complex, abstract, or unfamiliar aspects of the scenario (even though these are regarded by the researchers who have spent days or weeks devising and refining them as critically important). All of these factors are liable to produce response patterns of the kinds discussed earlier, which may make interesting reading in academic journals and give fresh insights into the rich and varied ways in which people process information, but which provide rather flimsy foundations for major decisions about the allocation of scarce resources between health and safety and a host of other things that may contribute to people's welfare.

Taking this view, some researchers have proposed that we try to harness the process of preference construction: As Gregory et al. (1993, p. 179) put it rather memorably, we should see ourselves "not as archaeologists, carefully uncovering what is there, but as architects, working to build a defensible expression of value."

Seductive though this imagery is, there remains the problem of how to implement it. Gregory et al. (1993) appear to favor organizing the process around the framework of multiattribute utility theory, and it would certainly be valuable to see how far and under what conditions this can be done – and what quantity and quality of research resources would be required. However, it seems highly likely that any such procedures would require far more time per respondent, so that unless funding for this kind of research is to be considerably increased, sample sizes will necessarily be rather smaller than for conventional one-shot, questionnaire-based surveys. Thus Gregory et al. (p. 189) talk in terms of studies involving "fewer than 100 people. Depth of value analysis is substituted for breadth of population sampling." No doubt, some researchers and policy makers will be nervous about such a relatively small sample combined with such a large input from the researcher/interviewer. It is certainly something that would require careful monitoring. On the other hand, it is now clear that large random sample surveys by themselves are not going to provide the necessary answers if the methods they employ are vulnerable to substantial biases and inconsistencies that are poorly understood and for which it is difficult to adjust.

Recently, those of us engaged in the HSE project have tried to explore approaches that are not as formal and highly structured as conventional multiattribute utility analysis, but that share the same broad strategy of presenting smaller samples/panels with questions that attempt to break down the tradeoff between money and risk of death into a number of simpler and conceptually more manageable steps. In a study carried out during the latter half of October and the first half of November 1997, we proceeded as follows:

1. Respondents were first presented with questions designed to elicit (a) their willingness to pay for the *certainty* of a quick and complete cure for a particular *nonfatal* road injury of lesser severity and (b) their willingness to accept compensation for the certainty of sustaining the same injury.
2. On the assumption that a respondent's underlying preferences obey minimal conditions of consistency and regularity, these WTP and WTA responses were used to derive a broad estimate of the rate at which the person concerned is willing to trade off wealth against risk of the nonfatal injury.
3. Respondents were then presented with SG questions aimed at eliciting their willingness to trade off the risk of the nonfatal injury against the risk of death.
4. Finally, the estimated rate of the tradeoff of wealth against the risk of the nonfatal injury derived from stage (2) was chained to the responses obtained at stage (3) in order to infer the respondent's implicit rate of tradeoff between wealth and risk of death.

This four-stage approach has several advantages over the procedure that was employed in the earlier studies. In stage 1, the valuation questions relate to a nonfatal injury of a type that most respondents can more readily conceptualize on the basis of their past experience of injury and illness. Moreover, these questions do not require respondents to trade off money directly against risk. To the extent that respondents *are* required to think about risk, the task involved in the questions in stage (3) is framed entirely within the domain of physical risk and is therefore a comparison of "like with like" – and is similar in principle to the kind of judgment entailed by many decisions about health care treatments that are intended to improve people's health but carry at least some risk that the patient could end up worse off.

In using this four-stage approach, we discovered that the vast majority of respondents found the various questions much more manageable than appears to have been the case with the direct money/risk of death tradeoffs used in the earlier studies. Moreover, responses showed clear evidence of sensitivity to variations in the severity of the nonfatal injury to which the questions related, as well as evidence of a broadly acceptable level of internal consistency.

After several rounds of piloting, the main study involved a quota sample of 167 respondents. Interviews were conducted on a one-to-one basis by members of the research team. Fuller details are given in Carthy et al. (1999), but the key results are as follows.

As tends to be the case in most studies eliciting values of this kind, the distribution of individual responses was widely spread, with the majority of respondents located at the lower end of the distribution, whereas a minority at the upper end appeared to have very high rates of trade-off. Indeed, a few responses were *so* much larger than the rest that there were serious doubts about their reliability (especially as they may well have been the result of a compounding of errors in the four-stage estimation process – about which more later), so that it seemed reasonable to compute means with these observations trimmed. On this basis, the mean estimate of VPF was in the range 1,000,000 to 1,500,000, with the VPF entailed by the median response being in the region of 500,000.

To the extent that aggregate willingness to pay for safety is reflected in mean rather than median responses, there was clearly a case for placing somewhat more emphasis on the range of VPFs entailed by mean responses. On the other hand, there is an argument that, if anything, people's responses to hypothetical WTP questions may overstate what they would *actually* be prepared to pay, which would suggest giving at least some weight to the more modest median response. Thus, all things considered, it seemed that any figure in the range £750,000 to £1,250,000 could be regarded as being broadly acceptable. Because this range encompassed the (then) current U.K. Department of the Environment, Transport and the Regions value of £850,000, the results provided a broad endorsement of the department's figure and no change in the latter was recommended.

Prospects for the Future

Although there were many encouraging aspects to the study just described, and although we have a reasonable degree of confidence in the policy recommendations that emerged from it, we recognize that there are still a number of difficulties to be addressed and further issues to be explored. Following are three examples; however, this is far from being an exhaustive list.

First, the multistage chained approach may have the advantage of breaking the overall task down into more digestible components; but the other side of this coin is that it thereby allows the possibility of errors and inconsistencies to creep in at more points in the process – and, as a result of the chaining procedure, to become magnified. One example of this problem was encountered in some very recent work for the New Zealand Land Transport Safety Authority, where a subsample of respondents was asked to undertake a matching exercise to establish some relativities between Minor and Temporary injuries, between Temporary and Permanent injuries, and between Permanent and Fatal injuries. In effect, these respondents were asked to say how many cases of one level of injury (e.g., Minor) would need to be prevented for this to be judged equivalent to preventing one case of the next level of injury (e.g., Temporary). Thus a respondent might say that one project would need to prevent 25 Minor injuries to be judged as good as another project that would prevent a single Temporary injury; that a project would need to prevent 50 Temporary injuries to be rated equivalent to one that prevented a single Permanent injury; and that preventing 20 Permanent injuries would be as good as preventing a single Fatality. If such a set of responses is chained together and attached to a value of preventing a Minor injury of NZ$100 (roughly US$60), the implied VPF is NZ$100 $\times$ 25 $\times$ 50 $\times$ 20 = NZ$2.5 million (which happens to be only slightly above the figure of NZ$2.25 million being used by the New Zealand government at the time of the study). However, it is easy to see how a couple of modest perturbations along the chain – or perhaps a single larger response at some point – could rapidly inflate the figure. A chain such as NZ$ 100 $\times$ 200 $\times$ 50 $\times$ 100 – no single element of which is obviously outrageous – would entail a VPF of NZ$100 million, a figure that would be wildly in excess of anything policymakers (or, we would conjecture, the vast majority of respondents themselves) would consider appropriate.

When analyzing the data generated by the New Zealand study, it became clear that the chained matching procedure outlined previously had generated a large enough number of very high individual VPFs to push the mean estimate derived from that procedure way out of line with estimates derived by the other approaches used in that study. Another variant used in that study, whereby relativities were estimated by modified SG questions rather than matching questions, was also susceptible to the problem of certain extreme responses being further magnified – or even becoming unusable – although such cases were not nearly as prevalent as with the matching procedure. Thus, although chaining procedures may have a good deal to recommend them, they are far from being a complete panacea, and they need to be handled with considerable care. Fortunately, we had taken the precaution of including other questions that were not subject to these particular effects – although, as is common in this kind of exercise, those other questions also produced an upper tail (albeit a more modest one) of very large values.

A second issue that we and our colleagues began to address in the latter part of the HSE study was whether different VPFs (and correspondingly different values for preventing nonfatal injuries/illnesses) should be used for different areas of health and safety. For example, should the prevention of deaths in railway accidents be accorded a different value than the prevention of deaths on the roads? Would it be in line with public preferences for more money – or less – to be spent preventing deaths in fires in public buildings (such as shops, offices, and hotels) than on preventing deaths in fires in people's own homes? Do the kinds of factors that psychological research has identified as feeding into people's *perceptions* of risk – such as the *voluntariness* of the risk, the degree of personal *responsibility* or *control*, the sense of *dread* evoked, or the extent (or lack) of *expert knowledge* about the risk – carry over into a desire for different values to be placed on preventing deaths in different contexts? Some earlier work (e.g., Jones-Lee and Loomes, 1995) had suggested that those who frequently travel both by car and by London Underground *would* subscribe to a somewhat (but not *greatly*) higher VPF being used in project evaluation for the Underground than the corresponding value for the roads.

Subsequent work for the HSE project on the relativities between different contexts has only recently been completed, and at the time of writing, the final report is not yet in the public domain. However, what we can say provisionally at this stage is that the kinds of differentials implicit in actual public policy do not necessarily coincide with the preferences elicited directly from members of the public. On the other hand, in the course of expressing their preferences in these matters, there appears to be at least some evidence that respondents are susceptible to yet other biases, including what seems (from the perspective of conventional wisdom) to be a disproportionate weight placed on the baseline level of risks in the various contexts, with this baseline information tending to obscure the extent to which respondents would themselves benefit to different degrees from safety improvements in those different contexts. Our initial hope was that trying to determine how VPFs in other contexts should be set relative to each other and to a "benchmark" VPF (such as the one used for road safety) might be less vulnerable to a host of undesirable effects, and provide a more robust and coherent "tariff" of values, than trying to estimate different VPFs via a series of separate WTP studies. However, once again, experience suggests that practice is rather less straightforward than theory and that although some problems may be avoided by taking this alternative route, there are others lying in wait to take their place.

Which brings us to our third sample of challenging issues: the more general question of the extent to which practical policy should be guided by the prescriptions of theories based on assumptions that have been found to be violated so regularly and so stubbornly in study after study. In the world of textbooks populated by individuals whose preferences are highly articulated, well behaved, and finely tuned, the rationale for using mean WTP-based values as the measure of the benefit of health and safety improvements seems entirely persuasive. But in the world of empirical research, which is populated by individuals with only partly formed and rather imprecise values, whose preferences prior to being confronted with decisions may exist only at a relatively basic level, and whose constructed responses may be vulnerable to a wide variety of influences not incorporated into the standard model, what use can/should public sector policy make of the results generated by the kinds of surveys discussed in this chapter?

Unfortunately, social science does not yet know enough about the nature of people's underlying values, and the process by which they develop and express their preferences, to be able to answer this question. What is clear to us, however, is that a body of research is now building up that is providing insights into the variety of factors that enter into people's judgments of value. To the extent that some effects may be identified as the source of bias and distortion, it may be possible for researchers to try to control for them and for decision makers to adjust for them. To the extent that other effects reflect genuine and robust elements of real concern to people, it may be possible for theorists to incorporate them and for practitioners to give them some weight.

Thus, although we acknowledge that there is still a substantial gap between the quality of the data we are currently able to gather and the information we would ideally like to have, we would still argue that it is better to use the results we *can* obtain, subject to a number of caveats, and moderated by a degree of (explicit) judgment on the part of those charged with the formulation of public policy, than to have policy determined by introspection, intuition, interest group pressure, and political expediency that would otherwise be the principal engines of resource allocation in the fields of health and safety.

Finally, although the imperfections and imprecision of people's preferences may pose many problems for those engaged in trying to elicit reliable values, there may be at least one silver lining to this particular cloud. For if it is true that people find it hard to be sure whether a response that implies a VPF of, say, £500,000 is really better or worse than a response that implies a VPF of, say, £2 million, and if it is hard for researchers to devise any methods that effectively distinguish between the two, this suggests that any value within that range might be regarded by many members of the public as no better or worse than any other, and may therefore be an acceptable basis for policy. Thus, demanding higher degrees of precision, or agonizing over which value within such a range is *the* correct one, may turn out to be less important than the conventional model of preferences might suggest. On the other hand, giving serious thought to the question of how to reformulate our model of preferences in light of the evidence, and considering the more general implications of such a model for public policy prescription, would seem to merit a prominent place on the research agenda.

References

Acton, J. P. (1973), *Evaluating Public Programs to Save Lives: The Case of Heart Attacks*, Research Report R-73-02, Santa Monica: Rand Corporation.

Baron, J. and Greene, J. (1996), "Determinants of Insensitivity to Quantity in Valuations of Public Goods: Contribution, Warm Glow, Budget Constraints, Availability and Prominence," *Journal of Experimental Psychology: Applied*, **2**, 107–25.

Beattie, J., Chilton, S., Cookson, R., Covey, J., Hopkins, L., Jones-Lee, M. W., Loomes, G., Pidgeon, N., Robinson, A. and Spencer, A. (1996), *Valuing Health and Safety Controls: A Literature Review*, Health and Safety Executive Research Report.

Beattie, J., Covey, J., Dolan, P., Hopkins, L., Jones-Lee, M., Loomes, G., Pidgeon, N., Robinson, A. and Spencer, A. (1998), "On the Contingent Valuation of Safety and the Safety of Contingent Valuation: Part 1 – *Caveat Investigator*," *Journal of Risk and Uncertainty*, **17**, 5–25.

Butler, D. and Loomes, G. (1988), "Decision Difficulty and Imprecise Preferences," *Acta Psychologica*, **68**, 183–96.

Carthy, T., Chilton, S., Covey, J., Hopkins, L., Jones-Lee, M., Loomes, G., Pidgeon, N. and Spencer, A. (1999), "On the Contingent Valuation of Safety and the Safety of Contingent Valuation: Part 2 – The CV/SG "Chained Approach," *Journal of Risk and Uncertainty*, **17**, 187–213.

Covey, J., Jones-Lee, M. W., Loomes, G. and Robinson, A. (1995), "The Exploratory Empirical Study," in Ives, D., Soby, B., Goats, G., Ball, D. J., Covey, J., Jones-Lee, M. W., Loomes, G., and Robinson, A., *Exploratory Study of Consumers' Willingness to Pay for Food Risk Reduction*, Report to the Ministry of Agriculture, Food and Fisheries.

Dolan, P., Jones-Lee, M. W. and Loomes, G. (1995), "Risk-Risk vs. Standard Gamble Procedures for Measuring Health State Utilities," *Applied Economics*, **27**, 1103–11.

Dubourg, W. R., Jones-Lee, M. W. and Loomes, G. (1994), "Imprecise Preferences and the WTP-WTA Disparity," *Journal of Risk and Uncertainty*, **9**, 115–33.

Dubourg, W. R., Jones-Lee, M. W. and Loomes, G. (1997), "Imprecise Preferences and Survey Design in Contingent Valuation," *Economica*, **64**, 681–702.

Frederick, S. and Fischhoff, B. (1997), "Magnitude Insensitivity in Elicited Valuations: Examining Conventional Explanations," mimeo, Department of Social and Decision Sciences, Carnegie Mellon University.

Gregory, R., Lichtenstein, S. and Slovic, P. (1993), "Valuing Environmental Resources: A Constructive Approach," *Journal of Risk and Uncertainty*, **7**, 177–97.

Jones-Lee, M. W. and Loomes, G. (1995), "Scale and Context Effects in the Valuation of Transport Safety," *Journal of Risk and Uncertainty*, **11**, 183–203.

Jones-Lee, M. W., Loomes, G. and Philips, P. R. (1995a), "Valuing the Prevention of Non-Fatal Road Injuries: Contingent Valuation vs. Standard Gambles," *Oxford Economic Papers*, **47**, 676–95.

Jones-Lee, M. W., Loomes, G. and Robinson, A. (1995b), "Why Did Two Theoretically Equivalent Methods Produce Two Very Different Values?" in *Contingent Valuation, Transport Safety and Value of Life*, eds Schwab, N. and Soguel, N., Boston: Kluwer.

Kahneman, D. and Knetsch, J. (1992), "Valuing Public Goods: The Purchase of Moral Satisfaction," *Journal of Environmental Economics and Management*, **22**, 57–70.

Kasperson, R. E. (1992), "The Social Amplification of Risk: Progress in Developing an Integrative Framework," in *Social Theories of Risk*, eds Krimsky, S. and Golding, D., Westport: Praeger.

Llewellyn-Thomas, H., Sutherland, H. J., Tibshirani, R., Ciampi, A., Till, J. E. and Boyd, N. F. (1982), "The Measurement of Patients' Values in Medicine," *Medical Decision Making*, **2**, 449–62.

Llewellyn-Thomas, H., Sutherland, H. J., Tibshirani, R., Ciampi, A., Till, J. E. and Boyd, N. F. (1984), "Describing Health States: Methodological Issues in Obtaining Values for Health States," *Medical Care*, **22**, 543–52.

Miller, T. and Guria, J. (1991), *The Value of Statistical Life in New Zealand: Market Research on Road Safety*, Wellington, New Zealand: Land Transport Division, Ministry of Transport.

Savage, L. J. (1954), *The Foundations of Statistics*, New York: Wiley.

Slovic, P. (1995), "The Construction of Preferences," *American Psychologist*, **50**, 364–71.

Thaler, R. (1985), "Mental Accounting and Consumer Choice," *Marketing Science*, **4**, 199–214.

Viscusi, W. K., Magat, W. A. and Huber, J. (1991), "Pricing Environmental Health Risks: Survey Assessments of Risk–Risk and Risk–Dollar Trade-offs for Chronic Bronchitis," *Journal of Environmental Economics and Management*, **21**, 35–51.

von Neumann, J. and Morgenstern, O. (1944), *Theory of Games and Economic Behavior*, Princeton: Princeton University Press.

10 Measuring Value Tradeoffs: Problems and Some Solutions

Jonathan Baron

The measurement of value tradeoffs is central to applied decision analysis. It was also a major concern of Jane Beattie from the time of her thesis to her work with Graham Loomes and others, described in chapter 9. In part of her thesis, Jane examined the use of holistic rating judgments of two-attribute stimuli as a way of measuring the tradeoff between the two attributes (Beattie & Baron, 1991).

One possible effect of difficulty is to make judgments of tradeoffs more labile, more influenced by extraneous factors. One kind of tradeoff judgment is to make holistic desirability ratings of stimuli in a set of stimuli that vary in at least two dimensions, such as the cost of a purchase and the travel time required to buy it. Tradeoffs between two dimensions can be assessed by asking how much of one dimension must be given up in order to compensate for a change in the other dimension with respect to the effect of these changes on the rating. This measure of tradeoffs should reflect the effect of these changes on the goals that motivate the judgments, such as the willingness to sacrifice time to save money. It should not be affected by the range of values on either dimension.

We found, in general, that tradeoffs were, in fact, unaffected by the range of variation, provided that the range conveyed no relevant information about utility. If this result is generally true, then holistic judgments would be a good way to measure tradeoffs for practical purposes. Mellers and Cooke (1994), however, found range effects in several similar tasks.

The research presented in this chapter has found an inconsistent pattern of sensitivity to ranges themselves. However, it also has found

This research was supported by National Science Foundation Grant SBR95-20288 and by a grant from the University of Pennsylvania Cancer Center.

substantial effects of magnitude of the values, which can be independent of the range of variation within a group of trials. For example, the
amount of money that must be saved to justify spending an extra hour is
greater when the purchase price is higher, as if the utility of money were
judged as a proportion of the price rather than as an absolute amount.
Some range effects may result from magnitude effects, but we still do not
understand the conditions that produce range effects when magnitude
is held constant.

Introduction

The measurement of value tradeoffs is central to applied decision analysis. How much money is a life worth? A year of health? An hour's relief
from pain? In choosing a cancer treatment, how should we trade off the
symptoms caused by the treatment against the probability of a cure? In
buying a car, how should we trade off the safety of the car for the driver
against its effects on air pollution? If we could answer these questions
on the average, then we could design policies designed to maximize
utility. For example, a health-care provider could provide all lifesaving
treatments up to the point at which the average cost per year of life
is more than its customers or citizens, on the average, think should be
paid. The same can be said for other public expenditures ranging from
highway safety to protection of wilderness.

A problem with this approach is that responses are often internally
inconsistent (Baron, 1997a). Some of the inconsistency is specific to the
methods used. For example, the use of hypothetical gambles seems to
be distorted by the certainty effect and, more generally, by the fact that
probabilities greater than 0 and less than 1 seem to be treated as more
similar than they should be.

Other sources of inconsistency are more ubiquitous. Primarily, people
are insensitive to quantity when they compare two attributes. People
find it surprisingly easy to say that health is more important than money,
without paying much attention to the amount of health or money in
question. For example, Jones-Lee, Loomes, and Philips (1995) asked
respondents to evaluate hypothetical automobile safety devices that
would reduce the risk of road injuries. The respondents indicated their
willingness to pay (WTP) for the devices. WTP judgments were, on the
average, only 20% higher for a risk reduction of 12 in 100,000 than for a
reduction of 4 in 100,000. Such results imply that the rate of substitution

between money and the good, the dollars per unit, depends strongly on the amount of the good. If a risk reduction of 12 is worth $120 and a risk reduction of 4 is worth $100, then the dollars per unit of risk reduction are 10 and 25, respectively. If we extrapolate downward linearly, a risk reduction of zero would be worth $90. Or we might think that the scale is logarithmic, so one-third of the risk reduction would be worth five-sixths of the price. So a risk reduction of $4 \cdot 1/3 \cdot 1/3$, or .44, would be worth $100 \cdot 5/6 \cdot 5/6$ or $69.44, or about $156 per unit of risk reduction. The dollars per unit could increase without limit. We cannot communicate the size of the error with a confidence interval – even on a logarithmic scale – because the confidence interval is potentially unbounded. This makes it difficult to generalize results to different amounts of money or risk, a generalization that is nearly always required. Even when such generalization is not required, such extreme insensitivity over small ranges raises questions about the validity of any single estimate.

The problem is not limited to WTP. It happens when respondents are asked to assign relative weights directly to nonmonetary attributes. Typically, the attributes are given with explicit ranges, such as "the difference between paying $10 and paying $20" or "the difference between a risk of 1 in 10,000 and a risk of 2 in 10,000." The weights are typically undersensitive to the range of the attributes. If risk is judged to be twice as important as cost, this judgment is relatively unaffected when risk reduction is doubled (Weber & Borcherding, 1993). Keeney (1992, p. 147) calls this kind of undersensitivity to range "the most common critical mistake."

A third type of judgment suffers from the same problem: the judgment of the relative utility of two intervals. In health contexts, respondents are often asked to evaluate some condition, such as blindness in one eye, on a scale anchored at normal health and at death. Implicitly, they are asked to compare two intervals: normal – blind-in-one-eye and normal – death. What happens when we change the standard, the second interval? Normatively, the judgment should change in proportion. For example, keeping normal at one end of each dimension, the utility of blind-in-one-eye relative to death should be the product of two other proportions: the utility of blind-in-one-eye relative to blindness (in both eyes), and the utility of blindness relative to death. In fact, people do not adjust sufficiently for changes in the standard (Ubel et al., 1996), just as they do not adjust sufficiently for changes in the magnitude of other dimensions involved in other judgments of tradeoffs. I shall call this phenomenon *ratio inconsistency* because it is based on a product of ratios (following Baron et al., 1999). I shall also view these various forms of insensitivity as manifestations of the same problem. In principle, all known manifestations of insensitivity could be understood as the tendency to give the same answer, regardless of the question. It is an open question whether the various forms of inconsistency can be explained in the same ways or not.

Undersensitivity to range can be reduced. Fischer (1995) found complete undersensitivity to range when respondents were asked simply to assign weights to ranges (e.g., to the difference between a starting salary of $25,000 and $35,000 and between 5 and 25 vacation days – or between 10 and 20 vacation days – for a job). When the range of vacation days doubled, the judged importance of the full range of days (10 vs. 20) relative to the range of salaries ($10,000) did not increase. Thus, respondents showed inconsistent rates of substitution, depending on the range considered. Respondents were more sensitive to the range, with their weights coming closer to the required doubling with a doubling of the range, when they used either direct tradeoffs or swing weights. In a direct tradeoff, the respondent changed one value of the more important dimension so that the two dimensions were equal in importance, for example, by lowering the top salary of the salary dimension. (Weights must then be inferred by either measuring or assuming a utility function on each dimension.) In the swing weight method, respondents judged the ratio between the less important and more important ranges, for example, "the difference between 5 and 25 vacation days is one-fifth of the difference between $25,000 and $35,000."

In the direct tradeoff method, the range is given for one dimension only. The task is thus analogous to a free-response contingent valuation (CV) judgment, so we might still expect – and Fischer still found – some insensitivity. Baron and Greene (1996) found that this insensitivity could be reduced still further by giving no specific ranges for *either* dimension. Respondents were asked to produce two intervals, one on one dimension and one on the other, that were equally large in utility. For example, instead of asking "How much would you be willing to pay in increased taxes per year to prevent a 10% reduction in acquisition of land for national parks?", the two-interval condition asked subjects to give an amount of taxes and a percentage reduction that they would find equivalent. Of course, one end of each interval was zero.

Holistic Ratings

Another way to measure tradeoffs is to ask for ratings of stimuli that vary in two or more dimensions. For example, the stimuli could be policies that differ in cost and amount of risk reduced. If the respondent produces enough of these judgments, we could fit simple models to her responses and infer how much of a change in one dimension is needed to make up for a change in another dimension, so that both changes together would yield the same rating. The rating response need not be a linear function of overall utility (but we could assume that it was for a first approximation). A large variety of methods use this general approach. The two most common terms are functional measurement (e.g., Anderson & Zalinski, 1988) and conjoint analysis (Green & Srinivasan, 1990; Green & Wind, 1973; Louviere, 1988).

In such a method, the numbers given to the respondent on each dimension represent attributes that the respondent values, such as minutes or dollars. The value of these attributes do not, we assume, depend on what other things are available. Thus the tradeoff between a given change on one dimension and a given change on the other should be unaffected by the range of either dimension within the experimental session. If a change from 50 to 100 minutes is worth a change from $20 to $40, then this should be true regardless of whether the dollar range is from $20 to $40 or from $2 to $400. The need for invariance in the substitution of time and money arises from the basic idea of utility itself, which is that it is about goal achievement (Baron, 1994). The extent to which goals are achieved depends on what happens, not on what options were considered.

Two exceptions should be noted, however. First, sometimes the options considered affect the outcome through their effects on emotions. Winning $80 may seem better if that is the first prize than if $160 is the first prize because of the disappointment of not winning the first prize. Second, in some cases, the *meaning* of a description in terms of goal achievement depends on the range. For example, the raw score on an examination can have a different effect on goal achievement as the range of scores is varied if the examination is graded on a curve. Even when this is not true, respondents who know little about a quantitative variable may think of it this way because they cannot evaluate the significance of the numbers (e.g., "total harmonic distortion" when buying an audio system; see Hsee, 1996).

Beattie and Baron (1991), using such a holistic rating task, found no effects of relative ranges on rates of substitution with several pairs of dimensions, but we found range effects with some dimensions, particularly those for which the numerical representation was not clearly connected to fundamental objectives, such as numerical grades on an exam. (The meaning of exam grades depends on the variance.) This gave us hope that holistic ratings could provide consistent and meaningful judgments of tradeoffs. Lynch et al. (1991) also found mostly no range effects for hypothetical car purchases, except in one study with novice consumers. (They used correlations rather than rates of substitution, however, so it is difficult to tell how much their results were due to changes in variance.) Mellers and Cooke (1994), however, found range effects in tasks where the relation of the numbers to fundamental objectives was clear, such as distance to the campus of apartments.

The experiments I report here have made me more pessimistic about holistic ratings. Although I cannot fully explain the discrepant results, I show that holistic ratings are generally subject to another effect that is potentially just as serious: a magnitude effect. People judge the utility of a change or a difference as a proportion of the overall magnitude of potential, even when the change alone is more closely related to the goal (Baron, 1997a). The result is that judgments are dependent on the maximum magnitude on each attribute scale. The classic example is the jacket-calculator problem of Tversky and Kahneman (1981; replicated under some conditions by Darke & Freedman, 1993).

Imagine that you are about to purchase a jacket for $125, and a calculator for $15. The calculator salesman informs you that the calculator you wish to buy is on sale for $10 at the other branch of the store, located 20 minutes' drive away. Would you make the trip to the other store? (Tversky & Kahneman, 1981, p. 457)

Most subjects asked were willing to make the trip to save the $5. Very few subjects were willing to make the trip to save $5 on the jacket, although, in an otherwise identical problem. In both cases, the "real" question is whether you would be willing to drive 20 minutes for $5. People judge the utility of saving $5 as a proportion of the total amount rather than in terms of its effects on other goals, that is, its opportunity cost. Baron (1997b) found a similar effect: Subjects were less willing to pay for government medical insurance for diseases when the number of people who could not be cured was higher, holding constant the number who could be cured. When many people were not cured, the effect of curing a few seemed like a "drop in the bucket" and was thus undervalued.

Typically, magnitude and range effects are confounded. *Magnitude* is defined as the difference between the maximum and zero, and *range* is defined as the difference between the maximum and minimum. Usually experimenters who vary the range manipulate the maximum as well. Indeed, both Beattie and Baron (1991) and Mellers and Cooke (1994) had higher magnitudes of the maximum on each attribute whenever the range was higher. Evidently, magnitude effects do not always occur. The fact that they occur, however, makes the measure untrustworthy. The point is that they would occur if magnitude were varied enough, so the tradeoff that subjects make is specific to the magnitudes of the dimensions they are given.

Baron (1997b) suggests that the magnitude effect is part of a more basic confusion between similar (and often correlated) quantitative measures. Just as young children answer questions about number as if they were about length (a correlated attribute), and vice versa, adults answer questions about differences as if they were about ratios, and vice versa. Differences and ratios are correlated. Thus, in discussions of drug effects on risk, people talk about relative risk (e.g., the ratio of breast cancer cases with the drug to the ratio of cases without it) rather than about change in risk (difference between cancer probability with and without the drug). It is the latter that is more relevant to decision making.

Both pure range effects and magnitude effects can result from the use of a *proportionality heuristic*. Someone who uses this heuristic evaluates a change on one attribute as a proportion of something else, even when it should be evaluated on its own. This is a reasonable heuristic to use when we know nothing about the meaning of an attribute. For example, when we evaluate the difference between 30 points and 40 points on a midterm exam, the meaning of this difference may well depend on whether the range of scores was 20–50 or 0–60.

Overview

In the rest of this chapter, I describe two sets of experiments. The first set shows the existence of magnitude effects on holistic ratings and describes some of the limits on their occurrence. The results are damaging to the idea of using holistic ratings to measure tradeoffs.

In the second set of experiments, I explore a different approach, picking up where Jones-Lee and Loomes left off in chapter 9. Perhaps we can measure value tradeoffs by working with the respondents, confronting them with the inconsistencies in their judgments and asking them to resolve these inconsistencies. Decision analysts claim that consistency checks usually do not violate the respondent's best judgment; for example: "... if the consistency checks produce discrepancies with the previous preferences indicated by the decision maker, these discrepancies must be called to his attention and parts of the assessment procedure should be repeated to acquire consistent preferences.... Of course, if the respondent has strong, crisp, unalterable views on all questions and if these are inconsistent, then we would be in a mess, wouldn't we? In practice, however, the respondent usually feels fuzzier about some of his answers than others, and it is this degree of fuzziness that usually makes a world of difference. For it then becomes usually possible to generate a final coherent set of responses that does not violently contradict any strongly held feelings" (Keeney & Raiffa, 1993, p. 271). Such checks can even improve the perceived validity of numerical judgments (e.g., Keeney & Raiffa, 1993, p. 200).

Baron et al. (1999) found evidence supporting these claims in studies of elicitation of health utilities. Consistency checks for the kind of ratio insensitivity described previously led to no serious objections from the subjects. Moreover, different kinds of utility measures were more likely to agree when each measure was adjusted, by the subject, to make it consistent.

Experiment 1

Experiment 1 built on the jacket-calculator problem. Subjects did three tasks:

> *Rating:* Subjects rated purchases that differed in price and time for attractiveness.
>
> *WTP:* Subjects expressed their WTP money to save time or time to save money.
>
> *Difference judgments:* Subjects compared a time interval (e.g., "the difference between 30 minutes and 1 hour") and a price interval (e.g., "the difference between $90 and $100"). They indicated which mattered more to them and the relative sizes of the intervals in terms of what mattered.

Magnitude and range varied somewhat independently. Magnitude was manipulated by multiplying the price by 4. Range was varied in the rating task by changing the first two items in each group of eight.

Method

Fifty-three subjects – 38% males, 92% students, aged 17–52 (median, 19) – completed a questionnaire on the World Wide Web. Subjects were solicited through postings on newsgroups and links from various web pages. They were paid $4, and they had to provide an address and a Social Security number in order to be paid.

The questionnaire had two orders. Order did not affect the results. The questionnaire had four sections: Ratings, WTP, Difference judgments, and Ratings again.

The ratings task began, "Imagine you are buying a portable compact-disk player and you have settled on a brand that lists for $120. It is available at several stores, which differ in travel time from where you live (round trip), sale price, and terms of the warranty. Rate the following options for attractiveness on a scale from 1 to 9, where 1 means that you are very unlikely to choose this option and 9 means that you are very likely to choose it. Try to use the entire scale. The first two items are the worst and best." The items differed in price, travel time, and warranty. The warranty was not analyzed. It was used simply to create variation to allow duplicate presentation of items that were otherwise the same. It was counterbalanced with all other variables. A typical list of items to be rated was the one shown in Table 10.1.

Notice that, in this list, the first two items in each group of eight have a price range of $40 and a time range of 1 hour. In the contrasting condition, the time range was 2 hours (0 to 2 hours) and the price range was $20 ($90 to $110). In the high-magnitude conditions, price was simply multiplied by 3, so that the range was also multiplied by 3. Two goods, a CD player and a TV set, appeared in two orders, given to different subjects. In one order, the conditions were:

> CD, low price, high price range (low time range)
> TV, high price, high price range
> CD, low price, high time range (low time range)
> TV, high price, high time range

In the other order, the conditions were reversed.

Between the first two and second two ratings were the WTP and Difference conditions (always in that order). A typical item in the WTP condition read, "You plan to buy a $110 CD player at a store that is 1 hour away. What is the most time you would be willing to spend traveling in order to buy it for $100 instead?" or "What is the most you

Table 10.1. *CD Players*

Price	Travel Time	Warranty	Rating
$120	1.5 hr	None	
$80	30 min	1 year	
$110	30 min	None	
$90	1.5 hr	1 year	
$100	30 min	None	
$110	1 hr	1 year	
$100	1.5 hr	None	
$90	1 hr	1 year	
$120	1.5 hr	1 year	
$80	30 min	None	
$110	30 min	1 year	
$90	1.5 hr	None	
$100	30 min	1 year	
$110	1 hr	None	
$100	1.5 hr	1 year	
$90	1 hr	None	

would be willing to pay for one that is 30 minutes away?" The subject was instructed to answer in terms of total price or time. For the first order, the WTP conditions were ordered as shown in Table 10.2, and these were reversed for the second order.

For the Difference judgment, a typical item was:

Which difference matters more to you?

1. The difference between $90 and $100 for a CD player.
2. The difference between 30 minutes and 1.5 hours of travel time.

What percent of the larger difference is the smaller difference in terms of how much it matters?

(In retrospect, the wording of this item is difficult to understand. In the data analysis, however, subjects who showed misunderstanding by responding in the reverse way were eliminated.)

For the first order, the items are shown in Table 10.3 (reversed for the second order). Notice that the range manipulation involves both price

Table 10.2. *Goods Used for WTP Conditions in Experiment 1*

	Initial		Change to:	
Good	Price	Time	Price or Time	Dollars/Hour
CD	$90	1.5 hr	30 min	$15.68
CD	$110	30 min	$90	$39.56
CD	$90	1.5 hr	1 hr	$21.63
CD	$110	30 min	$100	$30.52
TV	$270	1.5 hr	30 min	$29.44
TV	$330	30 min	$270	$76.02
TV	$270	1.5 hr	1 hr	$38.86
TV	$330	30 min	$300	$60.84

Note: In the rightmost column are the geometric means of the inferred dollars per hour.

and time: When the price range is higher, the time range is lower. This makes the range manipulation stronger.

Results

The design permitted an inference of the tradeoff between dollars and hours in all condition. For ratings, I calculated the orthogonal contrast for the price and time effects on ratings and took the ratio. I calculated the geometric mean across subjects and did statistical tests on the

Table 10.3. *Items Used in the Difference Task in Experiment 1*

CD	$90–$100 vs. 30 min–1.5 hr	$15.54
CD	$90–$110 vs. 30 min–1 hr	$24.06
TV	$270–$300 vs. 30 min–1.5 hr	$25.83
TV	$270–$330 vs. 30 min–1 hr	$56.47

Note: The table shows the good, the intervals compared, and the geometric mean–implied dollars per hour of the responses.

logarithms. (It is arbitrary whether to use the ratio or its reciprocal. Using the log means that this choice affects only the sign, not the distance from zero.)

For ratings, the inferred monetary value of time was affected by magnitude (confounded with range) but unaffected by range alone. The (geometric mean) values were (for subjects who had sufficient data in both conditions being compared) $20.32 for large amounts of money versus $89.33 for small amounts ($t_{47} = 13.71$, $p = .0000$) and $43.60 when the money range was small (and the time range was large) versus $46.13 when the money range was large (and the time range was small).

For WTP, geometric means of inferred dollars per hour are shown in Table 10.1. T tests on the means of the relevant conditions (e.g., all the high dollar amounts versus all the low dollar amounts) showed that time was worth more when the dollar amount was higher ($t_{52} = 11.4$, $p = .0000$) and when the subject responded with money rather than time ($t_{44} = 8.14$, $p = .0000$). Subjects also paid more for time when the range of time was small or when the range of money was large, holding magnitude constant ($t_{51} = 4.34$, $p = .0001$). In sum, the WTP measure showed both magnitude and range effects, whereas the rating measure showed only a magnitude effect.

Difference judgments also showed effects of both range ($t_{47} = 3.85$, $p = .0004$) and magnitude ($t_{47} = 5.69$, $p = .0000$), as shown in Table 10.2. Magnitude was confounded with range. Thus these effects can be seen as a replication of the finding that matching judgments are insensitive to range (e.g., Fischer, 1995; see Baron, 1997a, for discussion).

To summarize the results, all three measures – holistic ratings, willingness to pay, and difference judgment – were affected by magnitude (confounded with range), but only difference judgments and WTP were affected by range alone. One explanation of these results is that the WTP and difference tasks presented two ends of the range to be compared, and this encouraged subjects to consider these two ends as the relevant reference points. Holistic ratings, by contrast, may have allowed subjects to adopt an implicit zero as the low end of each range.

Whatever the explanation, the fact remains that magnitude effects render these tasks unsatisfactory as measures of tradeoffs.

Experiment 2

Experiment 2 manipulated the range and magnitude locally, within each group of four hypothetical purchases, by presenting two items to establish a range and then another two to test the effect of the first two. Range was manipulated by holding constant the top of each dimension and varying the bottom: In one condition, the money ranged from $120 to $80 and the time from 120 to 0 min; in the other condition, the money ranged from $120 to $100 and the time from 120 to 60 min. The magnitude manipulation simply added $100 to the price, holding the range constant.

Method

Eighty subjects – 25% males, 51% students, aged 16 to 51 (median, 23) – completed a questionnaire on the World Wide Web for $5. The questionnaire began:

Purchases: time and money

This is about how people make tradeoffs between time and money when they buy consumer goods. Imagine that all the items refer to some piece of audio or video equipment like a compact-disk player or a TV. You have decided to buy a certain model in the price range indicated on each screen. The issue is whether you are willing to travel some distance in order to save money on the price.

Half the time, you will evaluate one purchase at a time on a 9-point scale (1 = very unlikely to buy, 5 = indifferent, 9 = very likely to buy). The rest of the time, you will compare two purchases, also on a 9-point scale (1 = A is much better, 5 = equal, 9 = B is much better). Some purchases will be repeated several times. This is not to annoy you but to make sure that you pay attention to their existence. When you see these repeated purchases, you don't have to give the same answer you have given before, but you can if you want.

There are 56 screens of questions (2 or 4 questions on a screen), followed by a few questions about you.

Each single-purchase evaluation (evaluation, for short) screen had four purchases, and each purchase-comparison screen had two. The purchases were described in terms of price and time, for example, "$100, 60 minutes." Table 10.4 shows the base values used for both evaluation and comparison conditions.

Each comparison screen presented a comparison of A and B and of C and D. Each evaluation screen presented A, B, C, and D separately. Notice that within this basic design, the first seven purchases have a high range of times (0–120 min) for purchases A and B and a low range of prices ($100–$120). The second seven purchases are the reverse (60–120 min vs. $80–$120). The last two purchases in each screen are the same

Table 10.4. *Base Conditions for Experiment 2*

					Purchase			
	A		*B*		*C*		*D*	
Case	$	*Min*	$	*Min*	$	*Min*	$	*Min*
1	100	120	120	0	120	60	100	120
2	100	120	120	0	110	60	100	90
3	100	120	120	0	120	90	110	120
4	100	120	120	0	120	60	100	90
5	100	120	120	0	120	90	100	120
6	100	120	120	0	120	60	110	120
7	100	120	120	0	110	60	100	120
8	80	120	120	60	120	60	100	120
9	80	120	120	60	110	60	100	90
10	80	120	120	60	120	90	110	120
11	80	120	120	60	120	60	100	90
12	80	120	120	60	120	90	100	120
13	80	120	120	60	120	60	110	120
14	80	120	120	60	110	60	100	120

Note: Each row represents the items presented on one screen. In the comparison condition, the subject compared A and B and then C and D. In the evaluation condition, the subject evaluated A, B, C, and D. In cases 1–7, the time range is high (0–120) and the dollar range is low (100–120). In cases 8–14, the time range is high (60–120) and the dollar range is high (80–120).

for the corresponding items. Thus, effects of the relative ranges of times and prices are determined by examining the responses to purchases C and D. Notice also that the tops of the ranges ($120 and 120 min) are constant within the items in the basic design.

This basic design was replicated four times to make the 56 screens. Replications 1 and 2 were comparisons, and replications 3 and 4 were evaluations. (Because of a programming error, evaluation data were lost for 28 subjects, leaving 52.) Replications 2 and 4 extended the magnitude of prices, and the range, by adding $100 to each price. Comparisons of replications 2 with 1, and 4 with 3, then, test for a magnitude effect.

The order of the 56 screens was randomized separately for each subject.

Results

As a measure of the tradeoff, I computed the relative preference for the option with lower price (and higher time). If people evaluate price and time with respect to their ranges, this relative preference would be greater when the range of prices is small and the range of times is high. This result occurred in the evaluations ($t_{51} = 4.67$, $p = .0000$) but not in the comparisons ($t = 0.94$). For the evaluation items, when price range was small, subjects favored the low-priced item by a mean rating difference of .30, but when the range was high, they favored the low-time item by .34.

A simple explanation of this result is that, in the evaluation condition, subjects attended to all four items presented on each screen. When one of the items contained a very low price, they gave it a high rating, but then felt obliged to give a lower rating to the item that did not have such a low price. In sum, for the evaluation items, the first two items set up a range of responses. In the comparison items, on the other hand, subjects simply compared the two items they were given. They did not feel bound by their responses to other items on the same screen.

Subjects showed no significant magnitude effect in either condition. Although this result seems optimistic, the presence of a range effect undercuts the optimism about using this task to measure value tradeoffs. The magnitude effect may depend on encouraging the subject to use zero as one of the reference points. When both ends of the dimension are explicitly stated (e.g., 120 min and 80 min) – rather than leaving it implicit that one end is zero – range effects may take over.

Experiment 3

Experiments 1 and 2 show either range effects or magnitude effects in the holistic rating. Despite the promising results of Beattie and Baron (1991), the use of holistic rating tasks does not seem to provide a reliable means of measuring tradeoffs consistently. The measures it provides seem to depend on what subjects use as the top and bottom reference point of each scale.

Another approach to eliciting consistent tradeoffs is to confront respondents with their inconsistencies and ask them to resolve them. That is difficult to do in holistic rating tasks because respondents would have to deal with many responses at once. When respondents make direct judgments of relative magnitude, however, resolution of inconsistency might be easier.

Experiment 3 is an example of one method that might be used to help resolve inconsistency. It involves the comparison of utility intervals. Examples of possible intervals include "the difference between 60 and 120 min," "the difference between $90 and $120," and "the difference between normal health and complete hair loss." The last sort of difference is of interest for measurement of health utilities. For example, if we wanted to determine whether the benefit of chemotherapy for cancer is worth the cost, part of the cost might be the side effects of the therapy. A standard way to measure utilities in health is to compare everything to the interval between "normal health" and "death." Policy makers often assume that this interval has the same utility for everyone.

Experiment 3 concerns health intervals of this sort rather than those involving time and money. The subject judges the utility of interval A as a proportion of B, B as a proportion of C, and A as a proportion of C. The AC proportion should be the product of the AB proportion and the BC proportion. Typically, the AC proportion is too high (as I noted earlier), which is a kind of insensitivity to the standard of comparison.

In the method used here, the subject is forced to resolve the inconsistency but is not told how to do so. The subject answers three questions on a computer screen. Then, if the answers are inconsistent, buttons appear on the screen next to each judgment. Each button says "Increase" or "Decrease" according to whether the judgment is too low or too high, respectively, relative to the other two judgments. Each button raises or lowers its associated response by one unit. The subject can make the responses consistent by clicking any or all of the buttons.

This experiment used three different methods for comparing intervals: time tradeoff (TTO), standard gamble (SG), and direct rating (in two versions, DT and DP to be described). In the TTO method, the subject judged how many weeks with one health condition was equivalent to 100 weeks with a less serious health condition. The ratio of the answer to 100 is taken as a measure of the utility of the less serious health condition relative to the more serious one, on the assumption that time and utility multiply to give a total utility. In the SG method, the subject gives a probability of the more serious health condition, and this is taken as a measure of the utility of the less serious condition, on the assumption that the expected utility is what matters. The direct rating method simply asks for a comparison of the intervals.

The intervals to be compared were constructed by manipulating either the health condition or its probability or duration. Each interval was bounded by normal health at one end. Two health conditions were used for the other end of each set of intervals, one more severe and one less severe. For TTO and DP (where P stands for probability), the third condition was a 50% chance of developing the less severe health condition. For SG and DT (T for time), the third condition was 50 weeks of the less severe condition instead of 100 weeks.

The idea of manipulating a health condition by changing its probability comes from Bruner (1999). Bruner was interested in measuring the utilities of the major side effects of prostate cancer treatments, sexual impotence, and urinary incontinence. She used the TTO method. She asked subjects, in effect, how much of their life expectancy they would sacrifice rather than have a treatment that would give them an 80% chance or a 40% chance, for example, of impotence. Over a wide range of probabilities, the answer to this question was insensitive to probability. Subjects' willingness to sacrifice part of their life expectancy did not depend on whether the probability of impotence was 40% or 80% (although they were a little less willing when it went up to 99%). This insensitivity to probability makes the measure useless as a way of eliciting judgments of the utility of impotence.

The critical question is the one that compares the discounted less severe health condition (50% or 50 days) with the more severe condition. For this to be a good utility measure, the answer should be half of that to the question that compares the nondiscounted less severe condition to the more severe condition. Will the adjustment process lead to this result?

Method

Sixty-three subjects completed a questionnaire on the World Wide Web for $3. The subjects were 60% female, 51% students, and had a median age of 24 (range, 13 to 45). Three additional subjects were not used because they gave the same initial answer to every group of items.

The introduction to the study, called "Health judgments," began:

This study is about different ways of eliciting numerical judgments of health quality. If we could measure the loss in health quality from the side effects of various cancer treatments, for example, we could help patients and policy makers decide whether the benefits of treatment are worth the costs in loss of quality.

The side effects are always written in CAPITAL LETTERS. Here are the effects:

HAIR LOSS (complete)
NAUSEA (food consumption half normal)
DIARRHEA (three times per day)
FATIGUE (enough to be unable to work)
There are also combinations of effects.

In some question, you make two options equal by saying how much time with one side effect is equivalent to a longer time with some other side effect that isn't so bad. In some cases, the side effects are not certain.

Make sure to try the practice items before going on.

In one kind of question, you give a time. You must answer with a number from 0 to 20. Feel free to use decimals. Here is an example (using deafness):

A. 100 weeks with deafness.
B. $\boxed{50}$ weeks with blindness and deafness.

To answer this, you must pick a number for B so that the two options are equal. Try picking different numbers of weeks for B, going up and down, until you feel A and B are equal. Do this now by clicking on one of these two buttons:

The buttons were labeled "A is worse now" and "B is worse now." Clicking one button adjusted the number of days in the box by smaller amounts. The next practice item used probability instead of time to equate two options. Subjects were also told about the rating items, and they were told the number of items. Finally, they were told:

After you enter your answers, the buttons will suggest changes in your numbers. They will say "Increase" or "Decrease." Please choose the button that is most consistent with your true judgment of the conditions. Keep clicking one button or another until you are told you can go on. I am interested in how you choose to adjust your responses when you are forced to adjust them . . . .

The items were worded as follows, with S1 being the less severe of two symptoms and S2 the more severe. S1 was always one of the four symptoms listed. S2 was either two of the symptoms, including S1 (e.g., NAUSEA AND FATIGUE when S1 was NAUSEA) or all four. (Each symptom occurred equally often as a member of the pair.)

TTO

Fill in each blank so that the two options are equal.

A. 50% chance of S1 for 100 weeks
B. S1 for _____ weeks

A. *S*1 for 100 weeks
B. *S*2 for ___ weeks

A. 50% chance of *S*1 for 100 weeks
B. *S*2 for ___ weeks

SG

Fill in each blank so that the two options are equal.

A. *S*1 for 50 weeks
B. ___ % chance of *S*1 for 100 weeks

A. *S*1 for 100 weeks
B. ___ % chance of *S*2 for 100 weeks

A. *S*1 for 50 weeks
B. ___ % chance of *S*2 for 100 weeks

DJ

If the difference between normal health and 100 weeks of *S*1 is 100, how large is the difference between normal health and 50 weeks of *S*1?

If the difference between normal health and 100 weeks of *S*2 is 100, how large is the difference between normal health and 100 weeks of *S*1?

If the difference between normal health and 100 weeks of *S*2 is 100, how large is the difference between normal health and 50 weeks of *S*1?

DJ

If the difference between normal health and *S*1 is 100, how large is the difference between normal health and a 50% chance of *S*1? All the symptoms in this example are for 100 weeks.

If the difference between normal health and *S*2 is 100, how large is the difference between normal health and a 100% chance of *S*1?

If the difference between normal health and *S*2 is 100, how large is the difference between normal health and a 50% chance of *S*1?

To the right of each response box was a button, which was blank at the outset. After the responses were filled in, the program first checked whether the third response was less than each of the others and required a change of answers if it was not. Then the program checked to see whether they were consistent. Consistency was defined in terms of the relation of the three responses: After all the responses were divided by 100, the third response had to be the product of the other two to the nearest unit. If the responses were consistent, the subject could go on to the next screen. If the third response was too high, the word "Increase" appeared on the first two buttons and "Decrease" appeared on the third button. The subject clicked any of the three buttons until told to go on. Each button adjusted the response by one unit, up for increases and down for decreases. (The subject could also type in the response.) If the third response was too low, "Increase" and "Decrease" were switched. The subject had to make the responses consistent before going to the next screen.

Results

Subjects were initially inconsistent and insensitive to probability and time, as expected. The requirement for them to become consistent made them more sensitive to probability and time.

The measure of inconsistency for each screen was the log (base 10) of the ratio of the third answer to the product of the first two answers (after all answers were divided by 100). This would be zero if the responses were consistent. The mean inconsistency over all four elicitation methods was .0245 ($t_{63} = 3.45$, $p = .0010$), which implies that the third answer was about 6% too high, averaged in this way. The four methods differed in the size of this effect ($F_{3,189} = 5.57$, $p = .0011$): .0422 for TTO, .0335 for SG, .0098 for DP, and .0123 for DT.

The main measure of insensitivity to probability and time was the ratio of the third answer to the second minus .5. (The normative standard was .5.) This measure was positive, as expected, if subjects adjusted too little for the change in probability and time between the second and third answers. The mean was .0260 ($t_{63} = 2.96$, $p = .0043$). The four methods differed in the size of this effect ($F_{3,189} = 6.49$, $p = .0001$): .0145 for TTO, .0475 for SG, .0284 for DJ, and .0135 for DT. (Note that these differences cannot be understood as involving effects of time vs. probability.)

The response to the first question did not differ significantly from .5 overall, although the four methods differed ($F_{3,189} = 5.33$, $p = .0015$), with means of .4714 for TTO, .5083 for SG, .5042 for DT, and .5106 for DP.

The main result of interest concerned the ratio of the second and third questions. It should have been .5, but its mean, over all methods, was, as noted, too high by .0260. After the adjustment for consistency, the mean was .0050, not significantly different from zero. The change was significant ($t_{63} = 3.65$, $p = .0005$). However, this result could arise artifactually if the adjustment button on the third answer said Decrease more often than it said Increase, assuming that the direction of change did not affect the magnitude of change. Accordingly, I computed the measure for the Increase and Decrease trials separately. The average change for the Decrease trials was .0842 (in a downward direction), and the average for the Increase trials was .0479 (in an upward direction). For the 52 subjects who had data for both cases, the mean difference between these was .0382. That is, the downward change was greater than the upward change so that, on the whole, subjects became more consistent ($t_{51} = 3.36$, $p = .0015$). Thus, the benefit of the adjustment is not simply the result of forcing subjects to move in the required direction. When they were forced to move in this direction, they moved more than when they were forced to move in the opposite direction. They also moved more often in the former direction (66% of the possible cases vs. 56%; $t_{51} = 1.76$, $p = .0422$, one-tailed).

Experiment 4

Experiment 4 illustrates another approach to consistency adjustment. Subjects were given an estimate of what their responses would be if they were consistent. Unlike Experiment 3, the subjects did not have to adjust their responses. They were given the adjusted responses as a suggestion only. At issue is whether they would accept the suggestion and become more consistent.

Experiment 4 used three different health conditions rather than using two health conditions, one of which was discounted. It used only two methods, TTO and DJ.

Method

Fifty-eight subjects completed a questionnaire on the World Wide Web for $5. The subjects were 65% female, 38% students, and had a median age of 27 (range, 12 to 69).

The introduction to the study, called "Health judgments," began:

This study is about different ways of eliciting numerical judgments of health quality. If we could measure the loss in health quality from various conditions, we could measure the benefits of treating or preventing these conditions. This would allow more efficient allocation of resources.

The conditions we consider are:
NEARSIGHTEDNESS (need glasses)
BLINDNESS IN ONE EYE

TOTAL BLINDNESS
PARTIAL DEAFNESS (hearing aid restores normal hearing)
DEAFNESS IN ONE EAR (complete, hearing aid doesn't help)
TOTAL DEAFNESS
LOSS OF WALKING IN ONE LEG
LOSS OF WALKING IN BOTH LEGS
PARALYSIS OF ALL LIMBS
SPLINT ON INDEX FINGER (dominant hand)
SPLINT ON HAND (dominant side)
SPLINT ON ARM (dominant side)
CAST ON FOOT
CAST ON LEG
CAST ON BOTH LEGS
LOSS OF EYEBROWS
LOSS OF HAIR ON FACE AND HEAD
LOSS OF ALL HAIR (including face and head)

Notice that these conditions are in six groups of three. Within each group, the conditions are ordered in severity. The subject had to do a TTO practice item before beginning, as in the last experiment. They were also told about the rating items. They were told the number of questions and encouraged to use decimals in their answers.

The first 36 trials contained 18 TTO judgments and 18 DJ items. Each TTO item was introduced with "How many days makes these two outcomes equal?" The direct judgment items were worded the same way as the practice item.

The subject made each type of judgment three times for each of the six groups of conditions. Within each group of conditions, the subject compared the first and second, first and third, and second and third conditions. $S1$ and $S2$ thus stand for the conditions being judged, for example, "BLINDNESS IN ONE EYE" and "TOTAL BLINDNESS." By using all three comparisons, I could test for internal consistency. In particular, the judgment of the extremes (the first condition as a proportion of the third) should be the product of the other two judgments (as proportions). These 36 trials were presented in random order, each on its own screen, which disappeared when the subject responded.

After these 36 trials, the subject saw 24 screens with three judgments to a screen, again in a random order. These consisted of two types of judgments, each in a trained and an untrained version, for each of the six groups of conditions.

In both trained and untrained conditions, each screen began: "Please respond to all three items again in the boxes provided. You do not need

Table 10.5. *Sample Stimulus for Experiment 4*

Original Responses	Consistent Responses	Final Responses
PARTIAL DEAFNESS was 5% as bad as DEAFNESS IN ONE EAR	14%	
PARTIAL DEAFNESS was 5% as bad as TOTAL DEAFNESS	2%	
DEAFNESS IN ONE EAR was 5% as bad as TOTAL DEAFNESS	14%	

to give the same response you gave, and you do not need to make your answers consistent. Try to make your answers reflect your true judgment."

In the trained DJ condition, the next paragraph read, "The second column shows one way to make the ratios of your answers agree. The second row percentage is the product of the percentage in the first and third rows." In the trained TTO condition, the last sentence read, "The second row ratio of days (to 100) is the product of the ratios in the first and third rows. This assumes that all days count equally."

The subject then saw a table with the items on the left and either two or three columns of numbers, like the ones shown, for example, in Table 10.5.

For the TTO, the upper left entry would have read, "100 days of DEAFNESS IN ONE EAR was as bad as 5 days of PARTIAL DEAFNESS," and the second column would contain days instead of a percentage. For the untrained condition, the second column was omitted. Let us refer to the three comparisons as AB, BC, and AC, for the three rows, respectively. AB and BC are adjacent, and AC is extreme.

The consistent values in the second column were computed so as to preserve the ratio of the two adjacent comparisons and otherwise make the responses consistent. The two adjacent comparisons (AB and BC) were multiplied by a correction factor, and the extreme comparison (AC) was divided by the same factor. (The correction factor was not constrained to be more or less than one.) In particular, the correction factor was $[AC/(AB \cdot BC)]^{1/3}$. The correct values were rounded to the nearest unit, but the subject was encouraged to use decimals.

Results

For each condition group, I computed a measure of inconsistency: $log_{10}[AC/(AB \cdot BC)]$. (The direction of the ratio is arbitrary. It could be inverted. The log ensures that inversion would affect only the sign of the inconsistency, not its magnitude.) I averaged this measure over the six sets of conditions, for each of the two methods, in the initial, trained, and untrained conditions. I also computed an absolute-value inconsistency measure for each condition group and averaged it in the same way. Table 10.6 shows the means of these two measures for the two methods.

The trained items were more consistent than the untrained ones, which, in turn, were more consistent than the initial items by both signed and absolute measures. I tested this with four analyses of variance, one for initial versus untrained items and one for untrained versus trained items, for each of the two inconsistency measures. It is superfluous to compare initial and trained items. But the comparison of initial and untrained items tests the (confounded) effects of doing the items together in a group and doing them for the second time. The initial versus untrained effect was significant for both signed measures ($F_{1,57} = 68.2$, $p = .0000$) and unsigned measures ($F_{1,57} = 62.0$, $p = .0000$). The effect of TTO versus DJ was significant only for the absolute measures

Table 10.6. *Mean Inconsistency Measures for the Two Methods*

Method	Inconsistency (Signed)	Absolute Inconsistency
TTO, initial	.28	.45
TTO, untrained	.11	.29
TTO, trained	.05	.19
DJ, initial	.25	.35
DJ, untrained	.08	.21
DJ, trained	.04	.14

($F_{1,57} = 17.9$, $p = .0001$): TTO was less consistent. In neither case was the interaction between method and initial versus untrained condition significant. The improvement that resulted from presenting the items together and again was present for both methods.

Inconsistency was smaller in trained than in untrained items for both signed and unsigned measures ($F_{1,57} = 8.14$, $p = .0060$, and $F_{1,57} = 51.6$, $p = .0000$, respectively). Again, the effect of method was significant only for the absolute measure ($F_{1,57} = 13.1$, $p = .0006$). The interaction between training and method was not significant. Training improves consistency in both methods.

Discussion

The first two experiments add to existing demonstrations that holistic ratings are sometimes subject to extraneous influences in the form of range effects or magnitude effects. We can account for these effects in general by assuming that subjects adopt two reference points, top and bottom, for each dimension and evaluate the position of an item relative to these reference points, at least some of the time. That is, they think of variation along the dimension as a proportion of the distance from top to bottom rather than as an absolute change along a dimension whose units have value in their own right. This is sometimes a reasonable method of evaluation, for example, in evaluating examination grades. But it is used even when the subject can evaluate the units in their own right.

What is adopted as the top and bottom is somewhat variable and dependent on details of the task. Experiment 1 found magnitude effects in holistic ratings, WTP, and DJ, in the tradeoff of time and money. It found range effects in WTP and DJ but not in holistic ratings. As noted, the rating task may have differed from the others in that subjects might have found it easier to adopt zero as the implicit bottom of the range.

Experiment 2 used four items at a time, with the first two items setting the range. It found range effects when subjects evaluated items one at a time, but not when they compared one item to the other within a single question. A possible explanation of this result is that the comparison format provides its own context, so subjects ignore the context in previous questions. If so, the direct comparison may be helpful in overcoming range effects. This conclusion would be similar to that of Fischer (1995). Note, however, that the direct comparison is very similar to the direct judgment tasks used in Experiments 3 and 4.

In those experiments, subjects compared two intervals rather than making a judgment of a single two-attribute stimulus. As found in previous studies (Baron et al., 1999; Ubel et al., 1996), all of these measures showed ratio inconsistency: Subjects did not give small enough numbers when they compared a small interval to a much larger one (or, conversely, they did not give large enough numbers in their other responses). When this inconsistency was called to their attention, responses became more consistent. This is the recommended approach of applied decision analysis, and so far it seems to work, at least in the sense that it yields usable, consistent answers.

Holistic judgments have other problems. When respondents are asked to rate multiattribute stimuli with several attributes, they seem to attend only to a couple of attributes that they find particularly important, thus ignoring the less important attributes too much (Hoffman, 1960, Figs. 3–7; von Winterfeldt & Edwards, 1986, p. 365). However, this is likely to be a less serious problem when respondents rate two attributes at a time. Still, the existence of range and magnitude effects seems difficult to avoid. The only way to avoid it seems to be to present explicit intervals for comparison.

This claim is consistent with the finding of Birnbaum (1978) and Birnbaum and Sutton (1992) that subjects asked to judge the ratio of two stimuli respond (with a nonlinear response function) to the difference between the stimuli rather than to the ratio of their distances from zero (no stimulation, in a sensory task). However, when subjects are asked for *ratios of differences* – for example, "What is the ratio between the utility (loudness, etc.) difference between A and B and the difference between C and D?" – they base their responses on the ratio of the differences, not the difference of the differences. It would seem that the two-stimulus ratio task does involve four stimuli because a reference point is implied, for example, zero loudness or normal health. Birnbaum's result can be taken to imply, however, that we must state the reference point explicitly if we want subjects to use it, so we do this when we ask about differences.

Explicitness in stating the ends of ranges being compared is one of the prescriptions of decision analysis (Fischer, 1995), but it is not used routinely in other value-elicitation tasks. The results reported here suggest that such explicitness in the comparison of intervals is a good starting point for value elicitation. The rest of the process involves applying consistency checks and asking respondents to make adjustments. The checks used here are only examples of many others that could be used.

References

Anderson, N. H., & Zalinski, J. (1988). Functional measurement approach to self-estimation in multiattribute evaluation. *Journal of Behavioral Decision Making, 1,* 191–221.

Baron, J. (1994). *Thinking and deciding* (2nd ed.). New York: Cambridge University Press.

Baron, J. (1997a). Biases in the quantitative measurement of values for public decisions. *Psychological Bulletin, 122,* 72–88.

Baron, J. (1997b). Confusion of relative and absolute risk in valuation. *Journal of Risk and Uncertainty, 14,* 301–309.

Baron, J., & Greene, J. (1996). Determinants of insensitivity to quantity in valuation of public goods: Contribution, warm glow, budget constraints, availability, and prominence. *Journal of Experimental Psychology: Applied, 2,* 107–125.

Baron, J., Wu, Z., Brennan, D. J., Weeks, C., & Ubel, P. A. (1999). *Analog scale, ratio judgment and person trade-off as utility measures: Biases and their correction.* Manuscript.

Beattie, J., & Baron, J. (1991). Investigating the effect of stimulus range on attribute weight. *Journal of Experimental Psychology: Human Perception and Performance, 17,* 571–585.

Birnbaum, M. H. (1978). Differences and ratios in psychological measurement. In N. Castellan & F. Restle (Eds.), *Cognitive theory* (Vol. 3, pp. 33–74). Hillsdale, NJ: Erlbaum.

Birnbaum, M. H., & Sutton, S. E. (1992). Scale convergence and utility measurement. *Organizational Behavior and Human Decision Processes, 52,* 183–215.

Bruner, D. W. (1999). *Determination of preferences and utilities for the treatment of prostate cancer.* Doctoral dissertation, School of Nursing, University of Pennsylvania.

Darke, P. R., & Freedman, J. L. (1993). Deciding whether to seek a bargain: Effects of both amount and percentage off. *Journal of Applied Psychology, 78,* 960–965.

Fischer, G. W. (1995). Range sensitivity of attribute weights in multiattribute value models. *Organizational Behavior and Human Decision Processes, 62,* 252–266.

Green, P. E., & Srinivasan, V. (1990). Conjoint analysis in marketing: New developments with implications for research and practice. *Journal of Marketing, 45,* 33–41.

Green, P. E., & Wind, Y. (1973). *Multiattribute decisions in marketing: A measurement approach.* Hinsdale, IL: Dryden Press.

Hoffman, P. J. (1960). The paramorphic representation of clinical judgment. *Psychological Bulletin, 57,* 116–131.

Hsee, C. K. (1996). The evaluability hypothesis: An explanation of preference reversals between joint and separate evaluation of alternatives. *Organizational Behavior and Human Decision Processes, 46,* 247–257.

Jones-Lee, M. W., Loomes, G., & Philips, P. R. (1995). Valuing the prevention of nonfatal road injuries: Contingent valuation vs. standard gambles. *Oxford Economic Papers, 47,* 676–695.

Keeney, R. L. (1992). *Value-focused thinking: A path to creative decisionmaking.* Cambridge, MA: Harvard University Press.

Keeney, R. L., & Raiffa, H. (1993). *Decisions with multiple objectives.* New York: Cambridge University Press. (Originally published by Wiley, 1976)

Louviere, J. J. (1988). *Analyzing individual decision making: Metric conjoint analysis.* Newbury Park, CA: Sage.

Lynch, J. G., Jr., Chakravarti, D., & Mitra, A. (1991). Contrast effects in consumer judgments: Changes in mental representation of the anchoring of rating scales. *Journal of Consumer Research, 18,* 284–297.

Mellers, B. A., & Cooke, A. D. J. (1994). Tradeoffs depend on attribute range. *Journal of Experimental Psychology: Human Perception and Performance, 20,* 1055–1067.

Tversky, A., & Kahneman, D. (1981). The framing of decisions and the psychology of choice. *Science, 211,* 453–458.

Ubel, P. A., Loewenstein, G., Scanlon, D., & Kamlet, M. (1996). Individual utilities are inconsistent with rationing choices: A partial explanation of why Oregon's cost-effectiveness list failed. *Medical Decision Making, 16,* 108–116.

von Winterfeldt, D., & Edwards, W. (1986). *Decision analysis and behavioral research.* New York: Cambridge University Press.

Weber, M., & Borcherding, K. (1993). Behavioral influences on weight judgments in multiattribute decision making. *European Journal of Operations Research, 67,* 1–12.

11 Decisions with Multiple Stakeholders and Conflicting Objectives

Detlof von Winterfeldt

Introduction

The purpose of this chapter is to describe and illustrate a systematic process for framing and analyzing decisions involving multiple stakeholders with conflicting objectives. The process has evolved through many applications of decision analysis to highly controversial decision problems (see, e.g., Apostolakis and Pickett, 1998; Brown, 1984; Edwards and von Winterfeldt, 1987; Grygiel et al., 1991; Lathrop, 1994; von Winterfeldt, 1987; von Winterfeldt and Schweitzer, 1998; Woodward-Clyde Consultants, 1991). Many practitioners of decision analysis involve stakeholders in their applications, but they usually retain the term *decision analysis* for their activity. However, the involvement of multiple stakeholders in decision analysis led to a distinct paradigm, which I call here *stakeholder decision analysis (SDA)*.

Decision analysis traditionally has emphasized the notion of a single decision maker. The SDA extension of decision analysis was born out of necessity in the 1980s, when many practitioners of decision analysis, especially those working with government agencies, realized that there usually is no single decision maker. At best, there is an individual in an agency who attempts to reconcile conflicting interests; at worst, the agency itself has multiple constituencies with conflicting values. Other formal approaches, like game theory or negotiation analysis, proved impractical to provide a framework for these decisions. Informal

Preparation of this chapter was supported by the Institute for Civil Infrastructure Systems, New York University, under a grant from the National Science Foundation.

approaches, like arbitration or public involvement, although useful in conflict resolution, did not provide the same analytical capability and clarity that the decision-oriented approach creates.

The SDA process was developed through trial and error – and it is still evolving. The main criteria for success are whether the process generates a reasonable decision and whether that decision holds up throughout the inevitable period of legal and political challenges. Adjustments to the process are made primarily in response to feedback by decision makers and stakeholders. By and large, the process has "softened" from a rational decision-driven focus to an emphasis on decision facilitation.

The core of a stakeholder decision analysis is a controversial decision. Controversy typically arises because those with a stake in the consequences of the decision disagree about the preferred decision alternative. Stakeholders can disagree because of differences in values or differences in beliefs about the consequences of the decision, or both. The stakeholder decision analysis process systematically dissects these elements and subjects them to qualitative and quantitative analysis.

The purposes of a stakeholder decision analysis range from diagnosing a stakeholder conflict (e.g., is it about values or beliefs?) to helping stakeholders negotiate a preferred alternative. The most productive uses of this process are in prospective analyses to support decisions that have not yet been made. It is also possible to apply it to retrospective case studies to diagnose stakeholder conflicts.

This chapter illustrates the stakeholder decision analysis process with an example of a major infrastructure decision. It involves retrofitting electric transmission lines to reduce the possible health risks of exposure to electromagnetic fields (EMFs). The stakeholder conflict in this decision started with the EMF issue, but it was soon diagnosed as involving utility and ratepayers' cost concerns, property values, and issues about electrical systems reliability.

The structure of this chapter follows the steps of a stakeholder decision analysis: The second section introduces the concept of decision frames and how to involve stakeholders when developing a decision frame. The third section defines stakeholder values and procedures to elicit and structure them. The fourth section describes procedures to operationalize and measure stakeholder values. The fifth section provides guidance for estimating the consequences of decisions. The sixth section addresses the issue of evaluation once the consequences of the decision alternatives are estimated. The seventh section describes alternative ways in which stakeholders can be involved in making a decision and implementing it.

Decision Frames

Concepts

A decision can be characterized in many different ways – for example, as a problem or an opportunity, as a strategic choice or a tactical move, as an approach to balance multiple objectives, or as a means to meet a specific goal. Tversky and Kahneman (1981), realizing the powerful effect of these different characterizations on the ultimate decision, referred to them as *decision frames*. In one seminal study, McNeil et al. (1982) showed that public policy preferences among health programs change dramatically, depending on whether the same problem is framed in terms of saving lives (an opportunity) or preventing the loss of lives (a problem).

A decision frame is defined by four decision elements: the decision maker, the stakeholders, the decision alternatives, and the decision objectives. Framing a decision problem is analogous to locking in these four decision elements. The term *frame* is used quite literally in the sense of limiting the scope of the decision problem.

Defining a decision frame is the most important, most difficult, and least scientific task of decision making. It is important because it provides a screen for what alternatives and objectives are legitimate and thus defines the scope of the discourse about a decision. It is difficult because there are no clear-cut criteria for defining what is an appropriate frame for a decision. It is the least scientific part of a decision analysis, because it relies on the analyst's experience and his or her ability to manage the process of interacting with decision makers and stakeholders to elicit an appropriate frame.

In multiple stakeholder contexts, a decision frame is appropriate if the stakeholders can agree that the decision alternatives are defined at the right level of abstraction (e.g., strategic vs. tactical), that the alternatives include the ones they like, and that the objectives cover all of their concerns.

Decision Makers

Decision makers control the process of choosing from among a set of decision alternatives. A decision maker can be an individual, a group, or an organization. To identify a decision maker, one simply needs to ask, who controls the actions that make a difference in this problem?

Often, there is a hierarchy of decision makers within an organization, ranging from experts who make technical recommendations, to managers who mold these recommendations into a preferred decision alternative, to executives who sign off on the decision. Analysts have to be careful not to define the decision maker at too low or too high a level. Individuals at the lower level often focus on narrow alternatives and technical objectives, and they have no real control over the decision. High-level involvement, on the other hand, often consists of merely "rubber-stamping" the decision. The middle level, where technical information is combined with a broader set of objectives, is typically where the key decisions are made.

Frequently, decision makers interact laterally across organizations. For example, a regulatory agency may contemplate a set of standards, whereas the affected industry contemplates how to react to the possible standards and the individuals benefiting from the standards make specific choices about their behavior in reaction to the combination of a specific standard and the industry's response.

Stakeholders

Stakeholders are individuals, groups, or organizations that are either affected by or interested in a decision. Key stakeholders are affected by the consequences of the decision; for example, a regulated industry is affected by the cost of implementing a new regulation. Other stakeholders may be interested in the decision; for example, a professional engineering organization may be interested in the technical basis of a regulatory policy. A stakeholder decision analysis should always include stakeholders who are directly affected by a decision. Because of their possible influence on the decision, it is also useful to include other interested parties.

Alternatives

A decision maker controls the alternatives, and the alternatives control the consequences that are relevant to the stakeholders. For example, when considering choices for building a new transmission line, a utility decides on routes, line configurations, and load characteristics. These alternatives affect local residents, local governments, and regulatory agencies. Each of these stakeholders may have its own decision alternatives, for example, to intervene, regulate, move, or protest.

Objectives

Objectives are operational definitions of values in a specific decision frame. Values are the underlying principles that guide a decision maker's actions. An individual, for example, may have values that include a concern with family, health, and personal well-being. An organization may have values concerned with quality, growth, profit, and good citizenship. An objective is a specific formulation of a value that includes an object of value and a direction of preference. For example, an individual's value may be to improve his or her health. An organization's value may be to increase its growth.

Decisions are almost always made in the face of multiple conflicting objectives. For an individual, decisions about career choices, improving personal health, financial benefits, and the quality of family life are all objectives that may conflict. For an organizational decision about a new product development, increasing short-term profit, long-term market position, and reducing out-of-pocket costs may conflict.

Process Consideration

How can an analyst identify an appropriate decision frame? First of all, one needs to realize that there are many alternative frames and that no single one is correct. It is very useful to conduct discussions with decision makers and stakeholders to elicit their view of the decision frame. When interviewing decision makers, it is useful to move up and down the hierarchy of a specific organization and to interview decision makers in other organizations.

Identifying stakeholders is usually not very difficult because they make themselves heard, sometimes loudly. In many decision problems that involve contentious issues, there exists a track record of comments through public hearings and formal review processes. Hearings on environmental impact statements or city council meetings are good examples. Although identifying stakeholders is rarely a problem, this process almost always identifies too many stakeholders. The solution is to organize stakeholders around objectives and to let one or two stakeholders represent a particular objective. Another problem is that some obvious stakeholders have no voice. The solution is to invite members of the "silent" stakeholder groups to participate in the process. Sometimes, these stakeholders form an organization as a result. In an application to a problem of water resource planning in Arizona, for example, potentially affected farmers had no formal organization to participate in the process (Rozelle, 1982). As the process evolved, they were given a seat at the table, thus creating a de facto organization for their interest.

Identifying alternatives is difficult. Technical experts often generate too many alternatives, at too low a level, and with too much detail. High-level executives are not concerned with detail and may only sketch out two or three generic strategies. Again, the solution lies in the middle ground. Interviewing stakeholders is an efficient way to generate a set of alternatives. When involving stakeholders, it is important to include the preferred options of each stakeholder in the set of alternatives.

Identifying objectives involves interviews with decision makers and stakeholders and a series of steps to organize the interview results; more about that later.

EMF Illustration

The EMF issue has been part of the environmental debate since 1979, when Wertheimer and Leeper published an article suggesting a statistical association between certain characteristics of electrical power lines near homes and the incidence of childhood leukemia. They suspected a causal relationship between exposure to the EMFs from the power lines and cancer. Over the following 20 years, about $200 million in research funds were spent to determine the possible cause-and-effects relationships and the magnitude of this effect. In 1996, the National Research Council stated that "there is no conclusive evidence that EMF causes cancer" (National Research Council, 1996, p. 4). Nevertheless, the issue is still debated in the scientific community, and substantial concern among laypeople remains.

In 1995, the California Public Utilities Commission (CPUC) began funding a program to investigate various aspects of the EMF debate. The California Department of Health Services (CDHS) administered this program for the CPUC. One project, described in more detail in this chapter, was to identify and evaluate engineering and land use alternatives that could reduce the exposure to EMFs.

This project, like other projects funded by the CPUC, was monitored and reviewed by a stakeholder advisory committee (SAC). This committee had about 25 members, including representatives of the major investor-owned and municipal utilities in California, the unions, health organizations, environmental groups, residents living near electric power lines, ratepayer advocates, and others.

The original decision frame, described in a request for proposal issued by the CDHS with review by the SAC, was very general. It suggested that the analysis would support many different decision makers, including regulators, the utilities, and environmental and residents' groups. The request for proposal suggested an exploration of a variety of alternatives for reducing EMFs, including standard setting, engineering fixes, and land use restrictions. Regarding objectives, the request for proposal suggested that the analysis should consider a broad range of concerns, including health, costs, property values, environmental justice, and others.

Framing a more specific decision problem within this general framework consisted primarily of narrowing down the problem to a specific set of decisions. This process was complicated by several factors. First, there are many levels of decisions about EMFs. At the national level, research agencies have to make decisions about the appropriate levels of funding for EMF research projects. At the state level, public utilities commissions may consider setting standards to reduce EMF exposure. At the regional level, utilities need to make decisions about siting and engineering improvements of the electric power grid. At the local level, city councils make decisions about set-back regulations, undergrounding policies, and other ordinances. At the individual level, families make decisions about where to live and how much to pay for protection from this potential hazard.

To complicate matters more, there are at least four sources of EMFs in the electrical power grid: transmission lines, distribution lines, substations, and home grounding systems. Each of these involves special decision alternatives and objectives.

To develop more specific decision frames, the contractor (Decision Insights, Inc., 1996) proposed slicing the decision problem by the four sources of EMFs and by whether the sources were existing or new. This led to eight possible "modules" (see Table 11.1). This partitioning of the problem by the four sources of EMF exposure helped somewhat, but it still required definitions of decision makers, alternatives, and objectives for each of the cells in Table 11.1.

To define decision makers, stakeholders, alternatives, and objectives more clearly, four workshops were held in January 1997, three with potential decision makers and one with other stakeholder groups. Representatives of the major regional California utilities, state regulators, and smaller municipal utilities participated in the first three

Table 11.1. *EMF Sources in the Electric Power Grid*

Grid Component	Existing	New
Transmission lines		
Distribution lines		
Substations		
Home grounding systems		

workshops. Citizens opposed to power lines, ratepayer representatives, union representatives, and individuals concerned with health risks participated in the fourth workshop.

Questions raised in these workshops were as follows for each cell in Table 11.1:

1. Who can make decisions about the situation described in Table 11.1?
2. Who are the main stakeholders and those affected by the decision?
3. What are the major classes of alternatives that the decision makers can control?
4. What are the objectives that the decision makers and stakeholders need to satisfy?

The workshop produced four sets of results. Table 11.2 shows a list of decision makers; Table 11.3 shows several classes of stakeholders; Table 11.4 shows a list of alternatives; and Table 11.5 shows a set of high-level objectives. These tables provided the master lists, from which one can produce specific decision frames for each of the cells in Table 11.1.

Table 11.6 provides a more specific decision frame for the case of existing transmission lines. In particular, this case examined alternative ways to reduce EMF exposure for an existing transmission line located on a clear right-of-way through a 15-mile stretch of fairly dense residential housing. Once a decision is formulated at such a specific level, it is also possible to define the decision makers, stakeholders, alternatives, and objectives in more detail. Regarding alternatives, there are several specific engineering options to reduce EMF exposure, either by changing the phasing of the currents in the existing lines, by changing the

Table 11.2. *Decision Makers Involved in EMF Decisions*

Federal	Federal Energy Regulatory Commission
	Environmental Protection Agency
	Occupational Safety and Health Administration
	Consumer Products Safety Commission
	Bureau of Land Management
State	California state legislature
	California Public Utilities Commission
	California independent system operators
	Building Standards Commission
Regional	Councils of government
	Regional planning committees
	Investor-owned utilities
Local	City councils
	City planning departments
	Municipal utilities

line configuration, by increasing the height of utility poles or towers, by changing the load on the line, or by undergrounding the line. Undergrounding is the only alternative that virtually eliminates EMF exposure in this case, but it does so at a very high cost. All other engineering options reduce EMF exposure by between 10% and 80%. Nonengineering options include increasing the right-of-way (practical only where no houses exist) and restricting the use of the right-of-way (e.g., by fencing it in to avoid public use). Although there are many more objectives for this particular decision, Table 11.6 lists only the ones that differentiate among the alternatives.

Values and Objectives

Value Concepts

Values are the principles that guide people's decisions. They are expressed either as decision imperatives ("Though shalt not kill"), desired end states ("Peace"), or preferred directions ("Increase wealth"). Values help people manage their lives to produce consequences that they like. Without values, people would have to rethink every decision and examine its specific consequences and how they would feel about them (see Keeney, 1992).

Table 11.3. *Classes of Stakeholders for Reducing EMF Exposure*

Stakeholder	Major Concerns	Examples
Utilities	Service Reliability Cost	Pacific Gas and Electric Southern California Edison San Diego Gas and Electric Los Angeles Water and Power
Regulators	Safety Health Reliability Cost	California Public Utilities Commision California Energy Commission California EPA California independent systems operators City councils
Ratepayers	Utility rates	Ratepayers' association
Residents	EMF exposure Property values Rent	Citizens concerned about EMF Undergrounders
Environment groups	Environmental impacts Health	Sierra Club Environmental Defense Fund
Unions	Worker safety Worker health Salaries	Electric Utilities Union
Research agencies	EMF research base Competing research	Electric Power Res. Institute Natl. Institute for Env. Health Science U.S. EPA Cal. Energy Commission Cal. Dept. of Health Service
Professional organizations	Enhance professions	Bioelectromagnetic Society Physics Society American Industrial Health Council National Brain Tumor Foundation Parent-teacher organizations

When people express a preference or justify an action, they typically refer to their values. For example, when asked why they oppose the construction of a new power line near their home, residents may state that they value their children's health, the environment, their view, and their properties more than the need for improved electricity service. Values often come in packages like "religious values," "family values," or "environmental values."

Table 11.4. *Classes of Alternatives for Reducing EMF Exposure*

	Existing	New
Transmission lines	Line configuration Phasing Undergrounding Land use restrictions Standards Warning labels	Route selection Line configuration Undergrounding Land use restrictions Standards
Distribution lines	Balance load Undergrounding Raise pole height	Route selection Pole and line configuration Undergrounding
Substations	Relocate	Site selection
Grounding systems	Improve net return Insulate water pipe	Location of service drop

Objectives are specific expressions of values. An objective involves an object of value and a direction of preference (Keeney, 1992). For example, an object of value may be the health of a person, and the direction of preference may be to improve the person's health. Other examples are "to increase wealth" and "to improve one's psychological well-being."

Table 11.5. *Classes of Objectives for EMF Decisions*

Reduce EMF-related health risks
Reduce accidents due to EMF mitigation
Reduce life-cycle cost
Reduce property impacts
Increase service reliability
Reduce impact on the environment
Reduce socioeconomic impacts
Improve implementation
Increase equity and environmental justice

Table 11.6. *Specific Decision Frame for Existing Transmission Lines*

Decision maker(s)	California Public Utilities Commission Investor-owned utilities Municipal utilities
Stakeholders	Residents living near transmission lines Children in schools near transmission lines Workers with jobs near transmission lines Ratepayers Utility workers
Alternatives	Rephasing Split phasing Undergrounding Increase pole or tower height Decrease line sag Reduce load Increase right-of-way (ROW) Restrict activities in ROW

Objectives	Reduce EMF-related health risks
	    Leukemia
	    Brain cancer
	    Breast cancer
	    Alzheimer's disease
	Reduce costs
	    Total project costs
	    Operation and maintenance costs
	    Conductor losses
	Increase service reliability
	    Reduce outages
	Reduce property impacts
	    Reduce impacts on property values

Means, Ends, and Process Objectives

It is useful to distinguish among means, ends, and process objectives. Ends objectives are the ones that a decision maker truly cares about. For example, in medical decisions, patients typically care about prolonging the length and quality of their lives.

Ends objectives can be discovered with a simple test: Ask why a person cares about a stated objective. If the answer is "That is self-evident," it is an ends objective. If the answer is "Because achieving this objectives contributes to achieving another objective," it is a means objective. For example, a woman choosing a new car may state that one of her objectives is to buy a large car. When asked why, she may state that she likes the protection of a large car for safety. When asked why, she may say that a safer car reduces the risks of death or injury to her family and herself. When asked why this is important, she probably will just stare at you – it's a self-evident ends objective.

Means objectives are important because they contribute to achieving ends objectives. In the car example, the size of the car is a means to reducing the risks of death and injury. Reducing air pollution is a means to reduce the health impacts of people exposed to it. Even money is a means – to health, to enjoyment of life, and to helping others enjoy life.

Means and ends objectives can be used to evaluate decision alternatives. Process objectives, in contrast, do not differentiate among the alternatives, but they do differentiate among decision processes. Examples of process objectives are "fairness," "public involvement," and "accountability." In all examples, it is not the alternatives that are "fair," "involve the public," or "are accountable," but the decision process that is used to select from among them.

Objectives Networks and Trees

Means and ends objectives can be represented by a means-ends network (Keeney, 1992) or by an influence diagram (Clemen, 1990). Ends objectives can be represented as a hierarchy or tree (Keeney, 1992; von Winterfeldt and Edwards, 1986). The purposes of creating means-ends networks are to distinguish clearly between means and ends and to clarify their causal relationships. An arrow in a means-ends network means "to cause a change" or "to influence." Means-ends networks are also useful in building models that relate the alternatives to value-relevant consequences.

Figure 11.1 shows a simple means-ends network for an EMF decision. In this diagram, decisions are shown as boxes, means objectives as ellipses, and ends objectives as rounded boxes. A question mark on top of the arrow connecting "EMF Exposure" and "Health Effects" indicates that this relationship is uncertain.

Figure 11.2 shows a segment of a tree of ends objectives for the transmission line retrofitting decision. This tree defines the general areas of concern (at the root of the tree) and specifies these concerns by

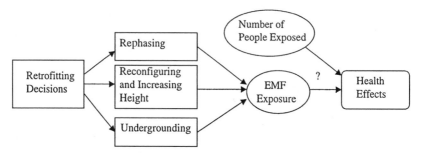

Figure 11.1. A simple means-ends network for EMF decisions. Squares denote decisions, ellipses denote means objectives, and the rounded rectangle denotes the ends objective.

subobjectives (as the branches of the tree). The arrow in an objectives tree means "is specified by."

Process Considerations

Constructing objectives for decision problems is more of an art than a science. It consists of individual or group interviews with the decision makers and stakeholders that focus on values, not on alternative ways to achieve them. Questions asked in these interviews are: What are your major concerns in this decision problem? What are some of the best consequences that can happen in this decision, and what are some of the worst consequences? What are the best features of your alternatives, and what are the worst features? Can you create a wish list for this decision problem? Keeney (1992) provides a more detailed list of questions that are useful to elicit objectives (see Table 11.7). Hammond, Keeney, and Raiffa (1998) provide additional guidance on how to identify objectives.

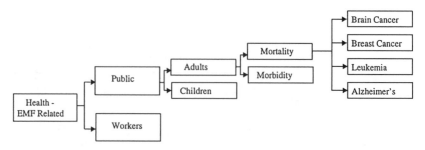

Figure 11.2. A segment of an ends objectives tree for an EMF decision.

Table 11.7. *How to Stimulate Thinking About Objectives*

Create a wish list
Compare alternatives
List problems and shortcomings of alternatives
List consequences of alternatives
Identify goals, constraints, and guidelines
Use different perspectives (e.g., different stakeholders' views)
Identify strategic objectives
Use generic objectives (e.g., from environmental impact statements)
Structure objectives (e.g., as an objectives tree or a means-ends network)
Quantify objectives (e.g., by defining specific measures for health effects)

Source: Adapted from Keeney (1992).

The answers obtained in an interview usually consist of a long list of items, which include means, ends, and process objectives at many different levels. If the interviews are conducted with different decision makers and stakeholder groups, there will be many such lists. The first task is to clean up the individual lists; sort them into ends, means, and process objectives; and obtain feedback from the individual stakeholders to determine whether these lists represent their values. In most cases, this process leads to minor revisions and additions to the lists. The main purpose of this task is to ensure that the lists are comprehensive reflections of each stakeholder's values.

The second task is to create a combined ends objectives tree. This tree should include all the ends objectives of the individual stakeholders. To ensure that it does, it is important to circulate the combined tree among the stakeholders and ask whether there are any omissions. Often stakeholders will reply that their means or process objectives are not included. In response, the relationship between their means objectives (documented in their individual lists of objectives) and the ends objectives in the combined tree should be pointed out. One should also clarify the role of process objectives.

EMF Illustration

A significant part of the EMF workshops described in the section on decision framing in this chapter was concerned with identifying objectives for four stakeholder groups: utilities, state regulatory agencies, local governments and city organizations, and citizens and environmental groups opposed to EMF exposure. Tables 11.8 to 11.11 show the set of objectives generated in these workshops for the four stakeholder groups.

The Stakeholder Advisory Committee had an opportunity to review these sets of objectives, but few changes were made as a result of this review. However, as the objectives were developed in more detail, some

Table 11.8. *Objectives of Utilities*

Ends Objectives	*Means Objectives*
Health and safety	Means affecting aesthetics
Public health (EMF)	Routing of power lines
Worker health (EMF)	Reliability
Indirect risks	Pole and tower height
Due to routing	Number and type of poles and towers
Due to reduced reliability	Number and configuration of lines
Environment	Means affecting ease and cost of maintenance
Aesthetics	Frequency of maintenance
Cost	Ease of access
Land	Time of maintenance
Construction	Training of crew
Maintenance	Means affecting outages
Local development	Number of outages
Growth	Duration of outages
Infrastructure	Means affecting property values
Reliability	Service reliability
Outages	Cost of service
Indirect impacts of outages	Power availability
Cost	
Lost revenue	*Process Objectives*
Possible damages	Public acceptance
Environmental impacts	Adaptability to deregulation
Crime, public safety	
Property values	
Due to EMF	
Due to other causes	
Planning and regulatory concerns	
Adaptability to deregulation	
Impact on long-term local planning	
Compliance with regulations	

Table 11.9. *Objectives of State Regulators*

Ends Objectives	Means Objectives
Health impacts	Implementation concerns
EMF risks to the public	Practicality
EMF risks to workers	Timeliness
Risk from EMF mitigation	Liability
Equity and fairness	
Cost equity	Process Objectives
Health equity	Implementation concerns
Property values equity	Political feasibility
Economic impacts	Political support
Growth	Value of information
Development	Validity of information
Reliability of electrical service	Clarity of information
Environmental impacts	Acceptance of information
Aesthetics	
Noise and disruption	
Flora and fauna	
Costs	
Construction	
Operation and maintenance	

Table 11.10. *Objectives of Local Governments*

Ends Objectives	Means Objectives
EMF risks	Means to liability
Public	Hassles
Workers	Other means
Property values	Value added to other alternatives
Liability	Compatibility with other alternatives
Compensation	
Punitive damages	Process Objectives
Maintenance and reliability	Public perceptions and reactions
Impacts on local development	Decision process concerns
Growth	Timeliness
Blight	Defensibility
Other social consequences	Justice and fairness – process
Environment	Process fairness
Justice and fairness – outcomes	Environmental justice

Table 11.11. *Objectives of Residents and Environmental Groups*

Ends Objectives	*Means Objectives*
Public health risks	Means affecting property values
Leukemia	Stigmatization
Brain cancer	Means affecting costs
Breast cancer	Impacts of risk avoidance
Electrocutions	Impacts of liability and lawsuits
Other health endpoints	Means affecting outages
Worker health risks	Storm hazards
From EMF exposure	Fires
From other causes	
Distribution of risks	*Process Objectives*
Children vs. adults	EMF management
Voluntary vs. involuntary	Flexibility
Minorities vs. others	Practicality
Across socioecon. groups	Credibility of information
Property value loss	Avoid alarming people
Visual impacts and aesthetics	Local autonomy
Justice and fairness – outcomes	Impacts of property rights
Fair distribution of costs	Local control
Fair distribution of risks	Impacts on land use
Cost	
Direct costs	
Social costs	
Due to EMF	
On housing	
Due to property devaluation	
Service reliability	
Outages	
Consistency with existing regulations	

stakeholders began to add to the objectives. The utilities added objectives related to the direct cost of transmission and distribution and asked for a specific cost breakdown. The residents added objectives related to the social costs of overhead transmission lines, such as air pollution, property damage due to fires, and loss of trees.

As a result of the workshops and the subsequent meetings, a final combined tree of ends objectives was created. This was done in an iterative process. First, the analysts created a master list of all ends objectives and sorted these ends objectives into major categories (e.g., "Health Effects – EMF"). Next, the analysts compared the subobjectives across stakeholders. Typically, one stakeholder had thought more deeply about one objective (e.g., utilities thought more about costs and reliability, whereas residents thought more about property values and health effects). The analysts selected the most detailed tree of subobjectives as a starting point. Subsequently, the analysts made sure that all stakeholders' concerns were expressed in this subtree. The tree that resulted from this process was presented to the stakeholders in several meetings, and requests for revisions and additions were incorporated. The final result is shown in Figure 11.3. The health and property impacts branches of this tree are defined in more detail as shown in Figures 11.4 and 11.5.

Measuring Objectives

Concepts

Up to this point, the stakeholder decision analysis process has been purely qualitative. Its results are a combined tree of ends objectives and a set of alternatives. Together, they can be represented as a consequence matrix (Hammond et al., 1998) in which the rows are the ends objectives (e.g., "Total Project Cost") and the columns are the alternatives. In the cells, the consequences of each alternative are described in terms of the specific ends objective. For example, a cell might contain the total project cost of undergrounding a stretch of transmission line.

For further analysis and comparison of the alternatives, it is useful to describe the consequences in terms that accurately measure the ends objectives. For example, Total Project Cost can be measured by the net present value (discounted at a specified rate) of the cash flow of all project costs expressed as 2000 dollars. The development of such measures for the ends objectives should not be confused with the actual estimation of the consequences for each alternative. A measure simply provides the yardstick by which to estimate consequences in the matrix. The actual estimation occurs when the yardstick is applied to a specific alternative.

Developing Measures

There are two types of measures: natural and constructed (see Keeney and von Winterfeldt, 1987; von Winterfeldt and Edwards, 1986). Natural measures have a common quantitative interpretation and use. Examples are the number of health effects, the percentage decrease in property values, and the net present value of a cash flow.

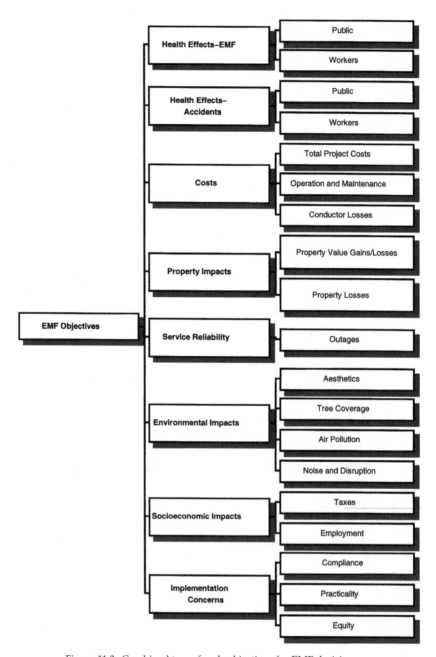

Figure 11.3. Combined tree of ends objectives for EMF decisions.

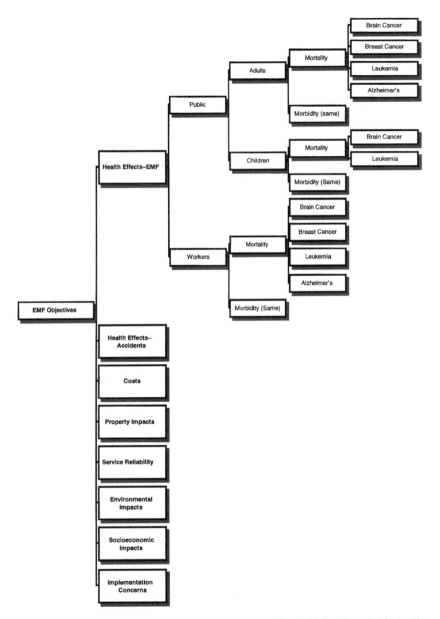

Figure 11.4. Combined tree of ends objectives for EMF decisions (with detail for EMF health effects).

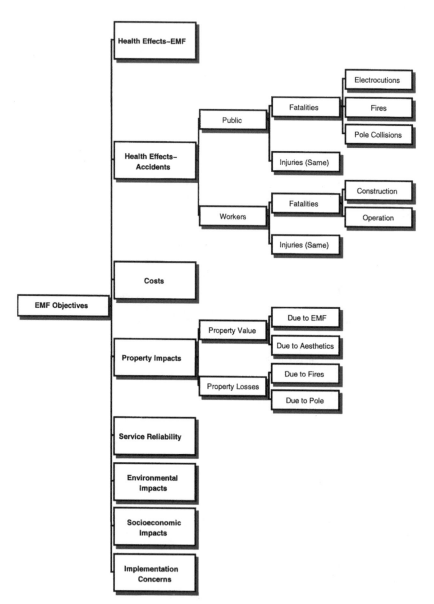

Figure 11.5. Combined tree of ends objectives for EMF decisions (with detail for accidents and property impacts).

Not all objectives have obvious natural measures. For example, there is no accepted quantitative scale for the ends objective "Aesthetics." Constructed measures provide specific guidance on how to score the consequences of alternatives with respect to an ends objective. When scoring the negative aesthetic impacts of alternative power line configurations, for example, it may be possible to develop a scale from 0 (no negative impact, clear view) to 5 (impact comparable to that of multiple lines on high transmission line towers mixed with distribution lines on poles).

Wertheimer and Leeper (1979) developed an interesting constructed measure of EMF exposure to investigate the relationship between EMF and health effects. Because they were not able to estimate the actual EMF exposure in residences directly, they visually scored the appearance of power lines and the distance of the residences to the lines in what they called *current configurations*. A very high current configuration (VHCC) was characterized by transmission lines with a thick set of conductors (indicating high loads) and a short distance from the residence (indicating high exposure). A very low current configuration (VLCC) was characterized by no power lines in the vicinity of the residence. Intermediate levels were low current configurations (LCC) and high current configurations (HCC), making up a total of four constructed measurement levels. In the study by Wertheimer and Leeper and in many subsequent studies, this constructed measure was used to code EMF exposure. Interestingly, the current configuration measure appears to be related more closely to health effects than to the actual measurements of EMF exposure. Some researchers have speculated that this constructed measure captures other features of the environment (e.g., traffic and pollution) that are, in fact, unrelated to EMF exposure.

Natural measures are preferable to constructed measures, because they prescribe more precisely how the measurement is to be done and leave little ambiguity or judgment in assigning consequences to alternatives. Constructed measures should be developed only when natural measures are not available or when they cannot capture the meaning of an ends objective. Constructing measures is an art that requires substantial experience. Keeney and von Winterfeldt (1987) and Keeney (1992) provide some guidelines.

Incorporating Uncertainties

It is often difficult to estimate the consequences of an alternative because they depend on events not under the control of the decision maker or because of lack of knowledge. For example, the health consequences of EMF exposure depend on whether or not there is a biological mechanism linking EMF exposure to health effects. Some researchers argue strongly that such a mechanism cannot exist because of the low energy level of EMFs. Others suspect that subtle mechanisms of hormonal changes and intercellular communication are responsible for an effect (for a summary, see National Research Council, 1996).

In case of uncertainty, it does not make sense to provide a point estimate of the consequences. Instead, consequences are characterized by probability distributions. In the case of EMF–health effects, for example, the probability distribution might have a finite probability for zero health effects (corresponding to the assumption that there is no credible biological mechanism) and a continuous density function over nonzero health effects conditional on the assumption that there is a credible biological mechanism with varying degrees of severity.

When the uncertainties are due to discrete events or discrete states of nature, a decision tree can often represent them. When uncertainties are due to lack of knowledge, they can be represented directly by a continuous probability distribution. In either case, a proper characterization of the consequences of an alternative should provide a best estimate (e.g., the expected value) and some characterization of the uncertainty of the estimate (e.g., the 90% credible interval of the probability distribution).

EMF Illustration

Table 11.12 shows the ends objectives with their associated measures for the transmission line retrofitting problem. Table 11.13 shows a schematic consequence matrix for this problem, considering only the four objectives that had the strongest impact on the decision. Note that the consequences were "rolled up" across several types of cancer and across several types of costs. This is possible whenever the measures for different objectives are commensurate.

Figure 11.6 shows a decision tree that characterizes the uncertainties about an EMF–health link. These uncertainties concern the eventual evolution of EMF research (positive, proving that there is a hazard; negative, proving that there is no hazard; and inconclusive, leaving the possibility of a hazard or no hazard). Some of the consequences of the EMF decision depend on the resolution of these uncertainties, notably the EMF health effects. If there is no hazard, the EMF health effects are zero. If there is a hazard, the EMF health effects can assume a range of possible values. Using probabilities for the uncertain branches in the decision tree, one can calculate the expected consequences, such as the expected

Table 11.12. *Measures for the Ends Objectives in EMF Decisions*

Ends Objective	Measure*
Health effects–EMF[†]	Person-years of life lost
Health effects–accidents[†]	Person-years of life lost
Cost[†]	Undiscounted 1998 dollars
Property impacts	
Property value	Change of property value in 1998 dollars
Property losses	Loss of property in 1998 dollars
Service reliability	
Outages	Person-hours of outages
Environmental impacts	
Aesthetics	Constructed measure
Tree coverage	Equivalent number of trees lost
Air pollution	Change of air pollutants in tons
Noise and disruption	Person-days of noise and disruption
Socioeconomic impacts	
Taxes	Changes in taxes in 1998 dollars
Employment	Changes in employment
Implementation concerns	
Compliance	Constructed measure
Practicality	Constructed measure
Equity	Constructed measure

* All measures are for a 30-year life span of power grid operations, except for property value changes, aesthetics, and implementation concerns, which are one-time changes.
[†] The same measure is used for all subobjectives, and the consequences are added up across subobjectives.

health effects from EMF exposure, considering all the paths through the decision tree. In addition to calculating expected values, it is useful to provide some sense of the range of possible consequences, perhaps even the full probability distribution over consequences.

Assessing the Consequences

Concepts

To assess the degree to which the alternatives achieve the objectives, it is necessary to fill out the consequence table with estimates, judgments,

Table 11.13. *Consequence Table for the EMF Decision (Four Main Ends Objectives Only)*

Objectives	Alternatives		
	No Change	*Rephasing*	*Undergrounding*
Health effects–EMF			
Costs			
Property values			
Outages			

or verbal descriptions of the consequences in each cell. In an ideal world, one should be able to determine consequences precisely and enter them as numerical point estimates. Practically, filling out the consequence table is a very difficult task involving data collection, modeling, and expert judgment.

Data Collection

In some cases, the consequences can be estimated using existing data. For example, operations and maintenance costs for overhead and underground transmission lines can be estimated fairly well using existing

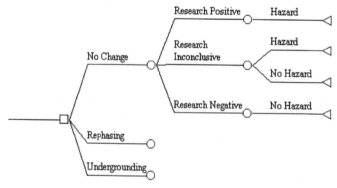

Figure 11.6. Decision tree of uncertainties about an EMF–health link. In a decision tree, squares denote decision nodes under the control of the decision maker, circles denote chance nodes, and triangles denote terminal nodes at which consequences accrue that depend on the paths of decisions and events.

data from utilities. Similarly, statistical databases can be used to determine the construction fatality risks for utility workers.

Even in these fairly trivial cases, judgment needs to be used in selecting and interpreting the data. Often, the data occur at a highly aggregate level (e.g., operation and maintenance costs for all transmission lines), and it is questionable whether they can be applied to a particular line (e.g., a new 115-kV line). Similarly, risk data are averages across many jobs (e.g., all utility workers), and it is questionable whether they can be applied to a specific job (e.g., lineman for transmission line service).

Modeling

When data are not available or are not directly applicable, models have to be built to estimate consequences. For example, when estimating the public health risks due to collisions with utility poles, models have to be constructed that relate the available data (pole collisions) to the relevant consequence estimate (collisions with utility poles). In this example, one would need to estimate the percentage of all pole collisions that involve utility poles, as well as the relative severity of nonutility pole collisions (e.g., street signs, lampposts) and utility pole collisions.

Similarly, to determine outages due to overhead transmission line failures, one would need to estimate the frequency and duration of overhead transmission line failures per mile of power line, as well as what percentage of these failures lead to customer outages and how many customers are typically affected. Based on these estimates, one could then make a model estimate of the person-hours of outages per year and per mile of overhead transmission lines.

Modeling can become very complicated, for example, when predicting EMF health effects. In this case, one needs to combine models of EMF exposure with spatial and time distributions of exposed people with dose–response functions to determine health risks.

Using Expert Judgment

Expert judgment is used in all steps of estimating consequences, even if a fairly good database exists. When data or models are inadequate, expert judgment often remains the sole source of consequence estimates. For example, only experts can reliably estimate wire codes. Similarly, experts are needed to estimate the aesthetic impacts of power lines.

When experts provide judgments, good measures, especially constructed ones, become important. Ambiguity in the definition of the measures can lead different experts to provide different judgments because of different interpretations. Good measures help to reduce ambiguity.

Expert judgments can be quantitative or qualitative. When using natural measures, experts should provide quantitative point estimates, ranges, or a probability distribution. When using constructed measures, experts should decide which level of the constructed measure best characterizes the consequences of each alternative. These levels can be defined qualitatively, using words to describe the consequences.

Representing Uncertainties

When data, models, and expert judgments involve uncertainty, this uncertainty should be expressed as a probability distribution over the consequences. This can be done either by providing distributions of data, ranges of inputs into models, or probability distributions directly assessed by experts (see, e.g., Keeney and von Winterfeldt, 1991; Merkhofer, 1987).

Decision trees are useful to facilitate the expression of uncertainties. With a decision tree like the one in Figure 11.4, some estimates are quite straightforward (e.g., the estimates of health effects) when there is no hazard (it should be zero). Probabilistic simulation can also be used to characterize uncertainties. In probabilistic simulations, a deterministic model is built with several input parameters, for example, a dose–response model, with input parameters that are defined by a threshold of exposure, the slope, and the shape of the function. Experts can assess probability distributions over the parameters, and a simulation algorithm can be used to calculate a probability distribution over the variable of interest, such as health effects (see, e.g., von Winterfeldt and Schweitzer, 1998).

In the end, the results of the consequence estimation are entered into the consequence table, either as point estimates, as ranges, or as complete probability distributions.

EMF Illustration

Table 11.14 shows the completed consequence table for the transmission line retrofitting decision. EMF health effects were calculated for a population of about 10,000 people living within 350 feet of a 115-kV

Table 11.14. *Completed Consequence Table*

Objectives	Alternatives		
	No Change	*Rephasing*	*Undergrounding*
Health effects–EMF	115.4	31.2	15.4
Costs	$18.30 million	$18.32 million	$47.9 million
Property values	($0.8 million)	($0.8 million)	($19.8 million)
Outages	28,890	28,890	483,500

Measures:
Health effects–EMF: number of person-years lost over 30 years of operation.
Costs: total undiscounted costs in 1998 dollars.
Property values: dollar apreciation of properties.
Outages: person-hours of outages over 30 years of operations.

transmission line. This calculation was based on some very complex exposure and health risk models. The numbers in the table reflect expected values, taken over all the scenarios shown in Figure 11.4.

The costs were calculated from component costs provided by an engineering firm. The property values were estimated using expert judgments of property value appreciation in the case of undergrounding the line. Outage estimates were based on a model using Canadian data of overhead versus underground transmission line failures and assumptions about the percentage of failures that lead to customer disruptions and the number of customers that would be disrupted.

This consequence table shows only the results of the four objectives that discriminated among the three alternatives. It is worthwhile to note that 18 other ends objectives turned out not to make much of a difference in selecting among the alternatives in this problem.

Evaluation

Concepts

In principle, an analyst could present the consequence table to the decision makers and stakeholders and let them decide. However, there are several complications.

First, it is not easy to make a decision based on the information provided in this table. Clearly, undergrounding is best in terms of health effects and property values, but it is worst in terms of cost and outages. The reverse is true for the "No Change" alternative. Rephasing settles somewhere in the middle: It leads to a significant reduction of health effects at a fairly small cost increment ($20,000) and no change in property values or in outages. Nevertheless, the final decision depends on the decision makers' and stakeholders' tradeoffs among the four objectives. These tradeoffs are based on their values.

Second, the numbers in the table are expected values and do not necessarily represent the range of consequences. For example, the range of EMF health effects for the "No Change" alternative is from zero health effects (in the case of no hazard) to about 10 times the effects shown in the table when compounding pessimistic scenarios in the decision tree.

There are five increasingly complex ways to evaluate the alternatives based on the results in Table 11.14: dominance analysis, cost-effectiveness analysis, cost-benefit analysis, multiattribute utility analysis, and Pareto analysis.

Dominance Analysis

Sometimes it is possible to eliminate an alternative because it is strictly better on all objectives than another one (or perhaps better on some objectives and the same or almost the same on others). To examine dominance, the analyst rank orders the alternatives for each objective and eliminates those that are inferior (or equal) to another alternative on all objectives.

A dominated alternative can be deleted from further consideration. Sometimes an alternative may not be strictly dominated, because it is slightly inferior on one or two objectives, even though it is vastly superior on all other objectives. In this case, we speak of *near dominance*, and we can eliminate the alternative that is nearly dominated.

If the stakeholders agree on the consequence table, there should be no disagreement about the rank order of alternatives within objectives. In many cases, stakeholders will disagree on some entries in the consequence table, and thus they will produce different rank orders. If this is the case, one stakeholder's dominated alternative may be another stakeholder's dominating alternative.

Cost-Effectiveness Analysis

If the issue is merely to search for the alternative that produces the most effectiveness for the least cost, one may consider ranking the alternatives by the ratio of cost-versus-effectiveness measure. For example, if the main purpose of an EMF decision analysis is to find the alternative that most cost-effectively reduces health effects, one could divide the cost of each alternative by the reduction of health effects it produces for a given cost.

Cost-Benefit Analysis

In cost-benefit analysis all consequences are assigned equivalent dollar costs, either on the basis of market studies or on willingness-to-pay surveys involving hypothetical transactions. In decision analytic practice, one often also uses direct assignments of equivalent costs based on the judgments of decision makers and stakeholders.

Cost-benefit analysis turns all consequences into the same unit: equivalent dollars. It is then easy to calculate the total equivalent costs or benefits for each alternative simply by adding the equivalent dollar consequences for each alternative across objectives. Of course, stakeholders and decision makers may disagree on the assignment of equivalent dollars to consequences, based on different values.

Multiattribute Utility Analysis

In multiattribute utility analysis, all consequences are first standardized to the same range of numbers, typically from 0 (worst plausible consequence) to 100 (best plausible consequence). Next, the decision makers and/or stakeholders assign weights to the objectives that reflect their relative importance and sum to 1. Then the weighted average is calculated for each alternative, using the formula

$$U(x_j) = \sum_{i=1}^{n} w_i * u_i(x_{ij})$$

where x_j is the jth alternative, w_i is the weight for objective i, u_i is the standardized utility function for objective i, and x_{ij} is the consequence of alternative j on objective i.

By the rules of standardization of the utility functions u_i and the normalization of the weights w_i, the resulting overall utility U will range from 0 to 100. This number, called a *multiattribute utility*, reflects the relative position of an alternative beween the best ($U = 100$) and the worst ($U = 0$).

Pareto Analysis

The previous types of analyses assumed that the stakeholders agree on the entries in the consequence table, the equivalent dollar costs (in cost-benefit analysis), or the weights (in multiattribute utility analysis). In practice, stakeholders will disagree – to some extent – on all of these elements. In practice, we have found that stakeholders include all combinations of disagreement: agreement on the consequence table but disagreement on weights (Grygiel et al., 1991; von Winterfeldt, 1987), disagreement on consequences but agreement on weights (the EMF study described here), and disagreement on both consequences and weights.

When stakeholders disagree about consequences or weights, their preferences will differ, as expressed both by their evaluation models and in their intuitive rank order of the alternatives. In this case, it is very useful to conduct a Pareto analysis, which is similar to a dominance analysis, except that alternatives are ordered by stakeholders, not by objectives. A Pareto-dominated alternative is one that is worse or the same for all stakeholders than another one. Pareto-dominated alternatives can be eliminated. Rank ordering alternatives by stakeholders also helps to identify contenders and losers.

EMF Illustration

Table 11.15 shows the dominance table equivalent of Table 11.14. Ignoring the numbers in parentheses for a moment, it turns out that none of the alternatives are dominated. "Rephasing" looks as though it might dominate "No Change," but it costs more. "Undergrounding" and "No Change" are very different.

It turns out, however, that rephasing does not cost very much; thus the difference between $18.30 million and $18.32 million might be considered irrelevant. If one substitutes a nearly identical rank order for cost, as shown in parentheses in Table 11.15, then "Rephasing" dominates the "No Change" alternative. This still leaves a tough choice between

Table 11.15. *Dominance Table*

	Alternatives		
Objectives	*No Change*	*Rephasing*	*Undergrounding*
Health effects–EMF	3	2	1
Costs	1(1)	2(1)	3(2)
Property values	2	2	1
Outages	1	1	2

Note: The numbers in the cells are the rank order (1 = most preferred, 3 = least preferred) of the alternatives for each objective. The numbers in parentheses for "Costs" reflect the near identity of the costs of "No Change" and "Rephasing."

undergrounding and rephasing. This choice turns out to depend largely on the value that one puts on property appreciation, again a value choice that stakeholders will probably disagree about.

To determine cost effectiveness, we calculate the ratio of cost versus life-years saved. For the rephasing alternative this is $21,758 per life-year saved; for undergrounding it is $479,000. Therefore, compared to the status quo, it is clearly more cost-effective to rephase than to underground. As a benchmark, studies of the value of life value a year of life expectancy lost at about $100,000 (Viscusi, 1992). This value implies that it would be appropriate to rephase the line, but not to underground it, if only cost and life expectancy are considered.

To estimate costs and benefits, we need to transform the life-years lost into equivalent costs. Using the value of $100,000 per life-year lost, which translates into about $4 million for the equivalent value of a statistical fatality of a person with a 40-year life expectancy (see, e.g., Viscusi, 1992). In addition, we need to turn a person-outage-hour into an equivalent cost. According to fairly standard loss-of-productivity estimates, this value is about $10 per hour. All other estimates in Table 11.14 are already in dollars. Table 11.16 shows the equivalent cost components of the consequences in Table 11.14 and the total equivalent costs.

According to Table 11.16, the best alternative is "Rephase," followed closely by "No Change" and by "Undergrounding" as a distant third. The table also indicates why this is the case: Rephasing substantially

Table 11.16. *Equivalent Costs of the Consequences of an EMF Decision*

Objectives	Alternatives		
	No Change	*Rephasing*	*Undergrounding*
Health effects–EMF	$11.54	$3.12	$1.54
Costs	$18.30	$18.32	$47.85
Property values	($0.81)	($0.81)	($19.81)
Outages	$0.28	$0.28	$4.84
TOTAL EQUIVALENT COST	$29.53	$21.13	$34.47

Note: All costs are in millions of dollars.

reduces health effects (by an equivalent cost of about $8 million) and otherwise is very similar to "No Change." Undergrounding costs much more, reduces health effects a little more, and increases property values. Nevertheless, these benefits do not make up for the increased costs.

In a multiattribute utility analysis of the same data, one first transforms all consequences into numbers from 0 (worst) to 100 (best). The range is picked with convenient consequences that cover the alternatives described in Table 11.14. In this analysis, the ranges were selected as shown in Table 11.17. By standardizing the consequences in Table 11.14 relative to this range of consequences, the entries in Table 11.18 are generated.

Table 11.17. *Ranges of Consequences*

Objective	Measure	Worst (0)	Best (100)
Health effects	Life-years lost	1,000	0
Costs	1998 dollars	$50 m	0
Property values	1998 dollars	0	($20 m)
Outages	Person-hours	500,000	0

Table 11.18. *Multiattribute Utility Analysis*

	Alternatives		
Objectives	*No Change*	*Rephasing*	*Undergrounding*
Health effects–EMF	42.30	84.40	92.30
Costs	63.40	63.36	4.20
Property values	0.40	0.40	99.00
Outages	94.22	94.22	3.30
MULTIATTRIBUTE UTILITY	49.7	58.1	40.7

When assigning weights, one needs to keep in mind that weights should reflect the relative value of each objective. This value depends on the range of the consequences of the objective. For example, if there were no or very little difference among alternatives in outages, this objective should receive a low weight (for a detailed discussion of these issues, see Fischer, 1995; von Winterfeldt and Edwards, 1986).

Keeping these range considerations in mind, a decision maker might assign the following weights: w(Health Effects) = 0.20, w(Costs) = .50, w(Property Values) = .20, w(Outages) = .10. The resulting multiattribute utility, using the weighted average formula, is shown in the last row of Table 11.18.

Pareto Analysis

An example of a Pareto analysis is shown in Table 11.19 for four stakeholders: utilities, residents living near the power lines, health officials, and ratepayers. The rank orders of the alternatives can be obtained either from direct judgments of the stakeholders or from the cost-benefit or multiattribute utility analysis. This Pareto analysis shows that there is no Pareto-dominated alternative. However, rephasing is a possible contender because it is best for health officials and second best for both the utilities and the residents.

It is also instructive to compare the stakeholders' equivalent costs (last row of Table 11.17) or the multiattribute utilities (last row of Table 11.18) in Table 11.19. This analysis provides more detailed

Table 11.19. *Pareto Analysis*

	Alternatives		
Objectives	*No Change*	*Rephasing*	*Undergrounding*
Utilities	1	2	3
Residents	3	2	1
Health officials	3	1	2
Ratepayers	1	2	3

Note: Entries are each stakeholder's rank order of the alternatives.

information about the relative differences between the stakeholders' value judgments.

Decision Making and Implementation

Concepts

The purpose of a stakeholder decision analysis process is to support decision making. It provides the decision makers with information about the beliefs and preferences of the stakeholders. In the end, however, decisions need to be made and implemented.

The stakeholder decision analysis process should lead to an identification of *contenders* and *losers* among the alternatives under consideration. The contenders are alternatives that rank high for all stakeholders. The losers rank low for all stakeholders. In the middle are *contested* alternatives that rank high for some stakeholders and low for others.

Losers can be discarded. Contenders and contestants are candidates for compromise solutions. Sometimes a compromise can be developed by redesigning an alternative to accommodate stakeholders who rank it low. In fact, several stakeholder decision analysis processes ended up with a compromise alternative that was not included in the original list (see, e.g., Edwards, 1979; Grygiel et al., 1991).

Once a decision is made, it needs to be implemented. This involves mobilizing support from the stakeholders in the implementation process or at least avoiding opposition from stakeholders who are not completely satisfied with the decision. Ultimately, it is the responsibility of the decision maker(s) to select and implement a decision, but lack of stakeholder support or outright opposition can create many obstacles in this process.

Even the best stakeholder decision analysis process can fail at this point, either because the disagreement among stakeholders is so strong that it fails to produce a decision or because a decision, once made, encounters stakeholder opposition at the implementation stage. It is therefore important to continue the process through the decision making and implementation phases. This can be done in several formats, including a consensus format, an advisory format, or a diagnostic format.

Consensus Format

In the consensus format, the stakeholders and decision makers work out a compromise alternative, either by choosing an acceptable alternative from the original set or by designing a new alternative. The stakeholder decision analysis process should provide detailed information about the pros and cons of each alternative seen from the perspective of the different stakeholders.

A consensus meeting begins with a presentation of the results for each of the stakeholders. At this point there should be no surprises. In particular, the stakeholders should agree with the results, at least in terms of how they represent their own beliefs and preferences. Next is the identification of contenders, contestants, and losers. Stakeholders should agree with the categorization of alternatives, even though they do not necessarily have to agree on the preferences among them. The first attempt at a consensus involves choosing one alternative from the set of contenders. Although rare, choosing an acceptable alternative is sometimes possible (see Brown, 1984).

If that is not possible, the stakeholder decision analysis should provide guidance about how to improve some of the contenders incrementally to make them winners for all stakeholders. Proposals for such changes should be examined through the evaluation models and fed back to the decision makers and stakeholders. If all stakeholders desire a consensus, this is the most likely path to a compromise.

If this step fails as well, it is time to examine the contested alternatives. Again, the analysis results should be able to guide the design of new alternatives that change one stakeholder's loser to a contender without hurting other stakeholders too much. An example of such an idea is discussed in Grygiel et al. (1991).

Advisory Format

Few decision makers set up a stakeholder advisory process that depends solely on consensus because the failure of consensus would mean that no decision can be made. Instead, many decision makers use stakeholder panels to advise them on the final decision.

In this format, the decision makers could still engage in a roundtable exchange with the stakeholders to discuss the contenders, the losers, and the contested alternatives. They could explore new alternatives to accommodate those stakeholders who stand to lose. But ultimately, the decision makers would have to select, weighing the preferences of the stakeholders.

Diagnostic Format

Sometimes the conflict among stakeholders is so fundamental that there is no hope of arriving at a compromise, and the analysis only clarifies that some stakeholders will win and others will lose. This is typically the case when the alternatives are arranged so that the values of one stakeholder are negatively correlated with the values of another stakeholder (see, e.g., von Winterfeldt, 1987).

If this is the case, the SDA process will merely inform the decision maker about the source of the conflict. It can be either in the beliefs or in the values of the stakeholders. If the conflict is in the beliefs, the decision makers legitimately can take sides by using data, models, and expert judgments that they trust. By taking sides about beliefs, the decision makers signal that they trust their own expertise more than that of other stakeholders, a legitimate and defensible position. It is much harder to justify a decision by taking sides about values than by taking sides about beliefs. By taking sides about values, the decision makers signal that their values align with some stakeholders (e.g., pro-growth) versus others (e.g., pro-environment) – a much harder and politically more sensitive position to take.

Implementation

Having come to a decision, the decision makers still need to marshal their own resources and the support of the stakeholders to implement it. Obviously, stakeholder consensus helps tremendously at this stage (see Brown, 1984; Edwards and von Winterfeldt, 1987). Making decisions with stakeholder advice helps too, especially if the chosen alternative reflects some accommodations of stakeholder values. In contrast, choosing against the expressed preferences of some stakeholders (e.g., in the diagnostic format) always invites opposition.

EMF Illustration

The EMF project is not completed yet, so little is known about decision making and implementation. However, the stakeholder decision analysis process has made it clear that it is unlikely to generate a consensus. The likely format for the *end game*, as the CDHS refers to it, is that the analysis results will feed into some kind of advice process. In this process, stakeholder beliefs and values will be considered quite explicitly, aided by the use of the models produced by the process. It is also likely that some design proposals will be made, for example about standards, construction guidelines, and land use restrictions.

The reason there will be no consensus is that there are two clearly opposed stakeholders: On the one hand are the utilities, which are primarily concerned with cost and service reliability. On the other hand are residents living near power lines, who are primarily concerned with property values. These values of the two stakeholder groups are diametrically opposed. Alternatives that satisfy the residents (e.g., undergrounding) are unacceptable to the utilities. Alternatives that are acceptable to the utilities (e.g., no change or low-cost technical fixes) are unacceptable to the residents. This creates a negative correlation among stakeholder values that reduces or makes impossible the chances for a compromise. In other words, all alternatives are contested, none are contenders, and none are losers.

There is a ray of hope in this story, though. It concerns the design of low-cost solutions to reduce EMF exposure and thus the potential health effects. Note that neither of the two antagonists in the EMF debate appears to feel strongly about health effects. Many utility representatives don't believe that there are health effects, and the residents, although believing that there are health effects, appear to be more concerned with property values. In the middle are solutions that reduce the potential for health effects at a fairly moderate cost – for example, rephasing power lines. These alternatives satisfy those concerned with a health-cost tradeoff and are perhaps acceptable to the utilities, which agree to a low- or no-cost mitigation policy.

References

Apostolakis, G. E. and Pickett, S. E. (1998). Deliberation: Integrating analytical results into environmental decisions involving multiple stakeholders. *Risk Analysis, 18*, 5, 621–634.

Armacost, L. L., von Winterfeldt, D., Creighton, J., and Robershotte, M. (1994). *Public values related to decisions in the Tank Waste Remediation System program.* Technical Report PNL-10107. Richland, WA: Pacific Northwest Laboratories.

Brown, C. A. (1984). The Central Arizona water study: A case for multiobjective planning and public involvement. *Water Resources Bulletin, 20*, 331–337.

Clemen, R. (1990). *Making hard decisions.* New York: PWT Kent.

Decision Insights, Inc. (1996). *Power grid and land use policy analysis.* Proposal submitted to the California Department of Health Services. Irvine, CA: Decision Insights, Inc.

Edwards, W. (1979). Multiattribute utility measurement: Evaluating desegregation plans in a highly political context. In R. Perloff (ed.), *Evaluator interventions: Pros and cons,* 13–54. Beverly Hills, CA: Sage.

Edwards, W. and von Winterfeldt, D. (1987). Public values in risk debates. *Risk Analysis, 7*, 141–158.

Fischer, G. W. (1995). Range sensitivity of attribute weights in multiattribute value models. *Organizational Behavior and Human Decision Processes, 62*, 252–266.

Grygiel, M., et al. (1991). *Tank waste disposal program redefinition.* Technical Report WHC-EP-0475. Richland, WA: Westinghouse Hanford Company.

Hammond, J. S., Keeney, R. L., and Raiffa, H. (1998). *Smart choices.* Cambridge, MA: Harvard Business School Press.

Keeney, R. L. (1992). *Value focused thinking.* Cambridge, MA: Harvard University Press.

Keeney, R. L. and von Winterfeldt, D. (1987). *Operational procedures to evaluate decisions with multiple objectives.* Technical Report No. RP-2141-10. Palo Alto, CA: Electric Power Research Institute.

Keeney, R. L. and von Winterfeldt, D. (1991). Eliciting probabilities from experts in complex technical problems. *IEEE Transactions on Engineering Management, 28*, 191–201.

Lathrop, J. (1994). Where the rubber meets the road: Consensus hits the fan in Santa Barbara County. *Proceedings of the Second Annual Conference of the International Association of Public Participation Practitioners.* Portland, OR: IAP3.

McNeil, B. J., Pauker, S., Sox, H. C., and Tversky, A. (1982). On the elicitation of preferences for alternative therapies. *New England Journal of Medicine, 306*, 1259–1262.

Merkhofer, M. L. (1987). Quantifying judgmental uncertainty. *IEE Transactions on Systems, Man, and Cybernetics, Vol. SMC-7*, 741–752.

Merkhofer, M. L. and Keeney, R. L. (1987). A multiattribute utility analysis of alternative sites for the disposal of nuclear wastes. *Risk Analysis, 7*, 173–194.

National Research Council. (1996). *Public health effects of exposure to residential electric and magnetic fields.* Washington, DC: National Academy Press.

Rozelle, M. A. (1982). *The incorporation of public values into public policy.* Ph.D. thesis, Arizona State University, Tempe, AZ.

Tversky, A. and Kahneman, D. (1981). The framing of decisions and the psychology of choice. *Science, 211*, 453–458.

Viscusi, K. (1992). *Fatal trade-offs*. New York: Oxford University Press.

von Winterfeldt, D. (1987). Value tree analysis: An introduction and an application to offshore oil drilling. In P. Kleindorfer and H. Kunreuther (eds.), *Insuring and managing hazardous risks: From Seveso to Bhopal and beyond*. New York: Springer, 349–377.

von Winterfeldt, D. and Edwards, W. (1986). *Decision analysis and behavioral research*. New York: Cambridge University Press.

von Winterfeldt, D. and Schweitzer, E. (1998). An assessment of tritium supply alternatives to support the U.S. nuclear weapons stockpile. *Interfaces, 28,* 92–112.

Wertheimer, N. and Leeper, E. (1979). Electrical wiring configurations and childhood leukemia in Rhode Island. *American Journal of Epidemiology, 109,* 273–284.

Woodward-Clyde Consultants. (1991). *Multi-unit coal capable site selection study: Phase V: Selection of a preferred site*. Prepared for the Florida Power Corporation. Wayne, NJ.

12 Designing Websites to Empower Health Care Consumers

Mark D. Spranca

Introduction

Of all the decisions that people make, decisions that have consequences for their own health are surely among the most difficult and important. Health care choices are difficult for a variety of reasons. For example, selecting a health plan can be difficult because plans vary on many complex dimensions (e.g., cost, coverage, quality, provider network, and type of plan) and consumers often face undesirable tradeoffs (e.g., deciding between a plan that covers fewer services but is rated highly or a plan that covers more services but is rated poorly). Deciding between surgery and radiation therapy for cancer can be difficult because the benefits are uncertain and the risks and side effects are serious. Managing a chronic condition can be extremely challenging because it requires a daily commitment, or decision, to a course of treatment sometimes involving difficult lifestyle changes (e.g., reducing fat intake, exercising, and stopping smoking). Complex, high-stakes decisions such as these are common in health care.

Jane Beattie was interested in what makes some decisions more difficult than others. Certain decision situations lead to a phenomenon she called *decision aversion*, a preference that a decision be made by fiat (Beattie et al., 1994). Her research found that decision aversion is more likely to occur when a decision maker anticipates regret, fears blame for poor outcomes, and does not wish to trade off certain attributes. Decision seeking is more likely to occur when making a decision that affects the decision maker alone. In real-life situations, decision aversion

Some of the research reported in this chapter was supported by the Aging for Healthcare Research and Quality and the Department of Labor as part of the Consumer Assessment of Health Plans Study.

often manifests itself as *decision avoidance*, a decision to avoid making a decision. If decision avoidance is not possible, the conditions that produce decision aversion may instead lead people to make suboptimal decisions.

Health care consumers are sometimes decision averse and at other times are decision seeking. It depends on the person, the decision, and the situation. Against the background of these moderators, a cultural shift is underway that is making decision seeking more common among health care consumers.

A powerful and widespread "consumer movement" is occurring in health care. Consumers are becoming more informed about and active in the decisions and behaviors that impact their health. Several concurrent forces are fueling the movement in the United States. (1) Health care organizations are trying to reduce their liability by shifting decision-making responsibility from providers to patients. (2) Managed care organizations are reducing costs by shortening the duration of patient–provider interactions. (3) Concerned that health care organizations are compromising on quality to save money, many consumers feel that they have to learn more about their health care options and take more responsibility for their health. (4) Policy makers are funding efforts to inform consumers so that the health care market will become more competitive and ultimately more efficient. (5) The Internet is providing easy access to enormous amounts of health care information especially written for consumer consumption. Together these trends are causing health care consumers to take a more active role in all aspects of their health care, from selecting health plans and doctors to learning about treatment options and adopting healthy lifestyles.

Historically, patients were passive and compliant in encounters with medical doctors. More often than not, doctors would recommend diagnostic tests and treatment procedures and patients would consent, usually with limited understanding of the risks and benefits and without a second opinion. This occurred because doctors had the medical training necessary to make informed medical decisions and patients trusted their doctors. Although the traditional doctor–patient relationship remains common today, many patients now share decision making with their provider (Brody, 1980; Quill, 1983; Charles et al., 1997). Consumers are participating more in medical decisions because they have access to more and better information and because they are increasingly skeptical about the intentions and ability of doctors. Although no one is quite sure why, there is some evidence that greater patient involvement in decision making can have a positive impact on health outcomes (Greenfield et al., 1985, 1988).

Compared to a generation ago, the consumer movement today also seems to be stronger in the areas of prevention of disease and management of chronic conditions. So far, the movement in these areas seems to be mostly a result of consumers being persuaded to take more responsibility for their own health. For example, there are information campaigns and tougher laws against drunk driving, public smoking, and drug use; press releases from the Food and Drug Administration, the Surgeon General, and academic journals such as the *New England Journal of Medicine* on the impact of diet and exercise on health; and efforts by managed care organizations to persuade their members with educational booklets and low copayment plans to seek preventive care and treat chronic conditions early. These efforts have produced some positive changes: Consumers are buckling up more often, smoking less often, and taking more steps earlier to detect cancer and other serious conditions.

Yet many public health officials and doctors lament the fact that consumers fail to do more to improve their own health. For example, they ask, Why do more people not eat well and exercise regularly? Why do more people not treat their depression, diabetes, and asthma? These questions may reflect some naiveté about human psychology and an exaggerated belief in the power of expert judgment to lead to behavior change. So far, the consumer movement has been driven primarily by sound medical research pointing out what consumers should and should not do to improve their health. But information alone can go only so far in producing lasting behavior change. Ongoing social support is also needed.

Patients have more responsibility for and difficulty with prevention and management decisions than they have with diagnostic and treatment decisions. With diagnostic and treatment decisions, patients can share responsibility with a doctor during an office visit. With prevention and management decisions, on the other hand, patients are confronted with daily decisions, usually at home or at work without a doctor present, that they must make themselves. Many factors make these decisions difficult. First, the decisions to prevent or manage must be made repeatedly to offer any benefit. It is easier for people to make one healthy decision (e.g., exercising once this year) than to develop a habit of making healthy decisions (e.g., exercising daily). Second, the positive impact is often uncertain and delayed. For example, regular flossing of teeth reduces the probability of developing gum disease, but the benefits of flossing are uncertain and delayed, which makes it difficult for consumers to commit to flossing. Third, the intervention sometimes requires difficult or painful lifestyle changes. For example, management of diabetes requires frequent skin pricks to monitor blood glucose levels and insulin injections. Fourth, people are reluctant to confront their mortality. Managing heart disease, for example, may be a constant reminder of one's vulnerability, which one would rather not face, regardless of the consequences.

Consumers are also becoming more involved in the selection of health plans. For example, private employers have historically decided which health plans to offer to their employees, and benefits counselors have often recommended plans to employees. Today employers are offering more choices, and benefits counselors are presenting more and better information that employees can use to compare plans. The Internet also has many sites that present comparative health plan information.

State Medicaid agencies in the United States are embracing managed care as a way of managing costs, which means that Medicaid beneficiaries are now being asked to select a health plan or to let the state assign them to a plan. Because states want consumers to discipline the heath care market, they are measuring health plan quality and developing easy-to-use guides to facilitate plan comparison along multiple dimensions. As a result, default-enrollment rates are dropping.

The purpose of this chapter is to discuss ways in which the Internet may aid health care consumers. The Internet promises to offer easy access to high-quality consumer-oriented health information and services. Website developers often claim that their sites will lead to more informed health care consumers, reduce costs for the health care industry and consumers, and ultimately improve health care outcomes. But these ideals are easier to express than to realize. To realize these ideals, developers need to embark on an iterative process of testing and development, followed by implementation, testing, and re-development. I will focus on website design. Among the problems with the design of current health sites are too much irrelevant information, not enough personalized information, lack of decision support, consumer-unfriendly language, and lack of social support. My review focuses on design techniques that address these problems.

My review comes from a program of applied research and development of Web-based tools to aid health care consumers in decision making. I review three tools, one nearing completion and the other two at the proposal stage. The first Web-based tool is designed to help consumers select a health plan. The second will be designed to help women considering genetic testing for breast and ovarian cancers to receive the information and support they need to make an appropriate decision. The third will be designed to help those suffering from depression to seek diagnosis and treatment and to manage their condition.

It is my hope that the ideas presented here will motivate new strands of basic and applied research in consumer decision making. Web developers need evidence-based principles to guide them on the best ways of reporting information and offering support over the Internet to consumers. Although decision analysis and prescriptive theories of choice provide suggestions for how to aid decision makers, most of them are more appropriate for experts. We need to know more about how to design decision aids for consumers. Finally, we need to know more about how to create useful websites – that is, sites that will enhance understanding, lead to better decisions, and motivate positive behavioral change.

Selecting a Health Plan

Choosing the right health plan is important because it can affect the amount one has to pay for care, as well as the quality of care one receives. To select the right health plan, consumers need comparative information about the factors that matter to them. Studies have consistently shown that consumers care about the services covered, out-of-pocket costs, maintaining their doctor, and freedom to choose other doctors (Moustafa, 1971; Mechanic, 1990; Marquis and Rogowski, 1991; Davis et al., 1995; Gibbs et al., 1996; Sainfort and Booske, 1996; Scanlon et al., 1997; Tumlinson et al., 1997).

Some recent studies have shown that consumers also care about plan quality (Hibbard and Jewett, 1996; Sainfort and Booske, 1996; Scanlon et al., 1997; Spranca et al., under review). Selecting the right one can be very difficult because the information needed is often unavailable and when it is available, it is sometimes incomprehensible or unreliable.

Fortunately, this situation is improving. More and better plan information is being developed for consumer consumption. Many dimensions of plan quality are being measured and reported to consumers by independent organizations. New techniques for estimating out-of-pocket costs are being developed and tested on consumers. Public and private websites are being developed to share comprehensive plan information with consumers.

For example, the National Committee of Quality Assurance (NCQA) began accrediting managed care organizations in 1991. For an organization to become accredited by NCQA, it must undergo a survey and meet certain standards designed to evaluate the health plan's clinical and administrative systems. Health plans are also required to submit Health Plan Employer Data and Information Set (HEDIS) data as part of the accreditation process. HEDIS evaluates the performance of health plans in dozens of key areas of care and service such as immunization rates, cholesterol management, and member satisfaction. NCQA widely disseminates accreditation status and HEDIS measures to purchasers and consumers through Report Cards, an Internet site, and a toll-free number.

The Consumer Assessment of Health Plans Study (CAHPS), funded by the Agency for Health Care Policy and Research (AHCPR), has developed a state-of-the-art survey for measuring consumers' experiences with their health plans. The survey consists of items that health plan members can reliably report on and consumers want to know about when selecting a plan. CAHPS has also developed and tested paper and computer reports for disseminating results of CAHPS surveys. These reports have been evaluated for usability with Medicaid and privately insured audiences. They have also been evaluated for their impact on plan selection in demonstration studies and laboratory experiments. This extensive evaluation has led to a number of innovations in the effective reporting of health plan information.

Better information with which to compare the cost of health plans is also becoming available. For example, the Washington *Checkbook* (Francis and *Checkbook*, 1997) publishes a book for federal employees that compares the total likely out-of-pocket costs of being in different plans under various family size and utilization assumptions. Shoshanna Sofaer and colleagues (1992) have developed a technique they call the *illness episode approach*, which can be used to estimate the annual cost of receiving care for particular conditions. With funding from the Department of Labor, I led a team to develop and test alternative ways of reporting health costs to consumers.

Understanding Out-of-Pocket Costs

It is important for consumers to understand expected out-of-pocket costs so that they can select a high-value plan. In general, consumers who want to compare expected out-of-pocket costs across plans need to consider differences in monthly premiums, deductibles, copayments/coinsurance, and stop-loss provisions; annual, per episode, and lifetime limits for covered services; what services are covered; the availability and terms for out-of-network coverage; and other factors. Consumers also need to consider what their and their dependents' own health service use might be in the next year, both if their health is as they expect and – more critically because they are buying insurance – if their health is worse than they expect.

Consumers who attempt to estimate their total annual health cost in available plans are faced with a daunting integration challenge. The basic procedure consists of multiplying expected utilization by the benefit structure of each plan. Although most consumers are given most of the basic information necessary to estimate their out-of-pocket costs, most of them probably do not know the basic procedure. Even those consumers who know the basic procedure probably lack the motivation to complete it.

The Internet offers a solution. Consumers could enter information about themselves, such as their age and gender, as well as the age and gender of any dependents. The computer could take those inputs and display a personalized table showing expected out-of-pocket costs under different utilization assumptions. Table 12.1 shows how four hypothetical plans compare in terms of total annual out-of-pocket cost. The columns refer to level of health care need, from no need to very high need. The top half of the table shows out-of-pocket costs if the consumer receives all care in the plan's network. The bottom half shows out-of-pocket costs if the consumer receives all care out of the plan's network. The table allows a consumer to see how high and low levels of coverage in health maintenance organizations (HMOs) and preferred provider organizations (PPOs) affect total out-of-pocket costs for five levels of health care need. Consumers can estimate their future level of health care need from past need as well as known risk factors. Because a health care plan is insurance, consumers should also compare costs if their needs turn out to be very high.

Comparing Quality

It is also important for consumers to be able to compare the quality of health plans. Until recently, consumers lacked reliable and valid information about plan quality. Instead they would ask people they trust, such as friends, family members, and their personal doctor, about the

Table 12.1. *Approximate Yearly Out-of-Pocket Cost (Including Premiums, Copayments, Deductibles, Coinsurance, etc.) in Four Hypothetical Plans*

		Level of Health Care Need (% of Insured Population with Each Level of Health Care Need)				
	*Level of Coverage and Type of Plan**	*No Need[†] (20% of Insured Population)*	*Low Need (20% of Insured Population)*	*Average Need (40% of Insured Population)*	*High Need (10% of Insured Population)*	*Very High Need (10% of Insured Population)*
				ALL CARE IN NETWORK		
Plan 1	*Low HMO*	300	415	800	1,630	2,335
Plan 2	*High HMO*	1,500	1,515	1,530	1,590	1,705
Plan 3	*Low PPO*	600	725	1,120	1,950	2,660
Plan 4	*High PPO*	1,800	1,825	1,850	1,910	2,030
				ALL CARE OUT OF NETWORK		
Plan 1	*Low HMO*	300	605[‡]	1,180[‡]	2,910[‡]	8,780[‡]
Plan 2	*High PPO*	1,500	1,705[‡]	1,910[‡]	2,870[‡]	8,180[‡]
Plan 3	*Low PPO*	600	905	1,360	2,370	4,130
Plan 4	*High PPO*	1,800	2,005	2,090	2,330	3,500

* "Low" plans cover fewer services than "high" plans.
[†] This is just the consumer's share of the annual premium.
[‡] Consumers in HMOs pay the full cost of care received outside of the network.

plans they were considering. They would hear anectodal evidence from a small sample of unknown representativeness. Today's consumers are more likely to have better information about plan quality when selecting a plan.

There are many challenges to presenting information about plan quality in a way that consumers can understand and integrate into the choice process. Consumers are not used to thinking about plan quality; they care more about the quality of their provider. They sometimes do not understand how plan quality can affect the quality of care they receive.

The CAHPS Decision Helper represents one attempt to overcome some of the challenges. Table 12.2 shows part of a screen from the CAHPS Decision Helper, a computer tool designed primarily for reporting the results of the CAHPS survey. The CAHPS survey consists of dozens of items that ask consumers about their experiences with their health plan. CAHPS uses several techniques to reduce the processing burden on consumers. (1) The several dozen items are integrated and presented as seven broad and distinct composites. (2) Instead of reporting means and standard deviations with significance levels, CAHPS presents one to three stars to indicate how well a plan did compared to the average for the plans that were surveyed. (3) Consumers are given the option of adding the stars to see at a glance how the plans compared overall across composites. (4) Consumers are encouraged to review how the plans did on the survey topics that are most important to them. Their "yes" or "no" answer will appear later in a partially completed worksheet for comparing plans on multiple dimensions.

Overcoming Obstacles to Making Tradeoffs

Table 12.3 shows part of another screen from the CAHPS Decision Helper. This worksheet is designed to make it easy for consumers to compare plans across all the major dimensions. In the basic version of Decision Helper, the computer automatically fills in the plan type and the consumer's assessment of how well the plan did on the survey. The other four columns are left blank. The risk of presenting only plan type and CAHPS survey information in the Decision Helper is that consumers will choose plans based on those dimensions alone. Therefore, CAHPS encourages sponsors of CAHPS projects to add modules to the Decision Helper for reporting information on doctors, benefits, and costs in each plan. If sponsors choose not to add these modules,

Table 12.2. *How Four Hypothetical Plans Compare on Seven Dimensions of Plan Quality*

	1 Getting Care That Is Needed	2 Getting Care Without Long Waits	3 How Well Doctors Communicate	4 How People Rated Their Health Care	5 Courtesy, Respect, and Helpfulness of Office Staff	6 Health Plan Customer Service	7 How People Rated Their Health Plan	**Total Stars**	Did the Plan Do Well on Survey Topic That You Care About?
Plan 1	*	**	**	*	**	*	**	11	Yes / No
Plan 2	***	**	**	***	**	**	***	17	Yes / No
Plan 3	**	***	***	***	**	***	**	18	Yes / No
Plan 4	**	**	*	*	*	**	*	10	Yes / No

* Plan did worse than the survey average.
** Plan did about the same as the survey average.
*** Plan did better than the survey average.

309

Table 12.3. *Sample Worksheet Showing a Hypothetical Individual's Assessment of How Four Plans Compare on Four Dimensions*

Plan Type	Did the Plan Do Well on *Survey* Topics That You Care About?	Does the Plan Have *Doctors* You Like?	Does the Plan Have *Benefits* You Like?	Does the Plan Have *Costs* You Can Afford?	Other Plan Info?
Plan 1	HMO	No	Yes	No	Yes
Plan 2	HMO	Yes	No	Yes	No
Plan 3	PPO	Yes	No	No	Yes
Plan 4	PPO	No	Yes	Yes	No

Decision Helper encourages consumers to collect this information and use it to complete the worksheet. Once consumers have completed the worksheet, they are given some advice on how to select the plan that best meets their needs.

Arguably, the easiest and most effective way of improving the quality of plan selection is to use decision analytic techniques to weight the attributes and integrate them for consumers. So why stop short of offering consumers this level of decision support? First, the health plans fear that the algorithm may be biased against them. Plans know approximately how unaided consumers select plans; they are unsure how aided consumers will select plans. Second, although consumers are free to reject the advice of a decision algorithm, consumer groups nevertheless sometimes object that algorithms take away the decision from consumers. Third, consumers often do not trust an algorithm that they do not understand. Even relatively simple weighted-additive decision algorithms are beyond the easy comprehension of most consumers. Although decision analysts will surely be disappointed, there is not broad support for decision support techniques that go beyond the modest ones found in Tables 12.2 and 12.3.

Genetic Testing for Breast and Ovarian Cancer

Women today have the option of undergoing tests for detecting genetic susceptibility to two common and treatable forms of cancer. One is breast cancer, which will affect about one in eight American women sometime in their lives. Of these, 5% to 10% have an inherited predisposition. The other is ovarian cancer, which will affect approximately 1 in 70 American women sometime in their lives. Of these, 5% to 10% have an inherited predisposition. Inherited breast and ovarian cancers are often associated with a mutation in a cancer susceptibility gene. Mutations in BRCA1 and BRCA2 genes are responsible for most cases of inherited breast and ovarian cancer susceptibility. Not all individuals with BRCA1 or BRCA2 gene mutations will develop these cancers but their risk is significantly increased. By age 70, a woman with one of three of the BRCA mutations has about a 56% risk of developing breast cancer and a 16% risk of developing ovarian cancer.

Several early detection and risk reduction options are available to patients who test positive for BRCA1 or BRCA2 gene mutations. One option is to undergo more frequent preventive screenings, such as mammography and self-exams. Another option is chemoprevention, which may decrease the chances of developing cancer. A third option is prophylactic surgery. Although effective for some women, this option is not suitable for all women given its radical nature. A final option includes improving the diet, increasing physical activity, and eliminating smoking and drinking.

Deciding whether to undergo genetic testing is not only cognitively demanding, but it is also emotionally taxing. Consumers need to consider a vast amount of complex medical and probabilistic information in order to make an informed choice about whether to undergo testing. The consequences of testing are both far-reaching and potentially life-changing. For example, a woman who tests positive for a genetic predisposition to breast and ovarian cancers learns that she has an increased risk of developing cancer herself, that she may pass the mutated gene to her children, and that her siblings may also carry the mutated gene. She must also decide how to respond to her own enhanced risk, whether to have children (if she has not already), and whether to inform her siblings.

Web-based tools can be developed to overcome some of the informational and emotional barriers to undergoing genetic testing (Figure 12.1). In this section I describe a possible Web-based tool that would enhance the usefulness and availability of information about and support for genetic testing. I focus the discussion on BRCA1 and BRCA2 tests for the predisposition to breast and ovarian cancers. Ideally, such a product would be designed to complement rather than replace the information

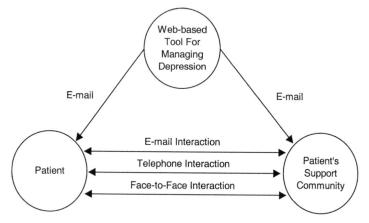

Figure 12.1. A Web-based tool could foster social support by sending e-mail messages that encourage patients and their support community to interact.

and support currently offered by genetic counselors, doctors, written materials, and videos. Moreover, it would feature (1) clear and engaging multimedia presentations, (2) easy-to-understand descriptions of the basics of genetic predisposition to disease, (3) up-to-date information on breast and ovarian cancers and BRCA1 and BRCA2 testing, (4) a searchable database of genetic counselors, (5) links to online support groups, (6) video testimonials from patients at different points in the genetic testing process, (7) a user-friendly host to guide users through the tool, (8) the option of entering the patient's family history to evaluate the personal relevance of genetic testing, and (9) the option of entering the patient's test result to assess the personal risk of cancer and the value of preventive measures.

Ignorance

Ignorance of genetics, cancer, and the implications of genetic testing prevents many consumers from considering, let alone undergoing, genetic testing. Consumers need convenient and inexpensive access to accurate and easy-to-understand information on many aspects of genetics, cancer, and genetic testing, including:

- Basic information about heritable diseases and genetic testing
- Basic information about breast and ovarian cancers and genetic tests for BRCA1 and BRCA2 mutations and others as they become available

- Drill-downs to detailed information about breast and ovarian cancers and genetic tests for BRCA1 and BRCA2 mutations and others, as they become available
- A description of the testing process (blood is drawn by a health professional, blood is sent to a genetic testing lab, test results are available 4 weeks later)
- Out-of-pocket costs of testing and counseling
- The qualitative risk of developing cancer (base rate in the general population; with a family history of cancer; with positive, negative, and uncertain test result)
- Errors associated with genetic testing (false positives and false negatives)
- The possible tests results and what they mean
- Risk management options associated with positive test results (surveillance, prophylactic surgery, risk avoidance, chemoprevention)
- Risk management options undergoing clinical trials (with estimates of their promise)
- The advantages and disadvantages of risk management options
- The qualitative risk of developing cancer with and without risk management
- The qualitative risk of passing on mutated genes to children
- The rapidly advancing law concerning discrimination
- Issues to consider when deciding whether to inform family members of test results
- Sources of additional information on breast and ovarian cancers and genetic testing

To help consumers find the information they want, the site could use proven techniques, such as layering, site maps, and key word searches, for organizing and presenting information.

Information Overload

Although having access to all the relevant information may be desirable, it can have the unintended effect of producing a sense of information overload, effectively overwhelming the decision maker. Consumers considering genetic testing may become overwhelmed while trying to process all the complex information that is relevant. One approach to helping consumers faced with information overload is to let the

Web-based tool do some of the processing. I will describe a risk assessment technique for reducing information overload and helping consumers to assess the relevance of genetic testing for them.

We know that about one in eight American women will develop breast cancer in her lifetime. But some women are more likely to develop breast cancer than others. An individual woman's risk depends on such *risk factors* as age, age at first menstrual period, age at first live birth, breast cancer among first-degree relatives, breast biopsies, race, and genetic test results. Risk assessment is a statistical technique for estimating an individual's probability of developing cancer based on that individual's risk factors. A Web-based tool could allow patients and medical professionals to enter (1) the patient's personal and family history to evaluate the personal relevance of genetic testing and (2) the patient's test result to assess the personal risk of cancer and the value of preventive measures.

Having accurate, patient-specific cancer risk estimates can be extremely valuable when deciding whether to undergo genetic testing or take preventive measures. Without risk assessment tools, genetics professionals and consumers are left to estimate risk using cognitive heuristics or rules of thumb. These heuristics sometimes lead to systematic errors. The errors are usually due to (1) considering some but not all known risk factors, (2) considering factors that are unrelated to the cancer risk, and (3) neglecting the population base rate for developing cancer. A related literature has consistently demonstrated the greater predictive validity of statistical judgments, such as those provided by a risk assessment tool, to clinical judgments, such as those offered by a doctor.

But risk assessment also raises serious concerns. One concern is the quality of the risk estimate. To ensure accuracy, the data from which a risk assessment model is built must be accurate. It is also essential that a tool consider all the known risk factors and only those factors. The tool cannot base its risk estimate on factors that are not known to be related to the cancer risk, even if practicing clinicians sometimes rely on such factors. As new studies demonstrate additional risk factors, the risk assessment tool will have to be updated. Another concern is misinterpretation of risk estimates. To reduce the chance for misinterpretation, it is important to present risk information in ways that genetics professionals and laypeople can understand and to provide instructions on how to interpret risk estimates.

Fear and Regret

The possible implications of genetic testing are frightening. They include learning that you may be at enhanced risk of developing a life-threatening condition. Fearing a positive test result, some consumers may ultimately decide not to undergo genetic testing, even if they were otherwise likely to do it.

Consumers also have plenty of reasons to anticipate regret. They may regret a decision to undergo testing and treatment if they develop cancer anyway or they may regret a decision to undergo prophylactic surgery if a cure for breast or ovarian cancer is developed later. Anticipating these sources of regret may lead consumers to forgo testing. Alternatively, some consumers may focus more on the regret they would experience if they were not to undergo testing and treatment and develop cancer later.

A Web-based tool can include features to enhance opportunities for receiving social support, which may help consumers to cope with their fears and appreciate that regret is possible whether they undergo testing or not. First, a Web-based tool can include a searchable database of genetic counselors and other genetics professionals, which may make it more likely that patients will speak to one. Genetic counselors are trained professionals who can help patients to interpret complex information, understand their emotions, and respond appropriately. Second, a Web-based tool can include links to online support groups. Typically these support groups consist of patients who are considering or have undergone genetic testing. They offer information and social and emotional support. Finally, a Web-based tool can include video testimonials from women and men deciding whether to be tested, cope with the waiting for the test result, decide on a course of treatment, and cope with the test result. Viewing testimonials from different kinds of people may help consumers to gain some perspective on how their own thoughts and feelings should affect their decision.

Managing Depression

Depression currently affects an estimated 17 million Americans (Regier et al., 1993) at an annual economic cost of approximately $43 billion (Greenberg et al., 1993). Those who suffer from depression may experience persistent feelings of sadness, helplessness, and worthlessness, loss of energy, loss of interest in pleasurable activities, fatigue, sleeping disturbances, appetite problems, social isolation, difficulty making decisions, and thoughts of suicide (American Psychiatric Association, 1994). Although depression can be both reliably diagnosed and effectively treated, it is both underdiagnosed (Wells et al., 1989; Simon et al., 1995) and undertreated (Robins and Reier, 1991; Keller et al., 1995). Barriers to diagnosis and treatment include patient embarrassment, lack of social support, brief and sporadic contact between patients and mental health professionals, and a treatment paradigm that frames depression as an episodic rather than a chronic condition (Hirschfeld et al., 1997). Moreover, when depression is diagnosed and treated, the positive effects are often short-lived because patient adherence is low.

Web technology presents a promising new opportunity to overcome these barriers in caring for depression. Web technology has a number of advantages over traditional mental health resources and services. The Web overcomes patient embarrassment by offering opportunities for anonymous social interaction and private, nonsocial interaction. The Web overcomes lack of social support by making it easy to build and maintain a large, supportive social network. The Web overcomes the brief problem of sporadic contact with providers because it is always accessible and can be used as often and as long as patients want. The Web can overcome the current paradigm that treats depression as episodic by becoming a daily source of information, support, and feedback – essential ingredients in the lifelong management of depression.

I will describe a possible Web-based tool that depressed patients could use alone or preferably as part of an overall treatment strategy in consultation with a provider. This tool would be built around two principles: connectivity and personalization. The tool would orchestrate and encourage social interaction between depressed people and their families, friends, medical professionals, and others suffering from depression. The tool would offer personalized feedback, suggested readings and tips of the day based on patients' entries in their daily logs. To encourage initial use, it would have to be fun and easy to use. To encourage sustained use, the tool would have to be helpful to patients.

Overcoming Inertia to Seeking Help

People suffering from depression often have tremendous difficulty taking the first steps to seeking help. Many factors contribute to this inertia, including denying being depressed, being too embarrassed to seek help, lacking enough energy to seek help, and having misconceptions about treatment options. Depressives need basic information and anonymous support to help them to take the first steps toward diagnosis and treatment.

Library of Information on Depression. The library would contain a large body of consumer-friendly information about depression. The library would cover a variety of topics, including types of depression, symptoms, diagnostic procedures for depression, causes of depression, and treatment alternatives, including talk therapy, drug therapy, and self-help methods. Special sections would include a list of self-care tips and articles on overcoming obstacles on the road to recovery. Articles would cover such topics as how to cope with difficult life events, how to recognize and avoid negative thoughts, how to be an effective problem solver, and how to talk to your therapist or provider. These sections would be linked to the "Tips of the Day" and "Suggested Reading" features within the Personalized Feedback section.

Depression Screening Questionnaire. People who visited the site could anonomously complete a brief screening questionnaire to help them decide whether they may be depressed and should see a mental health professional. Persons completing the screener would be provided with basic information to allow them to interpret their score.

Video Testimonials. Video testimonials offer compelling personal accounts of the struggles and triumphs faced by real people who are battling depression. The site would contain video testimonials on such themes as recognition and denial of depression, taking the first step to get help, common misconceptions about mental illness, attitudes toward talk therapy and drug therapy, managing depression for a lifetime, and relapse. Depressed people who watch these videos may feel encouraged, knowing that they are not alone and that they have others from whom they can learn and receive support.

Chat Rooms. Chat rooms allow people to communicate with others in real time and with complete anonymity. The site would offer several public chat rooms focusing on such themes as how to tell if you are depressed, drug versus talk therapy, and helping loved ones who are depressed. It would save and thread previous discussions so that when no one is available to talk, visitors can read past discussions. To encourage candor, it would also offer private chat rooms where two people can converse without others being able to "listen." It would also offer a special-event chat room where mental health professionals with expertise in the diagnosis and treatment of depression would appear during announced times. Patients may want to use the chat rooms to share experiences, ask questions, and receive support and encouragement. Families and friends of depressed people may also use the chat rooms to learn about depression, receive advice on how to help loved ones who suffer from it, and provide support to each other.

Emergency Hotline. Patients who are in crisis (e.g., considering suicide) need immediate attention. The site would direct patients who indicate that they are in crisis either to call a suicide hotline number or to use the site's emergency hotline. The site's hotline would offer a real-time written exchange between a patient and a mental health professional in order to address suicidal feelings immediately. The hotline differs from e-mail in that the request for and provision of help occur synchronously. Some patients may prefer the written exchange because it offers more anonymity than a telephone conversation.

Maintaining Positive Behavioral Change

Once patients are on the path to recovery, the challenge becomes keeping them there. Patients deviate from the path or relapse for many reasons, including skepticism about the effectiveness of their treatment, inadequate social support, and the challenge of committing daily to manage their depression. To stay on track, they need frequent and supportive social interaction, feedback on the course of their depression, and positive reinforcement.

Personal Support Community. A Web-based tool could encourage patients to supply their e-mail address so that it could contact them occasionally to ask how they are doing, provide positive reinforcement for use, and encourage social interaction (see Figure 12.1). Patients could also be encouraged to provide the e-mail addresses for any family members or friends whom they believe might help them by offering occasional social support. The site would automatically contact these social support persons and encourage them to periodically e-mail, call, or visit their friend for select purposes. The site would also remind a patient's support community whenever significant dates, such as the patient's birthday, are approaching.

Daily Log. The daily log would be an interactive form that patients fill out daily. The form would ask patients about their current mood, as well as about recent events, thoughts, and behaviors that may be related. For example, the form would ask about their symptoms, sleep, diet, exercise, treatment adherence, feelings, thoughts, social activity, professional life, and presence of stressful events. To reduce the respondent's burden, the form would accept only closed-ended responses. Patient inputs would be saved in a secure file so that patients could look later to see whether they can identify patterns in the way their environment, thoughts, and behaviors influence their mood.

Patients would be encouraged, but not required, to give their physician, psychologist, or other mental health provider access to their daily log. Reviewing the history of log entries together may help patients and their care providers to communicate more thoroughly and effectively. It also may help their care providers to make more informed and ultimately more effective treatment recommendations. For example, if a patient is adhering and the treatments are working, then his care provider may recommend continued adherence. On the other hand, if a patient is not adhering and is still suffering, then his care provider may suggest problem-solving techniques for reconciling the discrepancy that exists between the patient's goal of recovery and the lack of adherence. Finally, if a patient is adhering but the treatment is not working, then the care provider may recommend alternative treatments.

Patients who use the daily log may begin to understand that they have greater control over their mood and other symptoms than they had previously believed. This sense of control may make them more likely to develop a positive outlook on life and to develop and maintain healthy habits regarding diet, exercise, sleep, stress, and social and professional life. In addition, it may make them more likely to adhere to treatment recommendations. In the end, the daily log may help patients to manage their depression more regularly and over longer periods of time.

Personalized Feedback. As the website learns about an individual patient, it would begin to offer feedback, suggested readings, and tips of the day tailored to the needs of that patient. These personalized responses would be based on the patient's own entries in her daily log. The site would notify patients when personalized feedback is available.

Patients would be able to receive visual feedback on how their symptoms, behaviors, thoughts, and situation are changing over time. The data for these visual displays would come from a patient's own entries in her daily log. For example, by clicking on an icon labeled "graph of symptom severity," a patient could see how her symptom severity has changed since she began recording it. By highlighting trends in their progress and treatment, patients may begin to understand the relationships between the two. Ultimately, this feedback may reinforce good habits and discourage bad ones.

Patients who report problems in their daily log would receive "suggested reading" links to appropriate articles in the Library of Information. For example, if a patient reports experiencing insomnia in her daily log, the video host would suggest that she read an article on techniques for overcoming insomnia. Providing timely and relevant information without requiring much patient effort may help patients deal with their problems more quickly and effectively.

Patients who report problems would also receive personalized "tips of the day." This feature would provide patients with specific recommendations or suggestions for actions that they might find beneficial. For example, if a patient reports feeling stress, then the site would suggest using relaxation aids such as listening to soft music, reading a good book, or taking a warm bath or shower.

Behavioral Contract. Behavioral contracts are a commonly used means of codifying a behavioral goal set by a patient. The establishment of a contract usually follows a problem-solving session in which a patient identifies the nature and scope of the problem, develops possible solutions, and decides on a course of action. This technique has been shown to contribute to behavior change (Worthington, 1979; Kirschenbaum et al., 1982; Wilson et al., 1990). At the website, behavioral contracting could be used as one means of encouraging active self-regulation of depression, as well as its antecedents and consequences. Behavioral contracting would be introduced in the context of problem solving, and patients would be encouraged to commit to a plan of action to attempt to remediate a problem. The behavioral contract would allow them to specify a behavior that they will perform. Possible behaviors may include adhering to treatment recommendations and actions such as calling a friend, seeing a comedy, and taking a walk. Patients would also be able to type in a behavior not on the list. The site would also enable patients to send evidence of their commitment to someone in their support community should they choose to do so.

Conclusion

The Internet is revolutionizing the practice of health care. The greatest impact has been on health care consumers, who now have unprecedented access to an enormous amount of health care information. Information alone, though, will not sustain the changes that are occurring. I have tried to illustrate in three very different domains how websites may be designed to benefit health care consumers faced with difficult choices. To empower health care consumers, websites must first offer information that is accurate, consumer-friendly, comprehensive, and relevant. Second, websites need to employ decision support techniques to reduce the processing burden and enhance the value of information. Finally, social support must be built into websites to encourage decision making and motivate behavioral change. Jane would have been extremely interested in the creative uses of the Web to overcome decision aversion and promote good decision making.

References

American Psychiatric Association, *Diagnostic and Statistical Manual of Mental Disorders*, 4th ed. Washington, DC: American Psychiatric Association, 1994.

Beattie, J., Baron, J., Hershey, J. C., Spranca, M. D., "Psychological determinants of decision attitude," *Journal of Behavior Decision Making*, 1994; 7:129–144.

Brody, D. S., "The patient's role in clinical decision-making," *Annals of Internal Medicine*, 1980; 93:718–722.

Charles, C., Gafni, A., and Whelen, T., "Shared decision-making in the medical encounter: What does it mean (or it takes at least two to tango)," *Social Science and Medicine*, 1997; 44:681–692.

Davis, K., et al., "Choice matters: Enrollees' views of their health plans," *Health Affairs*, 1995; 14(2):99–112.

Francis, W., *Checkbook* magazine, eds., *Checkbook's Guide to Health Insurance Plans for Federal Employees*. Washington, DC: Center for the Study of Services, 1997.

Gibbs, D. A., Sangl, J. A., Burris, B., "Consumer perspectives on information needs for health plan choice," *Health Care Financing Review*, 1996; 18(1):31–54, 55–74.

Greenberg, P. E., Stiglin, L. E., Finkelstein, S. N., Berndt, E. R., "The economic burden of depression in 1990," *Journal of Clinical Psychiatry*, 1993; 54:405–418.

Greenfield, S., Kaplan, S., Ware, J. E., "Expanding patient involvement in care: Effects on patient outcomes," *Annals of Internal Medicine*, 1985; 102:520–528.

Greenfield, S., Kaplan, S., Ware, J. E., Yano, E. M., Frank, H. J., "Patients' participation in medical care: Effects on blood sugar control and quality of life in diabetes," *Journal of General Internal Medicine*, 1988; 3:448–457.

Hibbard, J. H., Jewett, J. J., "What type of quality information do consumers want in a health care report card?" *Medical Care Research and Review*, 1996; 53(1):28–47.

Hirschfeld, R., Keller, M., Panico, S., Arons, B., et al, "The National Depressive and Manic-Depressive Association Consensus Statement on the Undertreatment of Depression," *Journal of the American Medical Association*, 1997; 277:330–340.

Keller, M. B., Harrison, W., Fawcett, J. A., et al., "Treatment of chronic depression with sertraline and imipramine: Preliminary blinded response rates and high rates of undertreatment in the community," *Psychopharmacology Bulletin*, 1995; 31:205–212.

Kirschenbaum, D. S., Dielman, J. S., Karoly, P., "Efficacy of behavioral contracting: Target behaviors, performance criteria, and settings," *Behavior Modification*, 1982; 6(4):499–518.

Marquis, M. S., Rogowski, J. A., *Participation in Alternative Health Plans*. R-4105-HCFA. Santa Monica, CA: RAND.

Mechanic, D., Ettel, T., Davis, D., "Choosing among health insurance options: A study of new employees," *Inquiry*, 1990; 27:14–23.

Moustafa, A. T., Hopkins, C. E., Klein, B., "Determinants of choice and change in health insurance plan," *Medical Care*, 1971; 9(1):32–41.

Quill, T. E., "Partnership in patient care: A contractual approach," *Annals of Internal Medicine*, 1983; 98:228–234.

Regier, D. A., Narrow, W. E., Rae, D. S., Manderscheid, R. W., Locke, B. Z., Goodwin, F. K., "The de facto US Mental and Addictive Disorders Service System: Epidemiologic Catchment Area prospective 1-year prevalence rates of disorders and services," *Archives of General Psychiatry*, 1993; 50:84–94.

Robins, L. N., Reier, D. A., eds, *Psychiatric Disorders in America: The Epidemiologic Catchment Area Study*. New York: Free Press, 1991.

Sainfort, F., Booske, B. C., "Role of information in consumer selection of health plans," *Health Care Financing Review*, 1996; 18(1):31–54.

Scanlon, D. P., Chernew, M., Lave, J. R., "Consumer health plan choice: Current knowledge and future directions," *Annual Review of Public Health*, 1997; 18:507–528.

Schoenbaum, M., Spranca, M., Elliot, M., "Health plan choice and information about out-of-pocket costs: An experimental approach," under review.

Simon, G. E., von Korff, M., "Recognition, management, and outcomes of depression in primary care," *Archives of Family Medicine*, 1995; 4:99–105.

Sofaer, S., Kenney, E., and Davidson, B., "The effect of the illness episode approach on medicare beneficiaries' health insurance decisions." *Health Services Research*, 1992; 27:671–693.

Spranca, M., Danouse, D. E., Elliott, M., Short, F. S., Fareley, D. O., Hays, R. D., "Do consumer reports of health plan quality affect health plan selection?" In press.

Spranca, M., Schoenbaum, M., Elliott, M., "Attitudes towards alternative approaches to presenting out-of-pocket health costs," Manuscript in preparation.

Tumlinson, A., et al., "Choosing a health plan: What information will consumers use?" *Health Affairs*, 1997; 16(3):229–238.

Wells, K. B., Stewart, A., Hays, R. D., et al, "The functioning and well-being of depressed patients: Results from the Medical Outcomes Study," *Journal of the American Medical Association*, 1989; 262:914–919.

Wilson, D. K., Wallston, K. A., King, J. E., "Effects of contract framing, motivation to quit, and self-efficacy on smoking reduction," *Journal of Applied Social Psychology*, 1990; 20(7, Pt 2):531–547.

Worthington, E. L., "Behavioral self-control and the contract problem," *Teaching of Psychology*, 1979; 6(2):91–94.

13 Interpreting Conflicts Between Intuition and Formal Models

Deborah Frisch

A great deal of research has examined the ways in which people deal with different types of conflicts in decision making. Three main types of conflict have been studied by decision researchers. One type of conflict involves situations in which a person must decide what to believe on the basis of conflicting evidence. Research on hypothesis testing and judgment under uncertainty falls under this heading. The second type of conflict involves situations in which a person has to make trade-offs among different goals. Research on multiattribute choice addresses this type of conflict. The third type of conflict involves decisions under uncertainty. As Lopes (1990, p. 279) puts it, this type of situation involves the conflict between security (or avoidance of worst-case outcomes) and potential (or approach to best-case outcomes). As the chapters in this volume indicate, Jane Beattie contributed to each of these areas of research.

Much of the research that has been conducted on judgment and decision making (JDM) employs a methodology in which people's intuitive judgments or decisions are compared to normative models of rational behavior. In each of the three domains just described, researchers have found that people's judgments and decisions deviate from models of rational behavior. Throughout the history of the field of JDM, there has been conflict among researchers about how to interpret the discrepancy between intuitive judgments and normative models. Specifically, researchers have disagreed about whether this discrepancy is evidence of flaws in the subjects or flaws in the models of rationality. In this chapter, I discuss this meta-conflict with the hope of presenting a view that incorporates the important insights from researchers on both sides of the debate. In the first half of the chapter, I argue that deviations from normative models are more ambiguous than researchers usually assume when using examples from research on judgment under uncertainty. In the second half of the chapter, I show how this argument suggests a way to think about prescriptive issues in decision research (i.e., questions about how to improve the quality of decisions) that is not based on the controversial assumption that normative models provide standards to which people should aspire.

Ambiguity of the Heuristics and Biases Approach

One of the most general findings in decision research is that people's intuitive judgments and decisions systematically deviate from formal, axiomatic, normative models. Because Kahneman and Tversky published their first papers on the heuristics and biases approach to judgment under uncertainty (Kahneman, Slovic, & Tversky, 1982), there have been critics who have questioned their conclusions (Cohen, 1979, 1981; Einhorn & Hogarth, 1981; Gigerenzer, 1991, 1996; Lopes, 1981, 1991). The central claim that unites these critics is that the discrepancy between people's judgments and normative models such as subjective expected utility theory (SEU) and Bayesian probability theory (BPT) is not necessarily diagnostic of a flaw in people. Although the Bayesian view implies that as evidence accumulates, two sides that disagree will eventually converge on a single opinion, researchers in the field seem to be as polarized as they were 20 years ago (Gigerenzer, 1996; Kahneman & Tversky, 1996).

Kahneman and Tversky's novel and powerful claim was that the *systematic* discrepancies between people's judgments and normative models are diagnostic of the psychological processes involved in judgment. This enormously productive insight was based on an analogy between visual perception and judgment under uncertainty. Perceptual illusions are a useful source of information about the processes involved in normal perception. In a perceptual illusion, subjects' judgments systematically deviate from objective reality. For example, in the Ponzo (railroad track) illusion, the correct answer is that A = B (where A refers to the line that appears to be farther away). The two possible mistakes (A > B and B > A) do not occur with equal frequency. Rather, the mistake A > B is much more common than the mistake B > A. A systematic error in perception or judgment is more interesting and informative than a non-systematic (random) error. In the Ponzo illusion, the fact that the error A > B is more common than the error B > A suggests that apparent distance is used as a cue to judge size. Although apparent distance is usually an accurate cue, it also leads to systematic errors.

Based on the analogy between visual perception and judgment under uncertainty, Kahneman and Tversky argued that systematic errors in judgment arise as unintended consequences of subjects' reliance on imperfect cues or heuristics. No one wants to suffer from the Ponzo illusion, but it is a by-product of people's reliance on cues that generally lead to accurate judgments. Similarly, no one wants to suffer from the conjunction effect (Tversky & Kahneman, 1983), but it is a by-product of people's reliance on heuristics that usually lead to accurate judgments.

Tversky and Kahneman (1983) quote Helmholtz (1881/1903), who said, "It is just those cases that are not in accordance with reality which are particularly instructive for discovering the laws of the processes by which normal perception originates." They go on to say, "Helmholtz's position implies that perception is not usefully analyzed into a normal process that produces accurate percepts and a distorting process that produces errors and illusions" (p. 313). Kahneman and Tversky applied this type of reasoning to judgment under uncertainty and argued that both accurate and inaccurate judgments can be explained in terms of a single model.

In the domains of visual perception and judgment under uncertainty, the realization that a common set of mechanisms can explain both accurate and inaccurate judgments has been extremely productive. In the domain of perception, another insight has also been very important: Systematic errors in judgment can arise for two conceptually different reasons. One cause of systematic error is that subjects rely on a set of cues that are biased in the sense that they are more likely to lead to one mistake as opposed to the other. For example, it is widely believed that the procedure used to conduct the U.S. Census is biased and is more likely to miss people with low incomes than it is to miss people with high incomes. A second source of systematic error is that there are different costs associated with different types of mistakes. For example, if you measured all of the boards cut by a carpenter that were supposed to be 3 feet long, you would probably find more boards that were too long than boards that were too short. This systematic error is not due to the carpenter's reliance on heuristics. Rather, it is due to the fact that the cost of the mistake in which the board is too long is much lower than the cost of the mistake in which the board is too short. Weber (1994) demonstrates that a variety of phenomena in the judgment literature that have been explained in terms of perceptual bias can also be explained in terms of this type of *asymmetric loss function* (Birnbaum, Coffey, Mellers, & Weiss, 1992). The general point is that systematic error can arise either as the unintentional result of reliance on a biased set of cues or as the intentional result of an analysis of the costs associated with different types of mistakes.

Plous (1993) presents an interesting analysis of the fundamental attribution error that illustrates this idea. The *fundamental attribution error* refers to the social psychological finding that people tend to attribute other people's behavior to dispositional causes instead of situational ones. Plous analyzes this phenomenon from the perspective of expected utility theory.

	Actual cause of behavior	
	Dispositional	*Situational*
Attributed cause		
D	+3	−1
S	−3	+1

Imagine that you have observed a person engage in some behavior, and you need to decide whether to attribute the behavior to a disposition of the person (D) or a situational cause (S). The numbers in the table reflect the payoffs associated with the four possible outcomes. Plous justifies the payoffs by quoting Lopes (1982, p. 633): "Both physical and social survival require that we learn as well as we can to predict and control the effects that other people have on us. Thus, if an effect is predictable, even weakly, by the presence of some individual, then it is important that we find this out." That is, the payoff for attributing a dispositional cause is higher than the payoff for attributing a situational cause because you have learned something general and useful about the person. (This argument assumes that it is more useful to learn about a specific person than to learn about a situation.) To complete the analysis, Plous assumes that situational causes occur 60% of the time. He then asks what the "rational" response is in this situation. A simple application of expected utility theory shows that the EU(Dispositional) $= 1.2 - .6 = .6$ and EU(Situational) $= -1.2 + .6 = -.6$. That is, the expected utility of attributing a dispositional cause is greater than the expected utility of attributing a situational cause. If your goal is to maximize the probability of being correct, you should attribute a situational cause. If your goal is to maximize expected utility, you should attribute a dispositional cause.

Imagine that a person makes 100 judgments of the type described by Plous (1993). Each time, the person analyzes the situation in terms of the payoff matrix described previously and decides that the best bet is to make a dispositional attribution. This person's errors will not be random. She will make 60 errors in which the truth is S and she said D and no errors in which the truth is D and she said S. That is, her errors will be systematic. In this situation, the systematic error does not arise as a result of the person's reliance on heuristics. Rather, the systematic error is the result of the subject's assessment of the payoffs associated with the four possible outcomes. Because of the two asymmetries in the payoff matrix (i.e., the payoff for a hit is higher for D than for S, and the cost of a miss is higher for D than for S), a person who is trying to maximize the expected payoff will show a systematic error.

Although Kahneman and Tversky assume that systematic error is diagnostic of reliance on heuristics, systematic error is sometimes diagnostic of asymmetries in the payoff matrix (Weber, Tada, & Blais, 1998). An experimenter who was not aware of the subject's assessment of these payoffs might mistakenly conclude that the subject's systematic error was the unintentional consequence of the subject's reliance on heuristics. Kahneman and Tversky are correct in their claim that systematic errors are informative but incorrect in their claim that these errors provide unambiguous evidence that subjects are relying on heuristics. Systematic errors can arise as the *intentional* consequences of an analysis of the relative costs associated with different types of mistakes (and the relative benefits associated with different types of correct judgments). Many researchers recognize this fact and are careful to ensure that the subjects' goals in the task correspond to the experimenter's model. For example, if subjects are asked to imagine being in the role of a policy maker, the experimenter can ensure that the subject is not including goals (e.g., avoiding regret) that are relevant in personal decisions (e.g., Ritov & Baron, 1990). However, in discussions of the logic of the heuristics and biases approach, the fact that systematic errors can either be the intentional result of a cost-benefit analysis or the unintentional result of reliance on time-saving heuristics is usually not spelled out as explicitly as it could be. This might be a source of the ongoing controversy about how to interpret this body of research.

There is a second source of ambiguity in interpreting systematic deviations from normative models when we switch from the domain of visual perception to judgment under uncertainty. In visual perception, there is agreement about what the correct answer is. For example, most people believe there is a truth of the matter about how long a line is and also agree about how to measure it (e.g., with a ruler). In contrast, experts in the field of decision making do not all agree about the normative status of the models that Kahneman and Tversky used as standards of rationality (Bayesian probability theory and subjective expected utility theory). Therefore, the systematic discrepancy between people's judgments and the standards might occur because the subjects have different standards.

An example from outside the field of JDM might clarify this point. Several years ago, I received a paper in which a student misspelled the word *final* as *phinal*. Although I was used to seeing spelling errors, I was surprised at this particular error. A few weeks later, I saw a bumper sticker on a car that said *PHISH*. I did some research and found out that this is the name of a Grateful Dead-type band that is popular in Eugene, Oregon. Imagine that I gave a spelling test in which I read a sentence and the subjects had to write down what I said. Suppose my sentence was "Bob and Ted often argue about their very different attitudes toward fish." If there was a systematic error in how subjects spelled the word *their* (e.g., more errors in which it was spelled *there* than any other error), I would say that it was a mistake. I would hypothesize that the error was due to the fact that the word *there* is more common and therefore more available than the word *their*. I would predict that if I pointed this mistake out to the subjects, they would change their spelling of the word. In contrast, if I found a systematic error in how the students spelled the word *fish*, I would not necessarily conclude that it was a mistake. I would be more likely to think that the students thought I was saying *PHISH*. If so, what appeared from my perspective to be a mistake was actually a correct response. The point is that a systematic discrepancy between subjects' responses and the experimenter's idea of the correct answer can arise because subjects do not agree with the experimenter about what the correct answer is.

This analysis suggests that the systematic discrepancy between people's judgments and normative standards is more ambiguous than researchers typically acknowledge. In order to interpret any finding then, it is necessary to answer two questions. First, does the subject agree with the experimenter about what constitutes the correct answer?

Second, was the subject trying to maximize the probability of being correct or was the subject trying to maximize the expected utility of the response?

There are some findings in the heuristics and biases literature in which it is very likely that subjects accept the experimenter's definition of the correct answer and also are trying to maximize the probability of being correct. In these cases, it is reasonable to conclude that the systematic discrepancy between subjects' responses and the experimenter's standard occurred because subjects were relying on imperfect heuristics. For example, many studies on the availability heuristic involve comparisons between people's judgments and objective frequencies, such as the frequencies of different causes of death (Lichtenstein, Slovic, Fischhoff, Layman, & Combs, 1978). In these cases there is no controversy about what the correct answer is, and it is plausible that the subjects' only goal was to maximize the accuracy of their responses. Therefore, the standard explanation in terms of subjects' reliance on heuristics seems warranted. Another example in which the heuristic interpretation is very plausible is the following: Imagine a lottery in which six numbers are randomly chosen from the numbers 1–40. You have a choice between two tickets:

> Ticket 1: 1 2 3 4 5 6
> Ticket 2: 3 6 14 25 30 31

Which would you prefer? Many people would choose Ticket 2 because it looks more "random." However, the two tickets have the same chance of being the winning ticket. The intuition that Ticket 2 is more likely to be the winning ticket conflicts with the answer given by a simple application of probability theory.

Why does it seem that Ticket 2 is more likely to be the winning ticket? The concept of *representativeness* (Tversky & Kahneman, 1974) provides an explanation. Because Ticket 2 is more similar to the stereotype of a winning ticket, it appears to be more likely to win. That is, we know that in general "random-looking tickets" are the winning lottery tickets much more often than "tickets with a pattern." This belief leads us to assume mistakenly that in this particular case, Ticket 2 is more likely to be a winner than Ticket 1.

In this example, it is unlikely that subjects disagreed with the experimenter's definition of the correct answer. The two tickets do have the same chance of being the winning ticket. Is it possible that the subjects' systematic preference for Ticket 2 can be explained because the subjects have goals that were not included in the original analysis of the situation? Is there an alternative description of the payoff structure that could account for the preference for Ticket 2?

We can rule out the possibility that the observed pattern is due to subjects' beliefs about the relative costs associated with different mistakes because the cost of being wrong is the same in both cases. It is possible that subjects believe that the payoffs associated with being right differ for the two tickets. However, this line of reasoning would actually predict the opposite pattern of results from the pattern observed. A person might believe that the two tickets are equally likely to win but think that the payoff associated with winning for Ticket 1 is higher than the payoff associated with winning for Ticket 2. If you win with Ticket 1, you probably won't have to share the prize (because no normal person would choose such a nonrandom-looking ticket). On the other hand, if you win with Ticket 2, there's a higher probability that you'd have to share the prize. This line of reasoning predicts a preference for Ticket 1, not for Ticket 2. It's difficult to construct a similar scenario that would explain a preference for Ticket 2. Because there is no controversy about what the right answer is and there is no plausible payoff matrix that could account for the observed pattern, the claim that the systematic error is diagnostic of subjects' reliance on imperfect heuristics is justified. Almost everyone would agree that the discrepancy between people's judgments and the answer given by probability theory arises because of a flaw in subjects' reasoning.

Some examples in which subjects deviate from BPT can be explained by postulating that subjects' analyses of the payoffs associated with the four possible outcomes differ from the experimenter's analysis (as in the Plous, 1993, example described earlier). Consider how this approach would apply to the conjunction effect (Tversky & Kahneman, 1983). The well-known example states:

Linda is 31 years old, single, outspoken and very bright. She majored in philosophy. As a student, she was deeply concerned with issues of discrimination and social justice, and also participated in anti-nuclear demonstrations.

a. Linda is a teacher in elementary school.
b. Linda works in a bookstore and takes yoga classes.
c. Linda is active in the feminist movement.
d. Linda is a psychiatric social worker.
e. Linda is a member of the League of Women Voters.
f. Linda is a bank teller.
g. Linda is an insurance salesperson
h. Linda is a bank teller and is active in the feminist movement

The subjects' task was to rank these statements from most likely to least likely. Probability theory requires that "f" be ranked as more likely than "h." That is, the probability that Linda is a bank teller must be higher than the probability that she is a bank teller *and* a feminist. However, many people violate this basic principle of probability and rate "h" as more likely than "f." Kahneman and Tversky's explanation for this result is that Linda is very similar to the stereotype of a feminist and is not at all similar to the stereotype of a bank teller. Therefore, it seems much more plausible (and therefore likely) that she is a "feminist bank teller."

There are several reasons to be skeptical of the claim that the conjunction effect is a mistake that arises because of subjects' reliance on an imperfect heuristic. First, as Tversky and Kahneman (1983) note, the conjunction effect occurs even in extremely transparent situations. It's surprising that so many people would make such an obvious mistake. Second, some subjects defend their original response even when challenged. Tversky and Kahneman (1983, p. 300) quote one subject who said, "I thought you only asked for my opinion." Tversky and Kahneman (1983) attribute this persistence to a lack of statistical sophistication. However, it is also possible that subjects who defend their responses do not agree that the original judgment was a mistake. The biggest problem with Tversky and Kahneman's explanation is that some researchers (who are statistically sophisticated) agree with the subjects. For example, Wolford, Taylor, and Beck (1990) argue that the conjunction effect occurs because subjects make slightly different assumptions about the situation from those intended by Tversky and Kahneman (1983). Lopes and Oden (1991) argue that there is much more evidence supporting the claim that Linda is a feminist bank teller than the claim that she is a bank teller and that this accounts for subjects' responses. Gigerenzer (1991) also argues that the conjunction effect is not a mistake.

It is possible to construct an analysis that suggests that the conjunction effect is not a mistake that arises because of subjects' reliance on imperfect cues such as representativeness. The following analysis describes why I personally think Linda is more likely to be a feminist bank teller than a bank teller. It is based on the idea that the payoff associated with a hit varies as a function of the specific belief. In this situation, it is plausible to assume that the payoff for a hit is higher for the attribute feminist than for the attribute bank teller. If I know someone is a feminist, I know a lot about how to engage her in conversation. If I know she's a bank teller, it doesn't tell me very much. Therefore, assume that the payoff for correctly identifying a feminist is 3 and for identifying a bank teller it is 1. Furthermore, assume there is no cost for a false alarm. Finally, assume that the cost for a miss is the negative of the payoff for a hit (that is, the cost of a miss is the opportunity cost).

		TRUTH			TRUTH	
		F	not F		B	not B
ACT	F	3	0	B	1	0
	not F	−3	0	not B	−1	0

Combining these two tables yields the following payoff structure:

		TRUTH			
		FB	(not F) B	(not F)(not B)	F(not B)
ACT	FB	4	1	0	3
	B	−2	1	0	−3

If I had the payoff structure just described, then the action FB would dominate the action B. If you asked me, "Which is more likely, FB or B?" I could think about the columns (states of the world) or the rows (actions) in the table. That is, "feminist bank teller" corresponds to a state of the world but it also corresponds to an action. If I focus on the columns (states of the world), I'd obey the conjunction rule and say that B is more likely than FB. If I focused on the rows (actions), I'd see that the action FB dominates the action B and therefore I'd say that FB is more likely than B. Linda's more likely to be a bank teller but I'm more likely to act as if she's a feminist bank teller.

Of course, there's no real contradiction here. There are two separate questions: (1) Which is more likely to be true of Linda? and (2) Which belief are you more likely to act on? The answer to question (1) is B; the answer to question (2) is FB. In discussing the conjunction effect, Tversky and Kahneman (1983, pp. 313–314) state, "A comprehensive account of human judgment must reflect the tension between compelling logical rules and seductive nonextensional intuitions." My point is that the tension I personally feel about the Linda problem is between two equally compelling logical analyses: One assumes that the goal is to maximize the accuracy of the judgment; the other assumes that the goal is to maximize the expected utility of the judgment. Of course, I have not shown that all people who exhibit the conjunction effect do so for this reason. My point is just that the conjunction effect is not necessarily a mistake that arises because of people's reliance on heuristics.

Finally, some examples in which subjects systematically deviate from the experimenters' standard are best viewed as evidence that the subjects do not agree with the experimenter about what constitutes a correct answer. One of the most basic axioms of BPT is the *additivity axiom*, which states that $p(A) + p(\text{not A}) = 1$. In situations involving ambiguity, people sometimes violate this axiom (Einhorn & Hogarth, 1985). Is this a mistake? An alternative explanation is that people use the language of probability in a way that does not correspond to BPT (Frisch & Baron, 1988). BPT requires a person to express degree of belief as a single number reflecting the implication of evidence. In the theory, there is no meaningful difference between a situation in which you have a great deal of evidence suggesting that $p(X) = .5$ and a situation in which you have no evidence and therefore believe that $p(X) = .5$. However, these two situations differ with respect to the weight of evidence. If people try to convey both the implication and the weight of evidence in probability judgments, they will exhibit subadditive probabilities (and therefore violate the additivity axiom) in situations involving ambiguity. In a situation in which there is not much evidence relevant to the assessment of the probability of X, a judge might say that $p(X)$ is low but might also say that $p(\text{not } X)$ is low, leading to subadditive probability judgments.

Although BPT requires that probability judgments reflect the implication and not the weight of evidence, there is a long history of researchers who have argued otherwise. Einhorn and Hogarth (1985) present the following quote from Keynes (1921):

The magnitude of the probability . . . depends upon what may be termed the favourable and the unfavourable evidence; a new piece of evidence which leaves this balance unchanged, also leaves the probability of the argument unchanged. But it seems that there may be another respect in which some kind of quantitative comparison between argument is possible. This comparison turns upon a balance, not between the favourable and unfavourable evidence, but between the *absolute* amounts of relevant knowledge and of relevant ignorance respectively. (p. 71)

Keynes's (1921) point is that beliefs differ with respect to the balance (implication) of evidence but also with respect to the absolute amount of evidence on which they are based. Frisch and Baron (1988) quote Pierce (1932), who made an even stronger claim:

[T]o express the proper state of belief, not one number but two are requisite, the first depending on the inferred probability, the second on the amount of knowledge on which that probability is based. (p. 421)

Whereas Pierce argued that it was necessary to use two numbers to express degree of belief, some theories of probability try to incorporate both the weight and the implication of evidence in a single number. Some of these theories allow subadditive probabilities (Shafer, 1976). Therefore, it is plausible that people's judgments do not conform to the additivity axiom because they use a theory (language) of probability that is different from BPT.

In sum, there are three main reasons a person's judgments might deviate systematically from the experimenter's definition of the correct answer. One reason is that subjects are relying on imperfect cues or heuristics. This is the reason Kahneman and Tversky focus on and it was illustrated in the lottery ticket example. The second reason is that there were asymmetries in the payoffs that the subjects assigned to correct and incorrect judgments. This is the point of the Lopes/Plous example and my analysis of the conjunction effect. The third reason is that subjects do not agree with the researcher about what constitutes a correct answer. This was illustrated in the Phish example and the analysis of subadditive probabilities.

Prescriptive Implications: Decisions Under Uncertainty

This perspective has implications for how to think about prescriptive issues in decision research. In particular, this view makes it possible to talk about ways of improving the quality of decisions without assuming that normative models provide standards of rational behavior. In order to illustrate this, I turn from a focus on research on judgment under uncertainty to a discussion of research on risky choice. In the domain of risky choice, research has demonstrated that people's choices systematically deviate from the axioms of subjective expected utility theory (SEU). As in the case of judgment under uncertainty, there is controversy about how to interpret these findings. Many researchers have questioned whether SEU is an appropriate standard of judgment under uncertainty (e.g.,

Allais, 1953; Ellsberg, 1961; Lopes, 1981, 1983, 1996). Allais (1953) and Ellsberg (1961), the two researchers who first proposed counterexamples to SEU, both argued that deviations from the axioms of SEU were not necessarily mistakes. Similarly, Lopes (1996) argued that SEU is not an appropriate normative standard because people might have legitimate goals that are not subsumed by the goal of maximizing expected utility.

There are three types of reasons, analogous to the ones described in the first half of the chapter, that a person's choices might deviate systematically from the axioms of SEU. First, people might rely on heuristics that lead to mistakes. Second, people might have goals that are not reflected in the standard analysis of the task. Finally, people might interpret the concept of *utility* in a way that is different from its meaning in SEU. This would be analogous to the argument in the first half of the chapter that people might interpret the concept of *probability* in a way that is different from the meaning encoded in the axioms of BPT.

An obvious implication of this view is that some but not all violations of SEU are mistakes. Therefore, it does not make sense to view SEU as a standard of behavior that people should try to conform to. Rather, the purpose of SEU is to give the decision maker deeper insight into the factors that are influencing his or her decision. This perspective is similar to the view developed by Bell, Raiffa, and Tversky (1988), who argue that any violation of SEU can be viewed either as evidence of a mistake in the subjects or as evidence of a flaw in the model. They say, "There certainly are discrepancies between the tenets of SEU theory and descriptive behavior. Should we be changing the analytical procedures we propose for guiding real behavior or should we be applying a bit of psychological therapy? Or both?" (p. 25). That is, when people's choices violate an axiom of SEU, does the person need decision therapy or does the theory need to be modified?

The perspective I have presented is also very similar to the view described by Savage, who has been credited with being the first researcher to clearly differentiate the normative and descriptive interpretations of SEU (Shafer, 1986). Savage argued that the purpose of the axioms of SEU was to enable a person to detect inconsistencies among beliefs or preferences. In an analysis of the Allais paradox (pp. 101–103), he describes each of the three ways of resolving the inconsistency that I have described. The first option is to conclude that one of the choices was a mistake. This, in fact, is how Savage (1954) resolved the Allais paradox. The second option is to reject some aspect of SEU, such as the sure-thing principle. This option is equivalent to the idea attributed earlier to Allais (1953), Ellsberg (1961), and Lopes (1981) that people might have the goal of minimizing the probability of the worst-case outcome, in addition to other goals such as maximizing the expected payoff. Lopes (1987, 1990) discusses how rank-dependent models (Quiggen, 1982; Yaari, 1987) can be interpreted as allowing people to have these different goals. Someone who wanted to minimize the probability of the worst-case outcome would "overweight" outcomes at the low end of the distribution, relative to outcomes at the high end (Weber & Kirsner, 1997). Finally, Savage (1954, p. 101) says, "many apparent exceptions to the theory can be so reinterpreted as not to be exceptions at all." That is, it is possible to redefine the concept of utility to account for apparent violations of SEU. For example, if the utility of an outcome can depend on the other outcomes that might have occurred, then the Allais paradox is no longer a violation of SEU theory.

Although Savage's view implies that the function of SEU is a tool for gaining insight, many researchers have treated it as a standard of rational behavior (e.g., Kleinmuntz, 1991). In order to clarify the distinction between SEU as a standard for evaluating decisions and a tool for gaining insight, consider how decision therapy would be conducted from each of the perspectives. Imagine that a person exhibits the pattern of preferences in the Allais paradox:

Situation 1:	1	2–11	12–100
Gamble 1	500,000	500,000	500,000
Gamble 2	0	2,500,000	500,000
Situation 2:	1	2–11	12–100
Gamble 3	500,000	500,000	0
Gamble 4	0	2,500,000	0

Suppose that a person chose 1 in Situation 1 and 4 in Situation 2. What would the decision therapist who viewed SEU as a standard say? This therapist would try to get the client to change one of the two choices by pointing out that the client had violated the sure-thing principle. The therapist would remind the client that this principle is normatively very compelling. If the client was not persuaded by this appeal to logic, the therapist might point out that people who violate expected utility theory are sometimes susceptible to money pump arguments.

An article by Slovic and Tversky (1974) illustrates the problem with this approach. They present a hypothetical debate between an SEU advocate (Dr. S, for Savage) and a person who exhibited the pattern of preferences shown in the Allais paradox (Dr. A, for Allais). Dr. S tries to persuade Dr. A to change his choices in order to conform to SEU. Dr. A's position is summed up in the statement "What you call education, others may call brainwashing" (pp. 372–373). Dr. S's position is captured by his closing comment: "Yet I have observed, that, in general, the deeper the understanding of the axiom, the greater the readiness to accept it" (pp. 372–373). The standoff described by Slovic and Tversky (1974) still exists today (see Lopes, 1996; Schoemaker & Hershey, 1996).

The problem with this approach is that more than 45 years after the first counterexample to SEU was discovered (Allais, 1953), researchers still disagree about whether SEU is an appropriate normative standard. Many researchers who are extremely familiar with SEU do not accept it as a normative standard. This contradicts Dr. S's claim that the deeper the understanding of the theory, the greater the acceptance. Samuelson (1950) is famous for having said that he'd satisfy his preferences and let the axioms satisfy themselves. Lopes (1996, p. 187) says, "My own sense is that money pump and Dutch book arguments are logical bogeymen." Therefore, a decision therapist who tries to argue that SEU is a standard of rational behavior runs the risk of reaching this kind of impasse with a client whose choices deviate from the theory. A client who refused to accept SEU as a normative standard would have the company of researchers such as Allais (1953), Ellsberg (1961), and Lopes (1996).

In contrast, consider the therapist who acknowledges the fact that violations of normative models are ambiguous and who therefore views SEU as a tool for gaining insight. This therapist might tell the client that the pattern of choices exhibited is inconsistent with the axioms of SEU and that research on decision making suggests that there are several different reasons people deviate from the theory. One possibility is that one of the choices was a mistake. For example, one of the choices might involve a psychophysical bias. In Situation 1, the difference between a 99% chance of winning and a 100% chance of winning is very salient and has a big effect on your decision. In Situation 2, the difference between a 10% and an 11% chance of winning seems negligible. When you think about it, a 1% chance of a big payoff is worth paying attention to. This suggests that the client might want to consider the possibility that the choice in Situation 2 is a mistake that resulted from a lack of ability to discriminate small probabilities.

Another possibility is that the client has goals that are not captured by the obvious application of SEU to this situation. It is possible that in Situation 1, where one option guarantees a payoff, the client gives substantial weight to the goal of winning. This leads to a preference for the sure thing. In Situation 2, there is no option that guarantees a payoff, so the client gives less weight to the goal of winning. This would provide a justification for the original pattern of choices. The subject is willing to trade off expected value for certainty.

Finally, it is possible that the client is defining consequences differently from the way that the usual SEU analysis defines consequences. The client might believe that "winning $0 when you would definitely have won $500,000 had you chosen otherwise" is a different outcome from "winning $0 when you probably would have won $0 had you chosen otherwise." There are some emotions that arise in the context of making a decision including regret (Bell, 1982; Loomes & Sugden, 1982; Zeelenberg, Beattie, van der Pligt, & de Vries, 1996) and disappointment (Bell, 1985). Although SEU requires that the utilities of outcomes be independent of context, research suggests that context-induced emotions play an important role in people's decisions (Beattie, Baron, Hershey, & Spranca, 1994; Mellers, Schwartz, Ho, & Ritov, 1997). Furthermore, some research demonstrates that contextual factors such as framing can actually affect a person's experience of the outcomes of decisions (Levin & Gaeth, 1988). These findings suggest that some violations of SEU might arise because people define *consequences* in a way that differs from the way they are defined in SEU (Frisch & Jones, 1993; Kahneman & Tversky, 1984).

As this analysis demonstrates, there are (at least) three different explanations for the pattern of preferences known as the Allais paradox. Prescriptively, people should consider each of these reasons to see which one most accurately describes their thinking in the situation. On this view, one person might conclude that the Allais paradox is a mistake (e.g., if she found the psychophysical account most compelling) and another person might conclude that it is a perfectly sensible pattern of choices (e.g., if he found the multiple goals analysis most compelling).

Summary

In sum, violations of normative models such as BPT and SEU can arise for three different reasons (see Table 13.1). One reason is that people rely on imperfect heuristics (the subject made a mistake). A second reason

Table 13.1. *Reasons for Violation of Normative Models*

| | Source of Deviation | | |
Domain	Subject Made a Mistake	Model Fails to Include Some of Subjects' Goals	Subject and Experimenter Are Using Different Standards
Perception	Muller-Lyer illusion	Carpenter example	Phish example
Judgment under uncertainty	Lottery ticket	Conjunction effect	Subadditive probabilities
Risky choice	Psychophysical distortion	Rank-dependent weighting of outcomes	Experience of consequences affected by context

is that the subject had goals that the experimenter was not aware of. On this view, the subject's response actually is consistent with the (more comprehensive) rational analysis of the situation. A third reason is that the subject defines concepts (i.e., probability or utility) in ways that differ from the way they are defined in BPT or SEU. Therefore, the observation that people deviate from these models is not always due to their reliance on imperfect heuristics.

Because deviations from normative models are ambiguous, SEU is most appropriately viewed as a tool to gain insight as opposed to a standard that people should always aspire to. This perspective acknowledges the usefulness of SEU but also incorporates the insights from researchers who have argued that SEU is not an appropriate standard of rational behavior. Deviations can occur because of biases in the subjects such as psychophysical distortion of probabilities. This conclusion is most justified when subjects themselves agree on reflection that they have made a mistake or when it is difficult to explain the discrepancy as arising because subjects have goals that were not captured by the standard SEU analysis. For example, it is plausible that one of the responses in the loss/gain framing effect demonstrated by Kahneman and Tversky (1984) is a mistake since many subjects agree the two frames are equivalent when they are asked to directly compare them (Frisch, 1993).

It is also plausible that one of the responses exhibited in the preference reversal phenomenon (Lichtenstein & Slovic, 1971) is a mistake because it is difficult to construct an explanation for why a preference should depend on the type of response (buying price vs. choice) required. Other violations of the model arise because people have goals that are not captured in the SEU model. In these situations, people do not believe that they have made a mistake. The development of rank-dependent models (Quiggen, 1982; Yaari, 1987) captures the intuition that people might have goals that are not included in the standard SEU analysis, such as maximizing the probability of winning (Lopes, 1981). This explanation would apply to some violations of the independence axiom of SEU. Finally, people's experience of the consequences of decisions might depend on factors that are considered irrelevant from the perspective of SEU (Frisch & Jones, 1993).

In an article discussing the SEU perspective, Loewenstein (1996, p. 289) says, "The decision-making paradigm, as it has developed, is the product of a marriage between cognitive psychology and economics. From economics, decision theory inherited, or was socialized into, the language of preferences and beliefs and the religion of utility maximization that provides a unitary perspective for understanding all behavior. From cognitive psychology, decision theory inherited its descriptive focus, concern with process, and many specific theoretical insights."

Loewenstein's (1996) metaphors provide a way to summarize the two main themes of this chapter. First, Kahneman and Tversky's analogy between visual perception and judgment under uncertainty was the matchmaker that made possible the marriage of cognitive psychology and economics. This relationship has led to many insights into decision making that are unlikely to have been achieved by either group alone. Second, there has been chronic tension between researchers who accept the religion of utility maximization and those who do not. A way to characterize this tension is that the advocates of utility maximization sometimes act as if the critics need to be saved. This fundamentalist attitude might be responsible for the *normative agnosticism* (Kahneman & Tversky, 1996, p. 586) endorsed by some critics (Cohen, 1981; Gigerenzer, 1996). Perhaps the advocates could make the first move toward reconciliation by acknowledging that if our goal is to develop a rational theory of decision making, then we should be especially appreciative of critics who point out potential flaws in the theory. This is similar to an idea expressed in an article about Carl Sagan (Adler, 1997, p. 64) that stated, "A religion whose highest sacrament is heresy might have won Sagan's allegiance, but he never found one." Similarly, a field that is devoted to rationality ought to appreciate critics who point out the possible flaws and limitations in our current models of rationality.

Notes

1 Many violations of SEU can be modeled either by modifying the model or by redefining *consequence*. Researchers interested in describing behavior tend to prefer the first approach (see Machina, 1989, for a discussion of the costs and benefits of the two methods).

References

Adler, J. (1997, March 31). Unbeliever's quest. *Newsweek*, 64–65.

Allais, M. (1953). Le comportement de l'homme rationnel devant le risque: Critique des postulats et axiomes de l'école americaine. *Econometrica, 21*, 503–546.

Beattie, J., Baron, J., Hershey, J. C., & Spranca, M. D. (1994). Psychological determinants of decision attitude. *Journal of Behavioral Decision Making, 7*, 129–144.

Bell, D. E. (1982). Regret in decision-making under uncertainty. *Operations Research, 30*, 961–981.

Bell, D. E. (1985). Disappointment in decision-making under uncertainty. *Operations Research, 33*, 1–27.

Bell, D. E., Raiffa, H., & Tversky, A. (1988). Descriptive, normative, and prescriptive interactions in decision making. In D. E. Bell, H. Raiffa, & A. Tversky (Eds.), *Decision making: Descriptive, normative and prescriptive interactions* (pp. 9–30). Cambridge: Cambridge University Press.

Birnbaum, M. H., Coffey, G., Mellers, B. A., & Weiss, R. (1992). Utility measurement: Configural-weight theory and the judge's point of view. *Journal of Experimental Psychology: Human Perception and Performance, 18*, 331–346.

Cohen, L. J. (1979). On the psychology of prediction: Whose is the fallacy? *Cognition, 7*, 385–407.

Cohen, L. J. (1981). Can human irrationality be experimentally demonstrated? *The Behavioral and Brain Sciences, 4*, 317–331.

Einhorn, H., & Hogarth, R. (1981). Behavioral decision theory: Processes of judgment and choice. *Annual Review of Psychology, 32*, 53–88.

Einhorn, H. J., & Hogarth, R. M. (1985). Ambiguity and uncertainty in probabilistic inference. *Psychological Review, 92*, 433–461.

Ellsberg, D. (1961). Risk, ambiguity, and the Savage axioms. *Quarterly Journal of Economics, 75*, 643–699.

Frisch, D. (1993). Reasons for framing effects. *Organizational Behavior and Human Decision Processes, 54*, 399–429.

Frisch, D., & Baron, J. (1988). Ambiguity and rationality. *Journal of Behavioral Decision Making, 1*, 149–157.

Frisch, D., & Jones, S. (1993). Assessing the accuracy of decisions. *Theory and Psychology, 3*, 115–135.

Gigerenzer, G. (1991). How to make cognitive illusions disappear: Beyond "heuristics and biases." *European Review of Social Psychology, 2*, 83–115.

Gigerenzer, G. (1996). On narrow norms and vague heuristics: A reply to Kahneman and Tversky (1996). *Psychological Review, 103*, 592–596.

Helmholtz, H. von. (1903). *Popular lectures on scientific subjects* (E. Atkinson, Trans.) New York: Green. (Original work published 1881)

Kahneman, D. (1991). Judgment and decision making: A personal view. *Psychological Science, 2,* 142–145.

Kahneman, D., Slovic, P., & Tversky, A. (1982). *Judgment under uncertainty: Heuristics and biases.* New York: Cambridge University Press.

Kahneman, D., & Tversky, A. (1984). Choices, values, and frames. *American Psychologist, 39,* 341–350.

Kahneman, D., & Tversky, A. (1996). On the reality of cognitive illusions. *Psychological Review, 103,* 582–591.

Keynes, J. M. (1921). *A treatise on probability.* London: Macmillan.

Kleinmuntz, D. N. (1991). Decision making for professional decision makers. *Psychological Science, 2,* 135–141.

Levin, I. P., & Gaeth, G. J. (1988). How consumers are affected by the framing of attribute information before and after consuming the product. *Journal of Consumer Research, 15,* 374-378.

Lichtenstein, S., & Slovic, P. (1971). Reversal of preferences between bids and choices in gambling decisions. *Journal of Experimental Psychology, 89,* 46–55.

Lichtenstein, S., Slovic, P., Fischhoff, B., Layman, M., & Combs, B. (1978). Judged frequency of lethal events. *Journal of Experimental Psychology: Human Learning and Memory. 4,* 551–578.

Loewenstein, G. (1996). Out of control: Visceral influences on behavior. *Organizational Behavior and Human Decision Processes, 65,* 272–292.

Loomes, G., & Sugden, R. (1982). Regret theory: An alternative theory of rational choice under uncertainty. *Economic Journal, 92,* 805–824.

Lopes, L. L. (1981). Decision making in the short run. *Journal of Experimental Psychology: Human Learning and Memory, 7,* 377–385.

Lopes, L. L. (1982). Doing the impossible: A note on induction and the experience of randomness. *Journal of Experimental Psychology: Learning, Memory, and Cognition, 8,* 626–636.

Lopes, L. L. (1983). Some thoughts on the psychological concept of risk. *Journal of Experimental Psychology: Human Perception and Performance, 9,* 137–144.

Lopes, L. L. (1987). Between hope and fear: The psychology of risk. *Advances in Experimental Social Psychology, 20,* 255–295.

Lopes, L. L. (1990). Re-modeling risk aversion. In G. M. von Furstenberg (Ed.), *Acting under uncertainty: Multidisciplinary conceptions* (pp. 267–299). Boston: Kluwer.

Lopes, L. L. (1991). The rhetoric of irrationality. *Theory & Psychology, 1,* 65–82.

Lopes, L. L. (1996). When time is of the essence: Averaging, aspiration, and the short run. *Organizational Behavior and Human Decision Processes, 65,* 179–189.

Lopes, L. L., & Oden, G. C. (1991). The rationality of intelligence. In E. Eells & T. Maruszewski (Eds.), *Rationality and reasoning* (pp. 193–223). Amsterdam: Rodopi.

Machina, M. J. (1989). Dynamic consistency and non-expected utility models of choice under uncertainty. *Journal of Economic Literature, 27,* 1622–1668.

Mellers, B. A., Schwartz, A., Ho, K., & Ritov, I. (1997). Decision affect theory: Emotional reactions to the outcomes of risky options. *Psychological Science, 8,* 423–429.

Pierce, C. S. (1932). *Collected papers* (C. Hartshorne, and P. Weiss, Eds.). Cambridge, MA: Belknap Press.

Plous, S. (1993). *The psychology of judgment and decision making*. New York: McGraw-Hill.

Quiggen, J. (1982). A theory of anticipated utility. *Journal of Economic Behavior and Organization, 3*, 323–343.

Ritov, I., & Baron, J. (1990). Reluctance to vaccinate: Omission bias and ambiguity. *Journal of Behavioral Decision Making, 3*, 263–277.

Samuelson, P. (1950). Probability and the attempts to measure utility. *Economic Review*, 169–170.

Savage, L. J. (1954). *The foundations of statistics*. New York: Wiley.

Schoemaker, P. J. H., & Hershey, J. C. (1996). Maximizing your chance of winning: The long and short of it revisited. *Organizational Behavior and Human Decision Processes, 65*, 194–200.

Shafer, G. (1976). *A mathematical theory of evidence*. Princeton, NJ: Princeton University Press.

Shafer, G. (1986). Savage revisited (with discussion). *Statistical Science, 1*, 463–501.

Slovic, P., & Tversky, A. (1974). Who accepts Savage's axioms? *Behavioral Science, 19*, 368–373.

Tversky, A., & Kahneman, D. (1974). Judgment under uncertainty: Heuristics and biases. *Science, 185*, 1124–1130.

Tversky, A., & Kahneman, D. (1983). Extensional vs. intuitive reasoning: The conjunction fallacy in probability judgment. *Psychological Review, 90*, 293–315.

Weber, E. U. (1994). From subjective probabilities to decision weights: The effect of asymmetric loss functions on the evaluation of uncertain outcomes and events. *Psychological Bulletin, 115*, 228–242.

Weber, E. U., & Kirsner, B. (1997). Reasons for rank dependent utility evaluation. *Journal of Risk and Uncertainty, 14*, 41–61.

Weber, E. U., Tada, Y., & Blais, A.-R. (1998). From Shakespeare to Spielberg: Predicting modes of decision making. Presidential address, Annual Meeting of the Society for Judgment and Decision Making, Dallas, TX, November 21, 1998.

Wolford, G., Taylor, H. A., & Beck, J. R. (1990). The conjunction fallacy? *Memory & Cognition, 18*, 47–53.

Yaari, M. E. (1987). The dual theory of choice under risk. *Econometrica, 55*, 95–115.

Zeelenberg, M., Beattie, J., van der Pligt, J., & de Vries, N. K. (1996). Consequences of regret aversion: Effects of expected feedback on risky decision making. *Organizational Behavior and Human Decision Processes, 65*, 148–158.

Index

Note: When a concept is central to a chapter, the page listed refers to the first mention of that concept in the chapter.

WITHDRAWN